1990

The tragic and the sublime in medieval literature

The tragic and the sublime in medieval literature

PIERO BOITANI

Professor of English, University of Rome

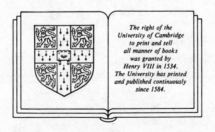

The right of the
University of Cambridge
to print and sell
all manner of books
was granted by
Henry VIII in 1534.
The University has printed
and published continuously
since 1584.

CAMBRIDGE UNIVERSITY PRESS

Cambridge

New York   New Rochelle

Melbourne   Sydney

Published by the Press Syndicate of the University of Cambridge
The Pitt Building. Trumpington Street, Cambridge CB2 1RP
32 East 57th Street, New York, NY 10022, USA
10 Stamford Road, Oakleigh, Melbourne 3166, Australia

First published 1989

Printed in Great Britain at
the University Press, Cambridge

British Library cataloguing in publication data
Boitani, Piero
The tragic and the sublime in medieval literature
1. European literature, 1100–1599 –
Critical studies
1. Title
809'.02

Library of Congress cataloguing in publication data
Boitani, Piero.
The tragic and the sublime in medieval literature / Piero Boitani.
p.   cm.
Includes index.
ISBN 0-521-35476-5
1. Literature, Medieval–History and criticism.   2. Tragic, The,
in literature.   3. Sublime, The, in literature.   I Title.
PN682.T68B65   1989
809'.02–dc 19   88-34451   CIP

ISBN 0 521 35476 5

Per Agostino e Uberto,
e alla memoria di Kenelm

Contents

Preface

This book explores two areas of medieval literature, the tragic and the sublime. It does so by concentrating on particular texts and themes and avoiding systematic treatment of theoretical issues. I am interested in what poems, narratives, and plays written over five hundred years ago mean to us today, whether what they say and the way in which they say it are still relevant to modern readers. Hence, the book begins with the problem of the 'alterity' and the 'modernity' of medieval literature and with the question of how we can interpret medieval texts. But this problem runs through all the chapters that constitute the present volume. For 'tragedy' and 'sublimity' may mean different things to medieval writers than they do to us, but it is only in the meeting between their medieval reenactments and the way we read them that we can find some significance.

To read medieval texts in this fashion, hoping for an encounter with our imagination, inevitably implies confronting on the one hand the literature of classical antiquity and the Bible, and on the other modern poetry, prose, and drama. Throughout the book, I compare medieval literary works with their ancestors and descendants, as well as one with the other. And although I often start from, or focus on texts written in English and Italian, I also try to keep in mind that there is a literary tradition, a world of the imagination, a philosophical and theological background, which go beyond national and linguistic boundaries. I often fly, therefore, across these as much as backward or forward in time; but since this book is meant to be read by students I have made the flight as smooth as possible by offering plot summaries, quotations, and translations so that any turbulence may be avoided.

'Tragic' and 'sublime' are terms invented by the Greeks and on which philosophers and men of letters have debated for two thousand years. What I mean by them is something that goes beyond considerations of style and genre (although these will be taken into account, especially in chapter 7). For me, 'tragic' is a scene, a plot, an image which shows us man's insoluble conflict with himself and the world around him, with his feelings, with his conscience and knowledge, his destiny, and his end. 'Sublime' is the opposite pole. As the first author of a treatise on the subject, a writer traditionally called Longinus, says, 'by some innate power the true sublime uplifts our souls; we are filled with a proud exaltation and a sense of vaunting joy, just as though we had ourselves produced what we had heard'. I do not of course deny that tragedy and sublimity often meet, that terror and uncanniness may produce, as eighteenth- and twentieth-century theorists have maintained, a sublime effect. Indeed, I see the sublime as arising from a contrast between opposed feelings. But its climax, which verges on the ineffable, is for me the supreme elation we feel at seeing the contrast pointed out and overcome in the words themselves employed by a particular writer.

In this book, therefore, I go from one type of tension to another. Having faced the tragic, uncanny mystery of the Old Man in the first chapter, I examine Dante's and Chaucer's versions of Ugolino's tragedy in the second. In both cases what we are confronted with is, quite simply, death. In chapter 3 I look at this problem ('O quike deth') as a conflict within the self, as the dying life and the living death of love and melancholy. Here, Petrarch's *Canzoniere* and Chaucer's *Troilus* constitute my main points of reference, and I therefore study the way in which the tragic is embodied in lyrical as well as narrative poetry.

Chapter 4 examines tragic themes from the point of view of imagery. The purpose is that of showing how the tragic setting is sketched by medieval authors (and how it changes in passing from one to another) by their use of those similes and metaphors which view man in the world of nature. In order to highlight the way in which we respond to the tragic quality of this setting because of the persistent vitality of those images, I make use of classical, Biblical, and modern passages here as before and after in this book. But in chapter 4 the very nature of the argument needs exemplification, and I am rather prodigal with quotations. Readers will at least enjoy the poetry.

Chapters 5 and 6 are transitional. In them I introduce knowledge as an element which further widens the gap between the tragic and the sublime. The protagonists of recognition scenes become aware of their plight. Thus, their tragedy is doubled, their elation in the case of a favourable denouement increases to reach the threshold of sublimity.

Preface

And we, as spectators of such scenes, are placed by complex manoeuvres on our knowledge in a position to feel with higher intensity our own tragic conflicts or man's possibility to attain supreme happiness. In both chapters, then, I outline an ideal itinerary from one pole to the other; passing, in the fifth, from religious works to romances; concentrating, in the sixth, on Dante's *Divine Comedy* and its gradual ascent from tragic encounters to sublime epiphanies.

With chapter 8 I definitely enter the sphere of sublimity, seeking a stylistic notion of it in the poetry of religion and love. Then, I leave the last two chapters of the book to Dante's *Paradiso*, where I look for the tensions and the struggles, the sense of going beyond into infinity that still makes us feel the sublime.

This book, then, is a study in comparative European literature dominated by Dante. If apologies are needed for the latter feature, I will say that any Italian critic must sooner or later confront his greatest poet (whose *Comedy* represents, in any case, the peak of medieval literature), and that moment has now come for me. The present volume has been a long time in the making. In the past fifteen years I have gradually realized that the lectures I gave, the papers and articles I wrote were increasingly revolving about the two areas of the tragic and the sublime I tackle here. Some of the following chapters were published as separate essays in different languages in periodicals or collections (and I thank publishers and editors for allowing me to use them here), but all have been rewritten or altered to fit the present purpose and because I felt the need to revisit texts I examined over the years in a new light. I hope that the continuity and the change, the unity and diversity to which the book is a witness will be useful to the reader.

A book such as this, composed as it were through time, owes something to many people – to the critics one mentions and with whom or against whom one travels, and above all to the friends and scholars one speaks with in continuous interchange. Here, for instance, the last chapter would simply not have been written had it not been for the presence, the help, the understanding, and the discrimination of Jonathan Steinberg, and if Anna Maria Chiavacci Leonardi, Robert Hollander, Alfonso Maierù, Giorgio Stabile, and Achille Tartaro had not made important suggestions. Chapter 1 would not be the same if Agostino Lombardo, Frank Kermode, Klaus Reichert, Przemyslaw Mroczkowski, Marcello Pagnini, Alessandro Serpieri, Margaret Bridges, and Paul Taylor had not heard it in an earlier version. John Burrow and Gianfranco Contini may have forgotten the points they made on the first drafts of chapter 2, section I – I have not. Chapters 3 and 7 are indebted to the observations of Jörg Fichte, Willi Erzgräber, Dieter Mehl, Friedrich Ohly, Karl Reichl. 'A spark of love' was profitably discussed with Jill Mann and, on a different occasion, with Peter Dronke. Whether they like it or not, I owe the project of this book to a visit to Rome by Jill Mann and Michael Lapidge. 'I know the signs of the ancient flame' is due to the generous invitation of Cormac O'Cuilleanain and the constant attention of Patrick Boyde. Francisco Rico provided me with precious information for chapters 3 and 5. In different ways David Benson, Winthrop Wetherbee, and Harold Bloom have stimulated my work on chapter 4.

I think, however, that my greatest debt is towards the two places that have shaped my way of reading literature, the English Department of Rome University and the Italian Department of the University of Cambridge. To Agostino Lombardo I owe the passion for analysing a text in all its nuances; to Uberto Limentani, the trust and warmth with which he sent me on to study *Inferno* XXXIII – the true beginning of this book. To them as teachers and as representatives of all my friends in Rome and Cambridge I therefore dedicate *The Tragic and the Sublime*. To complete this dedication I inscribe a 'memoria' for Kenelm Foster. Chapters 3, 6, 8, and 9 could not have been conceived without conversation with him and without his example as a man and as a critic. No one, however, except the writer himself, is responsible for his misunderstandings and errors. The present one is no exception to the rule.

PIERO BOITANI

Rome, *a. aet.* XL

Note on the texts

For Dante's *Divine Comedy* I have used the text (established by G. Petrocchi) and the translation of Charles S. Singleton (Princeton, 1970–1975) and often refer to his Commentary in that edition. The various works of Chaucer are quoted from *The Riverside Chaucer*, general editor L.D. Benson (Boston, 1987; Oxford, 1988), but I also refer to the second edition of *The Works of Geoffrey Chaucer* by F.N. Robinson (London, 1966). In the notes, these two volumes are called *Riverside Chaucer* and 'Robinson'.

Unless otherwise stated, Greek and Latin classics (and English translations from them) are taken from the Loeb series. The Vulgate Bible is the *Biblia Sacra iuxta Vulgatam Clementinam* (Madrid, 1965), and English translations are, unless otherwise specified, those of the King James Bible. All other texts and editions are indicated in the notes.

I

The old man and the earth: Alterity and otherness of a medieval story

We begin with the tragic: not with a literary genre or a specific type of drama such as tragedy, but with representations of the one single event of human life which is perceived by all of us as tragic. We begin, then, with dying and death, events which, like that of birth, cannot be described by those who experience them. How medieval literary artists manage to talk about these experiences is the subject of the first three chapters of this book.

There are, however, several questions that arise as soon as we start thinking about this problem. The most important one concerns the possibility of a difference, both mental and representational, between our modern attitude towards death and the medieval one. But this in turn reflects two basic problems – the way in which man faces this supreme mystery of his life, and the way, if any, in which *we* can read, that is, interpret, his written accounts of the mystery. Hence in this chapter I would like to begin by exploring two areas of the medieval 'other'. The first is the realm of the 'alterity' of medieval literature as such, that is to say, of its being alien to us moderns because it is allegedly the expression of a 'discarded image' of the universe by means of a 'language' that we no longer fully understand.[1] I shall argue that this alterity depends on a hermeneutic openness which is as wide as, if not actually wider than, that produced by modern texts, and that in fact this uncertainty and multiplicity of interpretation is what makes us feel the 'modernity' of medieval literature. In order to do this, I shall compare two stories, one medieval and one modern, where the central character is the same, an old man seemingly facing the world of nature and death.

Secondly, I shall focus on the figure of the 'other' such as it emerges in medieval narrative. The medieval story of the old man which I am going to use is, as I hope to show, an extraordinary literary example of the encounter with a mysterious, undefinable 'other'.[2]

Finally, I shall ask myself what the 'otherness' of the old man may mean to each of us. We shall see that cultural and literary alterity on the one hand, and human or trans-human diversity, unfamiliarity, otherness on the other entail, and at the same time are determined by, our interpretative approach – that, in other words, alterity and otherness are aspects not only of the production of literary texts, but also of their interpretation.

'He was an old man who fished alone in a skiff in the Gulf Stream and he had gone eighty-four days now without taking a fish'. This, as readers will undoubtedly remember, is the beginning of one of the most famous modern novellas, Hemingway's *The Old Man and the Sea*, published in 1952, nine years before the author killed himself. No one who has read it can forget the beautiful, if somewhat manneristic, tragic story which is a representation of man's destiny – his solitude, his fight against the elements and his own weakness, his defeat, and his victory.

The protagonist, Santiago, is a character whom Hemingway describes as follows, on the very first page:

The old man was thin and gaunt with deep wrinkles in the back of his neck. The brown blotches of the benevolent skin cancer the sun brings from its reflection on the tropic sea were on his cheeks. The blotches ran well down the sides of his face and his hands had the deep-creased scars from handling heavy fish on the cords. But none of these scars were fresh. They were as old as erosions in a fishless desert.

Everything about him was old except his eyes and they were the same colour as the sea and were cheerful and undefeated.[3]

No comment, I think, is needed to show how the writer's concentration on the particular 'signs' which mark Santiago's face culminates in a symbolic leap by which he becomes the representative of timeless, sterile, 'fishless' old age and, at the same time, of cheerful and undefeated humanity – a man whose eyes are the same colour as his enemy's, the sea. Hemingway hides nothing. He selects the characteristic elements – wrinkles, blotches, scars; neck, cheeks, face, hands, eyes – and shows them in full light, as it were in the sun's reflection on the tropic sea.

And here is the old man's adversary, or rather what the old man thinks of his adversary, *la mar*, the sea. Readers will notice that Santiago considers it a woman, a lover, rather than an enemy:

'. . . Why did they make birds so delicate and fine as those sea swallows when the ocean can be so cruel? She is kind and very beautiful. But she can be so cruel and it comes so suddenly and such birds that fly, dipping and hunting, with their small sad voices are made too delicately for the sea.'
    He always thought of the sea as *la mar* which is what people call her in Spanish when they love her . . . the old man always thought of her as feminine and as something that gave or withheld great favours, and if she did wild or wicked things it was because she could not help them. The moon affects her as it does a woman, he thought.   (pp. 23–4)

A constant flux of thoughts and solitary monologue fills the entire book. In this passage Santiago, in characteristically indirect fashion, asks himself one of the primeval questions: 'why did *they* make birds so delicate . . . when the ocean can be so cruel?' He will no more return to these whys. He will simply accept the reality of natural law, of the sea.

The old man catches his fish, and the fish drags him and his boat for three days on the ocean. At sunrise, as the third day begins, the fish starts to circle in its death-throes: its 'Passion' is drawing to an end – not towards resurrection, but towards death. The old man, who has already fought against hunger, sleep, cramps and tiredness, prepares himself for what he thinks will be the last battle:

'Fish', the old man said. 'Fish, you are going to have to die anyway. Do you have to kill me too?' . . . You are killing me, fish, the old man thought. But you have a right to. Never have I seen a greater, or more beautiful, or a calmer or more noble thing than you, brother. Come on and kill me. I do not care who kills who.
    Now you are getting confused in the head, he thought. You must keep your head clear. Keep your head clear and know how to suffer like a man. Or a fish, he thought.   (p. 82)

The struggle between life and death is a silent battle between brothers. At the beginning of the hunt, the old man had announced, ' "I'll kill him though . . . In all his greatness and his glory". Although it is unjust, he thought. But I will show him what a man can do and what a man endures.' Now, it is the fish that teaches the man how to suffer.

A worse struggle, however, is about to begin. The body of the fish is tied along the boat, 'they were sailing together lashed side by side and the old man thought, let him bring me in if it pleases him'. Soon, he is taken out of his reverie by sharks coming to their repast. Old man and fish become one thing, and Santiago fights against the sharks with all his might. '"Man is not made for defeat", he said. "A man can be destroyed but not defeated."' And yet, 'he knew quite well the pattern of what could happen when he reached the inner part of the current. But there was nothing to be done now.' Though 'tired inside' and painfully aware of his weakness, the old man goes on fighting, hopelessly, until he can. An inner duty drives him. Finally, he lands, and 'in the reflection from the street light', sees 'the great tail of the fish standing up well behind the skiff's stern'. All that is left of the great animal is the skeleton:

He saw the white naked line of his backbone and the dark mass of the head with the projecting bill and all the nakedness between.   (p. 109)

With the image of this 'nakedness' which is not simply death, but life-as-tending-towards-death – the absolute essence of life on earth – Santiago goes to bed in his shack, where, watched by a boy, he dreams about lions.

I would like readers to keep this powerful picture of a twentieth-century old man and his sea in mind while I leap six hundred years back to a fourteenth-century old man and his earth. I will take this figure, one of the apparently minor protagonists of Chaucer's *Pardoner's Tale*, in almost total isolation, by which I mean that I will consider him and the episode in which he appears not primarily as parts of a greater unit, the *Pardoner's Tale*, nor as atoms of the unfinished and infinite universe of the *Canterbury Tales*.

There are perhaps only two justifications for doing this. The first is that, with other critics, I believe that the '*Canterbury Tales* are a series of forays into the borderland of the exemplary and the mimetic' and explorations of 'the potentialities of narrative as a self-consistent and self-justifying literary form'[4] – which allows us to take each of them and read it as if it were an independent unit of a greater, incomplete and imperfect, whole. The second reason is that the section of the *Pardoner's Tale* on which I want to focus offers us twentieth-century readers a model of tragic narrative which we can still perceive as functional in spite of what Jauss would call its 'Alterität',[5] and above all that it raises not only problems of interpretation, but *the* problem of interpretation *tout court*.

The structure of the *Pardoner's Tale* is indeed peculiar and depends on the oral and dramatic fiction which dominates its relationship to the overall frame of the Canterbury stories. The Tale – which has recently been called 'The Death of a Salesman'[6] – begins with a long and fascinating Prologue–confession; the story itself, in contrast, has hardly begun when it is suddenly interrupted by a homiletic digression on the sins of gluttony, drunkenness, gambling and lying, seasoned with various *exempla* – that is, with short narrative digressions within the main narrative. The story is taken up again after about two hundred lines, and from then on it follows a straight path, with a construction based on ambiguity. It ends with another short homiletic tract, which develops first into an offer of relics by the Pardoner, and then into the quarrel between him and the Host, which is settled by the Knight.

The Pardoner's story is about three 'riotoures' who have been drinking since dawn in a tavern; they hear a funeral bell, and send a boy to ask who is dead. He reports that it is an old comrade of theirs, suddenly killed by a thief, commonly known as Death, who has claimed many victims during the plague. The three, who are drunk, decide to find Death and kill him. They set out towards the village where, according to the innkeeper, Death dwells. Along the way they meet the Old Man, who, when they threaten him, points out a certain oak tree under which Death cannot hide. The three proceed along the 'croked way' indicated by the Old Man, and find, under the oak, a huge pile of golden florins. Then they draw lots to decide which of them must go to the village to buy food and wine, while they wait for night to carry off the treasure. The lot falls to the youngest, who sets off on his way. The other two decide to kill him on his return, so as to get his share of the florins. But the third rioter has a plan of his own: he buys poison and puts it in two of the wine bottles, keeping the third for himself. When he returns to the oak, his companions murder him; then, to celebrate, they drink the poisoned wine and die. Thus all three have found death and shown themselves to be, much more grimly than in the Duke's words in *Measure for Measure*, Death's fools.[7]

The story, which was widespread in various forms during the Middle Ages, hinges on the ambiguity death = person, and on the ambiguity of the Old Man's directions: treasure = death. In this powerful tale, the three men's meeting with the Old Man occupies what in Aristotelian terms would be the 'middle' of the action; in itself it resolves nothing, but it sets in motion the process which will lead to the disastrous conclusion. The meeting takes place barely half a mile from the village where the three had gathered in the tavern and had decided to go out and kill Death. The old man is presented simply as old and poor, and he is first to speak. Meekly, he says, 'Now, lordes, God yow see!' But the 'proudeste' of the three insultingly asks him:

> Why artow al forwrapped save thy face?
> Why lyvestow so longe in so gret age? (718–19)

The first of these questions indirectly provides another detail of the Old Man's appearance: his body is completely covered. Is he wrapped, perhaps, in a shroud, or against the cold, or because of illness (perhaps the plague, which is raging in the neighbourhood)? The form of the question suggests all three hypotheses: in just a few words, it begins, indirectly, to build up a chilling image.

The second question makes no sense at all, except as a bit of insolence on the part of the criminal: 'Why do you live so long in such old age?' The Old Man looks into the face of the rioter and replies. What is the Old Man seeking in the gambler's face ('gan looke in his visage')? We are not told: and again we can speculate – we are indeed prompted to imagine. Is his gaze a sign of knowledge, of wise superiority, or is it perhaps mixed with fear? Is he trying to discover on the rioter's face his intentions? Or is he penetrating to the very heart of his interlocutor's nature? In any case the Old Man replies only to the second question:

> For I ne kan nat fynde
> A man, though that I walked into Ynde,
> Neither in citee ne in no village,
> That wolde chaunge his youthe for myn age;
> And therfore moot I han myn age stille,
> As longe tyme as it is Goddes wille.
> Ne Deeth, allas, ne wol nat han my lyf.
> Thus walke, I lyk a restelees kaityf,
> And on the ground, which is my moodres gate,
> I knokke with my staf, bothe erly and late,
> And seye 'Leeve mooder, leet me in!
> Lo how I vanysshe, flessh, and blood, and skyn!
> Allas, whan shul my bones been at reste?
> Mooder, with yow wolde I chaunge my cheste
> That in my chambre longe tyme hath be,
> Ye, for an heyre clowt to wrappe in me!'
> But yet to me she wol nat do that grace,
> For which ful pale and welked is my face. (721–38)

This is the heart of the episode, and no reader can be unaware of its density. The Old Man's reply is divided into two or, perhaps, three parts: first, he has lived to such a great age because he can find no one in all the world who is ready to exchange youth for old age; second, Death does not want his life;[8] third, he is a prisoner who knows no peace, who begs the earth to receive his body. We are, in a sense, far beyond that last scene in the play of human life envisaged by Jaques:

> Last scene of all,
> That ends this strange eventful history,
> Is second childishness and mere oblivion,
> Sans teeth, sans eyes, sans taste, sans everything.[9]

This Old Man is beyond childishness and above all beyond oblivion. If his body is vanishing, he is, like Deschamps in his 'Ballade des signes de la mort',[10] painfully aware of it. His death-wish is even stronger than the primeval one which Milton's Adam expresses when he discovers that punishment for his trespass has not been meted out fully and immediately:

> Be it so, for I submit, his doom is fair,
> That dust I am, and shall to dust return:
> O welcome hour whenever! Why delays
> His hand to execute what his decree
> Fixed on this day? Why do I overlive,
> Why am I mocked with death, and lengthened out
> To deathless pain? How gladly would I meet
> Mortality my sentence, and be earth
> Insensible, how glad would lay me down
> As in my mother's lap! There I should rest
> And sleep secure . . .   (*Paradise Lost* x, 769–79)

As his subsequent words show, Adam yearns for something he does not know. As soon as he starts meditating on death, he becomes uncertain, as much a coward as Hamlet and we all are made by conscience. Chaucer's Old Man, many generations after his progenitor, knows perfectly well what death is. Yet he stands at the opposite extreme of a similar figure in Aesop's *Fables*. Here, the *gēron* burdened by a pile of logs invokes Death, but when Death appears he says that all he asks is to be relieved of his load.[11] Chaucer's *gēron* is not afraid of death, and furthermore accepts his burden.

In fact, this Old Man is profoundly different from Hemingway's as well. There is no trace in him of 'cheerful and undefeated' eyes. We are not even shown his face, although that is the only part of his body which is not covered. All we know of his physical appearance is what he himself says is hidden under his shroud – vanishing flesh, blood and skin. The clarity, directness and immediacy of Hemingway's description are absent. Here, what dominates is indirectness, obscurity, mystery. The passage from reality to symbol was immediately perceptible from the very first page of *The Old Man and the Sea*, where the 'signs' on Santiago's body reveal what he represents – 'fishless' old age and undefeated humanity. Chaucer offers us no 'signs' that we can read and decipher; in fact, he seems to be deliberately playing a sort of 'hide and seek' game with his readers. He points to the enquiring eyes of the Old Man, but does not describe them. He has the rioter notice that the Old Man's body is 'al forwrapped', but then he makes the Old Man himself say that his body is decaying. Above all, Chaucer places at the centre of his portrait of the Old Man's a 'pale and welked' (i.e. withered, faded) face – a mute nakedness which is much more absolute than the naked backbone of Hemingway's fish. The face of Chaucer's old man is presented as a sphinx, pure 'absence' or blankness. Chaucer's 'alterity' reveals itself to be a surprising 'modernity'.

And finally, how are we to assess the meaning of Chaucer's character? In Hemingway, the significance of Santiago is pointed out clearly. By contrast, there is no overt indication in Chaucer's passage of what direction we should take in order to reach either the symbolic or the allegorical level. Yet we are convinced that some such meaning must be found – no author would introduce such a character and episode without purpose.

Being diligent medievalists, we start looking up the sources. After some time we discover, with Kittredge, Skeat and Robinson, that a late Roman poet called Maximian, obscure to us but well known in the Middle Ages, represents 'senectus' – old age – as knocking the ground with her staff and begging it to welcome her into its womb.[12] Thus, Chaucer's Old Man represents old age. This interpretation is supported by the opening of Boethius' *Consolation of Philosophy*, a work which Chaucer not only knew but translated into his own language. There, we find Boethius complaining about 'eelde' and about death's deafness towards old people's cries for him.[13]

All this, however, is not entirely satisfactory. We remember that the Old Man mentions God's will and later, quite explicitly, Holy Writ. We check our Vulgate Bible and see that he quotes Leviticus and indirectly refers to Matthew.[14] And of course we ask ourselves if in that all-embracing *summa* of stories which is the Bible there might not be a figure which resembles the old man.

Such a figure in fact exists and is one of the most extraordinary characters in the whole of Scripture – Job, the man who, deprived of wealth, family and health in spite of his being just, dares to call God Himself to trial. We recall that, having obtained permission from Jahweh, The Adversary touches Job's bone and flesh – 'skin for skin', as he says – covering his body 'with sore boils from the sole of his foot unto his crown'. Job himself shouts to his friends that man's body 'as a rotten thing consumeth, as a garment that is moth eaten' (13. 28), and invokes the earth: 'I have said to corruption: thou art my father; to the worm: thou art my mother, and my sister' (17. 14). Finally, we find a passage where Job pronounces a lament which is very similar to the old man's:

Wherefore is light given to him that is in misery, and life unto the bitter in soul; Which long for death, but it cometh not; and dig for it more than for hid treasures; Which rejoice exceedingly, and are glad, when they can find the grave? (3. 20–2)

These three verses come from chapter 3 of the Book of Job, the chapter in which the protagonist, having accepted 'good and evil' until now, curses the day of his birth with unparalleled fierceness and utters a complaint which is an indictment of God. In this lament, Job reverses traditional ideas about death and its unhappy domain of gloom, darkness and forgetfulness, calling it the land of repose, rest and freedom from turmoil. He then asks a series of terrible whys which express a desperate death-wish and culminate in a supreme existential question:

Why is light given to a man whose way is hid, and whom God hath hedged in? (3.23)

'It is not the suffering or bitterness of life as such that consumes [Job], but the misery of meaninglessness. The futility of existence has two clear features: the *derek* ('way') of life is hidden, and the one who hides it is God.'[15] In the mouth of a Biblical character, this statement is simply staggering. It has no precedent even in its non-Biblical, third-millenium BC Egyptian parallel, the 'Dispute over suicide';[16] and in the Middle Ages, Christian exegetes tried to soften its import by means of allegorical or moralizing interpretations.[17] Following this Christianization of the Biblical figure, Chaucer's old man accepts God's will:

> And, therfore moot I han myn age stille,
> As longe tyme as it is Goddes wille.

Our problems, however, are not over. Chaucer's Old Man invokes death

– and in that, of course, he is profoundly different from Hemingway's Santiago, who may accept death, but who in fact defends life at all costs. The Pardoner's Old Man can be seen as the human being who asks himself the primeval and perennial question about the mystery, paradox and absurdity of his life: 'why did I not give up the ghost', says Job, 'when I came out of the belly?'.[18] If man's way is 'hid' and, as the Vulgate puts it, God has surrounded him with darkness,[19] Chaucer's character would then seem to represent man's blindness, his being a prisoner of the mysteries of life, his inability to understand them. He would thus tend to become a Christian Job. On the other hand, Chaucer nowhere associates him directly with the suffering Jesus, of whom Job was, ever since Gregory the Great, seen as a 'figura'.[20]

Chaucer's Old Man is then culturally stratified, half a Biblical or pre-Biblical figure like Job, half a Christian one. To make textual interpretation even more complicated, Job 3. 21 states not only that human beings who live a life of misery 'long for death', but also that they 'dig for it more than for hid treasures'. Chaucer's Old Man does nothing of the sort. He asks mother earth to welcome him back into her womb, seeking that 'rest' which Job had already associated with Sheol, but he entertains no hope whatsoever of finding there a hidden treasure. Suddenly, however, there come into our minds two simultaneous thoughts – firstly, that the rioters are looking for Death as much as the old man; and secondly, that they do not find Death in person, but in fact a treasure: bushels of gold florins, which *will* be their death.[21] There can be little doubt that Chaucer is complicating the traditional *exemplum* of the three criminals by means of a complex play on several levels.

We have, in the first place, two quests for death – the furious one of the three ribalds, and the pathetic one of the Old Man. The rioters do not succeed in killing Death, but find a treasure that makes them kill each other. The Old Man fails to find death, patiently endures his old age, and then announces, 'I moot go thider as I have to go.' Job accepts the mystery of life only after God Himself speaks to him 'out of the whirlwind'. Exactly like Hemingway's Santiago, Chaucer's old man accepts his ineluctable fate. Yet the twentieth-century novelist and his character know 'the pattern of what could happen when [Santiago reaches] the inner part of the current', whereas Chaucer does not reveal *where* his old man has to go.

Secondly, we have three sets of interrelated questions, of 'whys'. The rioters ask the Old Man 'why artow al forwrapped save thy face' and 'why lyvestow so longe in so greet age'. The Old Man, as we shall presently see, answers these questions, but in doing so recalls Job's whys. Finally, these two inset series of questions raise *our* why: why do the rioters and the Old Man at the same time seek death? why do they not find him? why is the Old Man's body hidden and his face muffled? why does he look into the criminal's face? Why are we told that the Old Man has just left Death 'in that grove' 'under a tree', but nothing is revealed about what happened when the two met? The Old Man tells the rioters that Death will not have his life. Are we meant to surmise that he has just asked Death in person to take his life and that Death has refused? For a medieval text, Chaucer's passage is almost as 'interrogative' as a Kafkian story, and infinitely more ambiguous and mysterious than Hemingway's novella, where, as we have seen, the protagonist asks himself only once, 'why did they make birds so delicate . . . when the ocean can be so cruel?'

I shall return to this 'interrogative' structure of Chaucer's Tale in a moment. Let us now go back to the Old Man seeking death. 'His weariness of the world', says a recent critic, 'makes him see life as an exile, an imprisonment in which his soul is restless: "Thus walke I, lyk a restelees kaityf". Here he is echoing Paul . . ., as translated by Chaucer in the *Parson's Tale*.'[22] Is he then Christianity's 'spiritual man' who longs for the death of his corporeal nature? The last Scriptural allusion these lines contain seems to put all this into question and plunge us into total mystery. For the passage Chaucer echoes comes from the Book of Revelation (9. 6): 'And in those days shall men seek death, and shall not find it; and shall desire to die, and death shall flee from them.' This verse projects the Old Man's death-wish onto an eschatological perspective and in an ambiguous light. What kind of death will men desire when the angel sounds the fifth trumpet and opens the 'bottomless pit'? Will they want to kill themselves because the end of the world is approaching? What is certain is that the passage announces a complete upheaval of natural laws – men do not normally seek death – and casts an apocalyptic light on the rioters' and the old man's quest. The account of this quest, in sum, seems to be presented as a revelation, an *apokalypsis*.

In other words, our interpretation of the figure of the Old Man varies according to the text we decide Chaucer had in mind when he wrote the Tale. Or else, we must say that the Old Man contains *all* these meanings in a sort of polysemic concretion (which implies that Chaucer had the whole Bible at his fingertips *and* was constantly and deliberately making allusions to it). In any case, interpretation depends on our ability to find Biblical echoes and apply them properly to Chaucer's text. What takes place in *The Old Man and the Sea* is very different, not only because in six hundred years of Western culture the Bible has lost its fundamental relevance,[23] but because the story is itself generative of meaning without intertextual connections. When Hemingway says that the fish's death-throes begin at the third rising of the sun, he may be alluding to the three days Christ spent in the tomb or to those Jonah spent in the whale's belly. Such a viewpoint would add something to our interpretation of his novella – it does not *condition* it.

The difficulty we encounter in interpreting Chaucer's episode is further increased by the fact that his text is not static – being narrative, it is eminently dynamic, and the Scriptural allusions it contains are not the only factors that determine its meaning. Let us return to the narrative and its triple set of questions. The Old Man recognizes the will of God and says he continually asks the earth for a 'grace' which has not *yet* been granted him. In reality the Old Man's whole answer to the three criminals is based on impossibilities: of course it is impossible to find anyone willing to exchange his own youth for another person's old age; and it is impossible to hasten death and burial without doing violence to oneself. The Old Man's answer makes no sense at all in terms of logic; this corresponds very well to the senseless question that provoked it. We have overstepped the bounds of rationality, though not necessarily of nature. The Old Man is condemned to an indefinite suspension (but one which will end) between life and death: crystallized in old age, of which he has often been seen as the personification, he is a prisoner without peace. But his body is still subject to the ravages of life and time: a sort of cancer is devouring him, flesh, blood, and skin; his face gets ever nearer to the pallor and aridity of death; he disappears. The Old Man is the 'Other'. Unlike the character explicitly identified as such in Bergman's *The Seventh Seal*, he is not Death, as has often been said, nor Death's 'spy' or scout, as one of the rioters suspects; if anything he is Dying, the gradual extinction of life which has not yet reached final consummation. Perhaps this is why his body is completely covered, to avoid showing the signs of truth, of mortal life which is, as Dante says, but 'un correre a la morte' – a race to death.[24] Significantly, the fifteenth-century French poet Pierre de Nesson 'paraphrases' Job in the following manner:

> Job compere chair a vesture
> Car vestement est mis dessure
> Le corps affin qu'on ne le voye.

(Job compares the flesh to clothes, because clothes are put over the body so that it may not be seen.)[25]

And indeed we shall soon come back to this aspect of deliberate hiding of the truth.

The earth, on which the Old Man knocks with his staff, is our common mother. Once more, the image is different from Hemingway's parallel one. For Santiago, the sea is a woman he loves and who bestows or withholds her favours – a lover. Chaucer's old man asks the earth to let him re-enter its bosom and calls it 'mother', offering his chest with all his possessions in exchange for a hair-cloth shroud. Santiago's sea is an image of infinite, eternal, familiar, living, capricious, all-embracing *eros*. The Old Man's earth is the primeval correlative of *thanatos* as love for the mother – the finite abyss, the narrow womb (womb–tomb)[26] towards which we are irresistibly attracted.

The images are, however, once again indirect. The Old Man does not invoke death, but mother earth, which has given life and will receive it back again. Around the concept of death, which is mistakenly personified by the three gamblers and the boy, a broader perspective is gradually formed – by the stratification of images, by allusion, by Scriptural implications. At first the Old Man speaks of Death as a person (727) who does not want his life, thus echoing the ambiguous notion of the criminals. He sets youth against age (724) and death against life. Then the image of the ground, the gate of mother earth, broadens and modifies the perspective: the indirect message which the old man addresses to the three rioters is truth, something we must particularly note. The earth is the mother of man, made of dust, and to it man will return at the will of God. The Old Man speaks of life while seeming to beg for death. Knocking the ground with his staff he shows the criminals the *true* path towards death, and the impossibility of following it to the end without the grace of mother earth and the consent of God.

This exhausted prisoner of an old age that dies every day, this weary and shrinking pilgrim, has looked into the eyes of his questioner and seen there the boundless pride ('the proudeste'), the Lucifer-like arrogance, of one who wants to kill death – a privilege reserved for Christ. The figure of the Old Man emerges in all its greatness: he is neither an allegory of the 'vetus homo' nor a personification of Death or Old Age, nor merely an old man, but an image powerfully created through successive concretions, which in the end involves *all* of man and his destiny: 'I moot go thider as I *have* to go'. The Old Man is a 'metaphor' in Boncompagno da Signa's sense – 'a natural veil, beneath which the secrets of things are brought forth *more* hiddenly and *more* secretly'.[27] He is an 'enigma' in Isidore of Seville's definition of the

13

term: 'a dark meaning alone, adumbrated by means of certain images'.[28] Alive yet dying, he seems to be answering questions but does not, he says one thing with his words and another with his gestures and yet another with his appearance. He conceals the truth and at the same time points to it.

If we read further in the episode, we see that the humility and generosity of the Old Man are gradually deepened: he asks the rioters not to insult him, quoting a precept from Leviticus and paraphrasing Matthew. Then, with an ironic reference to the fact that the three rascals may live to old age ('if that ye so longe abyde'), he takes leave of them: 'God be with yow, where ye go or ryde!'. But the three understand nothing of all this, and threaten him:

> 'Nay, olde cherl, by God, thou shalt nat so,'
> Seyde this oother hasardour anon;
> 'Thou partest nat so lightly, by Seint John!
> Thou spak right now of thilke traytour Deeth.
> That in this contree alle oure freendes sleeth.
> Have heer my trouthe, as thou art his espye,
> Telle where he is or thou shalt it abye,
> By God and by the hooly sacrement!
> For soothly thou art oon of his assent
> To sleen us yonge folk, thou false theef!'   (750–9)

The Old Man then returns to the literal fiction: do you want Death? Death in person? Well, I've just left him under that great oak tree up there. Once again he tries to make them realize the truth: the path they must travel to reach Death is a 'croked way', the way of sin. That way they will indeed find Death – not the return to mother earth, not rest for their bones, but final, eternal death. The Old Man's farewell, which at first had been 'God yow see!' and then 'God be with yow', is now 'God *save* yow, that boghte agayn mankynde, and yow *amende*!' The Old Man has finished; he sets off again for his mysterious destination and with his last words disappears from the scene. At the end of the road, the three will find the treasure that is to be their death,[29] and 'No longer thanne after Deeth they soughte'. The gold now glistens under our eyes. Unlike the human being which has preceded them, the florins are 'fyne', 'faire', 'brighte', 'rounde', and 'newe': in short, they apparently embody the unambiguously clear, perfect, pristine, and unchangeable 'beautee' (839) that makes the three rioters 'glad' (773). Hidden decay is replaced by naked radiance, 'dying' by 'living'.

With its simple and powerful image of a poor old man condemned to a life of dying this episode, created by Chaucer through allusions, and without logical links, is in fact a parable. That is the way the old man acts and speaks, 'because they (the rioters) seeing see not; and hearing hear not, neither do they understand'.[30] This, it will be remembered, is Jesus' definition of a parable in Matthew, when his disciples ask him why he speaks to the multitudes in such way: 'Because', he says, 'it is given unto you to know the mysteries of the kingdom of heaven, but to them it is not given. For whosoever hath, to him shall be given, and he shall have more abundance: but whosoever hath not, from him shall be taken away even that he hath. Therefore speak I to them in parables: because they seeing see not; and hearing they hear not, neither do they understand.'

In the *Pardoner's Tale*, which has been called a parable *in toto*,[31] there is, then, a parable within the parable. The three men are like Jesus' multitudes. Advice had been offered to them by the boy:

> Beth redy for to meete hym [Death]*everemoore*;
> Thus taughte me my dame . . .   (683–4)

This warning had fallen on deaf ears; and the boy's mother ('my dame') is succeeded by the mother of all, the earth. The meeting reflects a total lack of comprehension between two cultures, that of the Old Man and that of the three gamblers. Communication between them is impossible: the three, desperately tied to their literal interpretation of 'death' and to the earth (not as common mother, but as pure materiality), cannot understand the profound meaning of the man's words and gestures. They seem to be completely outside Christian culture. From this point of view, they are the 'others', the true aliens.

But should we stop here? What Matthew seems to be saying is that Jesus speaks in parables because at least in this way the people, stupid as they are, will understand him. This is how the Gospel passage has always been taken. If this is so, the message of the Old Man at the moment he pronounces it (not, of course, later) is open to hope. What he is saying is, as I have remarked, the truth. As receivers of this cryptic but truthful message, the three rioters have, for one single moment, the possibility of finding an answer. And we, as readers and interpreters of the *Pardoner's Tale*, have some hope of understanding what the Old Man means.

However, there is another side to this coin. The synoptic, but earlier passage in Mark's Gospel reads in a slightly but very significantly different manner to the version given above. Here, Jesus says: 'Unto you it is given to know the mystery of the kingdom of God: but unto them that are without, all these things are done in parables: That seeing they may see, and *not* perceive; and hearing they may hear, and *not* understand; lest at any time they should be converted, and their sins should be forgiven them.'[32] This leaves the rioters inside the Tale but *outside* Christian culture no hope whatever. The Old Man tells them a parable so that they will *not* understand. This is why he keeps his body wrapped up and why his face is 'pale and welked' – to avoid, as I said before, showing the signs of truth. And we as readers have no hope of understanding the parable unless we are already inside, unless we already know what the story means.

One could of course follow the development of this concept of parable, prophecy and gospel back to its archetype in Isaiah (6. 9–10) and further to John (12. 40) and the Acts of the Apostles (28. 25–8). In this last case, the perspective would once more be reversed, for in that passage, which significantly concludes the whole book, Paul addresses the Jews of Rome quoting Isaiah (and therefore Mark), but adds: 'Be it known therefore unto you, that the salvation of God is sent unto the Gentiles, and that they will hear it.' If we consider either the criminals or ourselves as 'gentiles', our response to the message of the Old Man is obviously open to hope and understanding. But I should stop here. We are faced with two possibilities – either a sort of 'infinite interpretation' which grows further and further as we read Scripture,[33] or the 'genesis of secrecy' which, in Frank Kermode's conception,[34] constitutes the end of narrative, the mystery which produces interpretation.

The poetry of Chaucer's passage shows us Truth, but this truth is shrouded, veiled, vanishing away before our eyes. The poetry itself proceeds through *impossibilia* and *aenigmata*. The pathos which dominates the whole episode is the 'Passion', the *Passio* itself of human life – the tragic. In this story, Chaucer seems to have broken through all the poetic and aesthetic canons we associate with his age. It is only by total contrast that his Old Man reminds us of Hemingway's. Yet other powerful figures of English literature are evoked by the passage. Suicidal Gloucester,[35] dying Lear,[36] that Gerontion who, 'a dull head among windy spaces', has lost his 'sight, smell, hearing, taste and touch'[37] come immediately to mind. The closest descendant, however, is the Ancient Mariner, who tells us that

> The Night-mare Life-in-Death was she,
> Who thicks man's blood with cold.[38]

The old man and the earth

The fourteenth century does not seem to know the equivalent of Chaucer's figure, which anticipates Michault Taillevent's 'poor old man' who

> La mort huche, la mort appelle,
> A tout sa hoe, a tout sa pelle:
> Mais la Mort fait l'oreille sourde.
>
> . . .
>
> Mort requiert, mais Mort le refuse,
> Ne ja de plus prez ne l'aproche

(invokes death, calls death with a scream, with all his breath, but Death turns a deaf ear . . . He asks for death, but Death rejects him and does not come near him)[39]

Petrarch, who offers us the moving picture of a 'vecchierel canuto e bianco' who drags his aged limbs through the last days of his life on a pilgrimage to see the 'Veronica' in Rome, uses the image to tell us that in the same way he seeks in others the 'desired true form' of his beloved Laura.[40] Inspired, however, by Petrarch's words, a much later Italian poet elaborates the most powerful version of the icon of the old man I know. In his 'Canto notturno di un pastore errante dell'Asia' (1830), Leopardi presents us with a shocking equivalence between the old man and human life:

> Vecchierel bianco, infermo,
> mezzo vestito e scalzo,
> con gravissimo fascio in su le spalle,
> per montagna e per valle,
> per sassi acuti, ed alta rena, e fratte,
> al vento, alla tempesta, e quando avvampa
> l'ora, e quando poi gela,
> corre via, corre, anela,
> varca torrenti e stagni,
> cade, risorge, e piú e piú s'affretta,
> senza posa o ristoro,
> lacero, sanguinoso; infin ch'arriva
> colà dove la via
> e dove il tanto affaticar fu volto:
> abisso orrido, immenso,
> ov'ei precipitando, il tutto obblia.
> Vergine luna, tale
> è la vita mortale.

(Shrunken old man, white-haired, failing, half-naked, and barefoot, with a most heavy burden upon his shoulders, who runs through valleys and over

17

mountains, over sharp stones, deep sand, and brakes, in wind, in storm, when the hour is burning, and when it freezes – runs on, panting, crosses torrents and marshes, falls, rises again, and hurries more and more, without rest or refreshment, torn and bleeding; until he arrives where the road and all his travail have led: a horrible, vast abyss into which he falls headlong, and forgets everything. Virgin moon, such is mortal life.)[41]

The shepherd's song is, however, tremendously direct. Chaucer's narrative, as we have seen, is totally indirect. Indeed, Salvatore Battaglia said that the English poet 'turned the parable into a myth of the imagination'.[42] We must therefore ask ourselves how the parable becomes myth and where Chaucer's 'modernity' lies.

In his Introduction to the *Pardoner's Tale*, Nevill Coghill pointed out a long time ago that he did not think it possible to say which notion was present in Chaucer's mind when he created the mysterious figure of the Old Man – whether an allegory of Old Age, Death, the Wandering Jew, or the Old Adam 'within us all'. He maintained, however, that the 'supreme thing in the story . . . is the eeriness' – in other words, the reader's feeling of its 'otherness':

For my own part I . . . feel sure every sensitive reader will have that pricking of the scalp that comes when we have the intuition of some supernatural presence gliding into our experience, whether real or imaginative.[43]

Coghill in fact mentioned the 'uncanny neatness of the divine arithmetic' in the rioters' 'all-unlooked-for punishment' and called the Old Man 'weird'. There is indeed little doubt that the whole episode of the old man is uncanny and that this characteristic is the main source of the attraction we feel towards it. If we need any confirmation, we can turn to Chaucer's own picture of dying Arcite for comparison. In the *Knight's Tale*, we find an extremely precise description of physical death, from the swelling of Arcite's breast to the corruption of his 'clothered blood', from the 'cold' that mounts from his feet to his chest, to the 'dusking' of his eyes and failing of his breath.[44] The view we are offered is cruelly anatomical, dreadful both in itself and because of the detachment with which the Knight describes it, but it is wholly familiar. Arcite is a man dying in bed, such as any of us may have seen. We recognize his symptoms, expect his panting, wait for his last words. The Old Man is 'weird', unfamiliar, 'uncanny'.

But what, precisely, is the uncanny? Schelling said that 'unheimlich' 'is the name for everything that ought to have remained . . . secret and hidden but has come to light'.[45] More deeply perhaps than the German philosopher imagined, that is what happens in Chaucer's passage. Mysteriously and disconcertingly, the secret truth has emerged. The fact is, however, that we cannot pinpoint the nature of the truth which is shown to us. As Death says of himself to the plowman in *Der Ackermann aus Böhmen*, 'We are nothing and yet something. Nothing because we have neither life nor being, nor form, nor mind; we are not a spirit, not visible, not touchable; something because we are life's end, the end of being, the beginning of non-being, a link between these two'.[46] How can we catch the substance of this uncanny nothing-something? Perhaps we ought to find a more specific definition of the uncanny. In our search for it, we of course stumble upon Freud. Using Schelling, Freud came to the conclusion that our unconscious mind is dominated by a 'compulsion to repeat' 'proceeding from the instinctual impulses and probably inherent in the very nature of the instincts – a compulsion powerful enough to overrule the pleasure principle'. 'Whatever reminds us of this inner "compulsion to repeat" is perceived as uncanny.' For 'the uncanny is in reality nothing new or alien'; it is 'that class of the frightening' 'which is familiar and long-established in the mind and which has become alienated from it only through the process of repression'. Now, 'there is scarcely any other matter . . . upon which our thoughts and feelings have changed so little since the very earliest times, and in which discarded forms have been so completely preserved under a thin disguise, as our relation to death'.[47] Chaucer's episode of the Old Man explores, in an extreme, veiled form, not death, but our relation to death. Have we not always wished to kill death? Have we not known an Old Man such as this for a long time? He is there to remind us that dying is painful, inescapable, desirable, mysterious, familiar, uncanny – an-other and the same thing as living.[48] The Old Man incarnates the unbearable contrast we feel between on the one hand our notion of death as the opposite of life and on the other their equivalence. He represents the borderland, the *limen* or threshold where division is oneness, and his uncanniness is therefore supremely, 'sublimely' tragic.[49]

2

Two versions of tragedy: Ugolino and Hugelyn

I

One of the most tragic stories recounted in Dante's *Divine Comedy* is that of Ugolino in *Inferno* XXXIII. Compared to the uncanny episode of Chaucer's Old Man, this looks like a straightforward tragedy, a powerful and relentless horror story. We are beyond the old man's suspended state: in fact, we are now forced to follow an inexorable itinerary, a monstrous circle from damnation to life, to dying, death, and back to eternal death.

We are in the nethermost hell, that definitive death, which the Old Man in the *Pardoner's Tale* intimates to the three rioters awaits them, though neither author nor narrator mention it by name. In Dante, there is no ambiguity. We see before us not one but two tragedies strictly linked to each other. On the one hand, there is the tragedy of evil, so unbearable for us as to be ultimately unfathomable. A life spent in treachery is frozen into inescapable punishment by perfect Justice, the sinner that was a man is reduced to an animal. What dominates here is not a feeling of uncanniness, but one of sheer *phobos* – the Aristotelian terror. On the other hand, there is the tragedy of dying recounted by Ugolino, a tale that is meant to arouse *eleos*, pity, but which finally produces mere horror. What connects terror, pity, and horror is the way in which Dante makes Ugolino tell his story – the great, despairing 'dolor' which dominates and structures his speech.

In this chapter, I will examine the various levels of the tragic that the Ugolino episode unfolds within that primary dimension, the tragedy of evil. Then, I shall turn to Chaucer's version of the Hugelyn story.

The last three cantos of *Inferno* –from XXXII to XXXIV – make up a deliberate unity of matter and form. In the tenth *bolgia* of the eighth circle Dante and Virgil meet the giants. One of them, Antheaus, carries the poets down to the frozen lake of Cocytus, which constitutes the ninth circle of Hell. Here the traitors, the worst of all sinners, are punished, divided into four groups which occupy four adjacent areas of the lake (*Caina*, those who betrayed their relatives; *Antenora*, political traitors; *Tolomea*, traitors to their guests; *Giudecca*, traitors to their benefactors). Cantos XXXII–XXXIV describe this last circle of Hell, the sinners who inhabit it and Dante's encounter with some of them. Halfway through canto XXXIII we pass from *Antenora* (Ugolino and Ruggieri) to *Tolomea* (Frate Alberigo and Branca Doria). Halfway through canto XXXIV Dante and Virgil climb past Lucifer and, through a narrow passage, emerge – at the end of the canto – on the other side of the world, on the shore of the mountain of Purgatory, and finally see the stars again.

Cocytus dominates Dante's imagination and our reading throughout: the frozen lake which looks like glass (XXXII, 24–5), the eternal icy darkness (XXXII, 71–5), the 'gelate croste' form the immobile background against which Dante and Virgil move. The sinners' tears are frozen, too: the glazed tears of Alessandro and Napoleone degli Alberti in canto XXXII (46–8) are the same that Frate Alberigo will ask Dante to remove from his eyes later in canto XXXIII (127–8). All these sinners are tormented by the cold and the ice: some lie on the surface, some are half immersed, some are completely covered and shine through 'like straw in glass' (XXXIV, 12).

All the sinners of the ninth circle are – as befits their 'matta bestialità' – animal-like. Dante himself thinks it would have been better for them to be sheep or goats (XXXII, 15) rather than human beings, but they look like frogs, sound like storks (XXXII, 31–6), butt each other like rams (XXXII, 50); later, Ugolino is like a dog (XXXIII, 78), and Lucifer himself, the 'vermo reo', is like a horrible bird, or rather, a bat (XXXIV, 47–9). The tragedy of these sinners is that of men who have become brutish beasts.

The encounter with Ugolino takes place in the shade of the gigantic mouth of Evil which opens before us. From the very beginning, Dante evokes this image of horror by comparing the appearance of the two sinners – Ugolino and Ruggieri – to a famous episode of the tragic cycle *par excellence*, that of Thebes. There, dying Tydeus ate the brain of his enemy, Menalippus.[1] Here, one sinner is 'hood' to the other and, 'as bread is devoured for hunger', sets his teeth upon his victim 'where the brain joins with the nape':

> Noi eravam partiti già da ello,
> ch'io vidi due ghiacciati in una buca,

> sì che l'un capo a l'altro era cappello;
> e come 'l pan per fame si manduca,
> così 'l sovran li denti a l'altro pose
> là 've 'l cervel s'aggiugne con la nuca:
> non altrimenti Tidëo si rose
> le tempie a Menalippo per disdegno,
> che quei faceva il teschio e l'altre cose.   (XXXII, 124–32)

(We had already left him when I saw two frozen in one hole so close that the head of the one was a hood for the other; and as bread is devoured for hunger, so the upper one set his teeth upon the other where the brain joins with the nape. Not otherwise did Tydeus gnaw the temples of Menalippus for rage than this one was doing to the skull and the other parts.)

Tydeus' 'disdegno' – his raging spite – is the mark of the register that will dominate Ugolino's presentation. It is, as Dante says to the as yet unknown sinner, a 'beastly sign' of 'hatred', which the poet is afraid may be reflected in the drying up of his own tongue. The scene, and the story that follows it, are almost unspeakable. Sinner's mouth and poet's language are equally on the very edge of the human:

> 'O tu che mostri per sì bestial segno
> odio sovra colui che tu ti mangi,
> dimmi 'l perché,' diss' io, 'per tal convegno,
> che se tu a ragion di lui ti piangi,
> sappiendo chi voi siete e la sua pecca,
> nel mondo suso ancora io te ne cangi,
> se quella con ch'io parlo non si secca.'   (133–9)

(O you who by so bestial a sign show hatred against him whom you devour, tell me the wherefore, I said, on this condition, that if you with reason complain of him, I, knowing who you are and his offense, may yet requite you in the world above, if that with which I speak does not dry up.)

After this fitting 'preface' in canto XXXII, the Ugolino episode opens with the first line of canto XXXIII and ends at line 90. It is composed of four basic units (1–78) and by an appendix – Dante's own invective against Pisa (79–90). Schematically, the sequence is the following:

I (1–3): *Ugolino's first movement and metamorphosis.* By wiping his mouth on Ruggieri's head, the sinner changes. He is halfway between brute and civilized man. At the same time, the grammatical inversion with which the canto opens isolates Ugolino's mouth, the focus of the first seventy-eight lines of *Inferno* XXXIII, the cave of shade and darkness[2] from which the entire story issues and within which it takes place.

22

II (4–21): *Introduction.* Ugolino answers Dante's question at the end of the previous canto. He begins with a rhetorical echo of Virgil's Aeneas,[3] emphasising his own 'disperato dolor', the 'grief' which oppresses his heart. He then announces the purpose of his speech: if his words are to be 'seed' that may bear 'fruit of infamy' to the traitor whom he gnaws, Dante shall see him speak and weep together (7–9). His will be a peroration delivered in order to accuse Ruggieri and to defend himself.[4] Ugolino cares very little about Dante's identity and the reasons for his voyage to Hell (10–11). It is enough for him to know from his interlocutor's accent that he is a Florentine. Between sinner and pilgrim there is a common Tuscan background which makes it possible for the former to take for granted the latter's knowledge of his life. When, immediately afterwards, Ugolino introduces himself, he has but to pronounce his name and that of Ruggieri (13–14). He adds that there is no need to tell how, as a result of Ruggieri's ill devising, he who trusted the archbishop, was captured and then put to death (16–18). This is history – *historia* – known to all and particularly to fellow Tuscans. What Dante cannot know is 'how cruel' Ugolino's death was (19–21). No one had escaped from prison to tell the story in all its details, and Ugolino's present purpose is precisely that of recounting this *fabula*, the meta-history interred with his bones and lost to mankind. This is the reason that prompts him to speak (15), to show Dante why he is such a savage neighbour to Ruggieri here in Hell and how much the archbishop wronged him on earth (21). The past is going to be evoked in all its excruciating pain to arouse Dante's pity – the *eleos* of Aristotle's *Poetics*, which Ugolino's 'parlare e lagrimar . . . insieme' points to. Yet in this evocation, which links *historia* and *fabula* together in an inextricable narrative knot, hate seems to prevail for the moment. The powerful – and tragically ironical – contrast between the 'fui' (I *was* Count Ugolino) and the 'è' (this *is* archbishop Ruggieri) of lines 13–14, which emblematically marks the distance between past and present at the beginning of the story, points with pure scorn at a mere skull. Ruggieri, the author of Ugolino's ruin, is a simple 'this' ('questi', lines 14 and 28). In history, he was Ugolino's antagonist. In the *fabula*, he disappears. The stage is entirely taken over by his victim, by the monstrous ego of the narrator.

III (22–75): *Ugolino's own story (fabula).* This is divided into four sections: (a) definition of time and space (22–6); (b) prolepsis (forewarning dream, 26–36); (c) central development – first stage: agony (37–54); (d) central development – second stage: death (55–75).

IV (76–8): *Ugolino's last movement and metamorphosis.* With eyes 'askance', the sinner takes hold of the skull once more with his teeth, now strong on the bone like a dog's. We are back to the brute and back in Hell. The appendix, Dante's invective against Pisa, follows (79–90).

I shall return to the structure of the *fabula* – of the tragedy proper – presently. In the first place, however, we must see what kind of relationship exists between history and story. What we know of history is the following.

Ugolino, Count of Donoratico, was born in the first half of the thirteenth century. The Gherardeschi, Ugolino's family, were Ghibellines: Pisa itself, his native town, was Ghibelline at first. When he saw that the Guelphs, after the death of Manfredi at Benevento in 1266, were taking over all of Tuscany, Ugolino thought it better to become Guelph. Together with his son-in-law, Giovanni Visconti, he therefore tried, in the years 1274–75, to establish a Guelph government in Pisa, but he failed, was imprisoned, and finally exiled with other Guelphs. In 1276, however, he was allowed to return, accompanied by his nephew Nino Visconti, Giovanni's son. This time, Ugolino was successful in gaining the favour of the Pisans and became very powerful. When, in 1284, Pisa fought against Genoa, Ugolino himself led the Pisan fleet, which was defeated. Nevertheless, back in Pisa, and supported by the Guelphs of Florence, Ugolino became 'podestà' and 'capitano' of the city. A little later, Pisa found itself dangerously alone against an alliance of Genoa, Lucca and Florence. Ugolino decided to break it by buying off Genoa's associates: he let a few minor Pisan castles be given to Lucca and Florence. This move provoked harsh reactions in Pisa and Ugolino found himself at variance with Nino Visconti. The party split. Weakened by polemics and struggles, Ugolino drew closer to the surviving Ghibellines, headed by the Archbishop Ruggieri with the support of the Lanfranchi, Gualandi and Sismondi families. Ruggieri and his allies made Ugolino pay for their friendship: they demanded exile for Nino Visconti, and Ugolino accepted. Nino left Pisa before they could harm him, while Ugolino, 'to cover his treason', as Villani says,[5] retired to his castle of Settimo for a short time. He then returned to Pisa and took over again: Villani maintains that he had one of his antagonists, Anselmo di Capraia (his sister's son) poisoned. After this episode, events are not clear. It seems that Ruggieri, to show that he was not Ugolino's accomplice, accused him of having sold the famous castles to Lucca and Florence. The mob attacked Ugolino's palace: one of his sons and one of his nephews were killed, Ugolino taken with two of his sons and two (according to Dante) or three (according to Villani) of his grandsons (but, in order to arouse Dante's pity, they all appear as 'figli', children, in Ugolino's narrative). Ugolino's family and his allies were chased out of Pisa; he himself and the children imprisoned in the tower, where they died the following year, February, 1289. Thus, Ugolino betrayed first the Ghibellines, then the Guelphs (including his nephew Nino Visconti), and finally Anselmo di Capraia. These, his own treasons, he ignores in his narrative, while Dante obliquely refers to them in his invective against Pisa ('For if Count Ugolino had the name of betraying you of your castles . . .', lines 85–6). Ruggieri did not betray his party, for he remained a Ghibelline; but he betrayed Ugolino and made innocent people die in prison.

This, then, is history: Ugolino's tragedy, as everything in Dante, must be seen within the general frame of the political trends which characterize thirteenth-century Italy. It is history that condemns Ugolino to the frozen lake of Cocytus, history that gives him a place in the moral economy of the universe, history that echoes in the *contrappasso*. For Ugolino, the traitor, was betrayed by his enemy and condemned to die of hunger. An ancient Chronicle says that the Count 'made the people of Pisa die of starvation' because he sold wheat at an exorbitant price; 'then at last', it adds, 'he died of hunger with all his family'.[6] In the world of the living, human revenge already pointed to the nemesis of hunger. In the world of the dead, it becomes *contrappasso*. Here, the law of Dante's Hell gives the traitor his betrayer's skull to gnaw – Ruggieri will forever be, with his own brain, the object of his former victim's hunger. And yet Ugolino, too, is condemned to eternal hunger, for he will never satiate himself on the archbishop's head.

Thus, the episode of Ugolino is a perfect tragic knot of the earthly and the other-worldly, a superb concatenation of history, politics, ethics, and meta-history. If we now turn to this last dimension, we enter the 'segrete cose', the secret things unknown to all, where Dante and his narrator organize the *fabula*. At first sight, the structure of the story is extremely simple and linear. There is no more than one narrative thread,[7] and this begins 'in mediis rebus',[8] with Ugolino and the children in jail. The development itself seems to be inspired by the classical criteria of economy, unity, and inevitability. Ugolino's story – the *fabula* as such – is just eighteen terzinas, fifty-four lines in length, without narrative interpolations. It takes place entirely in the Mew, the tower where he is imprisoned, with four deliberate displacements: the dream, that suddenly brings us to 'the mountain because of which the Pisans cannot see Lucca' (30); and Ugolino's exclamations and apostrophes to Dante, which force us back to Hell and to the actual narrative situation three times (40–2, 66, 70). Finally, given the event described in the central ninth terzina, the nailing up of the tower's door (46–7),

25

death by hunger – the end of the story – is inevitable. Ugolino's narrative looks like a granitic monolith shooting past our eyes, and its total effect is in fact as shattering as that.

Yet if one looks more closely one begins to distinguish pauses and closures that mark the junctions between different blocks, and narrative patterns which are built up of materials at once diverse and coherent. Lines 26–7 announce the dream, and mark a pause in the description of the Mew and of passing time which sets our suspense in motion: what 'future' will the 'mal sonno' have in store for Ugolino? As we read the following three terzinas, we learn something about both the future and the past. Ugolino sees himself as a wolf and his children as whelps. They are chased by Ruggieri, now 'master and lord', from Pisa towards the mountain which separates it from Lucca. To pursue the Count, the archbishop employs 'lean and eager bitches' as well as the families of Gualandi, Sismondi, and Lanfranchi. Soon, father and children are weary, and the 'sharp fangs' of their enemies rip their flanks. Clearly, the nightmare is both a re-enactment of past events (the persecution to which Ugolino feels he has been subjected, the chasing of his family and allies out of Pisa) and an ominous foreboding of the future. The final line of the passage constitutes an appropriate closure:

> e con l'agute scane
> mi parea lor veder fender li fianchi.   (35–6)

(and it seemed to me I saw their flanks ripped by the sharp fangs.)

Yet on the one hand this closure leaves everything open (how is Ugolino, and how are we at this point in the story, to interpret this detail – to imagine his 'end'?), while on the other it evokes the effect of the 'bad dream' itself. This, says Ugolino, 'rent' ('squarciò') 'the veil of the future'. The rending is then echoed by the ripping ('fender') of the victims' flanks. Finally, it is only at the end of the episode that we fully understand the function of that closure. We are able to measure the full strength of the ripping (and hence of the rending) only after we see Ugolino bite his hands for grief and, later, take hold of Ruggieri's skull with teeth as strong as a dog's on a bone.

The suspension marked by lines 40–2, only a terzina after the end of the dream, is of a different nature. Ugolino has just told us that when he woke before dawn he heard his children cry in their sleep and ask for bread. Then, he suddenly interrupts the narrative and turns to Dante:

> Ben se' crudel, se tu già non ti duoli
> pensando ciò che 'l mio cor s'annunziava;
> e se non piangi, di che pianger suoli? (40–2)

(You are cruel indeed if you do not grieve already, to think what my heart was foreboding; and if you weep not, at what do you ever weep?)

This appeal to the interlocutor's pity comes at a crucial moment of the story, when we are waiting to hear what happened after the children woke up. Its function, besides arousing our *eleos*, is to keep up suspense.

By contrast, line 54 represents a true closure. We now know that the door of the tower has been nailed up. We have seen Ugolino turn to stone inside himself and Anselmuccio ask what ails him. All that day, and the night after, Ugolino neither weeps or answers –

> infin che l'altro sol nel mondo uscìo

(until the next sun came forth on the world)

The line echoes the famous ending of Ulysses' episode in *Inferno* XXVI ('infin che 'l mar fu sovra noi richiuso') and indeed it seals up a whole stage of Ugolino's story. One whole day and one whole night have passed since the beginning – since, after several months of imprisonment, Ugolino has had the dream. Now, 'another' sun appears, a 'new' day which is not just the next one, but a 'different' one as well ('altro'). Life is vanishing, death is coming. The tempo quickens. Ugolino tolls the days as he nears his end. Another pause, a single line, breaks into the sequence for a few seconds to give vent to Ugolino's despair – his sudden cry here in Hell pierces the general silence which dominates now in his story:

> ahi dura terra, perché non t'apristi? (66)

(ah, hard earth! why did you not open?)

Then, the *fabula* terminates:

> Poscia, più che 'l dolor, poté 'l digiuno (75)

(Then fasting did more than grief had done)

This line both climaxes and closes. Its structure has that unmistakable dying fall or, in Kermode's terms, 'the sense of an ending'. Yet it does not tell us directly that Ugolino died; it contrasts the power of grief with that of fasting, and fasting is stronger. Ugolino starves to death.

Yet, and this heightens the tension, Ugolino identifies with 'dolor'. It represents the dimension of his emotional existence. He *is*, and wants to present himself from the very beginning as, his 'disperato dolor'. 'Digiuno', on the other hand, is what his material life has been reduced to – mere starvation.

The system of pauses, suspensions, and closures in the *fabula* reveals that its tight construction responds to both an oratorical and a narrative purpose – the former: Ugolino's, the latter's: Dante's. The organization itself of the narrative turns out to be highly elaborate. Here, the narrator is also the protagonist of his own story. Thus, Ugolino is allowed – indeed prompted – by the supreme Narrator of the poem, Dante, to manipulate the *fabula*, his own part in it, and, finally, the role played by the deuteragonists (the children). And Ugolino organizes his narration in a typically specular and indirect fashion so as to underline his own predominant role in the story and its mysterious tragic core.

In the first twenty-eight lines of the canto (the first seven of the *fabula*) every event is referred by Ugolino to his own person: 'how I was taken', 'how cruel my death was', 'which because of me has the title of Hunger', 'had shown me', etc. Until we encounter the 'whelps' of the nightmare, we have no idea that the protagonist of this story of capture, hunger, and death, is accompanied by anyone. In the tower, he seems to stand alone, watching the moon wax and wane through a narrow hole. The children appear for the first time in Ugolino's dream as if they primarily existed in his own psyche. When, finally, they materialize, it is through their father's ears that we hear them cry in their sleep and ask for bread (38–9). Ugolino wakes up first (37), the children follow suit (43). The repetition of the word, 'desto' and 'desti', underlines the mirrored subordination of children to father. He, in short, is the wolf; they are his smaller images – whelps.

A particularly interesting case of Ugolino's narrative technique occurs at the end of the dream. He has just heard his children cry in their sleep. He turns to Dante, saying:

> Ben se' crudel, se tu già non ti duoli
> pensando ciò che 'l mio cor s'annunziava

We are, of course, not told precisely what the Count's heart fears, but since we have heard the children ask for bread in their sleep we are indirectly led to speculate. Ugolino's compressed anguish becomes Dante's and ours. Furthermore, a few lines later the narrator reveals that after the children woke up and while the hour approached when food was usually brought, each prisoner 'was apprehensive because of his dream' ('per suo sogno ciascun dubitava', 44). The 'dubitava' echoes the 'annunziava' of line 41, thus making it clear that Dante shapes the story by means of *repetitio* and *variatio* to give it a hammering beat. More significantly, however, this is the first time we hear that the children, too, have had a dream. And because this is so close to their father's nightmare and followed by equal foreboding and apprehension, the suggestion the text seems to make is that the children's dream mirrors the father's or in any case foreshadows the same future. Indirectness and reflection dominate.

This play continues throughout the *fabula*. For instance, the key event of the narrative is presented in a typically indirect fashion. Ugolino hears the nailing up of the tower door (46–7). No specific person performs the action, which is thus perceived as the product of some mysterious agent 'below' ('di sotto'). Chaucer who, as we shall see, replaces this sentence with 'the gayler shette the dores of the tour', changes the whole effect by moving from an indirect to a direct presentation. The nailing up of the door prompts Ugolino to look in silence at the faces of his children (47–8). Again, his gaze seems to be searching for their response to the same event. Finding no mirror there, he turns to stone inside himself (49). But his gaze comes back, doubly reflected in Anselmuccio's words: 'Tu guardi sì, padre! che hai?' (51) ('You look so, father, what ails you?'). The climax is finally reached at dawn the following day. As soon as a little light penetrates into the 'woeful' prison, Ugolino sees, as Seamus Heaney translates it, 'the image of [his] face in their four faces':[9]

scorsi
per quattro visi il mio aspetto stesso.   (56–7)

Once more, we are not told what Ugolino looks like, but we learn that his face is mirrored by the children's faces – that, virtually, they have become the same thing as he, images of unspeakable voids in which one can read hunger, despair, feelings turned to stone. The supreme moment of specularity at the end of life, this is tragically counterpointed by the total blankness that follows the children's death. Gaddo throws himself outstretched at his father's feet. Ugolino sees the other three fall one by one, but his gaze is in no way mirrored. Reduced to dead things, the 'figli' have become but the inert objects of their father's furious, blind 'groping'. There is no answer to his desperate calls (70–4).

Specularity is a way of keeping two things separate while making them identical and magnifying their characteristics. By having the children mirror him, Ugolino re-creates them in his image, after his likeness, and achieves a double effect. He makes himself the centre of the story and the only sentient being in it,[10] but he has his feelings multiplied by four – four images of his own tragedy.[11] What, then, the deuteragonists are allowed to do is to weep, to speak, to move. Without ever crying, the protagonist stands mute, immobile, isolated at the centre of the stage, casting his glances around. The children surround him like a choir, watching him, responding to his looks, calling him 'father' (51, 61, 69), reacting with sublime promptness, but with reflexes that we begin to suspect are almost conditioned. Seeing his own image in their faces, Ugolino bites his hands for 'grief' (58). Immediately ('di subito') they rise and, thinking that his gesture is dictated by hunger, they offer him their own 'wretched flesh'. Even now, however, they receive no answer. Father and sons remain separate. Dying, Gaddo lies at his father's *feet*. The only unity ever achieved is the total silence which reigns in the prison for two days:

lo dì e l'altro stemmo tutti muti (65)

(that day and the next we stayed all silent)

but this, too, is immediately broken by Gaddo's cry. And Ugolino manages to reach his children only when they have become corpses, merely groping *over* ('sovra') them with the blind man's touch.

Thus, the tragedy proceeds through alternate stages of indirect specularity, of oneness and separation, of immobility and extreme gestures. A theatrical crescendo of movements dominates the story. Anselmuccio merely speaks, Ugolino bites his hands, the four children rise up. Then, Gaddo throws himself outstretched at his father's feet, and the other three fall one by one. Finally, Ugolino gropes over their bodies. How can we reconcile these movements with the situation Ugolino is describing? Worn out by hunger as they must be, how can the children rise up so promptly? How can Gaddo 'throw' himself? And how can the other three 'fall' ('cascar')? Are they, after four days of fasting, standing up? The truth which Ugolino now claims for his account and which he compares to Dante's present perception with an extremely cunning 'authenticating device'[12] ('e come tu mi vedi, vid'io cascar li tre' (70–1); 'and even as you see me, I saw the three fall') is realistically implausible. It is an emotional truth which the narrator translates into the extreme, theatrical, melodramatic gestures of

Giovanni Pisano's statues or of 'gothic' art in general. His is in fact a 'parlare e lagrimar' – both speaking *and* weeping.

The present 'dolor' which prompts Ugolino to evoke his past 'grief', and the 'oratorical' purpose of his narrative, make him overcome plausibility and find truth in his own vision of the past ('vid'io', 'I saw'). Dante, who has been summoned as an indirect witness of the events recounted by the Count, does not challenge this climactic moment of subjectivity. Upon entering the ninth circle he has firmly stated his mimetic intention as a poet by asking the Muses to help him speak 'sì che dal fatto 'l dir non sia diverso' (XXXII, 12) ('that the telling may not be diverse from the fact') – and Ugolino's narration is after all part of this 'telling'.

The 'verisimilitude' of Ugolino's story such as he recounts it is skilfully supported by two more authenticating devices. When the narrator says that there is no need to tell how he was taken and put to death (16–18), we accept this as true because the facts to which he refers are historical. Immediately afterwards he adds:

> però quel che non puoi avere inteso,
> cioè come la morte mia fu cruda,
> udirai   (19–21)

(but what you cannot have heard, that is, how cruel my death was, you shall hear)

Through the mere contiguity of the two sentences, Ugolino implicitly establishes a parallel between history and meta-history, between what is known and real and what is unknown. *Historia* and *fabula* are placed on the same level of verisimilitude.

Finally, Ugolino announces that the dream 'rent the veil of the future', that is, the future turned out to be precisely what the dream prefigured under the 'veil' of Ruggieri's hunting the wolf and the whelps. In a sense, Ugolino is trying to authenticate the future by means of the dream, and the dream by means of the future. In the Middle Ages, early morning dreams were generally supposed to be premonitions of events which would really take place.

Ugolino's narrative is, then, a complex play on various registers: it is perceived as a monolith, but the monolith is composed of particles arranged in a very peculiar structure. If one looks carefully at the actual words employed in the canto, one sees, for instance, that many of them recur several times with variations, and indeed a reader can organize them into eight series of images which dominate the mimetic, emotional, and metaphorical dimensions of the story.

Let us take the two primary mimetic coordinates, time and space. Ugolino's story begins with two temporal displacements which paradoxically concentrate the time of the action into an extremely limited span. An analepsis – that is to say, a return to events that took place before the moment in the story from which the narrative starts – opens the *historia* when Ugolino recalls that he was captured (17).[13] Here, however, the 'poscia morto' (how I was thereafter put to death, killed) of line 18 moves to the end. A prolepsis – an anticipation of future events – opens the *fabula* with the 'bad dream'. As we have seen, however, the nightmare is both a re-enactment of something which happened in the past – Ruggieri's pursuit of the Count and his family – and a warning about the end, the 'ripping' of the flanks of wolf and whelps. In other words, *historia* and *fabula* begin with temporal distortions which cover the same events: chase and capture, dying and death.

It is the time and the tempo of dying and death that Ugolino describes in his story, beginning with the 'narrow hole' and the 'several moons' that bring us 'in medias res'. The hole – the 'opening' mentioned again three lines later ('forame', 25) – is the centre of both space and time. As part of the narrow room available in the Mew, the 'pertugio' constitutes a focalization of space and at once the means by which Ugolino and Dante measure time:

> Breve pertugio dentro da la Muda,
> la qual per me ha 'l titol de la fame,
> e che conviene ancor ch'altrui si chiuda,
> m'avea mostrato per lo suo forame
> più lune già   (22–6)

(A narrow hole in the Mew which because of me has the title of Hunger, and in which others are yet to be shut up, had, through its opening, already shown me several moons)

The hole is in fact not small, but 'breve' – short – and points to both space and time. The central chronometry of the narrative indicates both an analeptically indeterminate duration of external time (the 'several moons' of the world outside the Mew) and an extremely condensed, brief, internal time. The opposition between time and space outside and inside is a constant counterpoint of the story. The *fabula* begins with the 'dimane', the dawn after the dream (37); it progresses with 'the hour . . . when food was usually brought' (43–4); it pauses after 'all that day' and 'the night after', at the coming of the second day, 'until the next sun came forth on the world' (53–4). Here, the temporal notation is significantly referred to the outside world, and external time ends. The hole will measure time only inside the Mew. The 'other' sun, which shines on the world of the living, becomes a 'little ray' that makes its way into the 'woeful prison' of the *morituri* (55–6). And it is this faint light that now scans the last days of Ugolino's undoing. 'Lo dì e l'altro', 'quarto dì', 'tra 'l quinto dì e 'l sesto', 'due dì' – the narrator divides time obsessively, with a precise, hammering insistence, to underline the growing horror of his story, to make it terminate in the undeterminate 'poscia' (then) of line 75:

> Poscia, più che 'l dolor, poté 'l digiuno.

'Poscia' is really the last syllable of recorded time after which we go back to the eternal timelessness of Hell.

A similar process takes place in the dimension of space, confined within the narrow walls of the Mew ('pertugio', 'Muda', 'forame', 'carcere'), and finally sealed when the 'horrible tower' is nailed up. As if opposed to this closing, the sun 'comes out' ('uscìo', 54) in the open world outside, which goes on living but now ceases to exist for the protagonist. Immediately after Ugolino asks why the earth itself did not open wide (66), space is annihilated – blind, Ugolino gropes in a nowhere; only the children's dead bodies are points of reference.

Light is also progressively extinguished. From the beginning, faint moonlight seems to filter through the narrow hole of the tower ('più lune', 26). The sun of the outside world disappears later, becoming a 'little ray' in the 'woeful prison'. Then, with Ugolino's blindness, total darkness invades the scene, before plunging the Count into the starless air of Hell.

The six days of the children's agony and death are, then, an inverted version of the Creation (Adam was created on the sixth day), a monstrous Undoing of time, space and light which covers sun and moon, world and earth, human beings and God. Indirectly, Ruggieri is presented as the ultimate author of this Undoing, the great Enemy whom Ugolino, in supreme blasphemy, calls 'Magister' ('maestro') and 'Dominus' ('donno')[14] – Son and Father of iniquity. Ugolino himself is, on the other hand, the God being killed. When the children offer him their flesh, they call him 'father' and add an expression which is clearly reminiscent of a verse in the Book of Job:

tu ne vestisti
queste misere carni, e tu le spoglia   (6 2–3)

(you did clothe us with this wretched flesh, and do you strip us of it!)

After losing everything, Job says (1. 21): 'Naked came I out of my mother's womb, and naked shall I return thither: the Lord gave, and the Lord hath taken away.' Later, he speaks directly to God (10.11): 'Pelle et carnibus vestisti me' ('thou hast clothed me with skin and flesh'). Ugolino, this 'pater familias', this patriarch surrounded by his 'sons', presents himself as the Father – God – being undone by the forces of evil 'di sotto', below. Indirectness and obscurity are his ways of speaking, for mystery is the language of the Lord. Yet this inverted Creation does not end with a seventh day of rest, but with two days of desperate howling. Ugolino does not give his children's bodies any peace, nor indeed is he capable of resuscitating them. On the contrary, darkness is now upon the face of the deep, but the Spirit of God, instead of moving upon the waters, gropes blindly on the wrecks of his own creation. Only chaos is left to the 'padre' who had been acknowledged by his own children as 'padrone', but who had given them 'stone' ('sì dentro impetrai') instead of the bread they had begged for.[15]

Time, space, and light are the essential mimetic coordinates of the narrative. Sight is what joins this external dimension to the interior one. Ugolino talks about seeing throughout his speech, during which, he says, Dante will indeed see him speak and weep (9). Again, the people of Pisa cannot see Lucca because of the Monte San Giuliano (30). But it is in the story, in the *fabula* itself, that seeing becomes a complex play. In the dream, Ugolino seems to see the flanks of wolf and whelps ripped by the sharp fangs of the bitches ('mi parea . . . veder', 36). When the tragedy begins, no uncertainty is left. Ugolino's eyes become the filter through which the whole story is presented and, at the same time, the mirror of his reaction to the events that take place in the story. From his mute look at the children's faces after the door is nailed up (47–8) to his seeing three of them fall one by one at the end (71), the play of specularity that I have already examined develops without any pause. When Anselmuccio turns to his father, saying, 'Tu guardi sì, padre, che hai?' (51), we understand that Ugolino's glance is the external sign of the unspeakable horror he feels inside – of his turning to stone 'dentro' (49). Finally, when the protagonist becomes blind (73), we realize the end is near. The eyes that have witnessed the entire tragedy are now blank, clouded by hunger, ready for the 'blindness' that reigns in Hell.[16] Our all-seeing god is being punished by the Lord, who smites those who do not hearken unto His voice 'with madness, and blindness, and astonishment of heart' until they 'grope at noonday', 'in desolate places as dead men'.[17] Ugolino is about to turn into an animal, his eyes 'torti', contorted and distorted forever in Hell (76).

The feeling Ugolino tries to impress upon Dante and to express through the centrality of eyes in his story is that of 'grief'. The word 'dolor' opens and closes his speech, establishing a strong continuity between his suffering on earth, where 'grief' was overcome only by fasting, and the 'disperato dolor' that wrings his heart here in Hell (5). The word is, however, highly ambiguous. There is no question that on the one hand it means *tristitia* and it implies 'anger' and 'desire of revenge'[18] – that, in sum, it verges on the 'despair' recalled in line 5, moving towards the 'hate' which Ugolino expresses by devouring Ruggieri's head (XXXII, 134), thus constituting 'the ethically significant characterization' of the Count.[19] The climax of this 'fury' in the *fabula* itself will then be the 'dolor' for which Ugolino bites his hands (58). On the other hand, when Ugolino calls the prison 'doloroso' (56), it is equally clear that he is thinking of it as the place of sorrow and suffering. Likewise, when the children answer his bite by offering their own flesh, they point to 'doglia' as the feeling which prompts them:

> Padre, assai ci fia men doglia
> se tu mangi di noi   (61–2)

(Father, it will be far less painful to us if you eat of us)

Once more, Dante is playing on several levels. 'Doloroso', 'dolor', and 'doglia' occur within six lines, each at the beginning of a terzina. The accumulation must be deliberate, and its purpose to force the listener to superimpose the meanings of 'grief' and 'fury' in one single impression. After all, Ugolino appeals to Dante's 'grief' ('se tu già non ti duoli') – to his pity and tears (40–2). The Mew is the narrow hole of Ugolino's *tristitia*, of the children's pain, of everyone's sorrow. It is this 'dolor' that finally succumbs to 'fasting' in the last line of the story.

Hence, tears accurately define the emotional situation of the characters. Ugolino, who declares that he will narrate the story and simultaneously weep, never actually sheds a tear while living the last days of his life. The children, on the other hand, weep copiously, in their sleep (38) and after the door has been nailed up (50). The contrast is clearly underlined by the narrator himself: 'Io non piangea . . .

35

piangevan elli' (49–50). For the protagonist, the situation is now beyond weeping. One could apply to it the lines which Dante himself uses to describe, later in the same canto, the traitors of the *Tolomea*:

> Lo pianto stesso lì pianger non lascia,
> e 'l duol che truova in su li occhi rintoppo,
> si volge in entro a far crescer l'ambascia (94–6)

(The very weeping there prevents their weeping, and the grief, which finds a barrier upon their eyes, turns inward to increase the agony)

This is precisely what happens to Ugolino, who turns to stone within ('dentro impetrai', 49). Third metamorphosis of the sinner, who, identified as a beast from his very appearance, becomes then a wolf, this petrifying is the 'degree zero' of Ugolino's 'dolor'. For a second, in the total crystallization of every feeling, the fatherly sorrow of traditional, 'romantic' criticism[20] and the anger of the modern meet.

Then, tears dry up in the children's eyes as well, and what we have is a mere play of words and silence in the growing darkness. Throughout the story, the voices of Ugolino's sons have resounded in the tower, banging, as it were, against the wall of his silence. Their father looks at them 'without a word' (48), never answers their cry for bread, does not reply to Anselmuccio's question (52), says nothing to their offer of their own flesh, and keeps silent even after Gaddo begs him. He is a mute deity turned into an idol of stone, capable only of biting his own hands. Ugolino, who presents himself as all-seeing and all-knowing, is an impotent God. His tongue has indeed dried up. He opens his mouth only after the children's death to call them in the last remnant of human language before he is transformed into a dog. The children's words, on the other hand, proclaim them the true 'sons of man'. In a primeval cry – in the *Pater Noster* invocation of Christian mankind – they ask for bread (39). Like Christ in the Eucharist, they offer their own bodies in the supreme sacrifice (61–3). Like Jesus on the cross, Gaddo cries, 'Eli, Eli, lamma sabachtani?' ('My God, my God, why hast thou forsaken me?'):

> Padre mio, ché non m'aiuti? (69)

> (Father, why do you not help me?)

At the children's death, as before Jesus' cry, darkness comes upon the earth. Finally, Dante condemns Pisa for having put the children 'to such *cross*':

non dovei tu i figliuoi porre a tal croce.   (87)[21]

While Ugolino lives his and the children's tragedy as an inversion of the Creation, his sons' drama is a true Passion. After three days, however, Christ rises from the dead. A prey to their father's groping, Ugolino's children lie in death for two days. The third is never reached, and everything ends in the 'poscia' of line 75.

The last series of images in Ugolino's episode is one that no reader can fail to notice. Canto XXXII ends with the as yet unknown sinner setting his teeth upon the other where the brain joins with the nape – 'as bread is devoured for hunger'. Canto XXXIII opens with Ugolino's mouth rising from its 'savage repast' and mentioning the traitor he 'gnaws'. The episode ends with the sinner taking hold again of the wretched skull with his teeth, 'che furo a l'osso, come d'un can, forti'(78) ('which were strong on the bone like a dog's'). In the dream, the sharp fangs of the bitches rip the flesh of wolf and whelps. 'Bread' (39) becomes 'food' (44) and then 'misere carni' (63). The biting of the hands (58) is misinterpreted as 'voglia di manicar' (desire to eat, 59–60) and prompts the children to say: 'it will be far less painful to us if you *eat* of us' (61–2). Like that of the tower, the 'title' of Ugolino's narrative is Hunger. Fittingly, its last word is 'fasting':

Poscia, più che 'l dolor, poté 'l digiuno.

Fasting killed Ugolino. Was it also so much more powerful than grief that it prompted him to a 'savage repast' – a final, devilish Eucharist[22] – before he died? Rumours about his cannibalism were circulating, it seems, both before and after the *Inferno* was written,[23] and many hints in the text itself suggest that Dante may have had this conclusion in mind.[24] Finally, 'technophagy' – the eating of children by the father – would agree with the conception of tragedy that Dante borrowed from Hugutio of Pisa in his Letter to Cangrande.[25] Here, however, a 'lump of reticence in the throat'[26] stops Ugolino from telling us explicitly and allows Dante to use once more the technique of indirectness that is so typical of this canto. The tension of the episode rises to an unbearable climax of horror in the ambiguity of a sentence that cuts Ugolino's voice forever.

Ugolino's story is one which is told by, speaks about, and takes place within the mouth. For the 'bocca' that rises at the beginning of canto XXXIII is but the first in a series of cavities that open and close throughout the narration. The Mew is called *Hunger*: it is a mouth that swallows Ugolino and his children, and where 'others are yet to be shut up' (24). The 'narrow hole' of line 22 echoes in the 'forame' of line 25, and this in turn recurs with increased violence as the tear in the veil through which Ugolino has a glimpse of the future, and as the rip in the animals' bodies made by the bitches. To the 'breve pertugio' and its opening above corresponds the 'uscio di sotto', the door below, at the bottom of the horrible tower. That door is now nailed up the same way in which it will be closed after other prisoners in the future. Finally, Ugolino himself asks from his 'icy hole' (XXXII, 125): 'Ah, hard earth! why did you not open?' (XXXIII, 66). The ground is conceived as the great mouth which gulps men down to death.²⁷ In the next canto, each of Lucifer's three mouths will champ a sinner – a traitor – 'as with a heckle' (XXXIV, 55–6). Ugolino's mouth, the speaking tongue of the canto, anticipates the mouth of Evil that chews Brutus, Cassius, and Judas. The Mew is a prefiguration of the 'burella', the underground dungeon at the centre of which stands Satan (XXXIV, 98). The earth does eventually open to swallow the fallen angel (XXXIV, 121–6), as well as Ugolino, in an eternal 'grave' (XXXIV, 128). The 'breve pertugio' of the tower foreshadows the 'hole' where Ugolino lies, frozen, on top of Ruggieri (XXXII, 125) and the 'tristo buco' which, as Dante says in his grand *ouverture* to the last cantos of the *Inferno*, is the 'bottom of the entire universe':

> S'ïo avessi le rime aspre e chiocce,
>   come si converrebbe al tristo buco
>   sovra 'l qual pontan tutte l'altre rocce,
> io premerei di mio concetto il suco
>   più pienamente; ma perch'io non l'abbo,
>   non sanza tema a dicer mi conduco;
> ché non è impresa da pigliare a gabbo
>   discriver fondo a tutto l'universo,
>   né da lingua che chiami mamma o babbo.   (XXXII, 1–9)

(If I had harsh and grating rhymes, as would befit the dismal hole on which all the other rocks converge and weigh, I would press out more fully the juice of my conception; but since I do not have them, it is not without fear that I bring myself to speak; for to describe the bottom of the whole universe is not an enterprise to be taken up in sport, nor for a tongue that cries mamma and daddy.)

Thus, the story of Ugolino produces terror because it is one of Hell in life, a veritable tragedy of Evil recounted – supreme demonic transgression – as if it were sacred history. It is Lucifer's version of the

Creation, the ending of the Fall into the Mouth as if it were the fruit eaten by Adam and Eve. Dante fears he cannot describe the bottom of the universe with a tongue that cries 'Mummy' and 'Daddy' – both the innocent language of children and the universal, primary speech of human kind. Ugolino's mouth utters a howling narrative where the colloquial, tender 'babbo' is replaced by 'padre', but where 'mamma' (perhaps the first and last word every human being pronounces) cannot even be conceived. Dante proclaims he does not have 'harsh and grating rhymes'. Ugolino tells his story using alliteration ('*disperato dolor che* 'l *cor mi preme*'; '*e che conviene ancor ch*'altrui si *chiuda*') and sounds the repetition of which, combined with the alchemy of poetry, gives his lines a harsh, dim, dark quality. The 'r' and the 'u' become the marks of fury ('che *frutti* infamia al *traditor ch*'i' *rodo*') and despair:

> *Breve pertugio dentro da la Muda*
> *Poscia, più che 'l dolor, poté 'l digiuno*

Ugolino and Dante conceive this as the ultimate human tragedy, the last and worst of the *Inferno*.[28] The tragedy is the product of the basic contrast between the children's innocence and Ugolino's guilt. For the first and last time in the cantica, the story of a sinner's death is allowed to include the undoing of innocent people, who unjustly share his fate. It is this tragic contrast that prompts Dante's reaction:

> Che se 'l *conte Ugolino* aveva voce
>   d'aver tradita te de le castella,
>   non dovei tu i *figliuoi* porre a tal croce.
> *Innocenti* facea l'età novella,
>   novella Tebe, Uguiccione e 'l Brigata
>   e li altri due che 'l canto suso appella.   (85–90)

(For if Count Ugolino had the name of betraying you of your castles, you ought not to have put his children to such torture. Their youthful years, you modern Thebes, made Uguiccione and Brigata innocent, and the other two that my song names above.)

But on top of this an absolutely unbearable element is added, and that is Ugolino's attempt at making himself similar to his children, at exploiting them to proclaim his innocence. If, as the canto intimates at least twice, the children are Christ-like, then their father must be Jesus' Father. Dante, however, explodes this Lucifer-like fiction by counter-pointing the children's Biblical utterances with Ugolino's classical allusions. When the sinner first opens his mouth to speak, he echoes the words with which Aeneas begins his narration to Dido[29] – and the story Aeneas tells is the supreme tragedy of Troy's fall. When Ugolino cries, 'ahi dura terra, perché non t'apristi?', his models are Juturna lamenting Turnus' death,[30] Thyestes reacting to his savage repast,[31] Oedipus coming to know the truth.[32] The wild groping over the children's corpses recalls Niobe throwing herself on the cold bodies of her sons.[33] All the passages that Ugolino's speech echoes point to the dreadful ends, the climactic Doom of cities, men, and women. And Dante has framed the entire story with allusions to the tragic epos of Thebes and with borrowings from Statius' *Thebaid*. Thus, when he first appears in canto XXXII Ugolino is like Tydeus eating Menalippus' brain,[34] and his 'occhi torti' at the end of the episode recall Statius' 'lumina torva'.[35] Finally, Pisa is herself called 'new Thebes' in the poet's invective.[36] It is not by chance, then, that in the 'prologue' to Cocytus in canto XXXII Dante should choose for his invocation to the Muses an episode which is connected with Thebes – the aid they gave Amphion to build the walls of the city by inspiring his music:[37]

> Ma quelle donne aiutino il mio verso
> ch'aiutaro Anfione a chiuder Tebe,
> sì che dal fatto il dir non sia diverso.   (XXXII, 10–12)

(But may those ladies aid my verse who aided Amphion to wall in Thebes, so that the telling may not be diverse from the fact.)

For in the last cantos of *Inferno* Dante does indeed 'close in' Thebes and all its story of horror. With these classical counterpoints to Ugolino's demonic Scripture the poet succeeds in telling a story which is tragedy 'foul and horrible',[38] where discrepancies between the 'fact' and the 'word' are annulled by a mouth that speaks ambiguously, indirectly, specularly, for and against itself[39] – where language transforms events into a myth of the End at the bottom of the universe.

II

After thinking for a moment that he may well tell his fellow pilgrims the story of the life of Saint Edward the Confessor, the Monk of the *Canterbury Tales* decides to settle on 'tragedies', of which he says he has a hundred in his 'celle'.[40] He then proceeds to offer his audience the following definition of tragedy:

> Tragedie is to seyn a certeyn storie,
> As olde bookes maken us memorie,

40

> Of hym that stood in greet prosperitee,
> And is yfallen out of heigh degree
> Into myserie, and endeth wrecchedly.
> And they ben versified communely
> Of six feet, which men clepen *exametron*.
> In prose eek been endited many oon,
> And eek in meetre in many a sondry wyse.
> Lo, this declaryng oghte ynogh suffise. (1973–82)

To this conception the Monk goes back at the beginning of his Tale, adding that the stories he will tell are 'ensamples trewe and olde' – traditional, authoritative *exempla*:

> I wol biwaille in manere of tragedie
> The harm of hem that stoode in heigh degree,
> And fillen so that ther nas no remedie
> To brynge hem out of hir adversitee.
> For certein, whan that Fortune list to flee,
> Ther may no man the cours of hire withholde.
> Lat no man truste on blynd prosperitee;
> Be war by thise ensamples trewe and olde. (1991–8)

Not content with having already stated his theme twice, the Monk repeats it once more at the end of the story of Croesus, that is, if we accept the order of the majority of manuscripts, at the end of his Tale, before he is interrupted by the Knight:

> Tragediës noon oother maner thyng
> Ne kan in syngyng crie ne biwaille
> But that Fortune alwey wole assaille
> With unwar strook the regnes that been proude;
> For whan men trusteth hire, thanne wol she faille,
> And covere hire brighte face with a clowde. (2761–6)

It is clear that with a slightly pedantic insistence the Monk echoes Boethius' definition of tragedy:

What other thynge bywaylen the cryinges of tragedyes but oonly the dedes of Fortune, that with an unwar strook overturneth the realmes of greet nobleye? (*Boece* II, pr. 2, 67–70)

In the light of this conception, however, at least four problems arise immediately. The first is its being alien to us today, its alterity. We cannot accept as tragic the mere 'fall' of people in 'high degree' or of 'regnes that been proude', nor can we agree to its being determined only by the 'unwar strook' of Fortune. Indeed since at least 1789, the year of the French Revolution, such 'falls' would most likely fit in with the modern idea of justice or of social movements rather than that of fortune. For us, tragedy is inevitably linked to the names of Orestes, Oedipus, Philoctetes, Macbeth, Hamlet, King Lear, or, in a different realm, to Christ's Passion, to the sufferings of the Karamazovs and of Prince Myshkin. Our idea of tragedy involves the fallibility of man, his errors and sins, power and justice, ignorance and knowledge, madness and death.

The second problem is that the fictitious audience of the Monk's stories does not itself seem to appreciate them. The Knight complains of 'hevynesse' and of the 'greet disese' that listening to the sudden fall of great men produces. Indeed, he opposes to this 'the contrarie' – the 'climbing up' of people 'in povre estaat' – and may in fact be thinking of his own story, a tragedy that turns into romance.[41] The Host, more brutally, accuses the Monk of wearying the entire company and putting it to sleep.

The third problem is that Chaucer himself apparently holds a different, more complex idea of tragedy. Whatever the 'litel tragedye' of *Troilus and Criseyde* may be, it certainly is not the mere story of a downfall due to Fortune.[42] And we have seen with what kind of sense of the tragic the episode of the Old Man in the *Pardoner's Tale* is imbued.

Finally, the thematic pattern of the *Monk's Tale* itself does not look completely coherent. We begin with Lucifer and Adam, two very short episodes which seem to announce a grand, cosmic treatment of the Fall, and where 'sin' and 'mysgovernaunce', not Fortune, are the causes of final doom. With Samson, this universal theme is abandoned and, without ever mentioning Fortune, the Monk concentrates on the hero's strength and on his being betrayed by Delilah. Hercules, Samson's pagan counterpart in strength, follows. Here, Fortune appears in the teller's comment in the last stanza, but the hero's downfall is brought about by Deianira. With the 'proud' and 'elaat' Nebuchadnezzar we return to the Old Testament: appropriately, in this episode it is God who punishes the King, but his fall into madness and bestiality is only temporary, for he is restored and finally acknowledges God's power and grace. His son Belshazzar comes next, both a proud man and an 'ydolastre'. He is warned by God and destroyed by Darius – an example, says the Monk, of Fortune's way of acting. The story of

Zenobia, clearly indebted to Boccaccio's *De Casibus Virorum Illustrium* and *De Claris Mulieribus*, is a parabola in the course of which Virtue is overcome by a Fortune which cannot even pretend to be divine punishment. Zenobia is an exemplary woman, 'worthy in armes', chaste in the extreme, wise, 'large with mesure', ready to learn foreign languages and to read books. Her undoing is due to the turning of Fortune's wheel and to that alone. She does not die, but is made to walk in Aurelian's triumph and, instead of a sceptre, to hold a distaff in her hands to pay for her keep.

In most manuscripts, after Zenobia we encounter the so-called 'modern instances': Peter of Spain, Peter of Cyprus, Bernabò Visconti, and Hugelyn. These are all stories of treason and violent death. Fortune is absent only from the single stanza devoted to Bernabò. Nero, who comes next, is a vicious 'tyrant'[43] 'snatched from his seat' by Fortune through a popular rebellion and who finally commits suicide. Holofernes, strong and full of 'presumpcioun', is 'likerously kissed' by Fortune and beheaded by Judith. Antiochus, author of 'werkes venymus', is sorely smitten by God 'with invisible wounde' and starts rotting away precisely when Fortune favours his pride to the point that he considers himself omnipotent. With Alexander, Julius Caesar, and Croesus we leave the Bible for good. The first, a 'flower' 'of knyghthod and of fredom', is poisoned by his own men, Fortune thus 'turning' his 'six into an ace'. The second, a paragon of wisdom, manhood, and 'estaatly honestee', is fought by Fortune and stabbed by Brutus 'and his othere foon' (and the Monk takes the opportunity to 'biwaille' also Pompey, a victim of Fortune and of a 'fals traitour'). Finally, Croesus ends up gaping on the gallows thanks to Fortune herself.

In short, what we have is a string of stories that go in various directions and which do not correspond strictly to the three definitions of tragedy the Monk gives us.[44] The motivations for the 'falls' are disparate and often mixed with, or superimposed on each other (God, Fortune, treason). Furthermore, all the episodes are either brief allusions or, with the exception of the modern instances, more or less extensive *summaries* of various sources. They have no autonomous narrative development and no dramatic vigour. There is virtually no dialogue, and the protagonists have only an exemplary charàcterization.

This is not to say that powerful lines or stanzas are wholly lacking. At the end of the Zenobia story, for instance, the author resorts to

Boccaccio's *De Casibus*. There, he finds a series of sentences each rhetorically halved into two contraposed parts and all linked by *repetitio*:

Hec nuper persis syrisque tremenda regibus, nunc vilipenditur a privatis; hec nuper imperatoribus admiranda, nunc venit miseranda plebeis; hec nuper galeata contionari militibus assueta, nunc velata cogitur muliercularum audire fabellas; hec nuper Orienti presidens sceptra gestabat, nunc Rome subiacens colum sicut cetere baiulat.[45]

Chaucer keeps this structure and creates a stanza where not only the rhetorical balancing is maintained, but the epigraphic quality is intensified by alliteration. The language is that of *Troilus* and of the *Knight's Tale*:

> Allas, Fortune! She that whilom was
> Dredeful to kynges and to emperoures,
> Now gaureth al the peple on hire, allas!
> And she that helmed was in starke stoures
> And wan by force townes stronge and toures,
> Shal on hir heed now were a vitremyte;
> And she that bar the ceptre ful of floures
> Shal bere a distaf, hire cost for to quyte.   (2367–74)[46]

Another example is the terrifying description of Antiochus' end, with the inexorable progress of corruption that reduces him to a carcase even before he dies. The account of 2 Maccabees[47] is greatly intensified, and the picture is as vivid as that of Arcite's death in the *Knight's Tale*, as powerful as Boccaccio's description of the plague in the *Decameron*, as hair-raising as the evocation of Philoctetes' wounds in Sophocles:

> The wreche of God hym smoot so cruelly
> That thurgh his body wikked wormes crepte,
> And therwithal he stank so horribly
> That noon of al his meynee that hym kepte,
> Wheither so he wook or ellis slepte,
> Ne myghte noght the stynk of hym endure.
> In this meschief he wayled and eek wepte,
> And knew God lord of every creature.
>
> To al his hoost and to hymself also
> Ful wlatsom was the stynk of his careyne;
> No man ne myghte hym bere to ne fro.
> And in this stynk and this horrible peyne,
> He starf ful wrecchedly in a monteyne.   (2615–27)

Two versions of tragedy: Ugolino and Hugelyn

In other words, both Chaucer and the Monk are perfectly capable of speaking vigorously in the 'tragic' mode whenever they feel so inclined and particularly when they are relying on a written source and read it closely. The problem of the Tale as a whole must lie somewhere else. One comes closer to it by looking at the modern instances, three of which are not based on any written account. These, the stories of Peter of Spain, Peter of Cyprus, and Bernabò Visconti, are not in fact narratives. They sound rather like epitaphs which merely record the death by treason of the three men. Two begin with rhetorical addresses to the characters themselves, in a style which is typical of the complaint:[48]

> O noble, O worthy Petro, glorie of Spayne
> O worthy Petro, kyng of Cipre, also

The first 'epitaph', on Peter of Spain, is accompanied by a stanza which obliquely alludes to the men who helped Don Enrique of Trastamare betray the King. To this end, Chaucer makes the Monk employ a device – the coats of arms – used by French poetry and, most memorably, by Dante.[49] He adds the play on Ganelon and Olivier (Oliver Mauny, one of Peter's betrayers, was not like Charlemagne's trustworthy Olivier, but rather like the traitor Ganelon):

> The feeld of snow, with th'egle of blak therinne,
> Caught with the lymrod coloured as the gleede,
> He brew this cursednesse and al this synne.
> The wikked nest was werker of this nede.
> Noght Charles Olyver, that took ay heede
> Of trouthe and honour, but of Armorike
> Genylon-Olyver, corrupt for meede,
> Broghte this worthy kyng in swich a brike.   (2383–90)

The Spanish Peter is slain in his brother's tent by Enrique himself. Peter of Cyprus is killed in his bed by his own 'liges'. Why and how Bernabò, ousted by his 'double allye' – his nephew and son-in-law Giangaleazzo – was murdered the Monk professes not to know. But he underlines that the man who had been 'god of delit and scourge of Lumbardye' (a pretty incisive epitaph, too) was 'made to die' in his brother's son's prison. In the modern instances, then, Chaucer makes the Monk move between what Dante would have called the *Antenora* and the *Caina*, the areas of Hell where political traitors and those who betrayed their relatives are punished.[50] Furthermore, the actual scene of treason and death is gradually shifted from tent to bed and finally to prison. The stage for Ugolino's story is carefully set up. The 'plaintive epitaphs' of Bernabò and the two Peters will be magnified and deepened, to become articulated narrative for the first and only time in the *Monk's Tale*. The modern instances constitute Chaucer's closest equivalent to Dante's *Inferno* in one of the most non-Dantean contexts a reader can imagine.

For the problem of the *Monk's Tale* is a much wider one. Almost thirty years ago George Steiner wrote that 'Chaucer's definition [of tragedy] derives its force from contemporary awareness of sudden reversals of political and dynastic fortune', but also that 'the rise and fall of him that stood in high degree was the incarnation of the tragic sense for a much deeper reason: it made explicit the universal drama of the fall of man'.[51] In the *Monk's Tale*, this is proved not only by the examples of Lucifer and Adam, but also by that of Antiochus and by those of Nebuchadnezzar and Belshazzar. It is in this area that we as moderns can find the dimension of man's fallibility that embodies our sense of the tragic. When, however, the Monk tells the stories of Nero, Alexander, Julius Caesar, and Croesus, the focus has decidedly moved towards what Steiner calls the 'awareness of sudden reversals of political and dynastic fortune', an awareness which is increasingly 'secular', separated from strictly religious or moral considerations of man's intrinsic fallibility. This consciousness is even stronger in the modern instances, which are purposely inserted among Biblical and classical *exempla*.[52] Here, 'fortune' means struggle for power, treason a purely human, and particularly cruel game.

Now, this oscillation of the tragic between contrasting poles is a central feature of late fourteenth-century culture. An example is represented by Mussato's *Ecerinis* earlier in the century. In this 'Senechian' tragedy the notion of Fortune's wheel is still central.[53] More directly relevant to the *Monk's Tale*, Boccaccio maintains at the opening of his *De Casibus* that the cause of men's falls is divine Providence, yet he speaks of 'Fortune' throughout the work and at one point goes as far as to say that Fortune can do nothing against virtue.[54] Chaucer's Monk is a spokesman for these uncertainties. In his collection, he reviews the various possibilities of the tragic. Sin, pride, human cruelty, political struggle, treason, divine punishment – Fortune is precisely all this. It is the realm of those forces which, inside or outside man, dominate his life. The Monk piles up example after example, illustrating not only man's fallibility but above all his 'falling', his being a victim of powers that are from the beginning – or become if they grow inside him – far greater than the human being.

Samson and Hercules, the one Biblical, the other classical, are destroyed by their very strength, undone by the weaker sex! Zenobia is virtuous, yet she falls. Hugelyn has committed no crime, yet his fellow citizens condemn him to die of hunger and Fortune 'carves' him 'away'.[55]

The story of Hugelyn, then, is presented in more than one way as the climax of the *Monk's Tale*, the 'degree zero' of the Monk's sense of the tragic. Significantly, this is the only episode in the entire collection which is explicitly called 'tragedie' (2458), and the only one that is prefaced by Chaucer's version of the Dantean inexpressibility topos:

> Off the Erl Hugelyn of Pyze the langour
> Ther may no tonge telle for pitee. (2407–8)

What, then, has Chaucer done to Dante's tragedy to produce his own is the question we must turn to if we want to understand at what sense of the tragic he was aiming in the *Monk's Tale*.

The first thing one notices is that Chaucer has omitted the frame within which the Ugolino episode is inserted in the *Inferno*: his presentation, his self-introduction to Dante, his recommencing the 'savage repast', and Dante's invective against Pisa. Within the *fabula* itself, what is noticeably missing is Ugolino's dream. On the other hand, Chaucer has added several details. First and foremost, there is the fact that his Hugelyn is innocent, that he has been imprisoned because of a 'fals suggestioun' by bishop Roger as a consequence of which the people of Pisa revolt against the mighty Earl. Secondly, we are told that the children who went to jail with their father were three, and that their ages varied between a maximum of five and a minimum of three (2412 and 2431). Thirdly, Chaucer has specified that the Tower of Hunger was 'litel out of Pize' (2409).

It is fairly obvious that Chaucer's omissions depend on the nature of the Tale, which is told by the Monk and relies on his memory: Hugelyn is the subject of a narrative, not the narrator. But it also becomes clear that what the Monk leaves out of his story implies the loss of the animal and mouth images, of the ethical significance of Ugolino's place in Hell, of the strict connection between his hunger in life and his hunger after death (the gnawing of Ruggieri's skull), and finally of the indirectness with which the historical dimension is presented (the dream) and which allows it to border on meta-history. The political implications of Dante's narrative have also changed. Pisa is no longer a 'new Thebes'. On the bishop, Roger, falls the primary moral responsibility for Hugelyn's imprisonment (Ruggieri has become the only real traitor of

47

the story). The mob, instigated by him, is now the direct agent of Hugelyn's 'fall'. In other words, we are reading a perfectly ordinary episode of the struggle for power. The delicate Dantean balance between history and *fabula* has been altered. It is upon history, rather than meta-history, that this teller likes to dwell. The recent past, the two Peters, Bernabò, Ugolino, appeal to him – in a sense as if, in pre-Elizabethan fashion, the Mediterranean world of intrigue and murder were a mirror of the present, of the troubles contemporary England was going through and about which Chaucer could not of course speak directly. Thus, the Monk wishes to be precise (more precise than Dante) about the historical situation in which Hugelyn is 'carved away' by Fortune. And his 'historical' approach to the episode determines the method by which he sets up the background: first the name of the character, then the place (with the 'authenticating' detail of the tower's location), then number and age of the children, then why and how Hugelyn is in prison, finally that he has no food and no drink. Fortune frames the story (2413–14 and 2457) and appears in it, at the dead centre of Hugelyn's own consciousness:

> Allas, Fortune, and weylaway!
> Thy false wheel my wo al may I wyte. (2445–6)

Chaucer has adopted a new technique. Everything is pointed out with precision and in due order: first the introduction, then the reasons for Hugelyn's imprisonment, then the scarcity of food (first two stanzas, 2407–22). Only after this are we allowed to enter the 'secret things', to reach the 'medias res'. The action proper begins with the third stanza in the episode. The gaoler shuts 'the dores of the tour'. Hugelyn immediately thinks that 'they' are going to starve him to death. He weeps, exclaiming 'Allas that I was wroght!' (2429). The youngest child cries for food (fourth stanza, 2431–8), then dies (first half of the fifth stanza, 2439–42). Hugelyn bites his arms 'for wo' and complains against Fortune (second half of the fifth stanza, 2443–6). The remaining two children offer Hugelyn their flesh and die (sixth stanza, 2447–54). Finally, Hugelyn himself 'despeired, eek for hunger starf' (first line of the seventh stanza, 2455).

In this narrative, there is no major pause, none of the closures that characterize Dante's story, no temporal displacement. The plot unfolds in crescendo, cause is followed by effect, indirectness and specularity are replaced by directness. Ugolino's nightmare; the children begging for bread in their sleep; Ugolino's forebodings; the doubts of the prisoners; the sound of the nailing up of the tower; Ugolino's mute glance at the children; his turning to stone within himself; Anselmuccio's response to his father's gaze; Ugolino's seeing his own look reflected in the four faces: all these elements disappear. Instead, we have the *gaoler* shutting the door,[55] and Hugelyn consequently thinking 'that they for hunger wolde doon hym dyen' (2428). Between these two moments, there is only an instant of the dreadful, constant silence that petrifies Dante's Ugolino: 'He herde it wel, but he spak right noght' (2426). Then, Hugelyn speaks and weeps:

> 'Allas!' quod he, 'Allas, that I was wroght!'
> Therwith the teeris fillen from his yen.   (2429–30)

It is to these tears that the youngest child responds: 'Fader, why do ye wepe?' (2432). And a last remnant of Dante's indirect technique surfaces immediately afterwards. For, as if guessing his father's thoughts without having heard the gaoler shut the door, the child asks: 'Whanne wol the gayler bryngen oure potage?' (2433).

The protagonist of this fourth stanza is the 'yonge sone'. He sees his father's tears – and immediately forgets them because of his own plight. But in asking when the gaoler will bring the soup, he seems to understand what lies behind his father's tears. Dante's indirect 'e per suo sogno ciascun dubitava' refers to the dream and comes *before* the nailing of the door. In Chaucer, two direct expressions ('the gayler shette the dores of the tour' and 'whanne wol the gayler bryngen oure potage') are linked together in direct temporal sequence, representing the first and last stages in a series of causally connected statements. The process can be described as follows: 1. the gaoler shuts the doors of the tower; 2. Hugelyn (hears it, keeps silent and) thinks, because of (1), that they will let him die of hunger; 3. because of (2) and (1), he weeps; 4. the child asks why he weeps ((3), (2), and (1) implied); 5. the child asks when the gaoler will bring the soup (responding to (1), (2), and (3)).

In the Monk's fourth stanza, 'Fader, why do ye wepe?' recalls Anselmuccio's 'che hai?'. In Dante, however, this answers Ugolino's mute glance and tries to penetrate inside the stone that is now his heart. In Chaucer, by contrast, it prompts the child's own complaint, where the dominant images are those of food and hunger: 'potage', 'morsel breed', 'hungry', 'hunger', 'breed'. It is clear that Chaucer remembers here the 'domandar del pane' of Dante's children. But this, asked for by the children in their sleep, is the only food ever mentioned in *Inferno* XXXIII. As we have seen, it has a universal connotation – it is the daily bread of the Lord's prayer. Chaucer's bread comes after 'potage'. It is a scrap of bread: it is bread as such. The child, moreover, is anguished by the thought that his father may have some of it: 'Is ther no morsel breed that ye do kepe?' (2434). Then, hunger explodes in his words much more openly than it did in Dante's scene – becoming a figure of death:

> I am so hungry that I may nat slepe.
> Now wolde God that I myghte slepen evere!
> Thanne sholde nat hunger in my wombe crepe   (2435–7)

Creeping into his womb, hunger takes hold of the child's entire being: it prevents sleep and leads to eternal sleep. The child's womb is now the Mew – it bears the 'title of Hunger'.

The fourth stanza is above all the stanza of the 'yonge sone'. The emphasis lies on the *I* (repeated three times, with the addition of '*my* wombe' and '*me* were levere'). This contrasts with Anselmuccio's '*Tu* guardi sì, padre', and shifts the focus of attention from father to son. In the fifth stanza, the child reaches his father and dies. The attention here is divided between father and son and concentrates on the kiss which unites them, the child having already laid 'in his fadres barm'. Dante's Ugolino, on the other hand, cannot be reached. Again, the fifth stanza is organized in a series of causally connected statements, the first of which repeats, summarizing, the preceding stanza: 1. continuing to cry 'thus' (see preceding stanza), the child lies in his father's lap, says farewell, kisses his father, and *dies*; 2. Hugelyn sees him *dead* and bites his hands for *woe*; 3. Hugelyn complains against Fortune, who is responsible for his *woe*. The movement of the three clauses is very studied, providing an operatic scene which directly counterpoints Gaddo's death in Dante:

> Poscia che fummo *al quarto dì* venuti,
>   Gaddo mi si *gittò* disteso a' *piedi*,
>   dicendo: 'Padre mio, *ché non m'aiuti?*'
> *Quivi morì*

> Thus *day by day* this child bigan to crye,
>   Til in his fadres *barm* adoun it *lay*,
>   And seyde, '*Farewel*, fader, I moot dye!'
> And *kiste* his fader, and dyde the same day.

In Chaucer's fifth stanza, the images concentrate on death and grief. Food and hunger are left out. In the sixth stanza, the causal nexus works again, but not in the last two lines, which follow a different tempo. The children's offer of their own flesh appeals to Chaucer, but he significantly leaves out their sudden rising and, echoing Job more closely than Dante,[57] simplifies the rhetorical play of 'vestisti' and 'spoglia' with his 'Oure flessh thou *yaf* us, *take* oure flessh us fro' (2451). After this, there is a short pause ('and after that, withinne a day or two', 2453) which suspends the action. The last line of the stanza, slow and tense, comes in one breath:

> They leyde hem in his lappe adoun and deyde.

This line is one of the most powerful in the whole episode. It repeats the movement of the passage that describes the death of the youngest child in the preceding stanza, but omitting the farewell and the kiss. Chaucer focusses on the lying of the children in their father's lap, thus recalling the gesture of the 'yonge sone' ('lappe'–'barm'). Before dying, they all reach Hugelyn and, in contrast to Ugolino's solitude, the family forms a group. The slow, solemn rhythm of this line is set in deliberate contrast with the broken, abrupt cadence of the next:

> Hymself, despeired, eek for hunger starf.

In its terrible ambiguity, Dante's 'Poscia, più che 'l dolor, poté 'l digiuno' represents a climax without end. Chaucer has eliminated the two days of Ugolino's madness, his frenzied groping over the dead corpses, his calling. He has ignored any suggestion Dante's text could have made of Ugolino's cannibalism. He has made his line perfectly clear. He has transformed 'dolor' into despair and 'digiuno' into hunger. Hugelyn's children can die in his lap. At the end of their life, they can return to the flesh whence they sprang, to their father's bosom. Hugelyn's life ends in pure despair, as if anticipating the 'disperato dolor' that torments Dante's Ugolino in Hell. The tension of this line is all centred on 'despeired'. But the line ends with 'starf', with Hugelyn's death: the climax *is* the end. The epigraphic clarity, the sense of consummation it suggests are what makes the line so powerful.

Chaucer achieves poetic intensity with means exactly opposite to those which Dante uses. For instance, he keeps and amplifies the images of grief, tears, and hunger, but eliminates those of mouth and glances that dominate Dante's story. Above all, he does not play with light. His presentation looks like a black and white film of scenes from a concentration camp. No *chiaroscuro* gives particular relief to any of the sequences – they all have the same bare, gray background. Consequently, space does not exist: we have no 'pertugio'. Hugelyn and his children speak and move in a void, as if they were isolated from normal space, seen as statues suspended somewhere in the tower. What interests the Monk is not the staging of the story, but the bare human tragedy of it. Significantly, the only place ever focussed on is Hugelyn's lap. In this context, time has no relevance. The constant tolling of days in Ugolino's Mew is gone. A vague, loose succession of days replaces it: 'on a day bifil', 'day by day', 'the same day', 'withinne a day or two'. On the one hand, this is a kind of casual notation one would expect from a third person, oral narrator. On the other, if this teller, who shows himself to be as omniscient as Dante's Ugolino, ignores his predecessor's time sequence, it must be because he is not interested in its significance. Paradoxically, his tragedy is 'timeless' in a precise 'historical' context. What he is really getting at is the absolute essence of his story, the slow starvation of four human beings caused by a 'fals suggestioun' and a popular rising. The time of Creation − of Ugolino's satanic Undoing − is not relevant for him.

Likewise, the Monk drops all the classical allusions of the Ugolino episode. He does not care to establish implicit comparisons between his Hugelyn and Tydeus, Niobe, or Dido. And, as if to make his intentions absolutely clear, he excises all references to Christ's Passion. Gaddo's 'Padre mio, ché non m'aiuti?' has disappeared. Dante's reproach to Pisa, 'non dovei tu i figliuoi *porre a tal croce*', has been replaced by a complaint to Fortune:

> Allas, Fortune, it was greet crueltee
> Swiche briddes for *to putte in swich a cage*!   (2413–14)

The only allusions the Monk has kept are to Job. Hugelyn's children offer their flesh with the same readiness and resignation Job shows when the messengers announce that his sons and daughters have perished.[58] But the Monk's most significant move in this direction is to equate Hugelyn and his children by making them all Job-like figures. For when Hugelyn exclaims, 'Allas! . . . allas, that I was wroght!', the echo cannot be mistaken even if the intonation has changed.

After this opened Job his mouth, and cursed his day. And Job spake, and said, Let the day perish wherein I was born, and the night in which it was said, There is a man child conceived.   (3. 1–3)

Jesus' suffering has a purpose. Job can see none in his at this point, and many are the readers throughout the ages who have found none whatever in his entire experience. Like Job, Hugelyn is the 'victim of his people' after having been their 'idol'.[59] Like Job, Hugelyn falls 'from heigh estaat'. Unlike Job, however, he never hears God's voice, he is never restored. His is, consequently, a tragedy of woe that turns into despair. Unlike Job, Hugelyn never asks to what end he suffers. But *we* are meant to ask that question. And the answer can only be, with Hope Weissman: 'No end whatever.'[60]

Hugelyn is an example of what Dostoevsky will call 'useless suffering',[61] the victim of a small Holocaust. Speaking of this episode, critics have talked of 'pathos'.[62] That may well be the mode of the narration, but I find nothing more inescapably 'tragic' than the story of an innocent man condemned to die of hunger with his children for no reason whatever. Twentieth-century readers should know what I mean. And, after all, if Dante's tragedy of Ugolino is a complex play of *eleos* and *phobos*, Aristotle seems to have contemplated even *eleos* alone (the Monk's 'pitee') as the effect of tragedy. Hugelyn weeps and complains against Fortune — and these, we are told, are the marks of pathos. But does not Boethius himself, fallen from 'heigh estaat', lament his misfortune? What exactly is a man supposed to do when all has been taken away from him? 'All has vanished', says Goethe's Tasso, 'One thing only is left: nature has allowed us tears, the cry of pain, when man can no longer bear.'[63] Blind Oedipus and suffering Philoctetes had done precisely this two thousand years earlier.[64]

The Monk's story of Hugelyn is a new — yet very old — type of tragedy: it is the story of a man reduced to impotence, starved to death by his fellow countrymen ('they'). Options are kept open for Troilus almost to the end. Hugelyn has none. When the prison door is definitively shut on him and his children, he seems to remove mankind from his consciousness. He knows it is 'they' that want him dead; yet, as time goes by and the end approaches, Hugelyn accuses Fortune. The monstrous 'langour' which the Pisans have inflicted on him he perceives now as relentless fate, as a senseless machine for destruction: a wheel, as 'false' as Roger's 'suggestioun' earlier in the story. Hugelyn makes us understand the tragic essence of the entire *Monk's Tale* because his story faces an extreme case of it. Without ever knowing why, he must suffer a living Hell. For, quite simply, he is one of the millions who have been vanquished by history, and therefore becomes a timeless *exemplum*.

Chaucer has, then, created a tragedy which is in many ways the reverse of Dante's. Both still have a powerful effect on us. But the questions Chaucer's 'translation' raises are fundamental ones. Has he, for instance, accepted Ugolino's self-defence, read him the way he wants to be read? Is it for this reason that he makes Hugelyn innocent and stresses the 'pitee' of his story? Let us, for the sake of the argument, admit that he has done so unconsciously. What we have here, then, is the greatest witness ever to the power of persuasion of a fictional character. The Monk's praise of Dante at the end of the Hugelyn story is the proper acknowledgement of his indebtedness:

> Of this tragedie it oghte ynough suffise;
> Whoso wol here it in a lenger wise,
> Redeth the grete poete of Ytaille
> That highte Dant, for he kan al devyse
> Fro point to point, nat o word wol he faille.   (2458–62)

If, on the other hand, Chaucer has deliberately misread Dante, then the final eulogy is something we must reckon with still. Now, in order to take Ugolino's self-defence as truthful, Chaucer should have interpreted Dante's 'che se 'l conte Ugolino aveva voce d'aver tradito te de le castella' (for if Count Ugolino had the name of betraying you of your castles) as mere rumour. Above all, he should have taken the Ugolino story completely out of context, i.e. out of the final sequence of cantos in the *Inferno*, which is devoted to traitors. This is clearly unlikely for many reasons and especially in view of the fact that Chaucer stresses treason in the three preceding modern instances. So, Chaucer has deliberately 'misread',[65] 'deconstructed', and rebuilt Dante's narrative. His praise of *Inferno* XXXIII is, then, a precise pointer to his 'anxiety of influence'.[66]

The phenomenon is, however, more complex. In the first place, one could read the Monk's sentence with a strong stress on 'this': 'Of *this* tragedie it oghte ynough suffise'. Enough of my kind of tragedy: if anyone wants to read another account of the same story, he can turn to Dante. Chaucer's praise becomes an intertextual reference, a footnote that points to another narrative possibility and invites the reader to a different tragic experience. In other words, it indicates the difference itself between the two versions.

Finally, there is a third aspect of this stanza that must be examined. The Monk acknowledges that Dante's account is fuller ('in a lenger wise'). As the difference in length between the two narratives as such is hardly worth mention (fifty-four lines versus fifty), the Monk must be conceived of as thinking of the background and corollary of Dante's story, of the wider and different stage setting which he has eliminated.

The Monk adds that Dante 'kan al devyse – Fro point to point; nat o word wol he faille', i.e. that the great poet of Italy tells his story in detail, from beginning to end, 'pointing', as the narrator of *Troilus* would have it, Ugolino's 'wordes alle' and 'every look',[67] to produce a narrative in which no 'word' is out of place. The Monk then recognizes the overall fitness, consequentiality, and unrepeatable cohesion of Dante's story – the narrative omnipotence and infallibility of his predecessor. Yet the fact is that, after proclaiming the impossibility of recounting Hugelyn's 'langour', Chaucer's narrator shows himself to be as omniscient as Dante's Ugolino, who has suffered the experience in his flesh. The Monk knows Hugelyn's inner thoughts and all the events that took place in the tower and indeed points them out, but he was not there. The Monk's omniscience and Dante's omnipotence are on the same level. Dante, after all, was not there either. He uses the fiction of an eye-witness account to establish his own authority – his omnipotence – as a poet. While acknowledging this, Chaucer employs Dante's text as the very same device: the Monk's omniscience is based upon Dante's omnipotence. The Monk 'tells', Dante 'devises'. Dante invents a tragic fiction, Chaucer reads it. Aristotle says that the tragic poet 'may not indeed destroy the framework of the received legends – the fact, for instance, that Clytemnestra was slain by Orestes and Eriphyle by Alcmaeon – but he ought to show invention of his own, and skilfully handle the traditional material.'[68] What Chaucer presents us with in his eulogy of Dante is the complex, subtle, dramatic process by which a 'tragedy' remains the same while changing, is re-invented by being read. Ugolino and Hugelyn are *mythoi*, myths of our imagination.

3

O quike deth : Love, melancholy, and the divided self

In this chapter, I am going to explore a sphere of the tragic that centres around the interior dilemma which the individual human being faces when he is overwhelmed by the dominant passion of love. In order to do this, I will begin by looking at three of Petrarch's sonnets, numbers CXXXII to CXXXIV, which occupy a central position among the 263 lyrics that form the first part (*in vita di madonna Laura*) of his *Canzoniere*, which are typical of his style, and which have been widely influential in the European tradition. In the *Canzoniere* such as we read it now and such as Petrarch himself finally arranged it, they form a triptych with a unifying theme – that of the exploration of love and its phenomena – and a parallel structure, which is characterized mainly by opposition. The first sonnet is the famous 'S'amor non è':

> S'amor non è, che dunque è quel ch'io sento?
> Ma s'egli è amor, perdio, che cosa et quale?
> Se bona, onde l'effecto aspro mortale?
> Se ria, onde sí dolce ogni tormento?
>
> S'a mia voglia ardo, onde 'l pianto e lamento?
> S'a mal mio grado, il lamentar che vale?
> O viva morte, o dilectoso male,
> come puoi tanto in me, s'io nol consento?
>
> Et s'io 'l consento, a gran torto mi doglio.
> Fra sí contrari vènti in frale barca
> mi trovo in alto mar senza governo,
>
> sí lieve di saver, d'error sí carca
> ch'i' medesmo non so quel ch'io mi voglio,
> e tremo a mezza state, ardendo il verno.[1]
>
> (Can it be love that fills my heart and brain?
> If love, dear God, what is its quality?

56

If it is good, why does it torture me?
If evil, why this sweetness in my pain?
If I burn gladly, why do I complain?
If I hate burning, why do I never flee?
O life-in-death, O lovely agony,
How can you rule me so, if I'm not fain?
And if I'm willing, why do I suffer so? –
By such contrary winds I'm blown in terror
In a frail and rudderless bark on open seas,
Ballasted all with ignorance and error.
Even my own desire I do not know;
I burn in winter and in high summer freeze.)[2]

The first line of this sonnet, 'S'amor non è, che dunque è quel ch'io sento?', asks the basic question: what is it I feel if it is not love? The other six questions contained in the remaining seven lines of the octave stem from the first by a scholasticizing process of *divisio*. Thus, 2 – if it is love, *quid et quale est*? What is its nature? And which its characteristics? These are analysed in 3 and 4 (nature, defined by the object's effects), and in 5 and 6 (characteristics – psychological and emotional manifestations of love). The 3–4 unit (represented by lines 3 and 4) presents a further division: a – if the nature of love is good, whence an effect which is 'aspro mortale'?; b – if the nature of love is evil, whence is its pain sweet? Similarly, the 5–6 unit contains two pairs of *quaestiones*, the second of which occupies the first line of the sestet (line 9) abandoning the question mark and, but only apparently, 'concluding the intellectual argument':[3] a – if I burn gladly, whence my tears and my complaining?; b – if I burn against my will, what do I complain for?; c – how can this thing have so much power on me without my consent?; d – but, *contra*, if I consent, I am wrong in complaining. This nice, rhetorical as well as 'intellectual, rationative',[4] in sum, scholastic *quaestio* has in fact no answer, no *respondeo*, no *ad primum, ad secundum*, etc. Instead, we enter the realm of metaphor, where the field is at first taken by a frail bark, rudderless on open seas and blown by contrary winds. The bark itself has little wisdom and much error, and hence the 'I' of the poem does not himself know what he wants. Then we have a final outburst of imagery: I burn in winter and in high summer freeze. 'The first person appears in the very first line – "io sento". But this "I" that speaks is not so individualised that it must be Petrarch and no one else', wrote Leonard Forster.[5] This is true, but the impression one gets in reading the second stanza is that we are penetrating into a man's psyche, and the whole poem explores this dimension – feeling ('sento'), intellect ('non so'), and will ('voglio'). In fact, the conflict among these is an underlying theme throughout the composition ('a mia voglia', 'mal mio grado'; 'puoi', 'consento'; 'saver', 'error').

The central line of the sonnet, line 7, sums up the condition of the 'I', announcing my main topic: 'O viva morte, o dilectoso male', o life-in-death, o lovely agony. It is Love itself that is thus addressed by the poet and defined by two oxymora, which bring to perfection the traditional theme of 'bitter-sweet love'.[6] But how shall we translate 'male'? Bishop's 'agony' is a precise choice, which points to a predominantly physical and psychological – or, if one prefers, almost purely rhetorical – dimension. But what if 'male' indicates, as it certainly can in Petrarch's Italian, 'disease', 'illness' – in fact a disease that leads up to 'viva *morte*'? And could this 'illness' be considered also an 'evil', a moral 'male', as the 'ria' of line 4, opposed to the 'bona' of the previous verse, seems to announce? This is not to be ruled out without further thought. The word 'error' of line 12 is charged, according to a recent interpreter,[7] with moral connotations. It 'appears in the first and last poems of the *Canzoniere*' and is one of Petrarch's 'favourite terms for self-delusion'. Nor should we forget that 'the whole book is penetrated by the vigilant lucidity that Petrarch's use of these terms implies'.[8] If this is so – and the occurrence of 'saver' in line 12 seems to confirm it – sonnet CXXXII proposes to the reader not only an intellectual, psychological enigma, but a moral one as well, which would agree with the general construction of the *Canzoniere*. If we look at the end of the collection, we do indeed find the poet turning, after Laura's death, to God. He recalls with nostalgia and sadness the pleasant 'torture' ('stratio') of love, employing the oxymora that are typical of the first part of the *Canzoniere*. With them, he describes his old plight – that interior division between 'cold' and 'hot', between 'hope' and 'sorrow', which dominated his life while the beloved dazzled him like the sun. But Petrarch's turmoil is not yet placated. Although he invokes the Lord, Laura's disappearance makes him see his moral 'gain' and at once to feel regret. The 'freedom' he has found after the tragedy is 'oxymoronic' – 'bitter' and 'sweet' at the same time:

> Morte à spento quel sol ch'abagliar suolmi,
> e 'n tenebre son li occhi interi et saldi;
> terra è quella ond'io ebbi et *freddi et caldi*;
> spenti son i miei lauri, or querce et olmi:

di ch'io *veggio 'l mio ben, et parte duolmi*.
Non è chi faccia et *paventosi et baldi*
i miei penser', né chi li *agghiacci et scaldi*,
né chi gli empia di *speme*, et di *duol* colmi.

Fuor di man di colui che *punge* et *molce*,
che già fece di me sí lungo stratio,
mi trovo in libertate, *amara et dolce*;

et al Signor ch'i' adoro et ch'i' ringratio,
che pur col ciglio il ciel governa et folce,
torno stanco di viver, nonché satio.

(Death has extingished the sun that used tó dazzle me, and my eyes though whole and sound are in darkness; she is dust from whom I took chills and heat; my laurels are faded, are oaks and elms, in which I see my gain but am still pained. There is no one to make my thoughts fearful and bold, nor to freeze and scorch them, no one to fill them with hope and overflow them with sorrow. Out of the hands of him who pierces and heals [Love], who once made of me such a long torture, I find myself in bitter and sweet liberty; and to the Lord whom I adore and whom I thank, who governs and sustains the heavens with His brow, I return, weary of life, not merely satiated.)[9]

The poet's emotional and moral existence is coming to an end: he is both weary of, and satiated with life. It is this deep tiredness that prompts him to turn to God, in the hope of finding final peace in Him.

If we return to our initial sonnet, CXXXII, and compare it with its most famous precursor, Dante's 'Tutti li miei penser parlan d'Amore', we shall immediately notice interesting similarities and differences.

Tutti li miei penser parlan d'Amore;
e hanno in lor sì gran varietate,
ch'altro mi fa voler sua potestate,
altro folle ragiona il suo valore,

altro sperando m'apporta dolzore,
altro pianger mi fa spesse fiate:
e sol s'accordano in cherer pietate,
tremando di paura che è nel core.

Ond'io non so da qual matera prenda;
e vorrei dire, e non so ch'io mi dica:
così mi trovo in amorosa erranza!

E se con tutti vòi fare accordanza,
convenemi chiamar la mia nemica,
madonna la Pietà, che mi difenda.

(All my thoughts speak of Love, and they so differ among themselves that one makes me desire his dominion, another argues that it is madness, another with hope brings me joy, another often makes me weep; and they only agree in begging for pity, trembling with the fear that is in my heart.

Hence I don't know which to take as my theme, and I should like to write, but I don't know what – such is my uncertainty with regard to love! And if I would bring them all into harmony, I must call on my enemy, lady Pity, to take my side.)[10]

Like Petrarch, Dante focusses on the 'gran varietate' of his thoughts about love. A certain number of oppositions predominate here, too, but only in lines 4–6: one thought makes the poet desire love's dominion, another argues that it is madness, another with hope brings him joy, another often makes him weep. Petrarch's oxymora, however, are absent, and Dante's thoughts at least agree in begging for pity – a concept which, announced in the middle of the poem (lines 7–8), reaches a 'paradoxical climax'[11] at the end (lines 12–14). The scholasticizing *quaestio* is not developed. Nor does the poem contain any metaphor such as Petrarch's 'rudderless bark'. Dante trembles with the fear that is in his heart (line 8), Petrarch trembles, shakes with the cold in high summer and burns in winter.

The core of Dante's sonnet is constituted by the first tercet, lines 9–11. The concepts Dante expounds here are basically two: first, he does not know which to take as his theme (he would like to write, but does not know what); second, he finds himself 'in amorosa erranza'. Now, both ideas have their *raison d'être* in the particular stage that the 'autobiographical' story of the *Vita Nuova* has reached at this point. Following Beatrice's decision not to return Dante's 'saluto' (ch. x), there has been a crisis. A meeting between Dante and Love has prompted the poet to abandon the screen-ladies and look for new, more intimate, inspiration. In fact, this sonnet 'marks the beginning of a phase which is commonly called "Cavalcantian" or of painful love'.[12] For four chapters now (xii–xvi), Dante's *matera* will be precisely 'amore doloroso'. Later (xvii), he will turn to 'the *lode* and the disinterested love which finds satisfaction and fulfilment in itself'.[13] In other words, this sonnet describes a turning point in Dante's poetics of love. It is significant that he should devote two lines (9–10) to his inability to write, and to his uncertainty as to the subject of his writing. Whether or not this particular moment represents a moral and gnoseological crisis,[14] it does definitely indicate an expressive stumbling block. By contrast, the Petrarch of sonnet CXXXII has no such problem. For him, the subject is 'amorosa erranza' as such – the restlessness and the 'erring' of his love, of his whole soul. Dante complains about his uncertainty, Petrarch accepts it and even finds in it some pleasure. What Petrarch does not know is not, like Dante, what to say, but what to *want* (CXXXII, 13).

Dante's expression, 'amorosa erranza', is used by Boccaccio's Troiolo to describe his own inability to act when it becomes clear that Criseida will be exchanged for Antenore and Pandaro urges him to do something:

> Così piangendo, in amorosa erranza
> dimoro, lasso, e non so che mi fare

(Thus, weeping, I remain in this uncertainty of love, alas, and I don't know what to do)[15]

Dante does not know what to say, Petrarch does not know what to want, Boccaccio's Troiolo does not know what to do: the paralysis of love is increasing. Chaucer, who does not pick up these particular lines of the *Filostrato*, conveys their meaning with splendid variations in the *Troilus* (IV, 568–81), where his hero describes his uncertainty to Pandarus as determined by a conflict of 'desir' and 'reson' (572–4), of increasing love and decreasing hope (577–8) – a 'petrarchesque' presentation. In a sort of operatic crescendo, Troilus begins with 'Thus am I lost' (568), proceeds to 'Allas! how shal I, wrecche, fare?' (576), exclaims 'So weilaway, whi nyl myn herte breste?' (580), and concludes with the restlessness of love so typical of Petrarch's *Canzoniere*: 'For, as in love, ther is but litel reste' (581).

Let me now return to Petrarch and move to sonnet CXXXIII, the second of our triptych.

> Amor m'à posto come segno a strale,
> come al sol neve, come cera al foco,
> et come nebbia al vento; et son già roco,
> donna, mercé chiamando, et voi non cale.
>
> Dagli occhi vostri uscío 'l colpo mortale,
> contra cui non mi val tempo né loco;
> da voi sola procede, et parvi un gioco,
> il sole e 'l foco e 'l vento ond'io son tale.
>
> I pensier' son saette, e 'l viso un sole,
> e 'l desir foco: e 'nseme con quest'arme
> mi punge Amor, m'abbaglia et mi distrugge;

> et l'angelico canto et le parole,
> col dolce spirto ond'io non posso aitarme,
> son l'aura inanzi a cui mia vita fugge.

(Love has set me as a mark for the arrow, like snow to the sun, like wax to fire, and like mist to wind; and I am already harsh, my lady, through asking for your mercy, and you do not care. From your eyes came the mortal blow against which neither time nor place have power; from you alone come – to you it looks like a game! – the sun and the fire and the wind wherefore I am as I am. Thoughts are arrows, the face is a sun, and desire is a fire: and together with these weapons, Love stings, blinds and destroys me; and the angelic song and the words, with the sweet spirit from which I cannot save myself, are the breeze before which my life flees.)

Here, the first line is a decidedly 'impious' adaptation of Jeremiah's Lamentations (3. 12: 'et posuit me quasi signum ad sagittam'), which replaces God by 'Amor'. But in fact this is only the starting point for the construction of a new enigma, this time clearly reminiscent of the Provençal *dreit nien* rhymes. One interpreter calls the entire sonnet 'a true "devinalh" [riddle], in which the first quatrain, starting with a Biblical reminiscence, establishes the premises of the enigma, and the second quatrain and the two tercets offer, in a perfectly symmetrical movement, precise answers to the initial questions. The *blow*, the *sun*, the *fire* and the *wind* come from Laura's image; the thoughts are *arrows*, the face is the *sun*, desire is *fire*: with these weapons Love *stings*, *blinds*, and *destroys* him. Finally the *song* and the *sweet spirit* of the words are the wind (*l'aura*) before which his life flees',[16] 'l'aura' – the breeze – being of course also Laura, the lady. This is indeed a 'love theorem' with hidden 'syllogisms' and a perfectly logical construction. Where 'S'amor non è' ended with an open question, 'Amor m'ha posto' is beautifully closed, encircled by Love and Laura. At least, this is the formal solution. Yet the final image of Laura, the breeze–lady, brings no peace, for indeed the poet's very life flees before it. And we must ask ourselves: what life? His vital spirit, or also his true life, his existence? Is Petrarch seeing his life wasted, so to speak, after the dream of Laura, as the *Canzoniere* in general and the *Secretum* finally point out? What determines the tension here is precisely the conflict between the formally perfect "closedness" and the ultimately inescapable 'openness' of the two final terzine and of line 14.

The third sonnet under consideration, 'Pace non trovo' (CXXXIV), is one of the most typical of the so-called 'Petrarchan' and 'Petrarchist' manner. If one were to read it aloud, an English audience would hear it in Wyatt's rendering:

> Pace non trovo, et non ò da far guerra;
> e temo, et spero; et ardo, et son un ghiaccio;
> et volo sopra 'l cielo, et giaccio in terra;
> et nulla stringo, et tutto 'l mondo abbraccio.
>
> Tal m'à in pregion, che non m'apre né serra,
> né per suo mi riten né scioglie il laccio;
> et non m'ancide Amore, et non mi sferra,
> né mi vuol vivo, né mi trae d'impaccio.
>
> Veggio senza occhi, et non ò lingua et grido;
> et bramo di perir, et cheggio aita;
> et ò in odio me stesso, et amo altrui.
>
> Pascomi di dolor, piangendo rido;
> egualmente mi spiace morte et vita:
> in questo stato son, donna, per voi.
>
> I find no peace, and all my war is done,
> I fear and hope, I burn and freeze like ice,
> I fly above the wind, yet can I not arise,
> And nought I have, and all the world I season.
> That looseth nor locketh, holdeth me in prison,
> And holdeth me not, yet can I 'scape nowise,
> Nor letteth me live, nor die at my device,
> And yet of death it giveth me occasion.
> Without eyen I see, and without tongue I plain,
> I desire to perish, and yet I ask health,
> I love another, and thus I hate myself,
> I feed me in sorrow, and laugh in all my pain,
> Likewise displeaseth me both death and life:
> And my delight is causer of this strife.[17]

If one could sing, connoisseurs of opera would hear Petrarch's echo in Cherubino's words in Act I, Scene v of Mozart's *Nozze di Figaro*:

> Non so più cosa son, cosa faccio,
> Or di foco, ora sono di ghiaccio.

(I no longer know what I am, what I am doing; now I burn, now I freeze.)

Even more paralysed than Petrarch or Boccaccio's Troiolo, Cherubino is completely vanquished by love – every woman makes him tremble, he speaks of love to the whole natural world, he is in love with love. His

song of adolescent passion is presented as both pathetic and comic.
When, however, he blushingly addresses the Countess in Act II, Scene
v, his aria expresses the pure mystery of eros. And here, Mozart and
Lorenzo Da Ponte fully recapture the essence of the Petrarchan topos:

> Voi che sapete
> Che cosa è amor,
> Donne, vedete
> S'io l'ho nel cor.
> Quello ch'io provo
> Vi ridirò;
> E' per me nuovo,
> Capir nol so.
> Sento un affetto
> Pien di desir,
> Ch'ora è diletto,
> Ch'ora è martir.
> Gelo, e poi sento
> L'alma avvampar,
> E in un momento
> Torno a gelar.
> Ricerco un bene
> Fuori di me;
> Non so chi 'l tiene,
> Non so cos'è.
> Sospiro e gemo
> Senza voler,
> Palpito e tremo
> Senza saper;
> Non trovo pace
> Notte, né dì,
> Ma pur mi piace
> Languir così.
> Voi che sapete

(You Ladies, who know what love is, see if I have it in my heart. What I feel I
shall tell you; it is new to me, I am unable to understand it. I feel a sensation full
of desire, now a delight, now a torture. I freeze, and then I feel my soul burn,
and instantly I freeze again. I pursue a good which is outside myself – I do not
know who holds it, I do not know what it is. I sigh and tremble without
knowing; I find no peace at night nor in the day, yet I love to languish thus.
You who know what love is)

Nor, to stay with opera one more minute, do I find a more sublime
summary of Petrarch's ever-recurring oxymoron than in Alfredo's and

Violetta's joint celebration of the palpitating love of the whole universe, 'croce e delizia, delizia al cor' (cross and delight, delight to the heart), in Verdi's *La Traviata* (I, iii).

Over two centuries before this musical version of Dumas's *La Dame aux camélias*, a duke's majordomo masquerading as the Countess Trifaldi had, in a play inserted within a novel, invented a romance about herself. She had been in charge of the young and beautiful Princess Antonomasia of the kingdom of Candaya. To gain the favour of the girl, a private knight decides to 'seduce the keeper, so as to secure the keys of the fortress'. And what in fact wreaks her to his purpose and undermines her virtue is 'a cursed couple of verses' he sings one night under her window. The Countess proceeds to quote these – two quatrains composed respectively by the Italian Petrarchist, Serafino Aquilano, and the Spanish Comendador Escrivá – and then launches into a long harangue against those poets (*trovadores*) who write a kind of verse called *seguidillas*. These, she says, produce 'el brincar de las almas, el retozar de la risa, el desasosiego de los cuerpos, y, finalmente, el azogue de todos los sentidos' (the bouncing of the soul, the frolicking of laughter, restlessness of bodies, and finally a quicksilver in all the senses). Hence, all these 'poets' should be banished (as Plato, the Countess adds, would in fact banish all poets) to the Isles of the Lizards. Yet the poor lady recognizes that the fault does not really lie with the poets, but with those who believe them. She does, however, conclude with a splendid tirade against Petrarchism itself:

no me habían de mover sus *trasnochados conceptos*, ni había de creer ser verdad aquel decir: 'Vivo muriendo, ardo en el yelo, tiemblo en el fuego, espero sin esperanza, pártome y quédome', con otros *imposibles* desta ralea, de que están sus escritos llenos.

(I should not have allowed myself to be moved by such labored conceits, nor should I have believed that the poet was speaking the truth when he declared, 'I live dying, burn in ice, tremble in the fire, hope without hope, go and stay', along with other contradictory conceptions of this sort with which their writings are filled).[18]

Thus Cervantes, himself a translator and imitator of Petrarchan and Petrarchist lyrics, explodes the manner and the style of 'Pace non trovo'.

Petrarch's sonnet cxxxiv has illustrious ancestors – Rambaut de Vaqueiras' 'Savis e fols, humils et orgoillos', Roger of Apulia's 'Umile sono ed orgoglioso'.[19] With its *de oppositis* construction it represents, if one can formulate it so, a standard masterpiece of the European love lyric. Once more, we have here an apparent non-sense: thirteen out of fourteen lines – all, in fact, but the last – present to us a riddle formed by no less than thirty contrasting statements: 'Pace non trovo' – 'et non ò da far guerra'; 'e temo' – 'et spero', and so forth. We are given a first clue in the central line 7, with the mention of Amore (the 'tal' in line 5 announcing the enigma and alluding to both Love and Laura), and a final solution in line 14: for you, because of you (the ambiguity of 'per' I would not put past Petrarch, who might be offering himself to Laura such as he is as well as reproaching her for what he is), Lady, I am in such a state. The psychological situation is summed up beautifully in line 4, 'et nulla stringo, et tutto 'l mondo abbraccio', where the excruciating experience of love widens to cover the general condition of man, the feeling that he can embrace, comprehend the entire universe and at the same time cannot really clutch the essence, cannot grasp anything – the infinite openness and ultimately complete elusiveness of the inner and outer world to human beings.

The line which most interests me here is 'pascomi di dolor, piangendo rido' (12). This line, itself an example of that *coincidentia oppositorum* which dominates the literary tradition of love from classical antiquity down to Gottfried's *Tristan* and Chaucer's *Troilus*,[20] expresses that notion of the *dulce amarum*, the *glykypikron* of love which goes back at least as far as Sappho,[21] and which is also present in serious philosophical discussion. In his late dialogue *Philebus*, for instance, Plato has Socrates examine different kinds of sensations and maintain that there is one, 'common both to soul and body', which is a mixture of pleasure and pain. He gives a clinical account of this state:

Whenever, in the restoration or in the derangement of nature, a man experiences two opposite feelings; for example, when he is cold and is growing warm, or again, when he is hot and is becoming cool, and he wants to have the one and be rid of the other; – the sweet has a bitter (*pikrō glyky*), as the common saying is, and both together fasten upon him and create irritation and in time drive him to distraction.[22]

Later in the argument, Socrates adds that at least one type of union of pleasure and pain belongs to the sphere of pure 'mental feelings'. Love is one of these:

Why, do we not speak of anger, fear, desire, sorrow, love, emulation, envy, and the like, as pains which belong to the soul only? . . . And shall we not find them also full of the most wonderful pleasures?[23]

The heir of such illustrious tradition, Petrarch's oxymoron – 'pian-gendo rido' – is however profoundly different from its first ancestor in Western literature. In Book VI of the *Iliad*, Hector tries to take his son Astyanax in his arms, but the baby, 'scared at the dazzling helm, and nodding crest', clings 'crying to his nurse's breast'. Hector and Andromache smile 'with secret pleasure'. A moment later, Hector, having prayed to the gods for Astyanax and having removed the armour, returns the baby to his mother, and Andromache, 'the troubled pleasure soon chastised by fear', looks on both husband and son *dakruoen gelasasa* (484), smiling-weeping – for which Pope needs a whole line, 'She mingled with a smile a tender tear'. The difference lies not only in the different situation of the two scenes, but also in the fact that Petrarch's oxymoron is double, that the first half of his line, 'pascomi di dolor', adds the particular dimension of reflexiveness, of grief bending over itself and finding pleasure in its being grief.

In Petrarch, then, this line is a topos, even though he perfects it with great ability. Now, the formulation of this topos coincides with the description of the aspect of that *acedia* which Augustinus and Franciscus agree, in the second Book of the *Secretum*, is the 'plague of the soul' that dominates Petrarch: 'Et . . . sic lacrimis et doloribus pascor, atra quadam cum voluptate':[24] thus I feed on tears and grief, with a sort of dark, gloomy pleasure. Yet, in describing his *aegritudo* only a few lines before, Franciscus had said: 'Add to this that whereas with all the other passions by which I am oppressed is mixed something sweet (*aliquid dulcoris*) though false, in this sadness (*tristitia*) all is harsh, miserable and horrible; and the way is always open to despair (*ad desperationem*) and to all that brings unhappy souls to ruin' (p. 106). In other words, Franciscus' *acedia* is both total grief and 'dark pleasure', so much so that he cannot take himself away from it ('invitus avellar').

What, then, is Petrarch's *acedia*? 'This last evil', writes Kenelm Foster,[25] 'might be called sloth except that while this term suits, for example, the penitents on Dante's fourth Terrace, it is far too unsubtle for Petrarch's case, involving as this does a high dosage of melancholic depression.' In fact, 'careful analysis of the *Secretum* reveals that Petrarch understood *acedia* to mean grief, sorrow, depression, or (to use the Latin equivalent) *tristitia*'.[26] Augustinus himself 'eventually refers to it as *animi tristitia*'.[27] Furthermore, 'Petrarch's *acedia* in the *Secretum* is . . . conceptually a combination of the medieval chief vice and the Stoic main affect.'[28] Is this already 'melancholy' or *Weltschmerz*?

Lessing seemed to answer this question affirmatively when he said that it is precisely this 'sadness' that gives to Petrarch's poems a 'wollüstige Melancholie', a voluptuous melancholy.[29] Klibansky, Panofsky and Saxl, in their monumental study of *Saturn and Melancholy*, seem to answer it negatively and show that Petrarch did not conceive of the two opposed conditions – depression and enthusiasm – as two different aspects of one identical, substantially bipolar, disposition. Petrarch never calls 'melancholy' his *acedia*, and indeed rejects the Aristotelian notion of it.[30] Yet his symptoms are not very different.[31] Furthermore, it has more recently been pointed out that medieval *acedia* did not have a purely negative connotation and that there is a very ancient, indissoluble link between melancholy and eros,[32] such as Chaucer, too, is aware of in his description of Arcite's condition when he returns from Thebes to Athens:

> And in his geere for al the world he ferde
> Nat oonly lik the loveris maladye
> Of Hereos, but rather lyk manye,
> Engendred of humour malencolik
> Biforen, in his celle fantastik.[33]

Now, if the discussion of *acedia* takes up a good section of Book II of the *Secretum*, Book III is devoted to a thorough examination of the two 'adamantine chains' that bind Franciscus – Love (and specifically love for Laura) and Glory, the very passions which dominate the *Canzoniere* as well. The *Secretum* describes Petrarch as he sees himself at a certain point in his life (whether past or present) and as he struggles not to be anymore – it describes his crisis. And the three dominant factors in this crisis are Petrarch's feelings about *acedia*, love and glory. Is it possible that the *Canzoniere*, which, framed as it is by Sonnet I and Canzone CCCLXVI, divided as it is between a section 'in vita' and one 'in morte di madonna Laura', definitely shows that a 'conversion' did take place at one point in Petrarch's life – is it possible that the *Canzoniere* should make no mention of *acedia*? Is it possible that the *dolendi voluptas* of the *De Remediis* – a trait of *acedia* – is different from the pleasure-in-grief which characterizes Petrarch's vernacular lyrics in spite of all the verbal similarities?

A first answer is provided by Francisco Rico, who maintains that 'Petrarch never (outside the *Secretum*) attributes to the "aegritudo" the "dolendi voluptas" which he so often says hampers him for many reasons and which on the other hand the *De Remediis* impersonally singles out as exclusive of sloth.'[34] Elsewhere in his Latin works Petrarch always talks of *lugendi dulcedo* (the sweetness of weeping) in connection with someone's death, following the topos of consolation and of the sweetness that tears provide.[35] In his Italian lyrics, 'the image of the poet who proclaims "pasco 'l cor di sospir . . . e di lacrime vivo"'' is modelled on the Ovidian Orpheus who complains of his lost love, in the *Tristia* and the *Metamorphoses* as well as the Psalms, and it follows a 'copious courtly and troubadoresque vein' in the spirit of Sappho's *glykypikron*.[36] In other words for Rico there seem to be three kinds of *dolendi voluptas*, each with its own model in tradition. While I agree that Petrarch might have recalled a different topos depending on the circumstances he wanted to describe and the literary genre and convention he chose to follow, I would argue that the phenomenon is one, though probably produced by different causes. Thus, if there is no explicit treatment of *acedia* in the *Canzoniere*, it is enough to glance at the poems where words such as *noia, triste, angoscia* and *dolore* are used[37] to conclude, with Kenelm Foster, that 'restlessness is . . . a *leitmotiv* of the *Canzoniere*, but more especially of Part I'.[38] In fact, I find no better description of the central theme of Petrarch's Italian poems than the following, where Father Foster openly recalls the *atra voluptas* of the *Secretum*:

Much then of the *Canzoniere* is dominated by dissatisfaction – with Laura, with the poet himself, with the human condition as such. Moreover, it was a dissatisfaction consciously fostered and cherished, as we are told in *Secretum* II, with 'gloomy pleasure' . . . And as pleasure in sorrow gives sorrow permanence, so Petrarch's propensity to 'feed on tears' . . . becomes an element in that fixity in restlessness of some of his most characteristic poetry.[39]

This is, then, what Dante's *erranza* becomes in Petrarch. And it is this dissatisfaction which, *mutatis mutandis*, will prompt Hamlet to say: 'I have of late, but wherefore I know not, lost all my mirth, forgone all custom of exercises; and indeed it goes so heavily with my disposition that this goodly frame the earth seems to me a sterile promontory',[40] with all that follows. But we do not have to go all the way to Hamlet. In Book V of his *Troilus and Criseyde*, Chaucer uses the word 'melancholy' four times to sum up the plight of his hero conquered by love (*filostrato*) and defeated by betrayal.[41]

The first time, it is Pandarus who, replying to Troilus' instructions for his burial and to his description of the 'maladie' and the dreams that haunt him, exclaims:

> Thy swevnes ek and al swich fantasie
> Drif out and lat hem faren to meschaunce,
> For they procede of thi malencolie
> That doth the fele in slep al this penaunce. (358–61)[42]

Three hundred lines later, the Narrator himself uses the word, just before he puts into Troilus' mouth another *Canticus*, the last he pronounces, symmetrically placed towards the end of the story to parallel the one Troilus had uttered at the beginning, when he had realized he had fallen in love. This final song is preceded by a splendid description of the way in which Troilus' psyche is now split, projected outside himself, looking at Troilus with the eyes of the crowd:

> And of hymself ymagened he ofte
> To ben defet, and pale, and waxen lesse
> Than he was wont, and that men seyden softe,
> 'What may it be? Who kan the sothe gesse
> Whi Troilus hath al this hevynesse?' (617–21)

The Narrator comments:

> And al this nas but his malencolie,
> That he hadde of hymself swich fantasie. (622–3)[43]

Six hundred lines later, melancholy has become manic depression and anorexia: 'for his malencolye' Troilus eats and drinks no more and flees from all company (1215–18). People do not recognize him anymore, so lean, pale and feeble he has become. 'His harm', he says, is 'al aboute his herte', 'a grevous maladie'. Here, as nine hundred lines earlier, he thinks only of death (1232 and 295 ff). It is while he 'Stood on a day in his malencolie' (1646–7) that Deiphobus' coat-armor, 'rent fro Diomede' and bearing the famous brooch, appears to Troilus' eyes, the final proof of Criseyde's unfaithfulness. From now on, as if suddenly cured of his paralysing melancholy, Troilus actively seeks death in battle.

Book v of *Troilus* is the first great study of melancholy we have in English literature – it is also far superior to Boccaccio's description in the *Filostrato*. Disillusioned love ends in total disintegration of personality, but with the final recognition of betrayal, the paralysis and inactivity of Troilus' melancholy suddenly coagulate into a fury of active death-wish. But Troilus' divided self is present from the very beginning. When, after seeing Criseyde in the temple, he returns home and – typically – lies on his bed, he starts constructing images in his mind while sighing and groaning:

And first he gan to sike, and eft to grone,
And thought ay on hire so, withouten lette,
That, as he sat and wook, his spirit mette
That he hire saugh a-temple, and al the wise
Right of hire look, and gan it newe avise.   (I, 360–4)

Indeed in an extraordinary line Chaucer tells us:

Thus gan he make a mirour of his mynde
In which he saugh al holly hire figure   (365–6)

For the first time here, Troilus' mind literally re-flects. And if reflecting
the image of the beloved is a fairly common feature of medieval lovers,
Troilus' reflections soon take the inward way that his making a mirror
of his mind leads us to expect. For, as at the end of the story, Troilus
utters here a *Canticus* in which his divided mind emerges fully. He
analyses his feelings, dissects love, finds in it a 'quike deth', a 'swete
harm so queynte', a 'wondre maladie'. We are back where we started,
Petrarch's sonnet 'S'amor non è'. Chaucer translates and adapts it here,
departing from Boccaccio's *Filostrato* – which, significantly, only says
that Troiolo *'lieto* si diede a cantare', joyfully began to sing:[44]

If no love is, O God, what fele I so?
And if love is, what thing and which is he?
If love be good, from whennes cometh my woo?
If it be wikke, a wonder thynketh me,
When every torment and adversite
That cometh of hym may to me savory thinke,
For ay thurst I, the more that ich it drynke.

And if that at myn owen lust I brenne,
From whennes cometh my waillynge and my pleynte?
If harm agree me, wherto pleyne I thenne?
I noot, ne whi unwery that I feynte.
O quike deth, O swete harm so queynte,
How may of the in me swich quantite,
But if that I consente that it be?

And if that I consente, I wrongfully
Compleyne, iwis. Thus possed to and fro,
Al sterelees withinne a boot am I
Amydde the see, bitwixen wyndes two,
That in contrarie stonden evere mo.
Allas, what is this wondre maladie?
For hote of cold, for cold of hote, I dye.   (I, 400–20)

Ernest Hatch Wilkins and Patricia Thomson have said that Chaucer misunderstands Petrarch's sonnet, and in particular the first two lines.[45] This would be true only if we maintained that a medieval author is tied to the letter as well as to the spirit of his authority. But Chaucer adapts Petrarch's sonnet to his own needs and to his hero's plight. Troilus had mocked lovers, scorned Love. Chaucer, perhaps taking Petrarch's 'S'amor non è' as an absolute construction ('if love is not' instead of 'if it be not love'),[46] makes Troilus ask, 'If no love is, O God, what fele I so?', and 'And if love is, what thing and which is he?' Troilus is more of a philosopher than Boccaccio's Troiolo. If love is not, does not exist, what is it that I feel? And if love exists, *quid et quale est*? Both are indeed deeper questions, for the existence itself of love is here made dependent on subjective feeling. It is after this *Canticus* that Troilus addresses the God of Love for the first time (421–34), thus recognizing his, and love's, existence.

On the other hand, Chaucer makes a precise choice in his translation. He anticipates Bishop by six hundred years. Troilus' 'male' is not a moral evil in any way – it is 'harm' and 'maladie', a very physical disease, which produces in Troilus a sort of dreadful fever with double contrasting symptoms: 'for hote of cold, for cold of hote, I dye'. Nor, more significantly, is Troilus' 'sterelees boot' light of knowledge and heavy with error as Petrarch's bark was. And finally, Troilus knows very well, deep down, what he wants. He wants Criseyde, as the next fifty lines of the poem make clear. It will take a long time – the whole story in fact – for him to acquire that 'saver' and learn his 'error'. He will have to go through physical death and ascend to the eighth sphere to come to a recognition which is at once similar and much more extreme than Petrarch's crisis. His condemnation of the 'blynde lust' is radical.

The seeds of Troilus' melancholy are, however, present from the very moment he falls in love. With an extremely perceptive eye, Pandarus detects the signs of *dolendi voluptas* as soon as Troilus opens his mouth to reveal that his illness is eros:

> *Delyte nat in wo thi wo to seche,*
> As don thise foles that hire sorwes eche
> With sorwe, whan thei han mysaventure,
> And listen naught to seche hem other cure.

> (I, 704–7; italics mine)

Pandarus, the man who knows the world and its ways, tries to compose Troilus' divided mind into a higher, wiser unity – to make 'o lore' out 'of two contraries'. In preaching this, he places 'bitterness' and 'sweetness' in a sequence where the latter is considered as the inevitable complement of the former, but later in time; where in fact joy is known as such (is such), dialectically, only through experience of sorrow. The knot of the oxymoron is thus loosed:

> For how myghte evere swetnesse han ben knowe
> To him that nevere tasted bitternesse?
> Ne no man may ben inly glad, I trowe,
> That nevere was in sorwe or som destresse.
> Eke whit by blak, by shame ek worthinesse,
> Ech set by other, more for other semeth,
> As men may se, and so the wyse it demeth.   (I, 638–44)[47]

And the poet himself confirms the truth of this assertion when Troilus embraces Criseyde in the climactic love scene of Book III:

> O, sooth is seyd, that heled for to be
> As of a fevre or other gret siknesse,
> Men moste drynke, as men may ofte se,
> Ful bittre drynke; and for to han gladnesse
> Men drynken ofte peyne and gret distresse –
> I mene it here, as for this aventure,
> That thorugh a peyne hath founden al his cure.
>
> And now swetnesse semeth more swete,
> That bitternesse assaied was byforn;
> For out of wo in blisse now they flete;
> Non swich they felten sithen they were born.   (III, 1212–22)

In spite of this 'external' wisdom, however, the tragedy of Troilus as a character is that of having embarked upon a voyage which begins with interior death and fatally returns to interior death. In imagery, the first and last *Cantici* he pronounces are strongly linked one to the other. 'O quike deth', he exclaims in the first, when he feels he is dying of both heat and cold. There, he sees himself in a 'sterelees' boat in the middle of the sea between two opposed winds. A little later he wishes to reach the 'port' of death (I, 526–7) with his heart's sail (I, 606). In his last *Canticus*, the wind is astern, the lodestar is lost, and in darkness, night after night, his ship comes closer to the Charybdis that will devour it. Troilus 'dies' long before dying – before being killed by Achilles. And he knows it with every fibre of his being, he knows his destiny emotionally before discussing it philosophically: 'outrely he shop hym for to deye' (IV, 955). Tragically, this melancholic, deterministic awareness ('Thus to ben lorn, it is my destinee') of Troilus stays with us as a truth opposed to that of Pandarus and of the Narrator.

At bottom, then, the divided, oxymoronic essence of Petrarch's and Troilus' stories shows us, through the love plot, the paradox of life, the tragic gulf that separates and joins the 'contraries'. We should no longer wonder why Chaucer calls *Troilus* a 'little tragedy'. And indeed we respond to it in the apparently paradoxical – oxymoronic – fashion that Plato envisaged when he said that 'at the sight of tragedies the spectators smile through their tears'. For there are many 'combinations of pleasure and pain in lamentations, and in tragedy and comedy, not only on the stage, but on the greater stage of human life'.[48]

4

Sunset, flowers, and leaves: Tradition and tragic images

> La Nature est un temple où de vivants piliers
> Laissent parfois sortir de confuses paroles;
> L'homme y passe à travers des forêts de symboles
> Qui l'observent avec des regards familiers.

(Nature is a temple where living pillars at times let out confused words; man goes by it through forests of symbols which observe him with familiar looks).

This is the first stanza of the fourth poem, entitled 'Correspondances', in Baudelaire's *Les Fleurs du Mal*. Its meaning will perhaps be better clarified if we compare it to the following statement, made by Goethe in 1782:

Natur! . . . Wir leben mitten in ihr, und sind ihr fremde. Sie spricht unaufhörlich mit uns, und verrät uns ihr Geheimnis nicht.

(Nature! . . . We live right in her, and are alien to her. She speaks continuously with us, and yet she does not reveal to us her mystery.)[1]

Man and Nature, Goethe and Baudelaire say, are very close, yet they are not only distinct and separate, but also alien to each other. If, however, we read the two passages more closely, we begin to see important differences. Compared to Goethe's clearcut oppositions, Baudelaire's metaphorical approach is more complex and more oblique. Nature is a temple – a well-known image – a sacred building, but, apart from the living pillars which support it, it seems to be empty. Nature's message to man is not continuous ('unaufhörlich'), but occasional ('parfois'). Her words, intrinsically mysterious and incomprehensible for Goethe, are 'confused' for Baudelaire. For him, too, man does not 'live' in Nature: an accidental and transient visitor, he 'passes' through or by the temple. He is not totally 'alien' to the natural world, which shows him forests of symbols that look at him with familiarity. Indeed, as the poem

75

goes on to say, there is a correspondence between man and Nature, something like 'de longs échos qui de loin se confondent – Dans une ténébreuse et profonde unité'. Yet Baudelaire's image looks strangely distorted. Goethe's Nature does not reveal her secret to us, but this secret exists and we can continue to search for it, as Goethe himself did throughout his life. In 'Correspondances', it is the forests of symbols that look at man. Nature is no longer a passive object of endless investigation – she is a dark wood of signs, an intricate code which observes man from outside with familiar, but, I would suggest, also sardonic eyes. For man's flesh, spirit and senses being 'like' prairies, amber and moss (lines 9–14), distinction and comprehension between subject and object are impossible, and only fluid 'correspondences' are left – long echoes which merge from far away into a dark, deep unity. Seventy-five momentous years passed between Goethe's pronouncement and the publication of Baudelaire's poem in the *Fleurs du Mal*.

In this chapter I am going to study the tragic by examining three nature images. I therefore choose the comparison between Goethe's and Baudelaire's passages as an example of the critical method I intend to adopt. We have here four poles: nature and the tragic on the one hand; intertextuality and diachrony as poetic tradition on the other. As such, natural phenomena are of course not tragic. It is man who, by looking at himself in the world of nature, has identified some of them as tragic 'signs', as metaphors of his own condition. Since earliest times, human beings have done this through poetry, rather than philosophy or science, because poetry leaves more room for the imagination and feels free to associate the human soul and the external *cosmos*, bridging the gap between subject and object so as to grasp a meaning that neither philosophy nor science are capable of uncovering.

Medieval poets widely used the three images I deal with here – the sunset, flowers, and leaves – but they inherited them from classical antiquity or the Bible and in turn transmitted them to post-medieval literature. The transformations that these metaphors have undergone through the ages[2] must therefore be taken into account if we want to understand what they mean to us, twentieth-century readers. Our problem is then once more that of alterity and modernity: this time, however, not just of medieval literature, but of our whole literary corpus.

A purely intertextual approach to this problem would naturally lead to an inherently interminable research. While using such a method freely in the following pages, I have therefore introduced a genealogical criterion; that is, I have tried to concentrate on the various *direct* ancestors and descendants of our three images. Only after doing so can one analyse intertextual relationships and even compare more distant poems, entering the field of what Harold Bloom has called 'transumption' and 'transumptive criticism'.[3]

Let us begin, then, with the greatest medieval poem, Dante's *Divine Comedy*. After the general introduction of Canto I (the dark wood, the three animals, the meeting with Virgil), the *Inferno* proper starts with Canto II, where Dante shows himself afraid to undertake the journey through the other world and where Virgil persuades him to embark upon it by recounting how Beatrice herself has descended from Heaven expressly to command it. And here, one at the very beginning and the other at the end of the Canto, we meet the first two great Nature images of the poem, the sunset and the flowers:

> Lo giorno se n'andava, e l'aere bruno
> toglieva li animai che sono in terra
> da le fatiche loro; e io sol uno
> m'apparecchiava a sostener la guerra
> sí del cammino e sí de la pietate,
> che ritrarrà la mente che non erra.   (*Inferno* II, 1–6)[4]

(Day was departing, and the dark air was taking the creatures on earth from their labors; and I alone was making ready to sustain the strife, both of the journey and of the pity, which unerring memory shall retrace.)

> Quali fioretti dal notturno gelo
> chinati e chiusi, poi che 'l sol li 'mbianca,
> si drizzan tutti aperti in loro stelo,
> tal mi fec'io di mia virtude stanca   (*Inferno* II, 127–30)

(As little flowers, bent down and closed by chill of night, straighten and all unfold upon their stems when the sun brightens them, such in my faint strength did I become)

The third Nature image comes towards the end of Canto III, after Dante and Virgil have gone through the gate of Hell and, having reached the shores of Acheron, see the souls of the damned flock to Charon's boat:

> Come d'autunno si levan le foglie
> l'una appresso de l'altra, fin che 'l ramo
> vede a terra tutte le sue spoglie,
> similemente il mal seme d'Adamo
> gittansi di quel lito ad una ad una,
> per cenni come augel per suo richiamo.
>
> (*Inferno* III, 112–17)

(As the leaves fall away in autumn, one after another, till the bough sees all its spoils upon the ground, so there the evil seed of Adam: one by one they cast themselves from that shore at signals, like a bird at its call.)

In the first place, it is of primary importance to note at once the connection between the incipient night of the first image and the opening up of the flowers at sunrise in the second. Metaphorically, the two passages delineate the passing of a day in Dante's experience. Weary and fearsome, he begins his journey at sunset; shortly afterwards, comforted by Virgil and with Beatrice's words still echoing in his ears, he launches on his enterprise brightened, as it were, by the rising sun. The chill of night has disappeared.

Secondly, it is interesting to see how all three images are part of a complex pattern of nature metaphors which spans the whole of the beginning of the poem. Dante finds himself in a dark wood, sees a hill clothed by the rays of the sun, calls his heart a lake, compares his feelings at the end of the first night to those of a man emerging onto the shore from a stormy sea, encounters three animals in a desert as the sun climbs the sky with the stars that accompanied it when God created the universe (Canto I). Then, suddenly, the sun sets once more, while earthly animals go to sleep. And, as the poet finds himself 'su la fiumana ove 'l mar non ha vanto', he revives like flowers touched by the dawn sun. Finally, the poet sees human beings reduced to leaves which fall off the trees in autumn or to birds flocking to their call. In three cantos, we have gone through the whole world of nature and, within it, passed from allegory to metaphor: forest and desert; sun and stars; day and night; lake and river and sea; animals, flowers and leaves.

Let us now return to our first image, the sunset at the beginning of Canto II. There are several precedents for it in classical poetry. Statius, for instance, opens a twenty-five line long description of Polynices' hurried march through shattered forests, cloven mountains and overflowing streams in a stormy night, with a turgid passage which contrasts the coming of oblivious sleep over men and animals with the impending tempest and the upheaval of nature:

> Iamque per emeriti surgens confinia Phoebi
> Titanis late, mundo subvecta silenti,
> rorifera gelidum tenuaverat aera biga:
> iam pecudes volucresque tacent, iam Somnus avaris
> inrepsit curis pronusque ex aethere nutat,
> grata laboratae referens oblivia vitae.
> Sed nec puniceo rediturum nubila caelo

promisere iubar, nec rarescentibus umbris
longa repercusso nituere crepuscula Phoebo:
densior a terris et nulli pervia flammae
subtexit nox atra polos.   (*Thebaid* I, 336–46)

(But now through the wide domains which Phoebus, his day's work ended, had left bare, rose the Titanian queen, borne upward through a silent world, and with her dewy chariot cooled and rarefied the air; now birds and beasts are hushed, and Sleep steals o'er the greedy cares of men, and stoops and beckons from the sky, shrouding a toilsome life once more in sweet oblivion. Yet no reddening clouds gave promise of the light's return, nor as the shadows lessened did the twilight gleam with long shafts of sun-reflecting radiance; black night, blacker to earthward and shot by never a ray, veiled all the pole.)

To this, after the description of the storm, is added another contrast: the elements are raging, but Polynices continues to go. Yet there is also a deep correspondence between what King Lear will call 'this contentious storm' and the 'tempest in [his] mind'.[5] Uncertain, distraught, fearful of his brother and terrified by the dark silence surrounding him, Polynices is like a sailor caught, 'rationis inops' – 'beggared of resource' – by the tumult of sea and sky (370–6).

Statius of course unduly complicates, and thereby almost completely loses the effect of, a simple and powerful image used by Virgil no less than three times in the *Aeneid*. Aeneas has just founded Pergamea in Crete, but the city is being swept away by the plague. 'Nox erat', says the Trojan hero to Dido in recounting that episode, 'et terris animalia somnus habebat' – ''Twas night, when every creature void of cares, – The common gift of balmy slumber shares' (III, 147). The Phrygian Penates appear and exhort him to seek a country called Hesperia or Oenotria or Italia. Astonished, Aeneas cannot fall asleep, but starts from his couch and, after the appropriate sacrifices, runs to consult Anchises. Finally, they sail away from Crete.

Here, the contrast is implicit: everything sleeps; Aeneas, troubled by the vision of his gods, is awake. On another, similar occasion the opposition has altogether disappeared. Once more, it is night, and sleep holds all living beings, but this time Aeneas, too, lies down by the river and finds relief in slumber (VIII, 26–30). The Tiber then appears to him as if emerging through the shades of the poplars and prophesies victory in the war and the foundation of Alba. Man conforms to nature in almost complete bucolic harmony.

By far the most momentous use of this image by Virgil occurs, however, in a fully dramatic context, one nobody is likely to forget.

Aeneas, spurred by the gods, is leaving Carthage. Dido knows it and despairs. The picture of night and rest is expanded to include the whole natural world and extends over seven perfect Virgilian lines. Against it, stands the sad figure of Dido, who cannot accept night in her eyes or in her breast. Love and a storm of fury rage in her:

> Nox erat et placidum carpebant fessa soporem
> corpora per terras silvaeque et saeva quierant
> aequora, cum medio volvontur sidera lapsu,
> cum tacet omnis ager, pecudes pictaeque volucres,
> quaeque lacus late liquidos quaeque aspera dumis
> rura tenent, somno positae sub nocte silenti,
> lenibant curas et corda oblita laborum.
> At non infelix animi Phoenissa neque umquam
> solvitur in somnos oculisve aut pectore noctem
> accipit: ingeminant curae rursusque resurgens
> saevit amor magnoque irarum fluctuat aestu.

(*Aeneid* IV, 522–32)[6]

('Twas dead of night, when weary bodies close
Their eyes in balmy sleep, and soft repose:
The winds no longer whisper through the woods;
Nor murmuring tides disturb the gentle floods.
The stars in silent order moved around;
And Peace, with downy wings was brooding on the ground.
The flocks and herds, and particoloured fowl
Which haunt the woods or swim the weedy pool,
Stretched on the quiet earth, securely lay,
Forgetting the past labours of the day.
All else, of Nature's common gift partake;
Unhappy Dido was alone awake:
Nor sleep nor ease the furious queen can find:
Sleep fled her eyes, as quiet fled her mind.
Despair, and rage, and love, divide her heart;
Despair and rage had some, but love the greater part.)

Here, the opposition between man and nature is radical, and Virgil underlines it by employing key expressions in both sections of the image: *nox erat – neque umquam . . . pectore noctem accipit; carpebant soporem* and *somno positae – neque umquam solvitur in somnos oculisve; lenibant curas – ingeminant curae; saeva quierant aequora – saevit amor magnoque irarum fluctuat aestu.* Dido is totally insensitive to the peace which pervades all beings on earth: shut within her own tormented mind, she runs headlong towards madness and suicide. It is obvious that for a poet who, as the *Eclogues*, the *Georgics* and the *Aeneid* itself show, wholeheartedly responds to the rhythms of nature, Dido's deafness to and alienation from the natural world are most tragic features.

If we continue our journey back in time through poetic tradition, we can see that Virgil has brought to perfection an image twice consecrated by Apollonius Rhodius in his *Argonautica*, where on both occasions (III, 744–54 and IV, 1059–63) Medea's love and anguish are opposed to the quiet of night. The topos, however, must have been older. A fragment of Sappho (94 D) inserts it, with an original touch, within the context of disappointed eros:

> The moon has set and the Pleiades.
> The midst of night. Time goes by.
> And I sleep alone.[7]

But probably the earliest example is to be found in a fragment (58 D) by Alcman, the seventh-century poet who said he had found words and song by interpreting the language of partridges:

> The summits of mountains sleep and the valleys,
> crags and abysses,
> and the reptiles all that the dark earth feeds,
> and the mountain beasts and the swarms of bees;
> the monsters deep in the purple sea,
> and the races of wide-winged birds.[8]

This Nocturne is so extraordinarily pure and simple that it gives the impression of being in no need of the second part of the image – the contrast or opposition. But, as early Greek lyric was as, if not more, functional than later poetry, we must assume that the adversative clause was present here, too.

It is significant that no earlier use of the image, for instance in Homer, is recorded. Its birth seems to be tied to the emergence of lyric poetry or, as Bruno Snell would put it with a useful if perhaps too simplistic generalization, to the 'rise of the individual', the 'I', in the early Greek lyric.[9] The moment man acquires greater self-consciousness, Nature becomes something separate; and viceversa, the moment man's awareness of the natural world grows, he feels he has to measure himself against it. Nature and man are each other's mirror. A never-ending dialectic play starts which crystallizes in an image that soon becomes a topos, ever varied and renewed in lyric as well as narrative poetry and drama. Its basic mechanism rests on a contrast or correspondence. Thus: a – nature is quiet, but man is tortured (Virgil, Dido); b – nature and man are both at rest (Virgil, Aeneas and the Tiber); c – to the storm in nature corresponds one in man (Statius; Shakespeare, *King Lear*).[10]

In the purely lyrical tradition, and particularly during the medieval period, our image can be seen as complementary to the wider topos of the comparison or contrast of the lover's feelings and the forces of nature, 'especially as these are shown in the cycle of the seasons'.[11] The widely known 'De ramis cadunt folia'[12] is an example, but the most beautiful instances are Arnaut Daniel's 'Can chai la fueilla' and, directly inspired by it, Dante's 'Io son venuto al punto de la rota', where the opposition is repeated five times with astonishingly powerful variations. Dante himself further develops the topos in another of the so-called 'rime petrose', the marvellous sestina 'Al poco giorno e al gran cerchio d'ombra'. Petrarch, who echoes 'Io son venuto' in his own sestina 'L'aere gravato, et l'importuna nebbia', exploits Dante's technique and some of his images to expand the sunset–lover contrast in Canzone L, 'Ne la stagion che 'l ciel rapido inchina', where the elegiac tone, intensified by quotations from and reminiscences of Virgil's *Eclogues* and *Georgics*, spreads over the five stanzas that precede the envoy. Each of these contains one opposition. I quote one as an example of this lyrical version of our image:

> Come 'l sol volge le 'nfiammate rote
> per dar luogo a la notte, onde discende
> dagli altissimi monti maggior l'ombra,
> l'avaro zappador l'arme riprende,
> et con parole et con alpestri note
> ogni gravezza del suo petto sgombra;
> et poi la mensa ingombra
> di povere vivande,
> simili a quelle ghiande,
> le qua' fuggendo tutto 'l mondo honora.
> Ma chi vuol si rallegri ad ora ad ora,
> ch'i' pur non ebbi anchor, non dirò lieta,
> ma riposata un'hora,
> né per volger di ciel né di pianeta. (ll. 15–28)[13]

(When the sun turns its fiery wheels to make room for night and greater shade descends from the high mountains, the avid ploughman takes up his instrument and with words and mountain songs chases all heaviness out of his breast; then fills his table with poor food, similar to those acorns which the world honours but flees. Let anyone who wants to do so rejoice now. In spite of the turning of sky or of the planets I never had one hour of rest, let alone of joy.)

From Petrarch, of course, the image floods the European lyric, and we can still find it, laden with classical echoes and bright in its Mondschein–Sonata light and rhythm in Leopardi's 'La sera del dí di festa' (1820):[14]

> Dolce e chiara è la notte e senza vento,
> e queta sovra i tetti e in mezzo agli orti
> posa la luna, e di lontan rivela
> serena ogni montagna. O donna mia,
> già tace ogni sentiero, e pei balconi
> rara traluce la notturna lampa:
> tu dormi, che t'accolse agevol sonno
> . . .
> Tu dormi: io questo ciel, che sí benigno
> appare in vista, a salutar m'affaccio,
> e l'antica natura onnipossente,
> che mi fece all'affanno. A te la speme
> nego, mi disse, anche la speme; e d'altro
> non brillin gli occhi tuoi se non di pianto. (ll. 1–7, 11–16)

(Sweet and clear is the night and without wind, and the moon rests quietly over the roofs and in the orchards from far away revealing all the mountains in pure air. Oh my lady, every path is now still, and the night lamp sheds scarcely any light on the balconies: you sleep, for easy sleep has overcome you . . . You sleep: I go out to greet this sky, which seems so benevolent, and ancient, almighty Nature, who created me for torment. To you, she said, I deny even hope. Let your eyes shine but with tears.)

For Leopardi, then, the splendid nocturnal scene is but an illusion. Nature, an ancient, eternal, omnipotent, oppressive being, is an evil step-mother, who has destined the poet to a life of torment. Man, ever more frustrated by her splendid beauty, feels himself completely excluded from Nature's triumphal joys.[15] We have overtaken the Goethe of 1782 and almost reached Baudelaire. It may, however, be misleading to see matters in this fashion. Goethe himself wrote a famous short poem, not by chance entitled 'Ein Gleiches', where the topos is revisited with icastic simplicity to point to a total, but future and possibly ominous consonance between self and Nature:

Über allen Gipfeln
Ist Ruh,
In allen Wipfeln
Spürest du
Kaum einen Hauch;
Die Vögelein schweigen im Walde.
Warte nur, balde
Ruhest du auch.

(On every peak it is quiet, in the treetops you can scarcely feel a breath of air;
the birds are silent in the woods. Only wait, soon you too will lie as quiet.)

And Wordsworth composed a sonnet, 'It is a beauteous evening, calm
and free' (1802), in which Nature appears as 'the mighty Being' and a
'Temple', but where man, too, is divine and worships in the inner
shrine. In a passage of the 1805 *Prelude* (reproduced without alterations
in the 1850 version) the setting of the sun marks 'consummate
happiness' – 'wide-spreading, steady, calm, contemplative' – and
although the hour is neither 'winning' nor 'serene', the poet's soul

> Put off her veil, and, self-transmuted, stood
> Naked as in the presence of her God.   (IV, 127–42)

Indeed, in 'Tintern Abbey' the 'light of setting suns' is one of the
abodes of something in nature 'far more deeply interfused' which is
perceived not as tragic, but as a 'presence' that 'disturbs . . . with the
joy of elevated thoughts' – the 'sense sublime' that constitutes the
second pole of the present volume.

Dante, to go back to the beginning, is far from this kind of infatuation
and identification with a Nature which is but a projection and echo of
the self. No poet has perhaps managed as well as he to catch the
tranquillity and splendour of a full moon night with an image as pure
and 'classical' as any Alcman, Sappho or Virgil might have created:[16]

> Quale ne' plenilunii sereni
> Trivia ride tra le ninfe etterne
> che dipingon lo ciel per tutti i seni
>
> (*Paradiso* XXIII, 25–7)

(As in the clear skies at the full moon Trivia smiles among the eternal nymphs
that deck heaven through all its depths.)

But this is only a simile which he employs to tell us how the light of the
Virgin Mary appeared to him in Heaven. Dante's nature imagery is
always strictly functional to the narrative situation and absolutely

essential. As readers, we can lose ourselves in the infinite resonance of such images, but Dante the poet pauses only one moment looking at all the glory around him, then plunges headlong into his theme. This is true even of those passages where the pause, being longer, leaves a more lasting impression and determines, as it were, the atmosphere of a whole episode. The celebrated opening of *Purgatorio* VIII, which we can see as the 'mezzo del cammin' of Dante's sunset scenery, constitutes the introduction to the recognition scene with Judge Nino, one of the climaxes in the episode of the valley of Antepurgatory:

> Era già l'ora che volge il disio
> ai navicanti e 'ntenerisce il core
> lo dì c'han detto ai dolci amici addio;
> e che lo novo peregrin d'amore
> punge, se ode squilla di lontano
> che paia il giorno pianger che si more
>
> (*Purgatorio* VIII, 1–6)

(It was now the hour that turns back the longing of seafaring folk and melts their heart the day they have bidden sweet friends farewell, and that pierces the new pilgrim with love if he hears from afar a bell that seems to mourn the dying day.)

It is this passage that T.S. Eliot echoes in the third section of the *Waste Land*, 'The Fire Sermon', when Tiresias sees the typist home at teatime,

> At the violet hour, the evening hour that strives
> Homeward, and brings the sailor home from sea.   (220–1)[17]

Finally, with another incipient darkness simile, Dante definitively abandons both the tragic and the pathetic, and enters the *agon* of the sublime. In the Heaven of the Sun, a new 'crown' of blessed souls appears. On top of the bright sunlight, a new 'lustre' rises, 'per guisa d'orizzonte che rischiari' – like a brightening horizon. Then, suddenly, we find ourselves just after sunset, in the twilight between day and night. The new 'parvenze', appearances, are the emerging lights of the stars. Those *phainomena* paradoxically represent the imaginary vehicles of true 'subsistences':

> E sì come al salir di prima sera
> comincian per lo ciel nove parvenze,
> sì che la vista pare e non par vera,
> parvemi lì novelle sussistenze
> cominciare a vedere   (*Paradiso* XIV, 70–3)[18]

85

(And as, at rise of early evening, new lights begin to show in heaven, so that the sight does, and yet does not, seem real, it seemed to me that there I began to perceive new subsistences.)

When, at the beginning of *Inferno* II, Dante decides to use an image derived from classical tradition such as I have tried to sketch, and particularly from Virgil, he modifies it profoundly. In the first place, his background is not the night, but the dying out of day: 'lo giorno se n'andava'. This darkening of the air ('l'aere bruno') may well announce long-deserved rest to all living beings ('animai') on earth – it also constitutes the most appropriately sombre *ouverture* for a journey through the dim light and gloomy views of Hell. We have, to begin with, not a contrast, but a correspondence and foreboding. Coming as we do from the glorious morning of *Inferno* I, we are very likely not only to notice but also to feel this in our very bones. Yet the correspondence hides a contrast – between the earth on which the 'animalia' are about to fall asleep and the place, the here nowhere mentioned or specified, where Dante finds himself. The immense distance between the two worlds is underlined by the temporal identity: in both dimensions, the day is fading away.

Thus prepared and deepened, the traditional opposition between Nature and the human being emerges fully with 'e io'. Replacing fictional characters, the 'I' of the lyric, with all its dramatic urgency, enters the narrative. This is no Polynices, no Dido: it is the narrator himself, protagonist of his own poem. Terrible loneliness ('e io *sol* uno') isolates him from nature on earth, but also, it seems, from every other human being here and now. What an extraordinary thing to say after one has just been joined by Virgil! Dante, there is no doubt, is slightly depressed, and the rest of Canto II will show how much. Virgil, as he himself has said, is not a man, but a shade. Yet the solitude Dante feels here becomes more comprehensible if one sees it as a poetic dimension. The 'war of the journey and of pity'[19] opposed to the peace of all living beings on earth is the fictional visit to the other world, the first a man attempts, as Dante will soon say, after Aeneas and Paul, and the first a poet as such faces. It is not by chance that Dante now adds that his 'unerring' memory will recount this 'guerra' and that he invokes for the purpose the help of the Muses and above all of his own 'ingegno' and 'mente'. In the end, it is Dante's journey and the poetry which describes it that are opposed to nature.

The first three lines of *Inferno* II were used by Chaucer in the *Parliament of Fowls*. Here, the poetic persona who speaks in the first person singular has been reading the *Somnium Scipionis* all day. Then, sunset deprives him of light and therefore of his book:

> The day gan faylen, and the derke nyght,
> That reveth bestes from here besynesse,
> Berafte me my bok for lak of lyght,
> And to my bed I gan me for to dresse,
> Fulfyld of thought and busy hevynesse;
> For bothe I hadde thyng which that I nolde,
> And ek I ne hadde that thyng that I wolde.   (85–91)[20]

The traditional topos has changed considerably. If incipient night 'reveth bestes from here besynesse', the protagonist is neither tortured like Dido or Medea nor about to enter a 'war' of the Dantean kind. Quite simply, the lack of light prevents him from reading any further. And quite sensibly, the narrator gets himself ready for bed. In other words, we have no contrast, but conformity. What can you as a reader do if you have no candle and no electric light? You get into your pyjamas and go, or at least try to go, to sleep. The change of perspective lessens the dramatic quality of the image, inserting it into a common, everyday dimension. Soon, weary of the day's labour (92–4), the protagonist will be fast asleep. Man and nature follow the same rhythm. The only thing that distinguishes the former from the latter is the presence of consciousness. Dressing for bed, the narrator feels 'fulfyld of thought and busy hevynesse', whereas all other living beings are at this very moment getting rid of all 'besynesse'. The sense of perplexed meditation, of the slow and heavy revolving of thought, is very strong here. The reader keeps going mentally back to his book and is dissatisfied with it. He has what he did not want, he does not have what he wanted. It is out of this conscious dissatisfaction that his dream, and hence his poetic adventure, will take shape. In it he will, like Dante, go through a gate to explore not Hell, but the world of Nature herself, where all living beings, here blissfully asleep, will appear extremely busy.[21]

Within about eighty years – the same interval that separates our initial passages from Goethe and Baudelaire – an image which had lasted almost two thousand has entirely changed its meaning: no grand drama of man against nature, no heroic gesture of a poet alone in another world is presented to us, but just a picture of ourselves going to rest after a good read. Yet the tragic vitality of our image is persistent. 'The eleventh hour of the day', writes Caesarius of Heisterbach in the thirteenth century, 'draws the sun to its setting'. 'This', he adds in one breath, 'is the decrepit age which is nigh unto death', and he will therefore devote – significantly 'not without mystery' – the eleventh 'distinctio' of his *Dialogus Miraculorum* to the dying.[22]

Caesarius' interpretation may strike us as purely 'allegorical', and indeed he goes on to explain that the number eleven, 'as it passes one beyond ten in which number are embraced the commands of the divine law, denotes transgression. By the transgression of the first-created death entered into the world. Hence death (*mors*) took its name from "biting" (*morsus*). When man bit the apple of the forbidden tree, he incurred death and subjected himself with all his posterity to its certainty'. But it is the Jahwistic writer of Genesis who maintains that God's death sentence descended upon man 'in the cool of the day' (3. 8), in the late afternoon toward sundown, and Milton, for instance, is careful to follow the same pattern in *Paradise Lost* (x, 91–102). Sunset, Fall and dying are clearly linked.[23]

Yet even when religious overtones are not implied, the association between sunset and death is constant. Shakespeare's vicious Achilles threatens Hector and decrees the fall of Troy:

> Look, Hector, how the sun begins to set,
> How ugly night comes breathing at his heels;
> Even with the vail and dark'ning of the sun
> To close the day up, Hector's life is done.
> . . .
> So, Ilion, fall thou next! Come, Troy, sink down!
> (*Troilus and Cressida* v.viii.5–11)

Two centuries after Shakespeare, the 'allegory' of Caesarius has become explicit identification, but in a sense that the medieval monk would hardly have understood. Ugo Foscolo loves the evening precisely because it is 'the image of the fatal peace' and makes his thought wander 'upon the paths that go towards eternal nothingness'. The 'long, unquiet shades' that sundown brings to the 'universe' are 'prayed for': with darkness comes peace both outside and inside.[24] Man is at one with nature because nature dissolves his existential yearning, his attachment to, and suffering from life; because – supreme tragedy – nature evokes the 'nulla eterno'.

Even this is denied to later poets. In a sonnet composed in 1862 and significantly entitled 'Le Coucher du soleil romantique', Baudelaire hails the rising sun, beautiful and fresh when, like an explosion, it 'launches' its 'bonjour' to us. 'Happy is he', the poet continues, 'who can greet its setting, more glorious than a dream.' He himself would rush to the horizon to catch 'at least an oblique ray'. But,

> Mais je poursuis en vain le Dieu qui se retire;
> L'irrésistible Nuit établit son empire,
> Noire, humide, funeste et pleine de frissons;
>
> Une odeur de tombeau dans les ténèbres nage,
> Et mon pied peureux froisse, au bord du marécage,
> Des crapauds imprévus et de froids limaçons.

(But I vainly follow the God that withdraws; irresistible Night establishes its empire – black, humid, fatal, full of tremors; a smell of the grave floats in the darkness, and on the edge of the marsh my fearful foot crushes unforeseen toads and cold snails.)[25]

The setting sun, the withdrawing God, is ultimately elusive, for it immediately becomes 'irresistible Night'. Neither mankind nor its poetry (whether romantic or Baudelairean) can ever reach the climactic instant of light's transfiguration, what Dante would have called 'lo giorno . . . che si more'. Sublime dying is forbidden: what dominates is Death, full of little, slimy animals, trembling with 'frissons'. That is the poetry the age allows one to write. Fascinated by horror, the poet and his more traditional competitors now appear ironically (and it is a tragic irony) 'romantique'.

Thus, we should not wonder if the post-romantic lyric goes all the way down, well beyond Baudelaire's 'grave'. In 'Ein Herbstabend', for instance, Georg Trakl envisages a village 'dark' in an autumn evening. There, along the walls, there pass only 'Gestalten', forms or shades. These are men and women, 'and the dead go into cold rooms to make the beds for them'. We are far beyond Dante's *Inferno*, for what Trakl describes is the living hell of man's obscure, mysterious, heavy fate such as it looms *within* him. Nature – the evening – is a projection of man's anxiety. All we have, all that is ever ours in our constant 'Herbstabend', the poet concludes, is 'black and close': 'Doch immer ist das Eigne schwarz und nah'.[26]

What, then, is left to us is to 'go down' like the sun. And this 'solution', which appears as early as the second version of Hölderlin's 'Dichtermut',[27] is precisely what the ultimate representative of post-romantic man, Nietzsche's Zarathustra, announces he will adopt in his Prologue, when he addresses the sun itself:

Ich möchte verschenken und austheilen, bis die Weisen unter den Menschen wieder einmal ihrer Thorheit und die Armen wieder einmal ihres Reichtums froh geworden sind.
Dazu muss ich in die Tiefe steigen: wie du des Abends thust, wenn du hinter das Meer gehst und noch der Unterwelt Licht bringst, du überreiches Gestirn! Ich muss, gleich dir, *untergehen*, wie die Menschen es nennen, zu denen ich hinab will.

(I should like to give it [my wisdom] away and distribute it, until the wise among men have again become happy in their folly and the poor happy in their wealth.
To that end, I must descend into the depths: as you do at evening, when you go behind the sea and bring light to the underworld too, superabundant star! Like you, I must *go down* – as men, to whom I want to descend, call it.)[28]

Thus begins Zarathustra's down-going, his sun-setting, a momentous journey over the 'bridge' that is man, with 'old shattered law-tables around him and also new law-tables – half-written', until, finally, the hour comes 'when he who is going down shall bless himself'. Then, man's sunset ends, and the superman's new morning rises up to great noontide.[29] For the first time in the history of Western imagination, man *is* the sun. His 'untergehen' is a painful but exalted descent to the bottom of his self, to and *past* the tragic core of his essence, a voyage in the course of which the traditional universe of beliefs and mental images is subverted and laid waste so that a new soul may be born. Heathenly Christ-like, Zarathustra's 'sunset' is also supremely, and blissfully, Lucifer-like.

'Going down' can be dangerous. Thomas Mann understood this perfectly. 'I have a weakness', says his Adrian Leverkühn, 'for people who have been "down below". By below I mean in hell'; and he goes on to mention Paul, Aeneas, and Dante. His 'Apocalypsis cum figuris' draws not only on the whole apocalyptic tradition, but also on the various versions of a journey into hell and particularly on Dante's, from which as well as from Michelangelo's Last Judgement, the frightful oratorio derives its 'tönendes Gemälde', its tone-picture.[30] While writing *Doktor Faustus*, Mann himself had been reading the *Divine Comedy*.[31] For a novel that was to recount an artist's – and a whole world's – descent to Hell no epigraph would be more appropriate than the opening of *Inferno* II. Mann took it:

> Lo giorno se n'andava, e l'aere bruno . . .

Sunset, flowers and leaves

With our second image – the flowers opening up after night when the sun shines on them – we are in a completely different atmosphere. This is a simile, and its two terms are the flowers on the one side and Dante's own psychological reaction on the other. Alienated from nature at the beginning of the canto, the pilgrim is now, metaphorically, at one with her. The darkening air of sunset has given way to nightly chill ('notturno gelo') and this in turn yielded to the white light of the sun. After Dante's doubts, Virgil's account of Mary's and Beatrice's care for the moral health of the poet makes the journey begin with a dawn of hope. Like flowers bent down and closed by the frost of night, the failing strength, the 'virtute stanca' of Dante is now, with the coming of metaphorical sunlight, straightening up and opening out – in short, blooming. The 'war of the journey and of pity' can be faced. Nor will it be surprising to note that these flowers, henceforth banished from the *Inferno*, ultimately point to those under a cloud of which Beatrice herself will appear in *Purgatorio* XXX and, further, to the rose-flower of *Paradiso* XXXI–XXXIII. The 'blooming' of Dante's 'buono ardire' is in a sense fulfilled and rewarded only at the summit of Mount Purgatory by the actual appearance of the lady whose verbal evocation by Virgil has produced the pilgrim's resolution.[32] And finally, the flowers whitened by the sun will become the one immense 'candida rosa' of the Empyrean.

In *Inferno* II the image is, however, far away from the glorious plenitude of the *Purgatorio* and *Paradiso*, and one of the words used by Dante, 'stelo', suggests an ephemeral quality which is fundamental for the fascination the smile holds for us.[33] Enchanted by the sudden sunlight, we tend to forget that the stems of flowers are frail. Dante's simile promises future sublimation on the threshhold of the tragic.

The extraordinary impact of these lines does not depend on classical echoes. There seems to be no precedent in Antiquity for this kind of image. Dante is probably working with the new tradition of Provençal poetry and relying on contemporary popular sayings[34] as well as on more precise parallels elaborated by scientists and theologians.[35] There is, in other words, a medieval background for this simile. The dwarves can add something to what the giants, on whose shoulders they are borne, have said. Here, for instance, is a stanza from 'Ab la dolchor del temps novel', a poem by the very first troubadour, William IX of Aquitaine:

> La nostr'amor va enaissi
> Com la branca de l'albespi,

91

> Qu'esta sobre l'arbre tremblan
> La nuoit, a la ploia ez al gel,
> Tro l'endeman, quel·l sols s'espan
> Per la fueilla vert el ramel.

(Our love goes along the same way as the branch of the hawthorn, which stands trembling on the tree through the night, in rain and sleet, until the next day when the sun spreads through the green leaves on the twigs.'[36]

The phenomenon we witness with William's and Dante's similes is different from, and in a sense opposite to, what we have observed in the case of the sunset image. William and Dante crystallize into a few lines a new feeling towards nature and towards man's psyche. In their similes, the correspondence is not between nature and man as such, but between a common natural phenomenon and an event in the human heart, between outer and inner worlds.[37] A warrior is cut down in battle as a flower by the plough. A lady is as beautiful as a rose or as pure as a lily. These are topoi which compare two 'outsides', or two objects both viewed from outside. Even more than William, Dante internalizes one term of the comparison and the result is an interpenetration of both objects – the flowers acquire a living spirit, a heart, and the pilgrim becomes part of natural life. Furthermore, Dante is particularly fond of this image. He picks it up again in the blissful atmosphere of the *Paradiso* when, in Canto XXII, he meets St Benedict, whose loving words and appearance 'dilate', the poet says, his 'confidence'

> come 'l sol fa la rosa quando aperta
> tanto divien quant'ell'ha di possanza   (56–7)

(as the sun does the rose when it opens to its fullest bloom.)

The frailty of *Inferno* II has been replaced by the glorious 'might' of a rose fully open under the sun.

Dante's consecration of the flower–heart simile is a decisive cultural and poetic event. We have seen before how he exploits an image derived from the classics. Here, he himself becomes the classic. After him, 'Quali fioretti' turns into a topos. Poliziano uses it simply to indicate the coming of dawn,[38] but Tasso elaborates on it with a splendid manneristic touch to describe Armida's cheeks streaming with tears (a 'feigned woe', he adds) when Godfrey refuses to help her:

> Le guancie asperse di que' vivi umori
> che giù cadean sin de la veste al lembo,
> parean vermigli insieme e bianchi fiori,

> se pur gli irriga un rugiadoso nembo,
> quando su l'apparir de' primi albori
> spiegano a l'aure liete il chiuso grembo;
> e l'alba, che li mira e se n'appaga,
> d' adornarsene il crin diventa vaga.

(The cheeks, sprinkled by those living humours which fell down to the hem of her dress, looked like red and white flowers bathed by a cloud of dew when, at the first appearance of dawn, they open up to happy air their closed womb; and Dawn who, looking at them, is satisfied with them, desires to adorn with them her hair.)[39]

We have gone back to an 'outside' view. This time, it is precisely the 'surface' of the human being that the simile focusses upon, while Dante's 'stalk' has been replaced by 'womb', a word which, given Tasso's presentation of Armida, possesses an allusively strong sensual charge. The effect of the image rests on our perceiving the discrepancy between Armida's pretence and the natural phenomenon, and at the same time the fascination which her appearance exerts on the Christian warriors, on us, and indeed, by virtue of the last conceit, on dawn and nature itself.

Manzoni, who next picks up the topos, returns to Dante's psychological perception, but splits the image into two successive stages, one of relief and one of tragic passion. Ermengarda, Charlemagne's wife, is dead. The Choir comments on her unreciprocated love for her husband. At first, she had seemed to find consolation in love for God:

> Come rugiada al cespite
> Dell'erba inaridita
> Fresca negli arsi calami
> Fa rifluir la vita,
> Che verdi ancor risorgono
> Nel temperato albór

(As dew on the tufts of dried-up grass makes fresh life flow into the burnt stems, which rise up, green in the temperate dawn)

But immediately afterwards eros had come back in full force and laid her heart waste,

> come il sol che reduce
> L'érta infocata ascende,
> E con la vampa assidua
> L'immobil aura incende,

93

Risorti appena i gracili
Steli riarde al suol

(as the sun, returning from its journey, ascends through its fiery, steep way and with its continuous heat inflames the still air, burning once more to the ground the frail stalks which had just risen up.)[40]

Finally, Seamus Heaney employs Dante's simile in his *Station Island*, a poem published but five years ago where, in Dantean and Eliotian fashion, he recounts his pilgrimage to Saint Patrick's Purgatory in Ireland. In Section VI, the poet recalls his adolescence and the sudden illumination he had one night upon seeing a girl's 'honey-skinned − Shoulder-blades and the wheatlands of her back − Through the wide keyhole of her keyhole dress'. Then, in this revisitation of Dante's vision of Beatrice in the *Vita Nuova* and in the *Purgatorio*,

> a window facing the deep south of luck
> Opened and I inhaled the land of kindness.
> *As little flowers that were all bowed and shut*
> *By the night chills rise on their stems and open*
> *As soon as they have felt the touch of sunlight,*
> *So I revived in my own wilting powers*
> *And my heart flushed, like somebody set free.*
> Translated, given, under the oak tree.[41]

As any 'translation' should strive to do, this fully preserves the strength of Dante's lines. But Heaney goes one step beyond Dante, definitively overtaking the tragic: his flushing heart, his elation, his sense of newly acquired freedom, are total. Clearly, this indicates the key moment in the poet's experience when he grew from boy to man. A whole new world opened up before him. No one, however, can miss the sexual overtones of the image in the present context, and these seem of course entirely due to Heaney. Yet the fact is that the erotic potential of the simile, latent since the times of William IX, sublimated by Dante, subtly exploited by Tasso,[42] and retained by Manzoni, has now come to the fore.

Has 'poetic tradition' repressed it (in the Freudian sense of the word) all the way down to Seamus Heaney? Have poets used the trope to conceal 'unpleasant truths concerning dangers from within'?[43] Perhaps a look at some medieval instances will clarify the matter.

As far as the fourteenth century is concerned, it is Boccaccio's use of the image that interests us. In both *Filostrato* and *Teseida* he associates it with the figure of the young, meditative, lyrically-minded lover,

Troiolo or Arcita, his favourite characters. In the *Teseida*, the simile acquires particular pathos from the situation. At the end of the tournament, victorious Arcita lies wounded, knowing he will soon die. He asks to see Emilia and when she calls him 'dolce sposo' and declares she will stay with him forever, Arcita's heart rejoices. Dante's image is expanded, and the second term of the comparison is not only the hero's feelings, but also his outward appearance:

> Quali i fioretti richiusi ne' prati
> per lo notturno freddo, tutti quanti
> s'apron come dal sol son riscaldati,
> e 'l prato fanno con più be' sembianti
> rider fra le verdi erbe mescolati,
> dimostrandosi lieto a' riguardanti,
> cotal si fece vedendola Arcita,
> poscia che l'ebbe sì parlare udita.   (IX, 28)[44]

In the *Filostrato*, the context is totally different. Troiolo is not on the point of death, but is suffering the torment of unrequited love for Criseida. When Pandaro reports that Criseida's heart is not totally ill-disposed towards his friend, Troiolo's 'virtute stanca' revives as flowers brightened up by sunlight. Boccaccio follows Dante closely, keeping the comparison with his hero's state of mind:

> Quali i fioretti, dal notturno gelo
> chinati e chiusi, poi che 'l sol gl'imbianca,
> tutti s'apron diritti in loro stelo,
> cotal si fé di sua virtute stanca
> Troiolo allora   (II, 80, 1–5)

We may suspect these lines to contain a 'repressed' sexual allusion, but the fact is that the story of Boccaccio's Troiolo is significantly defined by flower images, and these belong to a much wider realm than the merely erotic one (though, as we shall presently see, eros plays an important role in the tradition). In the third Book of the *Filostrato* (12), the hero is full of joy as the world newly clothed with flowers by spring. When, later on, the Trojan parliament accepts the fatal exchange between Antenore and Criseida which will ultimately lead to the lovers' separation and Criseida's unfaithfulness, Troiolo falls to the ground in a swoon. The simile Boccaccio uses here is classical:

> Qual poscia ch'è dall'aratro intaccato
> ne' campi il giglio, per soverchio sole
> casca ed appassa, e 'l bel color cangiato
> pallido fassi, tale   (IV, 18, 1–4)

The parallel is with Virgil's famous young warrior, Euryalus, mortally wounded by Volcens and falling to the ground in a pool of blood, his head reclining on the shoulders:

> Volvitur Euryalus leto, pulchrosque per artus
> It cruor inque umeros cervix conlapsa recumbit:
> Purpureus veluti cum flos succisus aratro
> Languescit moriens lassove papavera collo
> Demisere caput, pluvia cum forte gravantur.   (IX, 433–7)[45]

> (Down fell the beauteous youth: the yawning wound
> Gushed out a purple stream, and stained the ground.
> His snowy neck reclines upon his breast,
> Like a fair flower by the keen share oppressed –
> Like a white poppy sinking on the plain,
> Whose heavy head is overcharged with rain.)

Boccaccio, one would be tempted to say, is applying a typically epic image to a melodramatic situation. But Virgil's simile is double, with the purple flower cut off by the plough on the one hand and with the poppy bowed down by heavy rain on the other. The second image goes back to Homer, *Iliad* VIII, 306–8, where Gorgythio, struck down by Teucer's arrow, falls

> As full-blown poppies, overcharged with rain,
> Decline the head, and drooping kiss the plain:
> So sinks the youth: his beauteous head, depress'd
> Beneath his helmet, drops upon his breast.[46]

Ovid expands the simile by introducing a human agent which replaces the rain. Appropriately, what he describes is the death of Hyacinthus, soon to be metamorphosed into the purple flower that still bears his name:

> ut, siquis violas rigidumve papaver in horto
> liliaque infringat fulvis horrentia linguis,
> marcida demittant subito caput illa vietum
> nec se sustineant spectentque cacumine terram:
> sic vultus moriens iacet et defecta vigore
> ipsa sibi est oneri cervix umeroque recumbit.
>
> (*Metamorphoses*, x, 190–5)

(Just as when in a garden, if someone has broken off violets or brittle poppies or lilies, still hanging from the yellow stems, fainting they suddenly droop their withered heads and can no longer stand erect, but gaze, with tops bowed low, upon the earth: so the dying face lies prone, the neck, its strength all gone, cannot sustain its own weight and falls back upon the shoulders.)

By the time the image reaches Quintus Smyrnaeus in the fourth century AD, the human agent is firmly installed at the beginning of the simile, interestingly enough employed to describe *Troilus'* own death:

> As when a gardener with a new-whetted scythe
> Mows down, ere it may seed, a blade of corn
> Or poppy, in a garden dewy-fresh
> And blossom-flushed   (*Posthomerica* IV, 424–7)

However, the poet from whom Virgil borrows his first comparison – the image of the flower cut off by the plough which Boccaccio will imitate – is not at all an epic poet. In asking his friends to bring Lesbia his final farewell, Catullus bitterly exhorts her to live with her three hundred studs and to forget his love for her. That love, he says, has collapsed through her fault like the flower at the edge of a meadow struck down by the plough. Here, like Boccaccio's Troiolo, is a lover truly and definitively 'filo-strato'!

> nec meum respectet, ut ante, amorem,
> qui illius culpa cecidit velut prati
> ultimi flos, praetereunte postquam
> tactus aratro est   (11, 21–4)

Almost certainly, Catullus' image is in turn inspired by a simile employed by Sappho in an epithalamium:

> as shepherds on mountains trample down
> a hyacinth with their feet – the purple
> flower falls to the ground[48]

What this genealogical tree shows is that one poet, Virgil, combines for the first time an epic image (ultimately Homeric) with an erotic one (ultimately Sapphic), because both belong to the bucolic sphere and so that, put together, they may acquire resonance from each other – *thanatos* from *eros* and viceversa. The fourteenth-century poet, Boccaccio, does not however know that Virgil's first simile has an epithalamic origin. He takes it from Virgil's poem, from what Dante calls the 'alta tragedìa'. He cannot but assume that such a simile is quite appropriate in an epic context. We must therefore conclude that he 'conceals' nothing. Boccaccio, then, uses this as a paradigmatically 'tragic' metaphor. What, on the other hand, is significant is that, quite unaware of its precedents, he applies it to describe the plight of a hero whose *love* story is coming to an *end*.

A second consideration is perhaps more important. Whether inserted within an epic, melodramatic or erotic context, all these similes share the gracefulness and pathos of elegy. In the first place, what interests Homer, Virgil and Ovid is not only their characters' death, but also the way in which they 'sink', the movement by which they invariably fall with head reclined. Secondly, for all the poets I have examined the flower, be it fading, bowed down by rain, cut off by a gardener or by the plough, is an image of man beaten by an external agent such as an enemy determined to kill, an unfaithful lady or pure chance. The equation established by these similes is of two kinds: 1 – one natural element (rain) overcomes another (poppy), and the effect this produces is similar to the manner in which the hero's head drops down on his shoulders or breast; 2 – man (gardener, plough) does violence to nature (flower) as man (or indeed woman) does violence to another man. In both cases, what is stressed is the pathetic element – heaviness, impotence, succumbing in the first, cruelty and frailty in the second. We are far from the stark, angry existential conciseness of Job's complaint to, and indictment of, God, where man is *qua* man, like a flower cut down by nature and by God Himself:

> Man that is born of a woman is of few days,
> and full of trouble. He cometh forth like a
> flower and is cut down. (14. 1–2)

It is the Bible that introduces into European culture the radical similarity of man and flower. Even when the register is softer than in Job, even when the intonation, following the natural course from blooming to fading, is almost elegiac, as in the Psalms (90. 5–6), Isaiah (40. 6–8), and the Letters of Peter (1. 1.24) and James (1. 10–11), the simile is not tied to a specific occasion such as death in battle, murder by chance or the end of a love story. It always possesses universal quality, it always goes to the roots of man's condition:

> As for man, his days are as grass: as
> a flower of the field, so he flourisheth.
> For the wind passeth over it, and
> it is gone; and the place thereof shall
> know it no more. (Psalm 103. 15–16)

In Chaucer's *Troilus and Criseyde*, the metaphorical parabola of the hero as flower is kept and stressed, but also significantly changed. When Pandarus brings Troilus good news of Criseyde's disposition, Chaucer follows Boccaccio's and Dante's 'Quali fioretti' closely, adding only the important notion of the flowers' 'kynde cours':

> But right as floures, thorugh the cold of nyght
> Iclosed, stoupen on hire stalke lowe,
> Redressen hem ayein the sonne bright,
> And spreden on hire kynde cours by rowe   (II, 967–70)

The love story of Troilus had begun in April,

> whan clothed is the mede
> With newe grene, of lusty Veer the pryme,
> And swote smellen floures white and red.   (I, 156–8)

It has continued, and definitely veered towards success, in May

> that moder is of monthes glade,
> That fresshe floures, blew and white and rede,
> Ben quike agayn, that wynter dede made,
> And ful of bawme is fletyng every mede.   (II, 50–4)

Soon, the triumph of love will be announced as imminent by Pandarus, and Troilus' heart will revive, full of joy,

> right so as thise holtes and thise hayis,
> That han in wynter dede ben and dreye,
> Revesten hem in grene whan that May is,
> Whan every lusty liketh best to pleye.   (III, 351–4)[49]

The 'natural course' of the flower Troilus is, however, broken off and changed by Fortune. As in the *Filostrato*, the decision of the Trojan parliament to accept the Antenor–Criseyde exchange prostrates Troilus. Chaucer, however, does not use Boccaccio's classicizing simile of the flower cut down by the plough, but replaces it with our third image, Dante's falling leaves from *Inferno* III:

> And as in wynter leves ben biraft,
> Ech after other, til the tree be bare,
> So that ther nys but bark and braunche ilaft,
> Lith Troilus, byraft of ech welfare,
> Ibounden in the blake bark of care,
> Disposed wood out of his wit to breyde,
> So sore hym sat the chaungynge of Criseyde.   (IV, 225–31)

The shift of emphasis operated by Chaucer by simply substituting one simile with another is enormous. The pathetic, elegiac element of Boccaccio's image is eliminated and replaced by the harsh, tragic quality of a simile applied by Dante to the souls of the damned and which, as we shall see, is for classical poetry what the floral metaphor is for the Bible – the emblem of the human condition.

Chaucer ignores Boccaccio and resorts to Dante. He establishes an ideal connection between the 'fioretti' of *Inferno* II and the 'foglie' of *Inferno* III. In doing so, he keeps the comparison between a natural phenomenon and man's inner feelings inaugurated by Dante, abandoning Boccaccio's melodramatic, 'external' view of the hero fainting like a flower mowed down by the plough. Chaucer, writes Winthrop Wetherbee, takes us 'to the very heart of Troilus' emotional condition'.[50] Whether or not there is irony in his rendering of the Dantean passage, 'the force of the comparison has been redirected towards the figure of Troilus, imagistically the tree itself'.[51] 'Ibounden in the blake bark of care' and 'byraft of ech welfare', Chaucer's Troilus stands – or rather, as Wetherbee remarks, lies down – like a bare tree, a vegetable skeleton of bark and branches, deprived of all its leaves. If his love had begun and triumphed in spring, when he himself had appeared like a flower surrounded by the glory of flowers, we are now, having skipped autumn (Dante's 'd'autunno'), plunged into winter, when leaves have, one after another, already 'ben biraft'. We should not be surprised to find Chaucer resorting at the end of his 'little tragedy' to the radical truth of the bible's imagery and condemning

This world that passeth soone as floures faire.   (V, 1841)[52]

By examining the 'floral' structure of Chaucer's *Troilus*, I have already entered the sphere of my third image – the falling leaves. I shall now return to its Dantean and classical origins, so that our picture of man in nature from Antiquity to the fourteenth century may be complete. We must remember that, with Dante, we have now gone through the gate of Hell. At the end of Canto III, the souls of 'those who die in the wrath of God' gather, as Virgil explains (121–9), from every land on the shores of Acheron to be ferried by Charon across to Hell proper. Their fear is turned into desire, because Divine Justice spurs them, so that they are eager to cross. It is precisely this complex movement and its deep motivation that the poet represents with his double simile. The souls of the damned flock one by one from the shore onto the boat like leaves falling in autumn, one after another, until the bough sees all its spoils on the ground. In doing so, the spirits obey Charon's 'signals' like birds being recalled. The final view we have of them – a slow and sombre one – is of their going over the dark water while a new throng gathers on the shore before they reach the other side:

Sunset, flowers and leaves

Cosí sen vanno su per l'onda bruna,
e avanti che sian di là discese,
anche di qua nuova schiera s'auna. (*Inferno*, III, 118–20)

Mankind and nature are one – in the first simile, both gradually declining, being slowly and painfully, piece by piece, despoiled; in the second, both called to ultimate destiny by an inner, unavoidable command. Yet there seem to be disquieting problems in this oneness of man and nature. Why, departing from the Virgilian original which I shall soon examine, does Dante introduce the point of view of the bough, which sees its spoils on the ground? By doing this, the poet paradoxically endows the tree with a soul and consciousness. He may possibly be inspired by a passage in Virgil's *Georgics* (II, 80–2),[53] but the context is far more tense in the *Inferno*. For what or whom does the bough represent – mankind in general looking, as it were, at itself falling to the ground? Or, even more strikingly, the 'evil seed of Adam', the souls of the damned, who, while flocking to Charon's boat, see themselves as the 'spoils' of human kind? An odd, ironical and tragic mirror-like effect is produced by this image. Detached, the bough looks at its spoils. By virtue of the position of 'similemente', its self-reflecting eyes project themselves on the ghosts of men, who are otherwise viewed as inanimate objects. On the other hand, we are presented with a metaphorical vegetable cycle which is both complex and perverted. We begin with autumnal leaves flying down, are then shown a bough and its remains, and finally brought to the 'seed' – the evil seed of Adam. We have, in other words, a film being rewound. But while the first and last frames are in motion, the central one is totally static and, as we have seen, with the eye of the camera bent upon its own ruins. A fourth frame is then superimposed, by which the souls of the damned appear as birds recalled – as the falcon called down by the lure.[54] Finally, we see the film reel forward, with the crowd going on the dark waves and another group gathering on the shore.

If then, at first sight, mankind may seem to be conforming to nature, at a second, more attentive reading, *this* particular section of mankind is viewed as going against nature and at once ineluctably towards its just destiny. For there is very little doubt that the general impression the passage leaves on the reader is of the inevitable fall of man into death and, further, into eternal death – a renewal of dying, and dying to eternal life, which is as perpetual as the seasonal falling of leaves every year and as alluring and binding as the 'call' for a bird. Divine Justice, such as celebrated in the inscription at the beginning of the Canto (III, 4), has its exacting toll. We are in a dimension far more definitively

101

tragic than we were introduced to by Chaucer in his corresponding passage. We are even beyond Job, reduced to 'a leaf driven to and fro', to a 'dry stubble' (13. 25), who shouts to his God:

> For there is hope of a tree, if it be cut
> down, that it will sprout again, and that
> the tender branch thereof will not cease.
> Though the root thereof wax old in the earth,
> and the stock thereof die in the ground;
> Yet through the scent of water it will bud,
> and bring forth boughs like a plant.
> But man dieth, and wasteth away: yea, man
> giveth up the ghost, and where is he?   (14. 7–10)

Dante knows perfectly well where men, and particularly the wicked, go after they die, and hence Job's pessimistic interrogation gives way to a bleak statement of fact: the evil seed of Adam has become a bough which contemplates its own remains fallen on the ground.

The factors that have produced such a radical view of the ultimate fate of the wicked are of course several, but the most important one from an imaginative point of view seems to me the way in which Dante has brought to its extreme logical consequences the Christian doctrine of Hell by working on classical imagery with daring inventiveness. It is well known that the present simile derives from a famous one in *Aeneid* VI, which describes almost exactly the same scene – the way, that is, in which the dead run to the shore of Acheron to be carried across by Charon, who accepts only those who have already been buried or those who have lain unburied for at least a hundred years:

> Quam multa in silvis autumni frigore primo
> Lapsa cadunt folia, aut ad terram gurgite ab alto
> Quam multae glomerantur aves, ubi frigidus annus
> Trans pontum fugat et terris inmittit apricis   (VI, 309–12)

Virgil's image is composed of *two* similes, both extremely powerful. In the first, the dead are compared to leaves which fall to the ground in the first cold spell of autumn. In the second, they are seen as similar to birds which gather on the earth, coming down from the sky, when the cold weather forces them to migrate across the sea towards sunny countries. The first simile has clearly influenced Dante, who changes it by adding the fundamental details we have noted. The second has only prompted Dante to create his own bird image. In the *Aeneid*, both similes stress four elements – the total conformity of man to nature, the 'falling' movement of leaves and birds, the coldness of the season, and, in consequence, the sadness of the occasion and the frailty of the world, which is shared by men, leaves and birds alike. An autumnal atmosphere pervades the whole scene – desolate and at the same time perfectly natural. What Virgil describes is the world of death; not, like Dante, that of *eternal* death.

In elaborating his double simile, Virgil puts together two images which in classical tradition are tied to two often interrelated themes, that of the numberless people in a crowd, and that of death or the human condition as such. Thus, to start with his second simile, the gathering of the Greeks before Troy is compared to the coming together of innumerable birds in the *Iliad* (II, 459–65). But in the Hades episode of *Odyssey* XI the dead surround the *psykhē* of Heracles with screams as shrill as those birds make when they flee in terror all over (605–6). And, even more significantly, in Sophocles' *Oedipus Rex* the Chorus sees the inhabitants of Thebes struck by the plague 'hurrying one after another, like winged birds, worse than irresistible flame, to the shores of the Western god', i.e. of Hades or Acheron (174–7) – an image which uncannily evokes the appeal as well as the inevitability of death, and where 'one after another' anticipates Dante by almost eighteen hundred years. If the bodies of the dead Suitors, 'lying fallen in their blood and in the dust', appear to Odysseus as numerous as, and similar to, 'fish whom the fishermen have taken in their net with many holes, and dragged out onto the hollow beach from the gray sea, and all of them lie piled on the sand, needing the restless salt water; but Helios, the shining sun, bakes the life out of them',[55] the faithless maids, hanged in a row, look 'like thrushes, who spread their wings, or pigeons, who have flown into a snare set up for them in a thicket'.[56] Finally, the souls of the Suitors, led by Hermes, proceed towards Hades 'as when bats in the depth of an awful cave flitter and gibber, when one of them has fallen out of his place in the chain they have formed by holding one another'.[57] The bodies of dead human beings are like the inanimate corpses of birds or fish – their spirits are represented by flittering, screaming birds.[58] A symbol of storm, violence and death, the image of the Harpies hovers in the background.

The ancestry of Virgil's first simile is less crude, but as old and illustrious and ultimately as desolate in purport as the bird image. Let me then complement Harold Bloom's treatment of what he has, after Wallace Stevens, called the 'fiction of the leaves'.[59] Bloom's 'transumptive chain' goes from Homer to Virgil and then, with the addition of Isaiah 34. 4 ('and all [the host of heaven] shall fall down, as the leaf falleth from the vine'), down to Dante and Milton. Coleridge inaugurates what Ruskin will consider the 'Pathetic Fallacy' in 'Christabel'; Shelley's 'Ode to the West Wind' transumes Milton and the entire previous tradition; Whitman consecrates the new 'mixed trope', 'leaves of grass'; Beckett's Estragon is invoked as the 'dead end' of the image; and finally, Wallace Stevens' 'The Course of a Particular' represents the 'definitive poem' where tradition is most authentically transumed and where the Pathetic Fallacy disappears.

My own chain is slightly more complex. In the first place, the simile is originally employed to denote a great number of people: Homer uses it in this sense at least three times.[60] Appollonius Rhodius, who is actually the first to compare men in a crowd with *falling* leaves, avoids the association with death. When, in the *Argonautica* (IV, 214–18), Jason and Medea leave, the Colchians pour to the banks of the river 'countless as the waves of the stormy sea when they rise crested by the wind, or as the leaves fall to the ground from the wood with its myriad branches in the month when leaves fall – who could reckon their tale?' But leaves and the souls of dead men had already been associated by Bacchylides. His Heracles sees 'the spirits of hapless mortals beside the stream of Cocytus like leaves a-quiver in the wind on the gleaming shoulders of Ida'.[61] It is this tradition that Virgil transumes by coupling in the falling leaves image both the idea of a numerous crowd and that of the dead. However, Virgil can do this only because tradition supplies him with a trope in which men as such are seen as leaves. When Homer's Diomedes asks Glaucus who he and his ancestors are, the Lycian warrior answers, 'Why do you enquire after my ancestry?', and adds a statement which is as radical as the Biblical imagery of grass and flowers:

> Like leaves on trees the race of man is found,
> Now green in youth, now withering on the ground;
> Another race the following spring supplies;
> They fall successive, and successive rise:
> So generations in their course decay;
> So flourish these, when those are passed away.[62]

By the seventh century BC this simile has become a topos. Semonides of Amorgos quotes Homer and comments on the *Iliad* passage, warning men that the time allotted to them is short:

Sunset, flowers and leaves

> The man from Chios said the most beautiful thing:
> 'The generation of men is like that of leaves.'[63]

Later, Aristophanes picks up the image, ironically putting it in the mouth of his Chorus of *Birds*:

> Ye men who are dimly existing below,
>   who perish and fade as the leaf,
> Pale, woebegone, shadowlike, spiritless folk,
>   life feeble and wingless and brief,
> Frail castings in clay, who are gone in a day,
>   like a dream full of sorrow and sighing,
> Come listen with care to the Birds of the air,
>   the ageless, the deathless[64]

The most elaborate version of the simile is, however, to be found in an elegy written in the seventh century BC by Mimnermus, the poet of youth and love. While Homer had looked at the generations of mortals succeeding each other on the earth in a grandiose fresco of the perennial rhythm of life and death through the ages, Mimnermus (and Semonides) consider the fate of the human being as such. Their subject, as befits lyric poets, is one life, the life of every individual. *Hēmeis, d'hoia te phylla*, Mimnermus begins,

> We, like leaves that spring's flowery season brings
> – quickly they grow in the rays of the sun –
> like them for a short time we enjoy
> the flowers of youth, and from the gods
> we know neither good nor evil.
> But dark dooms stand beside us: one
> holds the fate of painful old age,
> of death the other; and the fruit of youth
> lasts but a moment, for as long as the sun
> shines over the earth[65]

It will at once be noticed that Mimnermus' metaphor is not fully developed. We begin with leaves being born and growing in spring, but we never reach autumn. It is, I think, precisely this indeterminacy and suspension that make the poem so forceful. Mimnermus prefers to concentrate on the parabola of spring. His imagery opens with leaves budding in the season 'rich in flowers' (*polyanthemos*), returns to the 'flowers' of youth and concludes with youth's 'fruit'. The sun dominates the scene at the beginning and end, where it not only shines, but 'pervades' or 'floods' (*kidnatai*) the earth. The length of the day, or of a season (line 11) is only adumbrated. The gods do not let young people know either good or evil. Suspended in blissful ignorance, men live like leaves, flowers, fruit. But when he wants to indicate the end (*telos*) of all this, the poet leaves the realm of vegetable imagery and, right in the middle of his poem's *ouverture*, resorts to the language of myth and reality. Black shadows veil the sun. The *Kēres* stand beside every man, preparing either 'atrocious' old age or death. Bird-like and blood-thirsty, they seize human beings with their claws so that their souls descend to Hades.[66]

Mimnermus' precariously blooming leaves, basking in the sun for an instant – a miraculously balanced emblem of 'everything that grows' and 'holds in perfection but a little moment' – leave it to us to imagine their decay and fall in autumn. Ovid's Pythagoras completes the image, comparing the four ages of man to the four seasons of the year.[67] And, drawing directly on Ovid, Shakespeare will 'question make' of the beloved's, and the world's, beauty (Sonnet 12).

Virgil's transumption is, then, a complex phenomenon. A precise intertextual and genealogical reading reveals that the Latin poet is not simply troping on Homer's image – he is putting together at least six different though contiguous areas of imagery which he has inherited from at least seven major poets, i.e., from what must have appeared to him as a tradition pointing in one general direction. Thus:

leaves:—numberless in a crowd (Homer, Apollonius)
⌐dead souls (Bacchylides)
│ generations of men (Homer, Semonides, Aristophanes)
│ lives of individual men (Mimnermus, Semonides, Aristophanes)
birds: └innumerable people (Homer)
└the dead (Homer, Sophocles)

The next link in my chain introduces further complications. For the trope of the leaves is not absent from the Bible either. Distinct from that of grass, and independently of Isaiah's comparison with the falling host of heaven, it is to be found, already full-fledged, in Ecclesiasticus (14. 18–19):

Like foliage growing on a bushy tree, some leaves falling, others growing, so are the generations of flesh and blood: one dies, another is born.[68]

The simile is so strikingly Homeric that several scholars in the past have argued it proves a dependence of Ecclesiasticus on the *Iliad* or at least on the kind of Greek background I have sketched. Jesus Ben Sirach could of course have been using Biblical texts as well. The leaves image is present in the Psalms (1. 3), the Proverbs (11. 4 in the version of the Seventy), Jeremiah (8. 13; 17. 8), Ezekiel (47. 12), and Daniel (4. 9–11). However, it is never as radical here as in the Greek counterparts, for it does not define man's essence as such but rather takes into account his moral qualities or his changing material fortunes (those who trust in God shall not wither like leaves; those who sin against Him will be despoiled of everything). Even when it approaches or surpasses the strength of the Greek equivalent, the Biblical trope always relates man's condition to an external, supernatural agent. Thus, Job is a 'leaf driven to and fro', and fearful of being 'broken', by God (13. 25). Isaiah's Voice threatens transgressors (1. 30: 'For ye shall be as an oak whose leaf fadeth'), prophesies the fall of the heavenly host (34. 4), and proclaims it is because of iniquity that 'we all do fade as a leaf' (64. 6).

If, then, the author of Ecclesiasticus has troped on the Old Testament images, he has done so[69] in such a surprisingly new direction that only *we* as readers can talk of this as transumption. *His* is not a misreading, but a mortal sin against the Book or, to put it another way, a Freudian slip revealing a dangerous propensity to fall into alien wisdom.

It seems clear to me that Dante and Milton (whose devilish legions lie 'entranced', 'thick as autumnal leaves that strew the brooks – in Vallombrosa')[70] trope on both the classical and the Biblical images, for they apply the simile with obvious moral overtones, or, as Bloom rightly says, in the *Divine Comedy* and in *Paradise Lost* 'leaves fall from trees, generations of men die, *because* once one third of the heavenly host came falling down'.[71] But the topos employed by the Greeks, by Virgil, and by Ecclesiasticus has a vitality of its own, 'purged . . . of Miltonic moral splendour' long before Shelley and Milton himself. Chaucer, for one, uses it, as we have seen, in *Troilus* without any ethic connotation. Goethe's Werther sees himself at one point as a leaf turning yellow while the leaves of the trees around him have already fallen.[72] Besides Coleridge's 'one red leaf, the last of its clan – That dances as often as dance it can',[73] there is, in Shelley's *Triumph of Life*, 'a great stream of people . . . hurrying to and fro', 'all hastening onward', each 'borne amid the crowd, as through the sky – One of the million leaves of summer's bier'[74] – an authentically 'classical' and Dantean image. And, besides Whitman's 'frailest leaves of me', the tradition goes through poets as diverse as Tjutčev, Brentano, Baudelaire, Verlaine, Apollinaire, Yeats, Jiménez, Ungaretti, Frost,[75] Auden, Rilke, and Eliot before reaching its Beckettian 'dead end'. It is

García Lorca who calls this 'la *tragedia* otoñal – que los árboles llueven' (the autumnal tragedy that the trees rain down).[76] And I would consider the following poem by Auden, 'Autumn Song', as dead an end as one could imagine:

> Now the leaves are falling fast,
> Nurse's flowers will not last;
> Nurses to their graves are gone,
> And the prams go rolling on.
>
> Whispering neighbours, left and right,
> Pluck us from our real delight;
> And our active hands must freeze
> Lonely on our separate knees.
>
> Dead in hundreds at the back
> Follow wooden in our track,
> Arms raised stiffly to reprove
> In false attitudes of love.
>
> Starving through the leafless wood
> Trolls run scolding for their food;
> And the nightingale is dumb,
> And the angel will not come.
>
> Cold, impossible, ahead
> Lifts the mountain's lovely head
> Whose white waterfall could bless
> Travellers in their last distress.[77]

Rolling on after the nurses' death, the prams intimate a divorce between leaves and human beings which prefigures the total loss of meaning. And indeed a little later mankind disappears, leaving room for 'trolls', while the wood becomes 'leafless', the nightingale sings no longer, and the angel will not come. The worlds of nature, of man, and of God are gone.

Wallace Stevens' 'The Course of a Particular' celebrates the final divorce. For here the leaves cry, but they are completely and deliberately separated from men (and from God). They – the leaves of nature and of the poet's own book – 'do not transcend themselves', and their cry ultimately 'concerns no one at all':

> Today the leaves cry, hanging on branches swept by wind,
> Yet the nothingness of winter becomes a little less.
> It is still full of icy shades and shapen snow.

Sunset, flowers and leaves

The leaves cry . . . One holds off and merely hears the cry.
It is a busy cry, concerning someone else.
And though one says that one is part of everything,

There is a conflict, there is a resistance involved;
And being part is an exertion that declines:
One feels the life of that which gives life as it is.

The leaves cry. It is not a cry of divine attention,
Nor the smoke-drift of puffed-out heroes, nor human cry.
It is the cry of leaves that do not transcend themselves,

In the absence of fantasia, without meaning more
Than they are in the final finding of the ear, in the thing
Itself, until, at last, the cry concerns no one at all.[78]

My point is, however, that there is no end, and, at the same time, that
the end can be different. When Eliot, who uses the Dantean image in
Little Gidding (II, 30–4), writes in *The Dry Salvages* (II),

Where is there an end of it, the soundless wailing,
The silent withering of autumn flowers
Dropping their petals and remaining motionless . . .?

he combines the two traditional tropes of falling autumn leaves and
flowers in a splendid new concretion to ask the crucial question. His
withering flowers are silent and motionless, in a sense well beyond the
crying leaves of Stevens, because they partake of both the physical and
the metaphysical universe. 'Where is there an end of it?' His answer is
significant:

There is no end, but addition: the trailing
Consequence of further days and hours . . .
      . . .
There is no end of it, the voiceless wailing,
No end to the withering of withered flowers,
To the movement of pain that is painless and motionless,
To the drift of the sea and the drifting wreckage,
The bone's prayer to Death its God. Only the hardly, barely prayable
Prayer of the one Annunciation.

The voice that speaks here is, admittedly, not that of Isaiah, but it does
possess the full prophetic force of John the Baptist.

Or take Rilke:

Denn wir sind nur die Schale und das Blatt.
Der grosse Tod, den jeder in sich hat,
das ist die Frucht, um die sich alles dreht.

(For we are only the vase and the leaf. The great death, which everyone has in himself, that is the fruit, round which all revolves.)[79]

Here, Mimnermus' image is tragically inverted. Fruit is not youth, but death, and that death we have *inside* us. In another famous poem, 'Herbsttag', Rilke realizes that the 'time' has come ('Herr: es ist Zeit'). The heat of the summer was great, now may the Lord lay shade on the sundial and let the wind free over the plains; may He give two more warm days to bring the last fruit to ripeness. For

> Wer jetzt kein Haus hat, baut sich keines mehr.
> Wer jetzt allein ist, wird es lange bleiben,
> wird wachen, lesen, lange Briefe schreiben
> und wird in den Alleen hin und her
> unruhig wandern, wenn die Blätter treiben.

(He who has no house now will never build himself one. He who is alone now will long remain so, will lie awake, and read, and write long letters; will restlessly wander up and down the avenues, when the leaves drift away.)[80]

These leaves are being 'carried away', 'going adrift', and to their 'treiben' corresponds infinite loneliness, endless writing, uncertain wandering. Rilke suspends the end while intimating it: the result is unbearable tension. But the leaves do fall in 'Herbst', becoming the sign of a universal 'falling', a desolate, inevitable downcoming through cosmic distances to total emptiness. The fall of Isaiah's and Milton's heavenly host is wholly transumed because Rilke returns to the Greek trope and simultaneously transfigures it in the poem's last motion:

> Die Blätter fallen, fallen wie von weit,
> als welkten in den Himmeln ferne Gärten;
> sie fallen mit verneinender Gebärde.
>
> Und in den Nächten fällt die schwere Erde
> aus allen Sternen in die Einsamkeit.
>
> Wir alle fallen. Diese Hand da fällt.
> Und sieh dir andre an: es ist in allen.
>
> Und doch ist Einer, welcher dieses Fallen
> unendlich sanft in seinen Händen hält.

> (The leaves are falling, falling from afar
> as though from distant gardens in the heavens.
> They fall reluctantly and loathe to leave.

So, too, the heavy earth is falling through the night
far from all stars down into solitude.

We all are falling. See this hand? It falls
as all things do respond to heaven's laws.

Yet there is One who with unending tenderness
holds this falling in his hands.)[81]

Seen in this wider context, Shelley's 'Ode to the West Wind' becomes
the one real exception in the long transumptive chain. For, as if he were
Zarathustra going down like the sun, Shelley here becomes the wind.
The dead leaves are once more, as in the age-old tradition, 'like ghosts
from an enchanter fleeing', 'pestilence-stricken multitudes'. But man,
himself traditionally a leaf, is now the poet, the prophet, the Creator,
the 'Spirit'. His dead thoughts will be driven over the universe 'like
withered leaves to quicken a new birth'. The leaves have become pages
of a book, 'the incantation of this verse'. The 'fiction', as Stevens and
Bloom call it, is there, ready for Whitman to pick up.

No successor, I believe, is strong enough, or 'agonistic' enough, to
successfully wrestle with Shelley's prophetic, exalted version of that
fiction. But at least one ancestor had been, one whom Shelley knew
very well and one, finally, who had used the fiction of the leaves
precisely with the double meaning Stevens gives to the expression.
Dante, who in the *Convivio* (II xiii 10) refers to the passage in Horace's
Ars Poetica which inaugurates the equation between the poet's words
and falling leaves,[82] echoes its imagery in the *Paradiso*, where the first
speaker of the world, Adam, talks about the changes that occurred even
in primordial language:

> e ciò convene,
> ché l'uso d'i mortali è come fronda
> in ramo, che sen va e altra vene.   (XXVI, 136–8)

(and that must needs be, for the usage of mortals is as a leaf on a branch, which
goes away and another comes.)

But Dante who, as we shall see in a later chapter, envisages the essence
of God as a volume and the universe as its leaves, and who conceives of
his own last pages of poetry as the leaves of the Sibyl getting lost in the
wind, *is* the wind itself, as his ancestor Cacciaguida tells him:

> Questo tuo grido farà come vento,
> che le più alte cime più percuote
> ꞁ   (*Paradiso* XVII, 133–4)

(This cry of yours shall do as does the wind, which smites most upon the
loftiest summits.)

Leaves do not indeed cry – the wind does. 'In a wood that skirts the Arno, near Florence', 'at sunset' (!) on 25 October 1819[83] Shelley transumed Dante, who was in turn daringly rewriting Isaiah (40. 3–9) and the whole Book inspired by the Breath of God.

This sequence could of course take us a long way from the tragic vision of *Inferno* III, towards the sublime tensions we shall face in our last chapter: for Dante, after all, leaves and branches become in due course images of the blessed souls of Heaven.[84] But in fact Shelley's use of Dante leads us back to the core of our problem. Ruskin calls 'Pathetic Fallacy' the kind of 'falseness in all our impressions of external things' which is produced by 'violent feelings'. It is, he says, an 'error' which 'the mind admits when affected strongly by emotion' and which we are wont to consider 'as eminently a character of poetical description'. In order to give an example of this, Ruskin compares our passage from *Inferno* III and two lines from Coleridge's *Christabel*:

> Thus, when Dante describes the spirits falling from the bank of Acheron 'as dead leaves flutter from a bough', he gives the most perfect image possible of their utter lightness, feebleness, passiveness, and scattering agony of despair, without, however, for an intant losing his own clear perception that *these* are souls, and *those* are leaves; he makes no confusion of one with the other. But when Coleridge speaks of
>
> > The one red leaf, the last of its clan,
> > That dances as often as dance it can.
>
> he has a morbid, that is to say, a so far false, idea about the leaf: he fancies a life in it, and will, which there are not; confuses its powerlessness with choice, its fading death with merriment, and the wind that shakes it with music.[85]

Now, it is perfectly true that there is a difference between Dante's and Coleridge's presentations and that the latter 'fancies a life' and 'will' in his leaf 'which there are not'. But Dante's simile is, as we have seen, more complex than Ruskin thinks. By introducing the point of view of the bough that sees its spoils on the ground, Dante signals the ultimate tragedy of his scene (as well as his departure from Virgil), but in doing so he endows the tree with a soul and consciousness – and that is as 'pathetic' a 'fallacy' as Coleridge's. Similarly 'pathetic' and 'false' would be Dante's description of the full moon, Trivia, '*smiling* among the eternal nymphs', and his image of the bell 'that seems to mourn the dying day' in passages which I have already quoted. In other words, it seems to me that while Coleridge introduces the idea of the leaf's dance (and are we sure it is not the dance of death?), he is, in general, quite simply bringing to the extreme something which, as Troilus 'ibounden in the blake *bark* of care' proves, had already been experimented in the fourteenth century and indeed, as we have seen, by Virgil himself.[86] From an imaginative, 'metaphorical' point of view there is no difference between the medieval and the modern sense of the tragic, and no basic contrast between the ways in which we apprehend them. This is so not only because the nature of medieval and modern imagery is not essentially divergent, but also because our apprehension of them comes simultaneously with our reaction to the long chain of tropes I have examined (and in this sense classical and Biblical ancestors are parts of our present). The impact these images have on us does not depend only on the contexts within which they are inserted, but also on our feeling – deep-rooted, though fully conscious only if supported by wide and discriminating reading – that when we encounter them we hit some of the nervous centres of Western imagery, that is to say, of our metaphorical thinking. We know that, whether we be living or dead, the substance of our bodies, souls, and creations is like that of falling leaves or migrating birds. Suspended between life and death, truly *morituri*, we understand perfectly well what the poets mean when, in spite of their ever-changing attitudes towards the position of man in nature, they say that our heart is a flower and our essence a monad in the darkening air of sunset. To put it as plainly as (but more metaphorically than) one of the London citizens does in the middle of the turmoils that shake the world of *Richard III*:

> When clouds are seen, wise men put on their cloaks;
> When great leaves fall, then winter is at hand;
> When the sun sets, who doth not look for night?
> Untimely storms makes men expect a dearth.
>
> (II.iii. 32–5)

When any of these tropes appears under our eyes the division between our present, temporary condition of readers and our permanent nature of men suddenly hits us. We have always known that behind those 'fictions' there lies the truth, and we have normally filed it away. The slightest allusion by a poet is enough to remind us of our tragic plight because we instinctively recognize in the allusion the implications of the traditional image. Whether or not we are willing to partake of the anxiety and the struggle suffered and fought by the poet, that recognition gives us both pleasure and pain: pleasure as readers, pain as human beings. This, precisely, is the tragic effect.

The images we have read through the ages are, then, 'fictions', but surely not 'fallacies'. They are, as Harold Bloom says, 'tropes of action and desire' but only inasmuch as they are infallibly tragic tropes of being and knowledge. Let us look at the definitive example. In the space of two cantos, Dante draws an overarching view of man in nature passing from sunset to flowers and falling leaves. Within two Books, Chaucer moves from flowers to leaves. In the fourteen lines of an evanescent sonnet Shakespeare builds the 'supreme fiction' upon the leaves of life and writing, the after-sunset twilight of sleep and death, the ash-fire of love, age, and consummation. The leaves leave living:

> That time of year thou mayst in me behold
> When yellow leaves, or none, or few, do hang
> Upon those boughs which shake against the cold,
> Bare ruined choirs where late the sweet birds sang.
> In me thou seest the twilight of such day
> As after sunset fadeth in the west,
> Which by and by black night doth take away,
> Death's second self, that seals up all in rest.
> In me thou seest the glowing of such fire
> That on the ashes of his youth doth lie,
> As the deathbed whereon it must expire,
> Consumed with that which it was nourished by.
>   This thou perceiv'st, which makes thy love more strong,
>   To love that well which thou must leave ere long.

5

A spark of love: Medieval recognitions

Secular German literature begins, as far as we know, with the *Hildebrandslied*, an epic poem or 'song' probably composed in the seventh century AD in Northern Italy and of which only a fragment dating from the ninth century survives. Be it by chance or by literary predestination, that fragment contains the climactic scene of the poem, a scene of recognition. Old Hildebrand, who had been chased out of Italy with his king, Theodoric, returns after thirty years and faces the enemy army. The leader of the latter, the poet tells us immediately, is Hildebrand's son, Hadubrand.[1] The two do not know each other's identity. Hildebrand asks Hadubrand, calling him 'child', who he is, and the young warrior replies he is the son of Hildebrand, whom he venerates as a great hero of the past and who he believes is now dead. The old man answers: 'That knows the Highest above in Heaven, that you never until now have measured yourself in fight with a closer relative'. Not a word is said about what Hildebrand feels when he recognizes his son. He offers Hadubrand a gold armband as a sign of his 'grace' ('Huld'). Hadubrand thinks that the old warrior, a Hun in appearance, is trying to get close to kill him. He refuses to believe that this is his father, whom sailors have reported dead in war: 'Tot ist Hiltibrant, Heribrantes suno'. Hildebrand's cry comes from his heart: 'Alas, you ruling God, deadly fate approaches. Thirty summers and thirty winters have I wandered out of the country, always assigned to the archers' rank, and never did death meet me before a fortress. Now my own son must strike me with his sword, cut me down with the axe, or I be his murderer'. We know from other sources that Hildebrand will kill Hadubrand in the following duel, like Cuchulain his own son.

There is no doubt that this is one of the most powerful tragic scenes of medieval literature. In it, chance and fate meet to produce a crisis; misunderstanding, irony, the ethos and the passion of war dominate the encounter; old and young face each other; myth (the image of Hildebrand that Hadubrand has in his mind) and reality clash; suggestive indirectness dictates the poet's technique. Above all, knowledge is introduced to make the tragic effect unbearably sharp. For the tragedy lies precisely in the conflict between Hildebrand's recognition and Hadubrand's 'Verkennen', his 'méconnaissance' or refusal to recognize his father, and in the contrast between Hildebrand's recognition and his impotence before what he knows will happen. Hildebrand is old, experienced, full of memories, wise – he knows. Hadubrand is young, impulsive, without memory, blind – he does not know. On top of all this we, as readers of the poem, know everything from the very beginning. We watch this drama of recognition and *méconnaissance* with growing anxiety, suspense, and sense of impending doom. The tragic conflict takes us in.

In this chapter I am going to examine some medieval scenes of recognition, with an eye both to their broadly cultural or imaginative relevance and to their more strictly literary effects. For the way in which the Middle Ages treat this theme can tell us something about their view of the human condition, and at the same time take us to the crossroads where the tragic and its opposite, the sublimely comic, meet. Depending on what is being recognized and to which end it is being known, the effect of a poem will differ. Knowledge – in literary terms, recognition – is the mystery we are going to sound in this and the following chapter, where we shall reach one of its final, sublime outcomes. Here, I shall necessarily be selective, and will limit myself to treating essentially two themes, the mysteries of evangelical and para-evangelical recognitions, and the transformations of tragic conflicts.

Throughout these two chapters, I shall take as my theoretical frame the pages which Aristotle devotes to recognition – anagnorisis, as he calls it – in the *Poetics*, and which constitute the first organic treatment of this problem.[2] The Middle Ages did not know that particular book of the Aristotelian corpus (the first full translation into Latin, by William of Moerbeke, was composed as late as the thirteenth century, and was not widely known), but I shall use it only as a theory against which to measure the practice of poets. Divergences from, and similarities with that theory will therefore be constantly pointed out. It may then be opportune to recall here the essential lines of Aristotle's treatment of recognition.

For Aristotle, anagnorisis is a key element of plot in both tragedy and the epic, together with 'peripeteia' (reversal) and 'pathos' (catastrophe). It generates pity and fear (*eleos* and *phobos*), which is the purpose of the mimesis inherent in tragedy, and it produces a 'shock' of surprise and emotion tied to wonder. It is – thus his own definition – a change from ignorance to knowledge (*gnōsis*), and though this knowledge is of a particular person (or at times an object or an event), yet, because poetry is more philosophical than, say, history, and is concerned with universals, the knowledge that recognitions leads us to is, I infer, universal. Several combinations of ignorance, knowledge, error (*hamartia*), and anagnorisis, are possible. And several forms of anagnorisis are also possible. Indeed some people have seen in the list of types of recognition that Aristotle gives in chapter 16 a mirror of the ascending kinds of knowledge – senses, memory, intellect and 'intuition' – he describes in the *Metaphysics*. In the *Poetics* we have, in ascending order: 1 – recognition through signs, *sēmeia*, both natural (a birthmark) and acquired, the latter either on the body (scars) or external (rings, necklaces, etc.); 2 – recognition contrived by the poet, i.e. not stemming naturally from the plot; 3 – recognition through memory (Odysseus, who cries when the bard sings of Troy, is recognized by Alcinous); 4 – recognition based on reasoning (*syllogismos* – Electra and Orestes in Aeschylus), with its parallel type, that based on mistaken inference on the part of the audience (*paralogismos tou theatrou*); and finally, best of all, 5 – recognition which arises from the events themselves and coincides with *peripeteia* (*Oedipus Rex* is the model).

Aristotle leaves out other instances, though they are present in the literature known to him – for example recognition 'de facie', without complicated processes behind it (in the *Odyssey*, the people who inhabit Hades recognize, and are recognized by, Odysseus at first sight), or recognition 'by instinct' (such is the case of the dog, Argos, with Odysseus) or recognition by words, 'exchange of words' (I am – I am; Glaucus–Diomedes in the *Iliad*), or recognition–revelation of gods (Athena in the *Iliad* and the *Odyssey*, Demeter in the *Homeric Hymns*, Dionysus in Euripides' *Bacchae*). And of course we do not know what Aristotle thought of anagnorisis in comedy, as the second book of the *Poetics*, if he wrote it, has not come down to us.

However, before we turn, and in order to turn, to the Middle Ages proper, we ought to have a look at the way in which the other great Ur-branch of Western literature deals with the problem of recognition. The Bible does not theorize on this, but exhibits quite a few recognition scenes, especially in Genesis and in the New Testament. And in a sense, from Genesis to Exodus to the very first words of John's Gospel, one of the central themes of the Bible is precisely that of God who wants and struggles to be recognized by Israel and fails to do so except by recourse to exceptional means or through exceptional human beings like Abraham, Jacob, Joseph, Moses, David, Solomon, the prophets, and later the Apostles. The Bible stages this theme much more consistently and much more mysteriously than, say, does Euripides in the *Bacchae*, where Dionysus wants to be recognized by the Thebans and plays illusion tricks on Pentheus to achieve his purpose, with the final result that, after the god's epiphany, the true recognition is that by which Agave becomes aware that the head she is carrying is that of her own son, and that she has killed him.

The Bible goes one step further – it shows us with obsessive insistence two essential features: first, that in order to recognize God, man must have an inner readiness to do so and, as it were, a knowledge of himself as a human being, a capacity to turn inwards constantly and to be constantly open outwards and upwards. Translating this concept into Greek allegory, Philo of Alexandria views Abraham as (amongst other things) self-knowledge proceeding on to knowledge of God.[3] Secondly, the Bible tells us that, when it comes to the recognition of God by man, there is ultimately no proof. You have just got to believe it, you cannot rely either on signs, or memory, or inference. In New Testament Greek *pistis* does not mean 'proof', but 'faith', and *sēmeia* (signs) are Jesus' miracles. In Hebrew, *hakēr* – to recognize – is much less important, though by no means insignificant, than *jada'*, to know. But *jada'* in the sense of 'knowing' God always implies recognition, acknowledgement, confession, gratitude, or, as one German commentator puts it much more neatly, *Erkenntnis, Anerkenntnis, Bekenntnis*, and *Erkenntlichkeit*.[4] The most astonishing example of this is Job who, after listening to the voice of God exploding out of the whirlwind, exclaims: 'I had heard of thee by the hearing of the ear; but now mine eyes seeth thee . . . I know (*jada'*) thee'. Job re-cognizes, acknowledges, and 'confesses' his God.

Here, I shall leave aside the Old Testament, which would take us too far from the Middle Ages, and turn quickly to the New. The whole story of Jesus is seen as a struggle for recognition, from the moment when the Word becomes flesh, and the 'darkness comprehended it not' and 'the world knew him not' to John the Baptist's 'foetal' recognition of Jesus in the womb of Elizabeth, down to the various 'revelations' on the Jordan and on the mountain, to the recognition scenes after the resurrection.

I shall make three points here. The key pre-Passion scene of recognition in the Gospels occurs when Jesus asks his disciples who they think he is. Peter – the same Peter who will later deny knowledge of Jesus – replies: 'Thou art the Christ, the Son of the living God.' Jesus' answer to this is very interesting; 'Blessed art thou, Simon Bar-jona: for flesh and blood hath not revealed (*apekalypsen*) it unto thee, but my Father which is in heaven.'[5] Peter's recognition of the Christ has rightly been called a 'confessio', *Petri Confessio*. This is not based on material signs, on flesh and blood, but on God's direct *revelation* to which evidently, Peter the man has responded.

Second point. During the Last Supper we have a scene in which Jesus says: 'One of you shall betray me.' With different and interesting variations, all four Gospels tell us that the twelve start asking him 'is it I, Lord?'. Jesus does not answer directly: in Mark and Luke, all he says is that it will be one who dips in the sop with him. Matthew has Judas ask the question, and Jesus reply: 'Thou hast said.' John tells us that Judas was given the sop by Jesus (the sign that Peter, through the Beloved Disciple, had asked for) and then Jesus told him: 'that thou doest, do quickly'. Frank Kermode has written beautiful pages on these passages,[6] so I shall not analyse them. I merely point out that we have here a rather startling mystery: in Matthew Jesus answers Judas with a phrase that could mean anything. In John, the sign is clear, and Jesus' words to Judas are clearer than in Matthew. But the eleven do not hear, do not see, in fact totally fail to recognize Judas as the traitor, while we as readers are told beforehand and explicitly in all versions that Judas Iscariot was the man. For us, the recognition is clear. It is interesting to note that in the Chester Plays, when Judas asks Jesus 'ys yt not I – that shall doe thee this villanye?', Jesus answers: 'Thou hast read, Judas, redealye, – *for sycker thou art hee*',[7] where the medieval author makes explicit what was left mysterious by Matthew. *Méconnaissance* becomes recognition.

Third point. In John 20:25 Thomas Didymus doubts that Jesus has really risen and appeared to the others and says that he won't believe it unless he sees his hands with the print of the nails and puts his finger into those prints and thrusts his hands into his side. What Thomas wants is material evidence, like the scar Eurykleia washes in Odysseus' thigh. And he would get it, for Jesus, who appears once more now, invites him to reach hither his finger etc. But, as things are, John will not have a traditional recognition scene. Seeing, of course, *but without touching*, Thomas simply pronounces the New Testament version of the Old Testament faith formula: 'My Lord and my God', *ho Kyrios mou kai ho Theos mou*. The whole point is further clarified by what Jesus says immediately afterwards: 'Thomas, because thou hast seen me, thou hast believed: blessed are they that have not seen, and yet have believed' – where even the evidence of sight is denied value. No doubt Gregory the Great, John Chrysostom and Peter Lombard who quotes them[8] – and this means that the entire clerical culture of the Middle Ages knew it – were perfectly right, from this point of view and with this scene in mind, to say: 'Apparentia non habent fidem, sed agnitionem' (Gregory) or 'de visis enim non est fides, sed agnitio' (John Chrysostom). Things that appear, which can be seen, do not involve faith, but recognition.

Gregory, whose relevant passage is reproduced by Peter Lombard, solves the problem with a stroke of genius that picks up the substance of an argument developed by Augustine.[9] Both Augustine and Gregory maintain that Thomas *did* touch his Master's wounds, and Gregory adds that this was allowed by the Lord himself so that *we* can have solid faith.

Faith, says Gregory quoting the epistle to the Hebrews (11. 1) is, as Dante was to tell St Peter in Paradise, 'sustanza di cose sperate e argomento de le non parventi', 'the substance of things hoped for, the evidence of things not seen' (King James). So, says Gregory, Thomas' was not an act of faith, but one of recognition. 'Tactus est, et agnitus est', writes Augustine. But then, asks Gregory, why does Jesus tell Thomas, 'because thou hast seen me, thou hast believed'? The answer which both Augustine and Gregory give to this question is subtle, convincing and fundamental. Thomas, says Gregory, 'saw something, but believed something else'. A man cannot see the divinity, the divine nature. '*Thomas saw a man, but confessed God*': my Lord and my God. 'Hence by seeing he believed, because considering true the man (realizing he really was Jesus the man), he proclaimed him God, whom he could not see.' Thus, what we have here is a double scene: first, one of anagorisis, with the right 'signs' (Jesus' wounds, which, says Gregory, 'heal the wounds of *our* lack of faith'); then one of faith. This interpretation – a splendid fusion of Greek rationalism and Hebrew–Christian mystery – will, as we shall see in a moment, condition medieval versions of this episode.

However, to give readers an idea of the gap that separates this mentality from the modern one, I shall recall two examples from

A spark of love: Medieval recognitions

different countries and different centuries. In cantos XIV, XVII, and XIX of his epic oratorio, the *Messias* (composed between 1748 and 1773), Klopstock describes the post-resurrectional scenes one after the other and combining all the four Gospels. We have, then, the women at the tomb with John and Peter, Mary Magdalene, Emmaus, and the epiphany to the eleven in canto XIV; the Thomas scene in canto XVII; and that by the sea of Tiberias in canto XIX. The repetition of the 'miracle' underlines its fundamental importance and points to the overall cogency of the Gospels' design. But after the 'philological' revolution that Humanism and the Reformation introduce into Biblical exegesis, Klopstock cannot have Thomas touch Jesus. Thus, in canto XVII he reproduces the Johannine scene, emphasizing the stupor it produces and the sublime mystery it unfolds. Earlier on, however, in canto XIV, he solves the historico-cultural dilemma of Thomas in two complementary ways. In the first place, he interiorizes Thomas' doubts. After the eleven tell him of Jesus' appearance, the apostle spends a horrible night in the graveyard debating within himself and in total solitude the problems of death, resurrection, and faith. In his praying and in his delirium, Thomas cannot reach any conclusion by reasoning (or, as Aristotle would have called it, *syllogismos*), but – and this is the second, complementary instrument used by the poet – he is prompted to accept the mystery by a voice which speaks to him from the darkness. And the voice is that of Joseph, Jacob's son, the protagonist of one of the most spectacular recognition scenes ever invented: a scene which Klopstock's Jesus recounts to the two disciples walking towards Emmaus and which they quote to the apostles when they reach Jerusalem. The conflict between *agnitio* and *pistis* is solved by means of another miracle (Joseph's voice) and, ultimately, by implicitly resorting to the ancient exegetical method of typology. Joseph, a traditional *figura* of Jesus, manifested himself to, and was recognized by his brothers, who believed him dead – after resurrection, Jesus appears, is recognized, and 'believed in' by the apostles. In fact, Klopstock has the post-resurrectional recognition scenes culminate in a series of triumphal epiphanies and theophanies (canto XIII) which involve all the patriarchs and in one of which Joseph, talking to Benjamin, recalls 'the sweetest of (his) earthly hours', that of anagnorisis.[10]

My second example is closer to us in time. In chapter 9, Book 11 of the *Brothers Karamazov*, Ivan, the family intellectual, has a delirious conversation with the devil, who is also his own double. Ivan, we know, is obsessed by ideas about religion and God. Earlier on, chapter 5 of Book 5, he had told his younger brother Alyosha of a poem–parable he had intended to write, 'The Grand Inquisitor', in which Jesus reincarnates in the Spain of the Inquisition and is imprisoned and reprimanded by the Cardinal Inquisitor, who decides to burn him at the stake the following day. Jesus does not reply to the old man, but simply kisses him on the lips, and the Cardinal frees him saying: 'Go, and come no more – do not come at all – never, never!'[11]

Apparently, 'one of the finest passages', as Ivan says, of this poem would have come at the beginning. Jesus, he tells Alyosha, would have appeared 'quietly, inconspicuously, but everyone – and that is why it is so strange – *recognized* him'. That ('*why* they recognized (*iznajut*) him') might have been one of the finest passages in Ivan's poem. *We* might well ask why. And the answer, I suspect, would be that Dostoyevsky saw clearly how crucial for the whole of Christianity is the *mystery* of recognition, the *meaning* of man–God anagnorisis. Now, when the devil appears to Ivan as a 'démodé', 'hard-up' Russian gentleman later in the novel, he mentions 'The Grand Inquisitor' during the long discussion they have about God. But first of all the devil must prove to Ivan, who thinks he is only a projection, a double, of his own mind, that he really exists independently of him. And at the beginning of his speech, the devil has this to say: 'What is the good of believing against your will? Besides, so far as *faith* is concerned, *no proofs are of any help*, particularly *material ones*. Thomas believed not because he saw that Christ had risen, but because he *wanted to believe* before that.' The first part of this statement could have been written by John the Evangelist, or Gregory the Great. But when Ivan's devil adds that Thomas believed not because he saw but because even before he wanted to believe, he introduces an element of radical subjectivity – of personal will or wish to believe – which is totally alien to the mentality of the Gospels or the Middle Ages. Of course, one might rightly exclaim, after all it is the devil who is speaking. But this devil, I would rejoin, is the spokesman of nineteenth-century scepticism, the heir of Descartes' subjective rationalism (the devil will in fact say to Ivan, 'Je pense, donc je suis'), modern man who thinks he can authenticate existence by the simple fact that he 'thinks'. Though the devil also tells Ivan a legend (which his interlocutor says was made up by himself at the age of seventeen) that involves a rather different message, the 'gentleman' who talks about doubting Thomas not only denies the validity of 'proofs', of 'signs' in what concerns faith, but also implies that faith is not something which is given by God. He would agree with the Jesus of the Gospels up to when he says, 'Blessed art thou, Simon Bar-jona, for flesh and blood hath not revealed it unto thee'; but he would strongly object to the rest of the sentence, 'but my Father which is in heaven'.

Now, after this 'modern' excursus, let us ask ourselves what the Middle Ages do with the recognition–faith scene of John's Gospel. Briefly, the answer would be – they stress the element of anagnorisis to the detriment of mystery and faith.

The process started quite early, for even Luke – the Luke of the startlingly beautiful Emmaus scene – has Jesus tell the Apostles after the Resurrection: 'Videte manus meas et pedes, quia ego ipse sum: *palpate* et videte, quia spiritus carnem et ossa non habet, sicut me videbitis habere'.[12] Here, they do not after all, touch Jesus. But already in the apocryphal *Epistula Apostolorum*, they 'feel' and 'touch' him.[13] It will be the same in *Piers Plowman* B XIX, 167 (or C XXII, 172),[14] where Thomas touches Jesus' very 'flesshelich herte'. This is surprising in a long narrative poem where, unlike painters and playwrights who would need to represent such a scene visually, the writer could easily have kept silent on the whole issue, as after all does John's Gospel. And all the more surprising in a poem like *Piers Plowman*, where the author seems to have learnt the lesson of Old and New Testament to perfection in showing us what I think can only be called (and have been called by M. Goldsmith)[15] the 'epiphanies' of Piers – Peter – Christ with his changing identities and sudden revelations: thus at the beginning, B, V, 544 ff., where Piers emerges suddenly out of the crowd. Thus, more startlingly, in C XVI, 33 ff. (not in B), where Piers appears in the dress of Patience 'as he a palmere were' and Conscience 'knew hym wel' – a passage which recalls Emmaus, but with the basic difference that Conscience, appropriately for one who bears that name, has, unlike the disciples on the road to Emmaus, no 'holden eyes'. Sudden appearances and disappearances, mysterious epiphanies and recognitions, charac-terize Abraham–Faith, Spes, and the Samaritan, who disappears 'as wynde' in B XVII, 349–50. When the tourney is about to begin, here is one 'semblable to the Samaritan and somedel' to Piers the Plowman, who appears entering Jerusalem 'barfote on an asse bakke'. Faith says that he who will joust in Jerusalem is Jesus and he will fetch that which the fiend claims. Will asks, 'Is Piers in this place?', and Faith replies that Jesus will joust in Piers' 'armes, in his helme and his haberioun – *humana natura*; that Christ *be* nouȝt *biknowe here*, for *consummatus deus*'. The mysterious double nature of Christ–Piers appearing as the unknown knight of medieval romance and as the Samaritan (and Jesus) on an ass's back, prevents, and deliberately so, the recognition on the part of the crowd (not Will's or ours), in order to underline a fine theological point. The same point is made later when Will wakes up on Easter Sunday, goes to Mass, writes what he has dreamed, falls asleep and suddenly sees Piers Plowman 'paynted al blody, And come in with a croȝse bifor the comune peple, And niȝte lyke in all lymes to owre lorde Iesu.' Once more, when asked by Will if this is Jesus 'the Iuster' or Piers, Conscience answers: 'Thise aren Pieres armes, His coloures and his cote-armure ac he that cometh so blody is Cryst with his crosse.' One feels that Langland has fully understood, and translated in his own terms, the Gospels' point that after the Resurrection Jesus appears both with his old body that eats, drinks and shows his wounds and at the same time can go through walls or suddenly disappear. Langland also seems to have caught the full import of the Old Testament divine epiphanies when he shows us Christ appearing in all his power to Lucifer, a voice loud in the light. Satan recognizes this lord immediately and his question, 'What lorde artow', simply prompts the full revelation of divine glory': *rex glorie*, – and lorde of miȝte and mayne'. How different this *Christus triumphans* is from the Jesus of the Gospel's temptation scenes! How similar to the transfiguration or to God's revelation on Mount Sinai! It is clear that the epiphanies of Piers play a central role in the spiral-like structure of the poem. It is also clear that *méconnaissance*, recognition and revelation are themes, not just scenes, of fundamental import for the meaning of this work, and that these themes are treated in a very Gospel-like spirit. In a mysterious manner, they tell us the truth, and we pass from ignorance to knowledge.

Mediaeval plays deal with evangelical recognitions–epiphanies in a different manner and, as Otto Pächt has shown,[16] influence contemporary painting, or at least manuscript illumination. It would be impossible here to discuss even the English ones alone in detail, so I will limit myself to a few instances and considerations. All plays seem to imply that Thomas *did* touch Jesus' wounds: this is explicit in the Chester Cycle ('emittet manum in latus et vulnera'),[17] it is indicated implicitly in the Towneley play of 'Thomas Indie' when Jesus, after Thomas' cry for mercy, tells him: 'Thomas, for thou *felys* me and my woundes bare.'[18]

The York version is an exception; we have no indication – either explicit or implicit – that Thomas should touch the body. Here on the other hand, the proofs of Jesus' identity and divinity are clearly exhibited: when he first appears to the Apostles, they see a sight 'shynand so bright'. They believe this is a ghost – Jesus shows them his hands and feet and invites them to grope '(his) woundes wete', promising 'ensaumpill sere', the first of which is his eating of the honeycomb.[19] In this respect, the most interesting version is that of the Towneley Cycle, where the scene is much more elaborate than anywhere else and where doubting Thomas has a long discussion with the other apostles whom he considers mad because clearly, he says, what appeared to them was a phantom.[20] Both Peter *and* Paul tell him they have seen the Lord, but Thomas still holds this was no body, but a ghost. A third apostle then recalls the story of Jonah, but this, too, fails to convince Thomas. The fourth, fifth and sixth apostles tell Thomas that the Holy Ghost 'in Marye light' and 'cled' God's son 'in manhede'. When the fight which for love He had fought was over, He skipped out of the body that clothed Him. Thomas replies with perfect logic that 'if he skypt outt of his clethyng yit thou grauntys his cors was ded. It was his cors that maide shewyng unto you in his sted.' The others go on saying that He rescued the souls in hell and rose again in his body, 'Mighty god and man he rase'. Thomas then asks: if what you say is true, how could you distinguish a body from a ghost? The sixth apostle says: Well, man has got flesh and bone, hasn't he? Jesus took flesh and bone from Mary. What else do you need? The argument between the ten and Thomas goes on for what in an actual performance must be at least a quarter of an hour – with full use on the part of the ten, of all possible rational arguments, figural doctrine, quotation of authorities and, finally, even personal reference: 'If you don't believe us, then you're calling us liars.'

The whole point here is, surely, the discussion itself. This discussion shows us that the authors and the audience of the play are keenly aware of the difficulty of a recognition and of a belief (*pistis*) based purely on reasoning, or, as Aristotle would have it, on inference (*syllogismos*). For Thomas the only thing that counts is material evidence – touching the wound. This, and this only, will prove bodily resurrection. But then the rational soundness of Thomas' arguing is of course overthrown, because Jesus does in fact appear and thus proves that he has risen from the dead with his body, which Thomas can and does touch. This is not the point John makes in his Gospel.

As a tentative conclusion on the question of medieval treatments of the post-resurrectional recognition scenes, I would say, then, that these show a much more 'materialistic' approach than could be expected of

Christian authors. People want proofs, signs, as the scribes and the pharisees had demanded and such as Jesus had refused to give. *Piers Plowman* stands out in this context as the only exception.

So far I have examined a 'sacred' or pseudo-sacred type of medieval recognition—epiphany. There is another tradition which stems more or less directly from the obsession with recognition that apocryphal literature shows from the very beginning – for instance, from the *Acts of Pilate*, where Joseph of Arimathea relates to the high priest how he met and recognized the risen Christ.[21] To make clear how important this theme is, I will quote only two examples, which, in their 'extremism', are quite extraordinary.

In the supposedly fifth-century Apocalypse of John the Theologian, John asks the Lord 'if in the world of resurrection it will be possible to recognize (*gnōrisai*) each other, a brother his brother, or a friend his friend, a father his own children, the children their own parents'.[22] This question is one of the very first John asks, and it is obviously capital, for it shows us a fundamental need of human beings – a need for anagnorisis. What is the point of resurrection in the flesh if one cannot recognize friends, relatives, one's own flesh and blood? Life after death must be like life before death. Men must not only know, meet each other, but recognize each other after a separation. Without anagnorisis, resurrection as new life makes no sense. Without anagnorisis *this* life makes no sense.

But the answer which the Lord's voice gives John is also significant, though in a more restricted, Christian and medieval way. 'To the righteous', it says, 'there is recognition, but to the sinners not at all.' So, recognition is a reward. The bad guys don't even get that. Supreme punishment, they are not recognized even by their own flesh and blood.

My second example comes also from the Greek East. It is about two centuries later, and it occurs in the *Quaestiones* attributed to, but apparently not written by, St Anastasius the Sinaite.[23] In No. 91, the author asks himself the following rather curious question, based on Luke 16. 27–8: 'If those who descend to hell do not recognize (*epigignōskousin*) each other, how come that Dives prays to Lazarus and Abraham and moreover remembers the five brothers he left at home?' This passage of Luke's, in which Jesus is speaking, says the author, is not factual history, but a parable (*parabolikōs kai typikōs, all'ou pragmatikōs*). There are various reasons why the story is clearly impossible (for instance, the damned cannot see the righteous in heaven), but the most important for our writer is that no one will suffer the Gehennah or enter the Kingdom until the resurrection of bodies, until, that is, the situation envisaged by John the Theologian. This doctrine makes Dives' recognition of Lazarus and Abraham impossible. For, says Pseudo-Anastasius with a rather materialistic view of bodily corruption after death, 'when the body lies in the tomb, what can the speaking tongue of the rich man be like, and what the drop of water that may extinguish the fire?' For him, obviously, recognition is a question of flesh and blood only. Without eyes, hands, ears, anagnorisis makes no sense.

Pseudo-Anastasius' theory, however, is heretical for Western tradition. Catholic orthodoxy is more literal minded in its acceptance of the authority of Luke, who nowhere states that the story of Dives and Lazarus is a parable. Augustine, Gregory the Great, Bede, the *Glossa Ordinaria*, and the great scholastic writer who sums them all up, Peter Lombard, firmly believe that Dives recognized Abraham and Lazarus and that the souls of the damned can see those of the blessed and viceversa until Doomsday, when this sight will become impossible for those who are condemned to Hell.[24] Wisely, Augustine adds that he will not debate the question of how one should understand the tongue of Dives or the finger of Lazarus – the question, that is, of how 'material' all this might be.[25] But in his *Dialogues*, Gregory the Great maintains not only that the elect recognize even the patriarchs whom they have never seen before,[26] but also that recognition is, in the 'Kingdom', a criterion of retribution: 'The good rejoice more in seeing those whom they had loved be happy with them; the evil ones are tormented not only by their own pain but also by the pain of those whom, despising God, they had loved in this world, and who are tortured with them.'[27]

We shall have to take this tradition into account when, in the next chapter, we will read the many recognition scenes invented by Dante. In the fifth heaven he sees the blessed souls show an ardent desire to recover their dead bodies at the final resurrection

> forse non pur per lor, ma per le mamme,
> per li padri e per li altri che fuor cari
> anzi che fosser sempiterne fiamme. (*Paradiso* XIV, 64–6)

(perhaps not only for themselves, but also for their mothers, for their fathers, and for the others who were dear before they became eternal flames.)

What is important to note here is that the medieval view of anagnorisis hits the *affective* core of the mystery. Recognition can be a pleasure, or a punishment – a tragedy more tragic because it implies knowledge of itself as well as of the blood-relationship which it discloses; a sublime elation because it adds to reunion the awareness of it.

Let us go back to our apocryphal literature. Another instance brings us to a work where religious themes and romance plots meet: the *Clementine Recognitions*.[28] Clement, a Roman, is dissatisfied with pagan philosophy. He hears of Christ and meets and follows Barnabas, who takes him to Caesarea, where he becomes the Apostle Peter's attendant. While fighting against Simon Magus, Peter instructs Clement in the faith, talking about truth and knowledge. Clement tells Peter that he has lost mother, father, and brothers. Peter makes him recognize a beggar-woman as his mother. Peter's followers, Niceta and Aquila, are recognized as Clement's brothers. An old workman expounds his theory of 'genesis', which is then discussed. He is recognized as Clement's father, while Peter is celebrated.

The first thing to remark here is that the author is perfectly conscious of the affective, aesthetic, and simultaneously 'religious' effects that recognition scenes produce. Aristotle had seen these effects as consisting mainly of pity and fear and had inserted them within the general context of the shock of surprise and wonder that anagnorisis prompts. When Peter recounts Clement's recognitions to the crowd, the narrative is 'most pleasing' and the hearers weep 'through *wonder* at the events, and through *compassion* for sufferings incident to humanity', through *pity* of humanity.[29] Pseudo-Clement also shows clearly that recognition scenes are instrumental to a demonstration of how Providence directs human affairs (a long discussion of what he calls 'genesis', as opposed to Providence, leads to the third scene of recognition in the story), and that recognition and knowledge of truth are very strictly linked to each other. As Book VII shows, the point of recognition is reward for chastity and knowledge of eternal life; salvation is attained by knowledge of the truth through Peter, who is Clement's father, mother, and brother, and who effects his recognition of his carnal mother, brothers, and father. Finally, recognition is also, in the Biblical sense, acknowledgement: in Book I, Abraham 'recognizes' the Creator; in the same Book, the Jews refuse to recognize Christ; at the end of the work, Peter is solemnly acknowledged, and this in turn leads to full recognition of divine Providence.

Recognition of a person and recognition of the heretofore mysterious designs of Providence coincide. This characteristic of religious romance points to the positive pole of anagnorisis, the relief and the joy that we feel when we glimpse a higher hand at work in our favour, in our own world. In Chaucer's *Man of Law's Tale* King Alla and his wife Custance come to Rome independently and unaware of each other after many years of separation and after Custance's many adventures. Alla sees their child, Maurice, knowing that someone who purports to be his mother is alive. The recognition process begins immediately, with an increasing sense of wonder, as if all were a 'hallucination':

> Now was this child as lyk unto Custance
> As possible is a creature to be.
> This Alla hath the face in remembrance
> Of dame Custance, and ther on mused he
> If that the childes mooder were aught she
> That is his wyf, and pryvely he sighte,
> And spedde hym fro the table that he myghte.
>
> 'Parfay', thoghte he, 'fantome is in myn heed!
> I oghte deme, of skilful juggement,
> That in the salte see my wyf is deed'. (1030–9)

Then, Alla makes his 'argument'. This, however, is not the 'reasoning' we would expect from an Electra (I know the mother is alive and here; this child is Custance's living portrait; hence Custance is alive and here). Although the *syllogismos* is implied, what Alla thinks of immediately, and the only 'argument' the narrator recounts, points to Providence:

> What woot I if that Crist have hyder ysent
> My wyf by see, as wel as he hire sente
> To my contree fro thennes that she wente? (1041–3)

Chaucer is fully aware of the effects of a recognition scene. Alla goes to the house of the senator where Custance is staying, to see for himself 'this wonder chaunce'. She can hardly stand on her feet, he weeps copiously:

> Whan Alla saugh his wyf, faire he hire grette,
> And weep that it was routhe for to see;
> For at the firste look he on hir sette
> He knew wel verraily that it was she.
> And she, for sorwe, as doumb stant as a tree,
> So was hir herte shet in hir distresse,
> Whan she remembred his unkyndenesse. (1051–7)

The first effect of recognition is an unbearably bitter pain, which produces 'pitee', *eleos*. Then, when it becomes clear that Alla was not responsible for his wife's sufferings, sublime elation ensues. *Theos gar kai to gignōskein philous*, exclaims Euripides' Helen when she, who has been kept in Egypt during the ten years of the Trojan war, and her husband, Menelaus meet again: 'it is a *god* to recognize friends' – there is something godlike in recognition.[30] Chaucer, a Christian, is less extreme, but ultimately expresses the same feeling:

> And swich a blisse is ther bitwix hem two
> That, save the joye that lasteth everemo,
> Ther is noon lyk that any creature
> Hath seyn or shal, whil that the world may dure. (1075–8)

One can well understand, then, the medieval 'thirst' for recognition. Plots are often complicated and twisted around so that they may contain a scene of anagnorisis. Two examples, one pathetic and one tragic, will illustrate this. The first is the story of Gestas and Dimnas, the two criminals crucified with Jesus. In the supposedly late fourteenth-century *Libro de la infancia y muerte de Jesús* the two recognize Jesus as the child one of their fathers had saved during the flight to Egypt.[31] This is quite an ingenious and, as Aristotle would have said, 'complex' plot. It shows us that medieval imagination is capable of coupling in narrative what it believed was the supreme moment of divine and human history with . . . recognition.

The second example is the Judas legend, which has survived in many versions.[32] Here, Judas is not only the apostle who betrays Jesus, but an Oedipal figure on top. Without knowing it, he has killed his father and married his mother. The recognition scene between mother and son is effected without means of tokens or signs, but through words and memory. By recalling certain details the two establish their true and original relationship. Judas is condemned forever.

The Judas legend inevitably leads to the medieval versions of the Oedipus theme. Oedipus is not only the archetype of the complex which bears his name since the days of Sigmund Freud, but also – and in our context primarily – Aristotle's supreme example of tragedy, and of anagnorisis within a tragedy. How does medieval literature handle this figure? I choose two instances, distant in time and place, both of which direct us to a happy ending.

The first is the English romance, *Sir Degaré*.[33] Here, the Oedipus theme is treated in a very cautious way: Degaré *almost* lies with his mother, whom he has married having defeated her father the King in a tourney, but then he remembers the hermit's advice never to lie with a woman without first trying on her glove (which the faery knight left her and which she gave the infant as a recognition token together with a letter explaining all). Moreover, the author warns us in advance: 'He married his mother, but God, who guides all things, would not that they sin.' So Degaré (like Cinderella's prince with the shoe) tries on the gloves, and the recognition takes place without incest. Again Degaré *almost* kills his faery father in combat, but the father recognizes the pointless sword that Degaré's mother has given him, and the parricide is avoided. Once more, the author warns us in advance: 'The son rides against his father, and neither knew the other.' Then the knight asks Degaré where he was born, and he answers, 'in Litel Bretaigne, son of a king's daughter, but I do not know who my father was'. Seeing the pointless sword, the father recognizes his son, and both swoon. In *Sir Degaré*, then, a potentially tragic theme becomes purely 'romantic' (the situation is the opposite of that found in the *Hildebrandslied* and the Gaelic Cuchulain cycle). Providence, God, is firmly in control, the unknown knight makes himself known, recognition is effected simply by means of tokens (the glove and the sword), which replace Oedipus' splendid detective enquiry. Above all, recognition does not come as the culminating point of Oedipus' long, passionate quest for truth, and for what he significantly calls the *sperma*, his own origin and identity. It is quite by chance, and perhaps according to the design of Providence, that the medieval knight finds his parents.

Anagnorisis is still *gnōsis* – recognition is knowledge – but a very circumscribed, limited one. Yet the recognition technique of *Sir Degaré* agrees perfectly with Aristotle's theory that the plot which best produces pity and fear is that where someone intends to perform a crime, but discovers the relationship before he does it.

The story of Gregorius 'der gute Sünder' is half an Oedipus plot, and half a saint's legend inextricably intertwined with the themes of love, chivalry, repentance, confession, glorification, chance, the devil's plottings and God's mercy. In Hartmann von Aue's *Gregorius*,[34] the protagonist is the son of a brother and sister who have fallen in love with each other, only half aware of what they are doing, because the devil so wills. When the child is born, away from the court, his father leaves and dies of 'Sehnsucht'. The baby, placed like Moses in what Exodus would call an 'ark', and accompanied by precious material, gold, and a tablet which relates the whole story of his birth, is fished up off the coast of an island, where he is brought up as the foster-child of fishermen under the supervision of the Abbot who, after discovering the secret of his origins, has him taught in Latin and prepares him for a brilliant career as a monk. But when he grows up, Gregorius, after a fight with one of his step-brothers, becomes aware that he wants to be a knight and to seek adventure abroad. The Abbot reveals to him the secret of his parents' sin, gives him the tablet, the gold, and beautiful clothes made with the material found in the casket. Gregorius sails across the sea and lands near a city besieged by a foreign baron who wants to marry the ruling Lady. Gregorius engages in combat with the baron, defeats him, and falls in love with the lady. They marry. One day, through her chambermaid, the lady finds the tablet and recognizes Gregorius as her son. The two decide to separate and do penance for the rest of their lives. Gregorius is fastened to a rock in the middle of a lake and there he lies for seventeen years until, by means of a divinely inspired dream, the Roman conclave elects him as the new Pope. Recovered, fed, and dressed, he is brought to Rome, where he establishes himself as one of the greatest pontiffs ever. Several years later, his mother goes to Rome on pilgrimage, and the two recognize each other once more.

One could discuss Hartmann's romance at great length, taking into account all its themes. Here, I shall however make only a few remarks. Firstly, the two recognition scenes are the climaxes of the plot, one at the centre of the poem, the other at the end. Secondly, the first is a true recognition by means of tokens, the second is best described as a revelation, as it is Gregorius who, playing with his mother's inability to recognize him, finally tells her who he is. Thus we pass from ignorance to recognition to revelation – a movement which is consistent with the overall message of the poem. A crucial passage divides the first and the second stages, ignorance and recognition, of this process. When Gregorius is first introduced to her mother and both hearts start beating, she actually recognizes in his clothes the very same material which she with her own hands had laid beside the child (1942–54). Like Parzival on another occasion, she fails to ask the unknown knight who he is – something she will later regret deeply (2572–3) – and Hartmann, though not commenting directly on this, immediately adds that this was achieved 'by him whose plan corrupted Lady Eve' (1960–1). The *méconnaissance* is, I think, absolutely fundamental in Hartmann's story: for if Gregorius himself has no way of knowing that he is committing incest with his mother short of showing all women he might meet the tablet he carries with him – if, in other words, his is sinless ignorance – his mother could have pursued her recognition of the clothes ('confessed to herself', says Hartmann, 'wider sich selben si des jach', 1945) to full knowledge like Oedipus. Her *hamartia*, dictated by the devil through the impulses of the flesh, is persistence in *agnoia*, ignorance itself – quite the opposite of Eve's sin. Later on, when she discovers the tablet, she even deludes herself into thinking that perhaps Gregorius got it from someone else (2506–15). And finally, she does not recognize the Pope as her son even though she says she would be able to do so if she saw him. The truth comes to her from outside.

Gregorius, on the other hand, receives inner light as soon as he recognizes that his wife is also his mother. Faced by her despair, he immediately reacts with the knowledge that education in a monastery brings ('I have *read*', he says, that God forgives those who repent, 2700 ff.) and dictates penance for her and for himself. Comprehension will in fact be one of the chief characteristics of Gregorius as a Pope – he is the best 'healer' of 'sêle wunden' on Peter's chair (3790–2), and has a 'starken lêre' which makes 'God's honour' grow in 'the kingdom of Rome' (3827–30). Not even he, however, recognizes his mother when she arrives in Rome as a pilgrim, and does so significantly only when he receives her confession ('bîhte', 3842–56).

Confession, recognition, revelation – we are far from Oedipus, closer to Joseph and his brothers. *Gregorius* raises many questions – what is sin, what is love, what can man do when he is faced by the horrors of chance, evil, taboo – but the ultimate answer is God's Providence (3938–9), and the *lysis*, the denouement cannot end in catastrophe, *pathos*, but in salvation. The catharsis here is what Gregory and his mother undergo in those seventeen years – purgatory after the hell of sin and before the paradise where Hartmann tells us they will dwell forever as saints (3953–4).

The recognition scene between Gregorius and his mother wrings tears both of laughter and 'phantastic emotion' from the listeners of the grandiose musical suite composed by Adrian Leverkühn on the text of the *Gesta Romanorum* in Thomas Mann's *Dr Faustus*.[35] While writing those pages, Mann was already thinking of exploiting the Gregorius story, and in a few years' time this became in fact *Der Erwählte*, the 'chosen one'.[36] The final recognition scene in this subtle, ironical romance is a splendid piece of writing. The Pope confesses his mother and promises to her God's forgiveness. But she asks: what will the ultimate fate of my son-husband be? After all he was more innocent than I: I conceived a son with my brother, he only lay with his mother without knowing it. The Pope, however, contradicts her, – and here is the first surprise. Grigorss, he proclaims, knew very well that it was his mother he loved. What!?, she interrupts him. But yes, of course, he replies, 'a youth who sets out to find his mother and wins by conquest a wife who, however beautiful, could be his mother, must reckon with it that she might be his mother whom he marries. So much for his understanding. But to his blood the identity of wife and mother was familiar long before he learned the truth and play-acted about it.' Thus the value of the first recognition, the tragic anagnorisis of incest and accident, is put back into perspective. Grigorss' blood knew it: an inner, instinctive knowledge, which becomes awareness only with the passing of time, replaces all *sēmeia*.

This revelation of the Pope to his mother precipitates the second recognition. He shows her the famous tablet and finally declares: 'understand, Sybilla, we are your son'. But, and here is the second surprise, she replies, 'That I have known for long.' 'What? So you recognized me in the Pope's hood, after so many years?' 'Holiness, at first glance. *I know you always.*' 'And have you, light-headed woman, only played with us?' 'Since you would play with me yourself . . .'. 'We thought', the Pope concludes, 'to offer God an entertainment.' This is no longer anagnorisis, but meta-anagnorisis – it is recognition of recognition, that *wiedererkennen* which Mann, in harmony here with Freud,[37] celebrates in *Joseph and his Brothers*:[38] the myth recognizing itself in the story which narrates it.

In different ways, both Hartmann's *Gregorius* and Mann's *Der Erwählte* end up as 'comedies'. In them, recognition represents precisely the threshold, the door that can open up into either the tragic (first scene) or the sublime (second scene). The very same process takes place, though with much less humour, in another medieval German romance, Wolfram von Eschenbach's *Parzival*, written at about the same time as Hartmann's *Gregorius*. As its hero must pass from ignorance to knowledge, *Parzival* is in its entirety a recognition romance,[39] and the scenes of anagnorisis and *méconnaissance* in it add up to at least forty. At the centre of the plot lies Book IX, which begins with the recognition between Parzival and his cousin, Sigune, and culminates in the encounter between the hero and the hermit Trevrizent. In this meeting we have a double recognition process. On the one hand, Trevrizent must gradually learn that the knight now standing before him is not Lähelin, but his nephew, the son of Gahmuret and Herzeloyde. On the other, Parzival must recognize not only his uncle's identity, but also that he himself has killed one of his relatives, Ither; that Anfortas – of whom Parzival has failed to ask the question that could have cured the king – is also his uncle; and finally, that he is partly responsible for the death of his own mother.

These multiple recognitions bring Parzival to knowledge of the mysteries of the Grail, which Trevrizent reveals to him in order to explain the relationships the hero is unaware of. In other words, it is recognition of potentially tragic *philiai* that sends Parzival on to *wisheit*, to supreme knowledge. And the crucial moment of this recognition is when Trevrizent tells of the unknown knight who, at Munsalvaesche, did not ask Anfortas the famous question. Immediately afterwards, Parzival confesses he is that very knight. The play of ignorance, recognition, and knowledge in this scene is emblematic of the whole romance, where self-knowledge leads to knowledge of God. As Wagner, who significantly eliminates this scene and treats the theme in a much more 'mystical' fashion, puts it in his *Parsifal* (II, 771–4):

> Bekenntnis
> wird Schuld und Reue enden,
> Erkenntnis
> in Sinn die Torheit wenden.

(Confession will put an end to guilt and repentance; recognition will turn folly into sense.)

Having gone this far with one outcome of medieval recognition, we can now return to its tragic pole for the last time and simultaneously see it in all its ambiguity. In a previous chapter, I have examined the prolonged agony of self-division and melancholy that makes of Chaucer's *Troilus* a tragic poem. The suffering of Troilus reaches its climax in a recognition scene. After dreaming of Criseyde's betrayal (V, 1233–67) and after having his dream truthfully interpreted by Cassandra (V, 1457–1519), Troilus, who refuses to accept what he calls his sister's 'delusion' and who is in fact himself a 'fool of fantasie' (V, 1523), receives a letter from Criseyde which he considers a 'strange . . . beginning of change'. Finally, as one day he 'stands' 'in his malencolie', Deiphobus returns from the field with a coat which he has taken in battle from Diomedes:

> And whan this Troilus
> It saugh, he gan to taken of it hede,
> Avysyng of the lengthe and of the brede,
> And al the werk; but as he gan byholde,
> Ful sodeynly his herte gan to colde,

> As he that on the coler fond withinne
> A broch that he Criseyde yaf that morwe
> That she from Troie moste nedes twynne,
> In remembraunce of hym and of his sorwe.
> And she hym leyde ayeyn hire feith to borwe
> To kepe it ay! But now ful wel he wiste,
> His lady nas no lenger on to triste.   (1655–66)

The brooch is the 'inanimate object', as Aristotle would have called it, that Troilus recognizes. Furthermore, it is the 'sign', the material *sēmeion* that seals the tragic foreboding of Troilus' heart. Now, the hero truly re-cognizes ('ful wel he wiste') the truth he already knew. Criseyde has betrayed him. Yet Chaucer, though emphasizing the anguish and the pain that take hold of Troilus' psyche at this point, directs his recognition towards a deeper anagnorisis, one that underlines his inner division even more forcefully than before:

> Thorugh which I se that clene out of youre mynde
> Ye han me cast – and I ne kan nor may,
> For al this world, withinne myn herte fynde
> To unloven yow a quarter of a day!
> In corsed tyme I born was, weilaway,
> That yow, that doon me al this wo endure,
> Yet love I best of any creature!   (1695–701)

The bottom of one's own self-knowledge seems to have been reached, and Troilus has apparently become a completely modern hero. But soon, after death, Troilus' soul ascends to the eighth sphere, and from there looks down at our 'litel spot of erthe', despises the wretched world, considers it 'vanity' with respect to the full felicity of heaven, and laughs even at the woe of those who weep for his death. And with this Stoic recognition, the perspective has once more changed. Anagnorisis transcends tragedy, making man bend on himself, turn inwards, explore conscience in search of, or finally with his sight fixed on the gods.

Towards the end of the Middle Ages, at least one British poet clearly realized the dramatic potentialities of the recognition scene in the Troilus plot. In his *Testament of Cresseid*, which he himself calls a 'tragedie', Henryson stages a beautiful *méconnaissance*–recognition scene just before the end of the story. This comes as a total surprise to readers and is therefore all the more effective. Cresseid, who has betrayed Troilus and has been dismissed by Diomedes is now, punished by the gods, a leper. Troilus, returning in triumph to Troy after a raid, meets her in the crowd of begging lepers, 'not witting quhat scho was' (497). It is an extraordinary moment, for Troilus, without recognizing the disfigured face of Cresseid (501), yet thinks with 'ane blenk' that he has seen that face before (499–500), and in fact it reminds him of 'the sweit visage and amorous blenking – Of fair Cresseid, sumtyme his awin darling' (502–4). Troilus' reaction is predictable, but Henryson surpasses himself in describing it:

> Ane spark of lufe than till his hart culd spring
> And kendlit all his bodie in are fyre   (512–13)

Seized by a fever, Troilus sweats and trembles, can no longer bear his shield, changes 'hew' many times (514–17). Yet, as Henryson notes with a keen sense of pathos and drama, 'not one ane-uther knew' (518). Very appropriately, what is missing here is Troilus' *awareness* of his love,[40] in short, the recognition of recognition – what Virgil's Dido had exclaimed upon seeing Aeneas, 'Adgnosco veteris vestigia flammae', or what Dante, as we shall see in the next chapter, had tried to say to Virgil, quoting him, when, after the journey through Hell and Purgatory, he saw Beatrice again: 'Conosco i segni de l'antica fiamma' (I know the signs of the ancient flame). The whole effect of the *Testament* rests precisely on the fine psychological difference between awareness and unawareness. Troilus is unable to progress from the latter to the former, while we, as readers – and this is the second most important point – are conscious all the time.

For Troilus' instinctive *anamnēsis* of Cresseid upon seeing the leper's face Henryson offers an explanation which scholars have justly linked to Aristotelian psychology, and particularly to a passage in the *De Insomniis* (460b 1 ff.).[41] Yet Henryson's lines remind me of a sentence in Plato's *Theaetetus* where the word 'anagnorisis' appears as far as we know for the first time in the Greek language; when, that is, discussing false judgement, Socrates explains the function which memory performs in the process, that of a wax tablet:

When I, who know you and Theodorus and possess imprints of you both like seal-impressions in the waxen block, see you both at a distance indistinctly and am in a hurry to assign the proper imprint of each to the proper visual perception, like fitting a foot into its own footmark to effect a recognition[42]

This passage, which almost certainly refers to the beginning of the famous recognition scene between Electra and Orestes in Aeschylus'

Choephori, and which describes a mechanism that Proust will exploit *ad libitum* and *ad infinitum* in the *Recherche*, is also the ultimate ancestor of Henryson's 'psychological' explanation. In fact, the *Testament* scene, if I may put it boldly, stands half-way between Plato and Proust, or, rather, between Plato and Freud, with Aristotle:

> The idole of ane thing in cace may be
> Sa deip imprentit in the fantasy
> That it deludis the wittis outwardly,
> And sa appeiris in forme and lyke estait
> Within the mynd as it was figurait. (507–11)

Nor should we forget that this is only half of the scene. Cresseid receives from the unknown and unrecognized Troilus who, without speaking a word, rides away 'pensive in hart', a girdle and, upon asking her companions who that lord may be who 'hes done to us so greit humanitie', discovers it was Troilus himself. Undoubtedly, this is true recognition, and we must once more agree with Aristotle that, coming as it does together with the achievement of the reversal or *peripeteia* and without the use of signs (for the girdle here is only a token of Troilus' pity and humaneness), it is perfect.

This recognition brings Cresseid to ultimate, full, self-knowledge, on the road to which she has been ever since looking at her leprous face in the mirror, and to her final confession and testament. This recognition leads to the *pathos* or catastrophe, Cresseid's death, and to Troilus' despair when, through the *sēmeion* of the ring returned to him by the lepers, he learns of her end. And finally, in Henryson's mind it should lead us to recognize the moral of the story and of the world: 'Lo, fair ladyis', says the inscription that Troilus places on Cresseid's 'tombe of merbell gray',

> Cresseid of Troyis toun,
> Sumtyme countit the flour of wommanheid,
> Under this stane, lait liper, lyis deid.

We are at the end of the fifteenth century. Aristotle's *Poetics* is circulating again, and soon it will become an obsession. But recognition is still poised between tragedy and transcendence.

If, as J.A.W. Bennett said, 'the only scene that approaches Henryson's climax is the discovery of Tristram as Malory describes it',[43] the situation in *Sir Tristram* is profoundly different. In one word, it is neither tragic nor transcendental. Mad, Tristram is brought back to King Mark's castle where, bathed and fed, he recovers his memory. Isode decides to go and see the man who has returned from the forest:

> So they passed forth and spirred where was the syke man, and than a squyer tolde the quene that he was in the gardyne takyng hys reste to repose hym ayenst the sunne. So whan the quene loked uppon sir Trystramys she was nat remembird of hym, but ever she seyde unto dame Brangwayne,
>
> 'Mesemys I shulde have sene thys man here before in many placis.'
>
> But as sone as sir Trystramys sye her he knew her well inowe, and than he turned away hys vysage and wepte.
>
> Than the quene had allwayes a lytyll brachett that sir Trystramys gaff hir the first tyme that ever she cam into Cornwayle, and never wold that brachet departe frome her but yf sir Trystram were nyghe thereas was La Beall Isode. And thys brachet was firste sente frome the kynges doughter of Fraunce unto sir Trystrams for grete love.
>
> And anone thys lityll bracket felte a savoure of sir Trystram. He lepte uppon hym and lycked hys learys and hys earys, and than he whyned and quested, and she smelled at hys feete and at hys hondis and on all the partyes of hys body that she myght com to.
>
> 'A, my lady!' seyde dame Brangwayne, 'Alas! I se hit ys myne owne lorde sir Trystramys.'
>
> And thereuppon La Beall Isode felle downe in a sowne and so lay a grete whyle.[44]

This scene is highly pathetic, and if we consider that before entering the garden Isode believes Tristram dead, the impact it produces on us increases. Exile, madness, death, and resurrection are sanctioned by recognition, which follows *méconnaissance* upon its heels. Recognition, however, looks like a delicate mechanism which human beings can hardly handle. Thus, the little dog performs a function which is similar to, but more complex than, that of Argos in the *Odyssey*.[45] The instinct of the 'bracket' identifies Tristram, but the dog is itself presented as a token of love and an unfailing embodiment of the union between Tristram and Isode. The knowledge disclosed by the episode is neither tragic nor transcendental, but radically human – the very essence of the feeling that unites a man and a woman. And the medium of this knowledge, the dog, is itself the message. Love bridges the gap of separation, madness, and reported death. We are on the way to a fundamental change in the meaning and function of recognition. This will come to its extreme conclusion only in the exalted vision of Wagner's opera, where Tristan and Isolde sing together a hymn that

George Steiner has called 'an apocalypse of desire, an erotic consummation so complete that it annuls the autism of personal identity':[46]

> Du Isolde,
> Tristan ich,
> nicht mehr Tristan,
> nicht Isolde;
> ohne Nennen,
> ohne Trennen,
> neu *Erkennen*,
> neu Entbrennen;
> endlos ewig
> ein-bewusst.

> (Isolde, you, Tristan I, no longer
> Tristan, not Isolde; without naming,
> without parting, new *recognition*,
> new consuming; endless everlasting
> single-consciousness.)[47]

But long before Malory, the author of *Sir Orfeo* knew the secret that ties man and woman in reunion and recognition. When, after spending a long time in the woods as a poor, wild harpist, Orfeo sees a company of sixty faery ladies ride by a river, he approaches them and discovers that one is his own wife Heurodis, who had been carried off into the faery world. In the recognition scene, the feelings of the protagonists are set against the enchanted, alien company of the faeries. Upon this uncanny background, an extraordinary picture is drawn: an exchange of mute glances, the tears falling from Heurodis' eyes. Seeing on his face all the suffering he has undergone, she pities Orfeo. Then, the faery ladies take her away:

> To a leuedi he was y-come,
> Biheld, & haþ wele vnder-nome,
> & seþ bi al þing þat it is
> His owhen quen, Dam Heurodis.
> ӡern he biheld hir, & sche him eke,
> Ac noiþer to oþer a word no speke,
> For messais þat sche on him seiӡe,
> Þat had ben so riche & so heiӡe.
> Þe teres fel out of her eiӡe:
> Þe oþer leuedis þis y-seiӡe
> & maked hir oway to ride
> – Sche most wiþ him no lenger abide.[48]

A spark of love: Medieval recognitions

Here, we have no hint of supernatural intervention, no providential end in sight. The frozen instant of mutual recognition is entirely human: suspended between a tragic possibility and a happy ending, between joy and pain, the hearts of man and woman shiver on a threshold which we perceive as opening on to the sublime.

6

I know the signs of the ancient flame:
Dante's recognitions

'"*Miserere* di me", gridai a lui, "qual che tu sii, od ombra od omo certo!"' – Have pity on me whatever you are, shade or living man! This is the anguished cry with which Dante appeals to a vague human form as, faced by the three beasts, he is about to sink down the mountain back to the depths of the dark wood. We are at the beginning of the *Divine Comedy*, and about to read one of the greatest and most startling recognition scenes ever written. In the 'great desert' or waste land in which he finds himself Dante has just seen, as if emerging out of nothingness, a figure that seems 'faint through long silence' – 'chi per lungo silenzio parea fioco'. He does not describe this form, but suggestively evokes its shadowy appearance, the great silence that surrounds it, and the feeling of a long absence from his own consciousness it suddenly prompts.[1] In the following lines, the image does not come into focus visually (Dante in fact emphasizes its indistinctness and his own uncertainty by calling it 'od ombra od omo certo') but auditively. The voice that answers the poet comes from depths neither Dante nor we have yet sounded: 'Non omo, omo già fui', 'No, not a living man, though once I was, and my parents were Lombards, both Mantuans by birth. I was born *sub Julio*, although late, and I lived at Rome under the good Augustus, in the time of the false and lying gods. I was a poet, and I sang of that just son of Anchises who came from Troy after proud Ilium was burned.' So this is the author of the *Aeneid*, Virgil himself, the greatest poet of classical antiquity known to the Middle Ages.

Dante's surprise and emotion at meeting such a man, thirteen hundred years dead and yet inevitably at the centre of a medieval writer's meditations on his art, is almost undescribable. Dante the poet, however, can make us feel that shock or blow (Aristotle called it *ekplēxis*) which recognition always produces. 'Are you, then, that

Virgil, that fount which pours forth so broad a stream of speech?', he answers and for shame keeps his head bowed, 'O glory and light of other poets, may the long study and the great love that have made me search your volume avail me! You are my master and my author. You alone are he from whom I took the fair style that has done me honour.'

Surprise, shame, elation succeed each other quickly, and Dante finally erupts into a paean which is a deeper recognition, the recognition of the meaning Virgil's 'humanitas' and poetry have for him, for Dante Alighieri. Thus, what until now was merely a 'volume', a book, becomes a person, and Dante's recognition of that faint human form is presented to us as the trembling encounter of two people and the momentous coming together of two poets and two cultures across a gulf of one thousand three hundred years. 'In the realm of European literature', wrote Ernst Robert Curtius,[2] 'there is little which may be compared with this phenomenon . . . The awakening of Virgil by Dante is an arc of flame which leaps from one great soul to another . . . Historically, it is the sealing of the bond which the Latin Middle Ages made between the antique and the modern world.'

Dante has indeed begun to treat shades as solid things. If nothing in European poetry can be compared to this, no theory of literature has ever contemplated even the possibility of such a scene. As we have seen in the preceding chapter, Aristotle (whom Dante is soon going to see in the Castle of Limbo) had developed a theory of recognition throughout his *Poetics*, and had indeed noted its fundamental importance in a tragic or epic plot. Aristotle systematizes the various kinds of recognition arranging them on an ascending scale which corresponds to the successive stages of human knowledge and at the same time to the constituent 'elements' of tragedy. Thus, for instance, recognition by means of 'signs' is the moment of sense perception on the one hand, and of stage-spectacle on the other; recognition 'through memory' and 'through reasoning' belong to the sphere of imagination and rational thinking as well as to the inner 'thought' of a play; and recognition 'arising from the events themselves' corresponds to the action of the intellect (*nous*) catching the cause and essence of things and is simultaneously an integral part of the plot or *mythos*.[3] In this chapter, we shall try to see if and how this scheme applies to the recognition scenes Dante stages in the *Divine Comedy*. In doing so, we shall return once more to the problems of the tragic and the sublime. For knowledge, as we have already seen, adds to both a further dimension, that of their own conscious perception.

Aristotle nowhere mentions the recognition scenes between men and gods or between the living and the dead of which Greek literature could offer him many beautiful examples. This might indicate a more or less conscious unwillingness on his part to enter a realm where reason cannot acquire certainty and where anagnorisis appears as a mystery that can hardly be sounded by a philosopher. Yet poets cannot and do not avoid plunging into those depths. Aristotle chose several recognition scenes of the *Odyssey* as examples of his types of anagnorisis, but neglected those of Book XI. Anyone who has read those six hundred lines will never forget the inimitable *Nekyia*, or evocation of the dead, in which Odysseus recognizes, and is recognized by, his companion Elpenor, the prophet Tiresias, his own mother Anticlea, the heroes and heroines of the past, and his own friends, the Greek warriors at Troy – Agamemnon, Achilles, Ajax. His encounter and conversations with the nerveless and boneless *psykhai*, the insubstantial shades of the dead, reveal to Odysseus the meaning of death and life, show him the whole mythic past of his race, bring him back to the epic days of the war, unveil his future, and transform him into the symbol of a timeless civilization based on travelling and discovering. Neither Proust nor Joyce forgot that lesson.[4] And, what is more to the point for us, Virgil proved an apt pupil. In Book VI of the *Aeneid*, he makes Aeneas visit Avernus and there recognize, and be recognized by, his pilot Palinurus, his former lover Queen Dido, the Trojan Deiphobus and, finally, his father Anchises, who shows him the future heroes of Rome down to the emperor Augustus. Here, then, recognition comprises not only one's roots (symbolized by the father, who replaces Odysseus' mother) and the tragic past (the destruction of Troy), but also love (Dido) and the racial and political future (foundation and glory of the 'Urbs'). Aeneas finds his meaning as the founder of an historical civilization – that of Rome.

Walter Otto once wrote that the recognition scenes in *Odyssey* XI uncover 'das Sein des Gewesenen', the 'being of having been'.[5] The first thing we shall notice in studying Dante's equivalent episodes is that the knowledge the pilgrim and we acquire through them is not merely that of a 'being' irremediably vanishing away, receding into the past, but the knowledge of a concrete, present entity which, while containing the past and projecting itself into the future of eternity, embodies a permanent essence, at once individual and universal. Thus, Dantean recognition is truly Aristotelian in spirit: it is the apprehension of the *tode ti*, of substance in individuality.

Homer's and Virgil's versions of the Nekyia, with their similarities and differences, tell us a great deal about ancient conceptions of life after death, but they also show us that a voyage to the other world is almost meaningless without recognition. As we have seen in the preceding chapter, anagnorisis remains central also in medieval Christian imagination. For the dead, recognition is a punishment and a reward. Dante handles this tradition in his own peculiar manner. For instance, when he meets the avaricious in the fourth circle of Hell, he tells Virgil that he should be able to 'recognize' some of them (VII, 49–51). His guide replies that a 'contrappasso' applies to these sinners, a 'contrappasso' that hinges on recognition:

> la sconoscente vita che i fé sozzi,
> ad ogne conoscenza or li fa bruni.   (VII, 53–4)

(the undiscerning life that made them foul now makes them dim to all discernment.)

On the other hand, we have seen how the notion of reward and joy in recognition and reunion applies to the fourth Heaven, where the blessed souls of the 'sapientes' show themselves eager to recover their bodies at Doomsday 'perhaps not only for themselves, but also for their mothers, for their fathers, and for the others who were dear before they became eternal flames' (*Paradiso* XIV, 64–6). Recognition, which brings human beings together, means life as knowledge of each other. It is no mere philological pedantry to observe that the Biblical 'to know' (*jada'*) also means 'to make love'.

Dante, then, is the heir to a complex tradition. Orpheus' voyage to the other world was, for the Middle Ages, a 'figure' of Christ's own descent to Hell,[6] and the way was thus open towards an integration of pagan and Christian views of the journey to Hades and of the place anagnorisis has in it. Dante himself proclaims he has been preceded by Aeneas and St Paul (*Inferno* II, 13–33). Now, one particular interpretation of *Aeneid* VI may clarify the process that leads to the *Divine Comedy*. In his twelfth-century commentary on Virgil's poem, Bernardus Silvestris follows a well-established tradition in seeing Aeneas' peregrinations as an allegory of man's itinerary through the various ages of life and through a whole series of moral 'errors' (for instance lust, represented by Dido's episode). The Nekyia marks the beginning of maturity and means the discovery of true knowledge – theology. In visiting the underworld, Aeneas encounters his old 'errors', experiences them again with a new consciousness, and is finally able to reach knowledge of God. Thus, Aeneas comes to contemplation of the Creator (Anchises) only after passing through five degrees of 'creaturarum agnitiones' (of recognition of creatures), from inanimate beings up to men and angels.[7]

This allegory might be seen as a kind of potential grid for the actual plot of the *Divine Comedy*. In Dante's poem, the protagonist's encounters with a series of characters who exemplify a sin or a virtue or who expound a particularly important doctrine lead to his salvation and ultimately to his seeing God. In this sense, anagnorisis is always self-recognition. When, on the first terrace of Purgatory, Dante meets the proud, he is recognized by one of them, Oderisi da Gubbio, a famous illuminator. In the ensuing conversation, Oderisi preaches a beautiful sermon on the vanity of human glory which touches Dante's very being because it mentions not only Cimabue and Giotto, but also Guinizelli, Cavalcanti and, implicitly, Dante Alighieri as the successive leaders in Italian art. Dante declares that Oderisi's words have instilled in his heart 'good humility' (XI, 118–19) and will later admit his fear of being condemned, after death, to the punishment of the proud (XIII, 136–8). Thus, the self is mirrored in the other. Recognition becomes – as for a Christian it always should – confession.

Dante's journey in the *Comedy* is, then, a recognition: a growth and rediscovery *in the flesh* of the Biblical knowledge of good and evil, leading to cognition of, and immersion in, God. The *Divine Comedy* as a whole presents itself as a grandiose anagnorisis, a slow and ever more intense passage from ignorance to knowledge. In particular, each single instance of recognition in the poem points, as Aristotle would have it, to *philia* (friendship) or *ekhthra* (hostility), not only in the sense of revealing to Dante whether the characters he meets are relatives, friends, or enemies of his, but also in the deeper sense of unveiling man's varying degrees of *philia* or *ekhthra* to God and His law. And those characters will indeed, as Aristotle would wish, be 'marked out for' or 'defined with reference to' 'good or bad fortune' (*eutykhia* or *dystykhia*). They will illustrate the final, eternal *eutykhia* or *dystykhia* of man's immortal soul. The sublime, or tragic, potential of such scenes is therefore immense.

To recognize someone is for Dante to penetrate his or her personality to its very essence – to understand and to stage dramatically the ultimate truth his interlocutors incarnate in their gestures, faces, stories. Recognition opens up for him their historical identity as frozen in the 'here and now' of the other world. Shades in Hell and Purgatory, lights in Paradise, the souls of his Nekyia appear suddenly, manifest themselves, are recognized and recognize without the complex mechanisms of signs, memory, and reasoning about which Aristotle writes in his *Poetics*, but, as it were, by their mere appearance, their words, their self-revelation. With her lover Paolo, Francesca da Rimini comes out of the group of the lustful and tells Dante the tale of their love and death. That story, and the details Francesca adds, are enough for the pilgrim to recognize her and to make him faint for pity (*Inferno* v, 73–142). On the enchanted beach of Purgatory, a soul moves out of the crowd to embrace Dante. The spirit's love is so obvious that it prompts the poet to do the same. He tries three times, but in vain, to clasp his friend's shade (thus repeating the gesture of Odysseus with his mother and of Aeneas with his father). He shows his wonder; the soul smiles, withdraws, tells Dante to stop, and finally the poet recognizes him. Casella sings for him Dante's own canzone, 'Amor che ne la mente mi ragiona' (*Purgatorio* II, 76–117).

Similar scenes occur throughout the *Inferno* and the *Purgatorio* and are the cause of so much of the *Comedy*'s appeal through the miracle of surprise and wonder they produce in the protagonist and in the reader. I shall now explore some of their basic mechanisms and meanings, paying particular attention to the two recurring themes of recognition of poets and self-recognition. A few preliminary remarks are, however, necessary.

In the first place, we must remember that, following Aristotle, Dante believes that 'Nature wills that in our attainment of knowledge, progress should be made with order, that is, by going on from that which we know better, to that which we know less well.'[8] This, clearly, is also the ideal itinerary of the *Comedy*, for we know sin and earthly passions much better than the bliss and mysteries of Heaven. Yet as far as recognition of single human souls is concerned, things are similar, but at the same time more complex: for different reasons it is difficult for Dante to recognize the shades of Hell and Purgatory, but it is impossible for him to know the identity of his interlocutors in Paradise. There, the souls of the blessed appear to him as lights on a background of light; hence, they must manifest themselves to the pilgrim and declare who they are. Recognition as a poetic and gnoseological mechanism is, appropriately for God's own realm, replaced by revelation – a process which, as we shall see, starts in the *Purgatorio*. Furthermore, the very means of this gnoseological mechanism change in passing from one cantica to another. In Hell and, partly, in

Purgatory, we have a semblance of the first stages in the process of knowledge such as Dante conceives them.[9] The pilgrim recognizes his interlocutors through his senses (in particular through sight and hearing) and through their transmission of 'sensible forms' to memory as well as to the cogitative and imaginative virtues of the soul. In Heaven, the object of revelation is of course perceived through sight or hearing, but the intellectual process simply does not begin. What we encounter is a sudden, complete 'il-lumination' that strikes the pilgrim's perception and intellect. These, in turn, grow higher, more intense, and more god-like by virtue of divine grace the higher the pilgrim ascends through the spheres.

Secondly, one should perhaps ask oneself how Dante recognizes his characters in *Inferno* and *Purgatorio* if these are but shades. Dante himself has provided an answer to this question in *Purgatorio* xxv, where Statius explains why the souls of the gluttonous can be punished and purged by means of hunger and thirst. How, asks Dante, can shades suffer these and become thinner? It is the question medieval exegetes asked about Dives. Statius replies with a long exposition, central in many ways to the thought underlying Dante's poem and which concerns the generation and growth of man and finally the nature of shadow-bodies after death. According to Statius, as soon as the soul of the disembodied dead reaches the banks of the Acheron or the mouth of the Tiber thence to depart towards Hell or Purgatory, its 'virtus formativa' projects a phantom body alike in size and appearance to the earthly body; and 'as air, when it is full of moisture, becomes many-coloured by reflection, so the air surrounding the soul near the two rivers shapes itself in that form which is imprinted on it by the "virtue" of the soul. Then, like the flame which follows the fire wheresoever it moves, the spirit is followed by its new form' (88–99). This is what an 'ombra' or fictive body is. The shade then forms the organs of every sense, from the lowest to the highest, the sense of sight. It is by this 'sentire' that the inhabitants of Hell and Purgatory speak, laugh, weep, and sigh, and therefore recognize and appear as 'forms' – 'ombre vane, fuor che ne l'aspetto' – that can be recognized.[10] The changing lineaments and bearing of the shade body reveal the inner emotions, just as happens with the earthly body. It should, finally, be added that in Dante's view the soul of a dead man possesses memory, intellect, and will 'far more "acutely" actualized ("in atto") than before'.

This complex explanation, the reasons for which are both philo-sophical and poetic, points to something which is borne out in the actual scenes of recognition in Dante's poem. The heightening of the soul's faculties after death, the fact that the shade changes appearance according to its 'affections' and desires indicate that for the souls of Dante's Hell and Purgatory recognition may represent an exceptionally intense experience. His shades do not only have an 'aspetto', a physical appearance; they are, in a sense, naked human feelings and minds. They cannot, as Erich Auerbach once remarked,[11] hide any of their passions. Between shades thus inclined and a man such as Dante the protagonist, inherently motivated to acquire knowledge and naturally open to the emotions of a living person on a journey to the other world, recognition will therefore be a unique moment of contact. In other words, the anagnorisis scenes of the *Comedy* are not only narrative devices.[12] They are the technical means by which Dante stresses the central process of the poem, the acquisition of knowledge in the flesh, and its dramatic quality.

Thirdly, there is a quantitative and qualitative difference between anagnorisis in Hell and in Purgatory. Fully staged recognition scenes are much more numerous in the latter. If one excepts the encounter with Virgil in canto I, which is a general prologue to the poem and whose events take place outside Hell proper, in the *Inferno* we have only one major scene of recognition, that between Dante and Brunetto Latini in canto XV. In the *Purgatorio*, on the other hand, we have at least eight such episodes, which include the meetings with Casella, Belacqua, Sordello, Judge Nino, Oderisi, Statius, Forese Donati, and finally Beatrice. There is a quite simple explanation for this: with a few exceptions, the souls of the damned are not particularly keen on being identified by Dante as this, they feel, will only bring shame to them. An example is Filippo Argenti, one of the wrathful in the fifth circle. Covered with mud, he rises from the Stygian marsh as Dante and Virgil are crossing it on Phlegyas' boat. Dante asks him who he is, but he angrily replies, 'You see that I am one who weeps.' In spite of this, the poet recognizes and curses him (VIII, 31–9). Furthermore, the souls of the damned are very often disfigured both by their punishment and their own inner anguish. In the third circle, among the gluttonous, Ciacco defies Dante:

> riconoscimi, se sai:
> tu fosti, prima ch'io disfatto, fatto

(recognize me if you can: you were made before I was unmade);

but the poet cannot do so because of the sinner's 'angoscia' (VI, 40–8).

Metamorphosis, *méconnaissance*, blindness, oblivion, inability to recognize characterize the sphere of anagnorisis in Hell. The *Inferno* is the place where recognition tends towards its negation; not its degree zero, but, so to speak, below zero. Where it takes place, it is a difficult, agonizing process, as with Ciacco and Brunetto. Its tragic essence is infinitely increased by a tension which, though allowing wonder, has no release. The souls of Dante's Hell have no escape. They have but a single moment in all eternity to be, or not to be recognized by a fellow human being. Recognition is their only chance of being remembered – of living – and at the same time of being damned forever in human memory. For them, anagnorisis coincides not with 'peripeteia', a reversal of circumstances, but with 'pathos', a catastrophe which has already taken place in history and is there forever present outside history. The knowledge anagnorisis brings to the damned is in fact totally useless and hopeless. For Dante, and presumably for us, this knowledge will eventually constitute a means of real Christian catharsis and salvation. Its effect will indeed be pity – the Aristotelian *eleos* – but one inextricably mixed with terror (*phobos*) and horror, one, as Dante tells us, transformed into a 'war', the 'guerra de la pietate'.[13] Hence, to study the development of recognition in Hell means to become aware of the double bottom, as it were, of tragedy: to acquire consciousness of the tragic while realizing its total uselessness for the actors themselves.

The situation is profoundly different in Purgatory. Recognition is easier in its regained light, for here Dante's own body projects, to the perennial wonder of his interlocutors, a shadow that makes him very visible. What is more important, however, is that the souls who inhabit what Jacques Le Goff has called the 'third place', the 'in-between',[14] know that they are saved. Indeed, being recognized by Dante and thereby being remembered by their relatives in prayer will shorten their purifying pains. Anagnorisis is for them a joy, a pleasure. It is this feeling that Dante himself expresses when, in the little valley of Antepurgatory, he sees a soul who, as if he would recognize him, gazes at him alone. The air around is darkening, yet it is not so dark as to impede the movement and the penetration of the eyes of the dead and those of the living and their mutual understanding. The senses meet directly. The shade moves towards Dante, the pilgrim towards the soul – 'noble Judge Nino, how I *rejoiced* to see you there, and not among the damned!':

> Solo tre passi credo ch'i' scendesse,
> e fui di sotto, e vidi un che mirava
> pur me, come conoscer mi volesse.
>   Temp'era già che l'aere s'annerava,
> ma non sí che tra li occhi suoi e' miei
> non dichiarisse ciò che pria serrava.
>   Ver' me si fece, e io ver' lui mi fei:
> giudice Nin gentil, quanto mi piacque
> quando ti vidi non esser tra' rei!   (*Purgatorio* VIII, 46–54)

And this is the joy, the feeling almost of divine 'grace', that prompts Forese Donati to cry loudly, when he turns his deepset eyes and fixes them on Dante: 'Qual grazia m'è questa?' This emotion and this voice trigger off Dante's recognition. The shades of the gluttonous are so lean and covered with scurf, the sockets of their eyes seem such 'rings without gems', that it is impossible for the pilgrim to identify them. Forese's voice discloses 'what his countenance had suppressed'. It is like a spark rekindling Dante's whole knowledge, and the poet recognizes his interlocutor's face:

> ed ecco del profondo de la testa
> volse a me li occhi un'ombra e guardò fiso;
> poi gridò forte: 'Qual grazia m'è questa?'
>   Mai non l'avrei riconosciuto al viso;
> ma ne la voce sua mi fu palese
> ciò che l'aspetto in sé avea conquiso.
>   Questa favilla tutta mi raccese
> mia conoscenza a la cangiata labbia,
> e ravvisai la faccia di Forese.   (*Purgatorio* XXIII, 40–8)

Here, then, the shade's voice is the seed and the 'sign' ('favilla') from which anagnorisis springs, and anagnorisis itself appears as a sudden illumination, a wholesome flame kindled by a spark. Once more, this is an image that conveys excitement and joy. At its centre stands the key word – 'conoscenza' – with all the overtones which Dante's 'mind in love' carries with it.

The same word marks the climax of the recognition scene between Dante and Brunetto in *Inferno* XV.[15] If one compares the two episodes, however, the nature of the difference between anagnorisis in Hell and Purgatory becomes immediately evident. Brunetto is less disfigured than Forese, but in Hell Dante's face, as we know from *Purgatorio* I (95–9), is dirty from the 'sucidume' of the place, and his eyes are dimmed by 'mist'. When the crowd of sinners against Nature approach Dante and Virgil across the expanse of sand under the broad flakes of falling fire, they look at the two poets 'as men look at one another under a new moon at dusk' and then 'knit their brows as the old tailor does at the eye of his needle' (*Inferno* xv, 18–21). Uncertainty, difficulty, painful efforts are the characteristics of sight in Hell. The first simile Dante employs here ('come suol da sera guardare uno altro sotto nova luna') conflates two passages from *Aeneid* vi, the first of which describes the scenery of Dis and the dark landscape through which Aeneas and the Sibyl are now walking:

> Ibant obscuri sola sub nocte per umbram
> perque domos Ditis vacuas et inania regna:
> quale per incertam lunam sub luce maligna
> est iter in silvis, ubi caelum condidit umbra
> Iuppiter et rebus nox abstulit atra colorem.

> (Obscure they went through dreary shades, that led
> Along the waste dominions of the dead.
> Thus wander travellers in woods by night,
> By the moon's doubtful and malignant light,
> When Jove in dusky clouds involves the skies,
> And the faint crescent shoots by fits before their eyes.)[16]

The second, significantly enough, marks the moment of the hero's recognition of Dido:

> Quam Troius heros
> ut primum iuxta stetit adgnovitque per umbras
> obscuram, qualem primo qui surgere mense
> aut videt aut vidisse putat per nubila lunam

> (Whom when the Trojan hero hardly knew,
> Obscure in shades, and with a doubtful view
> [Doubtful as he who sees, through dusky night,
> Or thinks he sees, the moon's uncertain light].)[17]

As we shall again see, Virgilian echoes and Virgil's own presence signal the high points of recognition throughout the *Comedy*. Agonizingly and uncertainly 'eyed' by the entire group ('famiglia') under the rain of fire, Dante is then recognized ('conosciuto') by one of the spirits, who takes him by the hem of his cloak and cries, 'Qual maraviglia!' We pass from a general view to an individual one, from vision to recognition, to wonder, and to a familiar gesture which indicates a desperate effort at establishing, or re-establishing, human contact. Surprised by that arm which is reaching out for him, Dante fixes his eyes on the man's scorched face. In spite of the 'cotto aspetto', knowledge and recognition are full, but not immediate:

> E io, quando 'l suo braccio a me distese,
> ficcai li occhi per lo cotto aspetto,
> sí che 'l viso abbrusciato non difese
> la conoscenza sua al mio 'ntelletto   (*Inferno* xv, 25–8)

Like the tailor through the eye of his needle, Dante has to look hard before he sees, and his lines give us the impression that he must twice peer through 'scorched face' and 'viso abbrusciato' so that his 'intellect' might pierce that 'defence' and obtain 'conosoenza'. The full realization of his interlocutor's identity is not instantaneous, but in fact a slow 'intellectual' process which comes to completion only with the pilgrim's final gesture and his words:

> e chinando la mano a la sua faccia,
> rispuosi: 'Siete voi qui, ser Brunetto?' (29–30)

Like Brunetto before him, Dante tries to establish physical contact with his interlocutor. By reaching down his hand towards his face, however, he shows not only a human reaction of affection and pity, but also one of uncertainty, as if he were attempting to prove through touch the intellectual knowledge he has obtained through sight.

Profoundly different as the two recognition scenes are – and the essence of this difference may be seen in the exclamations of the two souls, 'Qual maraviglia!' and 'Qual grazia m'è questa?' – they have at least one element in common, which is shared also by the episodes of Judge Nino and Oderisi da Gubbio: the total attention of Dante's poetry to the face and particularly to the eyes of his actors. As in Giotto's frescoes, the 'ficcarsi' and 'fissarsi' of eye into eye is a continuously repeated motion, or rather the coming of that motion to a standstill in a concentrated instant. It is one of the two central mechanisms employed by Dante in his recognition scenes – anagnorisis 'by means of the eyes'. Nor is this by chance, for 'occhio', the most frequent noun in the poem, represents an essential dimension of the *Comedy* (that of 'vision') and indicates the main organ through which Dante can satisfy his ever present desire to know. Furthermore, it is in the visage of man that the 'last *potentia* of matter comes into *actus*'; and the 'anima' operates most intensely in two parts of a human face – mouth and eyes, where 'almost all the three natures of the soul [vegetative, sensitive and intellective] dominate'.[18]

In *Inferno* xxix, after the beautifully indirect and incomplete recognition scene between Dante and Geri del Bello (1–36), the poets meet the falsifiers. One of them, Capocchio, a notorious counterfeiter of metals, pictures and men – in fact an excellent 'ape of Nature' – asks Dante to 'sharpen' his eyes towards him so as to recognize his now leprous face:

> Ma perché sappi chi sí ti seconda
> contra i Sanesi, aguzza ver' me l'occhio,
> sí che la faccia mia ben ti risponda:
> sí vedrai ch'io son l'ombra di Capocchio,
> che falsai li metalli con l'alchímia;
> e te dee ricordar, se ben t'adocchio,
> com'io fui di natura buona scimia. (133–9)

In Hell, no 'imitation' will hold, and the true nature of a man will be open to acute sight. For, as Dante repeats in an apparently mere aside towards the end of *Purgatorio* xxi (111), it is

> ne li occhi ove 'l sembiante più si ficca.

When the enquiring eyes of a human being are fixed without impediment on the eyes of another, they acquire a knowledge which is not mere recognition of an identity, but penetration into the soul, the very essence of their interlocutor. Such is the intensity and directness of Dantean anagnorisis that it can do without signs, memory or reasoning.

The line I have just quoted from *Purgatorio* xxi belongs to one of the most famous episodes of the entire *Comedy*, that in which the soul of Statius, having expiated his sin of excessive prodigality and his 'tepidezza' in showing himself a Christian, is free from Purgatory and enabled to ascend to Paradise.[19] With the encounter between Virgil, Dante and Statius we enter a realm where 'recognition' must be understood in at least two unusual acceptions – as 'agnitio' or 'acknowledgement' of poets, and as epiphany.

Statius, Dante and Virgil have never met before and therefore, strictly speaking and according to all medieval authorities,[20] cannot 'recognize' each other. Yet apart from the fact (which Dante would have known only if he had read William of Moerbeke's translation of the *Poetics*) that 'anagnorisis' primarily means not 're-cognition', but a shift

154

from ignorance to knowledge,[21] there is a deeper sense in which this episode can be called a recognition scene. The pattern has been set by the encounter between Virgil and Dante at the beginning of the poem, and is repeated in *Purgatorio* VI–VII in the meeting between Virgil, Dante and Sordello. It is a pattern which revolves around Virgil, with the pilgrim playing the role of spectator or deuteragonist, and Dante the writer that of stage director.

The fact is that Dante, Sordello and Statius do know Virgil before they meet him. And who would not know the great shade of Western poetry and wisdom, which even our non-classicizing century makes the protagonist of a splendid 'novel', Hermann Broch's *Death of Virgil*? To find Virgil in the other world, to have him recognized three times, is the supreme dramatization and personalization of a culture that questions and celebrates itself. Virgil himself, though setting the example, had been less daring. In his Dis, Aeneas does not encounter Homer (Aeneas is not, of course, the poetic persona of Publius Vergilius Maro), but only the remote Ur-poets, the 'Poetae theologi' Orpheus and Musaeus, symbols of religion as much as of poetry.[22] And Aristophanes, who in his *Frogs* has Dionysus himself, the god of tragedy, descend to Hades and there be present at the contest between Aeschylus and Euripides, stages no recognition scene in that play. Anagnorisis of poets in the other world is in fact a Dantean invention.

Here, then, is medieval poetry coming face to face with antiquity —the troubadour Sordello meeting Virgil in Antepurgatory. Looking around like a lion 'quando si posa', slow, solemn, full of dignity, Sordello answers Virgil's enquiry about the best way up the mountain by asking the two travellers from what country they come. And the name of Mantua is enough to prompt self-revelation and an embrace between the two shades:

> e 'l dolce duca incominciava
> 'Mantua . . .', e l'ombra, tutta in sé romita,
>   surse ver' lui del loco ove pria stava,
>   dicendo: 'O Mantoano, io son Sordello
>   de la tua terra!'; e l'un l'altro abbracciava.
>
> (*Purgatorio* VI, 71–5)

After Dante's invective against Italy, the emperor and Florence, which occupies the remainder of canto VI, the scene resumes at the beginning of the following canto, when Sordello asks his interlocutors who they are. Dante answers not a word, but leaves the stage to Virgil: 'Io son

Virgilio' (7). The words are as direct and simple as Aeneas' 'Sum pius Aeneas' (I, 378) and Odysseus' 'I am Odysseus, son of Laertes' (XI, 19). Sordello's reaction, however, is very different from those of Venus in the *Aeneid* and of the Phaeacians in the *Odyssey*. It rather resembles that of the apostles at Jesus' 'ego sum' after the resurrection.[23] What Sordello sees before him now is a miracle, and he is uncertain whether in his wonder he should 'believe' it or not. Then, he signals his acceptance by lowering his eyes and turning to Virgil in humility, bowing to embrace him and immediately afterwards greeting him with a true 'Gloria', which significantly ends with the words, 'what merit or what grace shows you to me?':

> 'O gloria di Latin', disse, 'per cui
> mostrò ciò che potea la lingua nostra,
> o pregio etterno del loco ond'io fui,
> qual merito o qual grazia mi ti mostra?
>
> (*Purgatorio* VII, 16–19)

The words, as Eliot said in another recognition scene derived from Dante, 'suffice . . . to compel the recognition they precede'.[24] A sacral aura pervades this second part of the episode. Anagnorisis takes place in the atmosphere of epiphany. Sordello looks like a man who suddenly sees something before him, wonders at it, believes and at the same time distrusts it:

> Qual è colui che cosa innanzi sé
> súbita vede ond'e' si maraviglia,
> che crede e non, dicendo 'Ella è . . . non è . . .',
> tal parve quelli   (10–13)

The numinous, indeed divine quality of the Virgil–Sordello revelation increases when Statius appears on the scene later in the *Purgatorio*. When the episode begins, in canto XX, a sudden earthquake announces a crucial event. If we were unwilling to associate this with the earthquake that made Jerusalem tremble at Jesus' death,[25] Dante himself compares it to the convulsions of the surface of the island of Delos just before Latona gave birth there to Apollo and Diana, the two 'eyes of the sky', sun and moon (XX, 130–3). And if this pagan Nativity is still not enough, here is a general singing of 'Gloria in excelsis Deo', and here are Virgil and Dante 'immobili e sospesi' 'like the shepherds who first heard that song' (XX, 136–41), transporting us to the familiar account of Christmas.[26] From this proclamation of an event unique in human history Dante (obviously immersed here in the epiphanies of

Luke's Gospel) brings us to the end of that salvation story by comparing the appearance of a 'shade' to one of the most startling and beautiful of the so-called post-resurrectional appearances, that of Jesus to the two disciples on the road to Emmaus:[27]

> Ed ecco, sí come ne scrive Luca
> che Cristo apparve a' due ch'erano in via,
> già surto fuor de la sepulcral buca,
> ci apparve un'ombra   (*Purgatorio* XXI, 7–10)

Thus the 'ombra', 'born' like Jesus, resurrects like him 'out of the sepulchral hole' and as suddenly and mysteriously materializes before the two travellers, following them (and 'who', writes Eliot in *The Waste Land*, 'is the third who walks always beside you?') while they, unawares, watch the crowd that lies at their feet. The words of greeting spoken by the shade, similarly Christ-like and post-resurrectional ('Pax vobiscum')[28], make Dante and Virgil suddenly turn, the latter replying with the appropriate salutation in words ('Et cum spirito tuo') or gesture ('cenno') and immediately adding:

> Nel beato concilio
> ti ponga in pace la verace corte
> che me rilega ne l'etterno essilio.   (16–18)

(May the true court which binds me in the eternal exile bring you in peace to the assembly of the blest.)

It is with this greeting, which highlights Virgil's strong feeling of the contrast between his own 'eternal exile' and the shade's ultimate belonging to the 'blessed council' that the play begins. It will unfold in five movements or sections of dialogue,[29] with the third, a true central 'act', constituting the climax. The prologue which I have just examined, and the first scene, are a 'divine comedy'. The play becomes more and more human in the following stages. We begin with the Nativity, the Resurrection, a soul's liberation from Purgatory and ascension to Paradise (from XX, 124 to XXI, 72). Then, with Statius' revelation of his identity, we go back to earth to learn about the early stage of his life (XXI, 73–102). We return to Purgatory in the central act, the recognition scene proper (XXI, 103–36). We descend to Limbo in the first part of the fourth section, to pass once more to earth for Statius' story of the second stage of his life (XXII, 1–54). In the fifth and final movement we follow the third stage of Statius' life in the world of the living and are then plunged again into the first circle of the 'blind prison' (XXII, 55–114). A short, but significant pause ensues; then the ascent up Purgatory's mountain resumes.

In the first movement of this extraordinary play, the as yet unknown spirit shows himself astonished at Virgil's declaration. If you are shades whom God forbids from entering His kingdom, he asks, who has brought you so high up the mountain? (XXI, 19–21). Virgil's reply describes, as usual, the purpose of Dante's journey through the other world and his own role as guide. Thus, it is with Dante's ascent that our play opens, and with a rather elaborate indication that this is being done before death, in the living body (25–7); we are also reminded that the pilgrim's soul is the spirit's 'sister' (28) – a reminder of common immortality and perhaps a foretaste of the community of poetry that is soon going to be revealed.

Virgil's first question, rather surprisingly, does not concern the spirit's name, but the earthquake which he and Dante have witnessed and which, the poet tells us,[30] has been the source of his intellectual 'thirst' and curiosity ever since. The mysterious epiphany has made us expect the revelation of the shade's identity. Dante delays it, thus keeping up suspense; but by having his persona's extreme desire for knowledge satisfied first, he implicitly explains precisely why the preceding events are epiphanic – that is, why they are visible signs which 'manifest' something of higher import. To cut the spirit's long explanation short, the cause of the earthquake is entirely super-natural[31] – such a phenomenon takes place whenever a soul has completed its term of purification and 'feels' it can ascend to Paradise (XXI, 40–72).

The very first sentence uttered by Statius contains, probably, an indirect compliment to Virgil: the 'religione de la montagna' (41–2) sounds like an echo of the Aeneid's 'religio . . . loci' (VIII, 349). But in the second movement of the play, when the spirit finally reveals his name, the presence of Virgil acquires a new, more substantial, dimension. For what we are told now is not only that this is Statius, that his fame in the world was that which most endures and gives honour – the name of poet – and that he wrote the Thebaid and the Achilleid, but also that the seeds for his poetic 'ardour' were planted by the sparks of a divine flame, the Aeneid, 'mother' and 'nurse' of his poetry. Indeed Statius would gladly pay with an extra year of Purgatory for having lived at the time of Virgil:

Al mio ardor fuor seme le faville,
che mi scaldar, de la divina fiamma

onde sono allumati più di mille;
de l'Eneida dico, la qual mamma
fummi, e fummi nutrice, poetando:
sanz'essa non fermai peso di dramma.
E per esser vivuto di là quando
visse Virgilio, assentirei un sole
più che non deggio al mio uscir di bando. (94–102)

There is a clear echo of *Inferno* I and of Dante's own acknowledgement of Virgil as supreme master and author, but with the difference that if Dante, there, recognizes the Latin poet as the 'only' one from whom he has learnt the 'bello stilo', he goes on throughout the *Comedy* to pay his respects to various 'fathers' and masters, from Brunetto Latini to Guido Guinizelli, whereas Statius' poetic and moral life is presented here as entirely dominated by Virgil, and Virgil alone.

Statius' last words trigger off the third and central act of the play. Once more, literary history becomes drama. For the author of the *Aeneid* is present, and anagnorisis cannot be delayed any longer. To enact it, the poet sets a scene in which a man and his smile stand at the centre: it is the medieval poet who acts as intermediary between the two classics, who 'invents' his own tradition. Virgil turns to Dante with a mute expression which orders him to keep silent. But 'smiling and crying are so tied to the emotion that produces them that they cannot be controlled by the will'. Dante smiles, as if he were winking. Statius falls silent, looks at his interlocutor 'ne li occhi ove 'l sembiante più si ficca', and asks him why a smile has flashed across his face. Dante, caught between the opposing desires of Virgil and Statius, utters a sigh. Virgil understands him and allows him to tell the truth. And Dante opens his mouth to unveil the great wonder:

Questi che guida in alto li occhi miei,
è quel Virgilio dal qual tu togliesti
forte a cantar de li uomini e d'i' dèi. (124–6)

(This one who guides my eyes on high is that Virgil from whom you derived the strength to sing of men and of the gods.)

Statius says not a word, but bows down to embrace Virgil's feet. The master, however, stops him:

Già s'inchinava ad abbracciar li piedi
al mio dottor, ma el li disse: 'Frate,
non far, ché tu se' ombra e ombra vedi'.

159

> Ed ei surgendo: 'Or puoi la quantitate
> comprender de l'amor ch'a te mi scalda,
> quando'io dismento nostra vanitate,
> trattando l'ombre come cosa salda'. (130–6)

(Already he was stooping to embrace my teacher's feet; but he said to him, 'Brother, do not so, for you are a shade and a shade you see'. And he, rising, 'Now you may comprehend the measure of the love that burns in me for you, when I forget our emptiness and treat shades as solid things.)

In the first part of this scene, the divine comedy of epiphany has definitively become human. Dante smiles here for the second time in the poem.[32] We must remember that according to his own, as he thought, Aristotelian conception laughter is an exclusively and distinguishing human phenomenon.[33] The smile that irrepressibly surfaces on his lips at Statius' words is an 'ammicco' – a wink, a nod, in a short a 'sign' – which puzzles his interlocutor and makes him ask the crucial question. In other words, what we have here is a sort of Dantean version of Aristotle's anagnorisis by means of signs: one, though, in which the *sēmeion* acts not as proof, but as signifier of something which is ultimately impenetrable to other men. This is neither an 'external' nor a 'bodily' sign, neither an 'inherited' one like a birthmark nor an 'acquired' one like a scar, but rather, as Dante tells us while using it, the inevitable 'follower' of the emotion from which it comes or, as he says in the *Convivio* (III viii 11), a 'flashing' or 'sparkling'[34] of the soul's pleasure, 'that is to say, a light showing outside what is inside'. Hence, Statius' look probes Dante's very soul by questioning his eyes, where the outer expression of the inner feeling, the 'sembiante', is 'most fixed'.

Once more, therefore, when we read this scene in which the action consists of a smile in the middle of a continuous exchange of glances, we penetrate into a man's innermost essence – here, interestingly, the root of his pleasure. The 'dilettazione' of the soul which Dante's smile betrays[35] remains, for a few moments, enigmatic to Statius. Virgil, of course, knows its cause and so, undoubtedly, do the readers. It is with our recognition that Dante has been playing throughout the episode,[36] devising an inexorable, clockwork 'comic' mechanism which we cannot escape and the successive stages of which we ask ourselves about in anticipation, then follow with attention and increasing wonder, and finally accept with a smile of pleasure. Dante's delight becomes ours. When the enigma is explained to Statius – 'This is

Virgil', and the cause of my smile was what you said about him (124–9) – what comes into full light is not only Statius' passage from ignorance to knowledge, his anagnorisis, nor simply that Dante's pleasure lay in the expectation of that revelation, but also our realization that Dante the poet has manoeuvred Dante the character in such a way as to make that recognition inevitable and coinciding with our knowledge, to make Statius' acquisition of knowledge a 'shock' or *ekplēxis* to him and to us, thereby producing a feeling of pleasure. We understand, in the end, why Aristotle says that the pleasure of mimesis, and hence of all poetry, lies in recognition,[37] and why the Greek words for 'reading' – *anagignōskein* and *anagnōsis* – are so close to 'anagnorisis'.

Of this *Freude am Wiedererkennen* (as Freud describes it in an essay on the theme)[38] we are apparently shown no trace in Statius himself. He, who has found again someone indeed familiar, his mother's and nurse's father, neither smiles nor speaks nor looks around with the wonder Dante anticipated (121–3). These are feelings Dante the poet projects on Statius through Dante the character. Statius' movement in stooping down to clasp Virgil's feet expresses recognition in the form of worship. The 'flame', 'ardour', and warmth that characterize the Statius–Virgil relationship are no longer just filial feelings; they have become veneration. And, like the angel in Revelation,[39] Virgil rescues Statius from idolatry by reminding him of their brotherhood in being shades. Until now, the living body of Dante has physically dominated the stage, while Virgil is celebrated. Suddenly, Virgil himself brings us back to the other world, to the 'non omo, omo già fui' of *Inferno* I, and proposes a deeper, sobering, and sombre recognition:

> Frate,
> non far, ché tu se' ombra e ombra vedi.

Rising from the ground, Statius accepts this truth in his answer, but the four lines with which he concludes the canto go beyond the present situation and, in one extraordinary leap, reach the kernel itself of the *Divine Comedy*, where a poet's love for other poets and for poetry makes him forget their emptiness and treat shades as solid things. With this meta-poetic recognition in which humility and exaltation are perfectly balanced (and with which T.S. Eliot inagurated modern poetry in his *Prufrock*) the canto ends.

The play, however, continues in canto XXII with a persistent oscillation between shades and solid things. Virgil acknowledges Statius' love and declares he has known it ever since Juvenal descended to Limbo and told him about it (XXII, 10–18) – another dramatization of literary relationships. Immediately afterwards, we return to the past and to earth to learn more of Statius' life, and we discover that his entire existence has been a Virgilian itinerary. The *Aeneid* was his mother and nurse in poetry, two lines of *Aeneid* III made him repent of his prodigality (XXII, 37–45), and Eclogue IV showed him the way to the Christian God (XXII, 64–75). Virgil is poet, 'famous sage', and prophet. Yet, and this is the tragedy Dante makes us experience while presenting to us a sublime comedy, Virgil is condemned to Limbo whereas Statius is saved.

As Statius' own account of his life reaches its culminating point, his conversion to Christianity, his attention significantly turns to the community of classical poetry. 'Tell me', he asks Virgil, 'where are our ancient Terence, Caecilius (Statius), Plautus and Varius, if you know; tell me if they are damned, and in which circle' (97–9). The 'ubi sunt' motif is transformed – shades or not, these poets seem to be more 'solid' in Statius' mind than anything else. With Virgil's answer we do not merely return to Limbo; we review classical tradition from Homer (101–2) to Euripides and Simonides, from Virgil himself to Persius, to the writers Statius is enquiring about, and finally to the mythological characters of Statius' own poems (100–14). The mountain of Purgatory, with the miraculous quaking of which the episode began, seems to be forgotten. Before us rises in its stead, twice evoked by the Latin poets (65, 104–5), Mount Parnassus. Its 'suckling', 'nursing', and 'thirst-quenching' function (102, 105, 65) occupies the inhabitants of Limbo (104) as well as the travellers here in Purgatory, where Virgil and Statius continue their conversation while Dante, walking behind them, listens to their 'sermoni' from which, as if drinking in the caves of Parnassus, he acquires further comprehension of the art of poetry – 'ch'a poetar mi davano intelletto' (129). And if one needs an example of recognition as interpretation, it will be enough to compare lines 128–9 of *Purgatorio* XXII with their model in Psalm 118[40] to understand that for Dante the two poets' speeches are as illuminating to the apprentice of poetry as, for the Psalmist, the words of God's revelation are to the intellect of the simple.

Anagnorisis of poetic masters takes place within an epiphany and has a reflective and reflexive quality – perhaps Joyce's 'Stephen Hero' learnt it from Dante as well as from Thomas Aquinas. When, shortly afterwards, Dante meets his true 'father' in the Stilnovo, Guido Guinizelli, in a recognition scene which is not described, but which is significantly compared through simile to an episode of Statius' *Thebaid* (v, 715–30), he looks 'pensively' at his interlocutor for a while without speaking or indeed hearing (xxvi, 94–105). We have no way of judging precisely which thoughts are revolving in Dante's mind at this point, but we can be sure that they regard vernacular poets and poetry as well as other matters, for the entire passage is a dramatization of Dante's meditations on that topic. In it, as well as in *Purgatorio* xxiv, a 'modern' school emerges to complement the ancient one of Limbo and *Purgatorio* xxii and to complete Oderisi's hints in canto xi.

As he ascends the purgatorial mountain, Dante moves backwards through his past poetic identities to find and renew his roots in a great sequence of self-recognition, the only modern equivalent of which is Stephen's in Joyce's *Portrait of an Artist*.

The climax of this movement is reached in *Purgatorio* xxx with the disappearance of Virgil and the triumph of Beatrice, a scene where 'peripeteia', 'pathos', and anagnorisis combine with epiphany to produce, as Dante had announced in the *Vita Nuova* (xlii, 2), 'what had never been said of any other woman before'. Jorge Luis Borges once wrote that Dante 'built the triple architecture of his poem in order to insert this encounter into it'.[41] There is some exaggeration in this pronouncement, but also a profound truth, for this meeting constitutes the ideal climax of a human and poetic story, joins together Dante's past and present, prepares him for the future and, on the allegorical level, replaces Reason (Virgil) with Wisdom or Theology (Beatrice), cleanses the pilgrim entirely from sin and finally launches him towards the ultimate end of his journey: the knowledge of God.

It would be impossible and inappropriate to take all these elements into account here.[42] I shall therefore analyse this episode only as a recognition scene. A preliminary observation seems to me opportune. There is only one passage in the whole of Western literature that can compare with this in intensity as well as general theme: that in which Penelope and Odysseus face each other in the hall of their palace after twenty years. As soon as one says this, however, one realizes the fundamental difference between the two episodes. In the *Odyssey*, where the hero is constantly called *dios* and protected by the supernatural power of Athena, the encounter is a totally and sublimely human affair; in the *Comedy* the beginning and end of the scene are surrounded by a divine aura. Beatrice appears to Dante on a chariot at the end of a solemn, allegorical procession. Her arrival is greeted by Latin invocations from the Song of Songs, from the Gospels and the liturgy, and, as we should by now expect, from the *Aeneid*,[43] while the scenery is compared to the resurrection of the blessed at Doomsday (13–18). The rosy-fingered dawn that Athena prevents from breaking upon the love-making and story-telling of Odysseus and Penelope shines here in a simile,[44] where the sun veiled by vapour stands for Beatrice surrounded by a cloud of flowers:

> Io vidi già nel cominciar del giorno
> la parte orïental tutta rosata,
> e l'altro ciel di bel sereno addorno;
> e la faccia del sol nascere ombrata,
> sì che per temperanza di vapori
> l'occhio la sostenea lunga fïata:
> così dentro una nuvola di fiori
> che da le mani angeliche saliva
> e ricadeva in giù dentro e di fori (22–30)

(Sometimes I have seen at the beginning of the day the eastern region all rosy, while the rest of the heaven was adorned with fair clear sky, and the face of the sun rise shaded, so that through the tempering of vapours the eye sustained it a long while: so within a cloud of flowers, which rose from the angelic hands and fell down again within and without.)

At last a Lady (not, we notice, a shade, nor yet a light) appears, 'olive-crowned over a white veil' and 'clad, under a green mantle, in colour of living flame'.[45] She wears the wreath of wisdom and the colours of faith, hope and charity, but she is also, unmistakably, the 'donna' of the *Vita Nuova*.[46] To the unforgettable experience of his adolescence Dante now leads us back, as he will again at the end of the canto (115–45) and in the following one, where his 'vita nova' will be revisited with a new consciousness.[47] The 'theophany' with which the scene opened becomes 'recherche du temps perdu' and at the same time anagnorisis.

When she sees her husband after the slaying of the Suitors, Penelope looks at him both knowing and not recognizing Odysseus (XXIII, 94–5). When Pierre Bezuhov returns to Moscow and to Natasha at the end of *War and Peace*, he does not recognize his beloved 'because of the immense change in her' and above all because there is no trace of the old smile in her eyes.[48] It is this phenomenon that Proust describes with marvellous precision and insight towards the end of *Time Regained*, when Marcel fails to recognize his old friends during the 'Matinée' at the Guermantes:

For to 'recognise' someone, and, *a fortiori*, to learn someone's identity after having failed to recognise him, is to predicate two contradictory things of a single subject, it is to admit that what was here, the person whom one remembers, no longer exists, and also that what is now here is a person whom one did not know to exist; and to do this we have to apprehend a mystery almost as disturbing as that of death, of which it is, indeed, as it were the preface and the harbinger.[49]

Dante overcomes this terrible contradiction with a magnificent leap. He does not recognize Beatrice, but himself and his old love for her. Before having visual cognition of her, his soul feels the same wonder, trembling, and crush it used to feel in adolescence:[50]

> E lo spirito mio, che già cotanto
> tempo era stato ch'a la sua presenza
> non era di stupor, tremando, affranto,
> sanza de li occhi aver più conoscenza,
> per occulta virtù che da lei mosse,
> d'antico amor sentì la gran potenza.   (34–9)

(And my spirit, which now for so long a time trembling with awe in her presence had not been overcome, without having more knowledge by the eyes, through occult virtue that proceeded from her, felt old love's great power.)

Recognition is instantaneous (though syntactically delayed as much as in the cases of Brunetto and Forese) because, as Borges says, 'for Dante Beatrice existed infinitely'.[51] Time has elapsed, but it does not have to be regained. Beatrice's presence is enough to join past and present without the help of memory, for the 'signs' of anagnorisis are inner motions which the character knows as he knows himself. Those 'signs' come to life again, ten years after Beatrice's death, resurrected by a 'power' that moves from her. The mystery Proust speaks of is present here, too, the 'virtue' which flows from the Lady being hidden; it is not, however, the mystery that prefaces death, but that of love's might, which radiates in the world and transfixes human beings.[52]

The indelible mark left on the heart by this power replaces all external signs. In order to recognize Odysseus, Penelope must ask him to reveal the 'secret sign' of their bed. In Dante, this has become 'occulta virtù'. And if, as Singleton says,[53] 'recognition "by occult virtue" is common enough in medieval narrative', it is Dante alone that transforms it into an 'earthquake' of his heart. When the 'occulta virtù' becomes 'lofty' through visual power – when it openly explodes – recognition is completed:

> Tosto che ne la vista mi percosse
> l'alta virtù che già m'avea trafitto
> prima ch'io fuor di puerizia fosse   (40–2)

(As soon as on my sight the lofty virtue smote that had already pierced me before I was out of my boyhood)

Yet, significantly, Dante does not say that he recognized Beatrice, and this is what makes his scene so different, for instance, from the parallel one in *Pearl*. In the English poem, the protagonist sees, beyond the marvellous river, 'a crystal clyffe ful relusaunt' from which spring rays of splendour. A child-maiden sits by the rock, gleaming in her white mantle. The protagonist recognizes her immediately and tells us so:

> I knew hyr wel, I hade sen hyr ere.
> As glysnande golde þat man con schere,
> So schon þat schene anvnder schore.
> On lenghe I loked to hyr þere;
> On lenghe I knew hyr more and more.

Dante, on the other hand, turns to Virgil, and to him he quotes – paying a supreme compliment to his master and guide – the line of the *Aeneid*[55] in which Dido reveals to her sister Anna that she now feels for Aeneas the same passion she felt for her husband:

> Adgnosco veteris vestigia flammae
> conosco i segni de l'antica fiamma

Dante does not recognize Beatrice, but the tokens of his old love for her. He feels the 'gran potenza', then voices it, transforming it into an 'ancient flame'. A few instants earlier, Beatrice appeared as if bathed in the colour of charity, of a 'living flame'. When Dante feels and then recognizes in himself the signs of the ancient flame, both images ('fiamma viva' and 'antica fiamma') acquire new poignancy, opposing, as it were, and completing each other beyond time, suspended between old love and present charity, between sight and inner feeling, appearance and recognition. And if in the utterance of this recognition we can hear a distant echo of the 'fiamma antica' which envelops Dante's Ulysses,[56] the Virgilian quotation at once undoubtedly evokes love for the 'divina fiamma' of *Purgatorio* XXI: the *Aeneid*. Compared to this line, pronounced in Beatrice's presence and addressed to its own source (Virgil), even the cry of Racine's Phèdre – 'Je reconnus Vénus et ses feux redoutables'[57] – nearly pales into pompous insignificance.

Beatrice is surprisingly remote from the pilgrim's consciousness, and his exclamation is addressed to Virgil. And suddenly, the realization that Virgil is no longer there breaks into Dante's awareness and interrupts the anagnorisis with 'pathos' and 'peripeteia'. As unexpectedly as the shade of the 'dolcissimo padre' had appeared in the dark wood, so has it now faded away, as it were 'on the crowing of the cock'. At the 'trumpet to the morn' sounded by Beatrice's dawn epiphany, Virgil silently 'hies to his confine', and Dante inconsolably weeps:

> Ma Virgilio n'avea lasciati scemi
>   di sé, Virgilio dolcissimo patre,
>   Virgilio a cui per mia salute die'mi;
> né quantunque perdeo l'antica matre,
>   valse a le guance nette di rugiada
>   che, lagrimando, non tornasser atre. (49–54)

(But Virgil had left us bereft of himself, Virgil sweetest father, Virgil to whom I gave myself for my salvation; nor did all that our ancient mother lost keep my dew-washed cheeks from turning dark again with tears.)

Shades have indeed become solid things . . . and irremediably returned to their 'emptiness'. As anagnorisis progresses to the recovery of the past and towards the ultimate acquisition of divine knowledge, a human loss has thus made itself felt.

There is no joy in Dante's recognition of Beatrice. His reaction is one of fear and distress (45), of being 'affranto' (broken and overpowered) by the appearance of his long lost Lady. Once more, the movement is different in *Pearl*, where a gladdening exultation precedes the protagonist's confusion, amazement, and fear (169–84). When Beatrice finally addresses the pilgrim, he sees her as an admiral (58), a stern royal figure (70), and a harsh mother (79–80). Nor is recognition completed here. Dante sees Beatrice's eyes turning to him, but cannot distinguish her fully under the veil (67–9). Only her own words finally declare her identity:

> Guardaci ben! Ben son, ben son Beatrice.

In *Sir Orfeo*, as we have seen in chapter 5, Orfeo and Heurodis recognize each other at once and face each other, like Odysseus and Penelope, in total silence. They can do so because they are equals, and their temporary reunion is the sublime meeting of two human beings. Beatrice, on the other hand, is both human and trans-human. She is the poetic incarnation of a divine virtue and the embodiment not only of Dante's memory and love, but also of his conscience. To recognize her is both an overwhelming joy and a painful tragedy, because it means sounding one's innermost errors.

Dante, however, surprises us once more. Another anagnorisis has already struck the reader. The Everyman pilgrim of Hell and Purgatory, the nameless narrator of *Inferno* and *Purgatorio* is called 'Dante' for the first and last time in the poem (55); and the sound of this name which, he says, 'of necessity is registered here', as if wedged between those of Virgil and Beatrice, has a curiously moving effect on readers who have known it all along. His signature, inserted with humility by a writer who will call his poem 'sacred', makes us rediscover, with Yeats' *Hic*, that this

> chief imagination of Christendom,
> Dante Alighieri, so utterly found himself
> That he has made that hollow face of his
> More plain to the mind's eye than any face
> But that of Christ.[58]

His and our recognition of this human personality and poetic imagination at precisely the moment when he finds 'the most exalted lady loved by man' shows that Dante, alone perhaps of all poets, has gone through the 'tragic war' in the flesh and found happiness after it. For the drama of anagnorisis which I have tried to trace throughout the *Inferno* and the *Purgatorio* culminates in canto XXXI of the second cantica with Dante's contrition and confession, a supreme act of Christian self-recognition (66, 88), which makes him finally recognize Beatrice with infinite joy and, in her, with her and through her, see for the first time a 'splendour of living light eternal' which radiates through the air and which no poet will ever be able to describe:

> O isplendor di viva luce etterna,
> chi palido si fece sotto l'ombra
> sí di Parnaso, o bevve in sua cisterna,
>   che non paresse aver la mente ingombra,
> tentando a render te qual tu paresti
> là dove armonizzando il ciel t'adombra,
>   quando ne l'aere aperto ti solvesti?

> (O splendour of the live eternal light,
> Who is there who has grown pale under the shade
> Of Mount Parnassus, or has drunk from its basins,

Who would not find that his mind was encumbered,
Trying to render you as you appeared
When you showed yourself openly in the air

Where heaven in its harmony adumbrates you.)[59]

For the first time in the poem, full recognition is explicitly ineffable. Yet the way in which Dante uses the inexpressibility topos points to the constant tensions that characterize his struggle for the sublime. Sublimity does not simply derive from the subject matter of a poem: the equation between supreme mysteries and the sublime is reductive. Nor is sublimity merely a question of style. As we shall see in the last chapter of this book, Dante's sublime is a more complex phenomenon – it is the technique by which the poet makes us feel the infinity and ineffability of his scenes by describing them with words stretched to their utmost limit. Here, this tension is already present. The glorious opening of this passage is immediately contrasted with the tiring work of the poet; the splendour of living light eternal opposed, with a significant variation on the image derived from Persius,[60] to the paleness of the human writer. And Mount Parnassus, in the 'caves' of which Statius drank, prompted by Virgil's example (XXII, 64–5), and where ancient poets dreamt of Eden (XXVIII, 139–41), appears now as a shade. The painful work of the poet becomes a vanishing pallor, an insubstantial shadow. Paradoxically, the lightness of this image is at once translated into heaviness: growing pale, the poetic mind becomes full, confused, inert, as if paralysed by its own weight. Hence, the poet only *tries* to represent that light.

Yet this poet has not just become pale in the shade of Parnassus, studying, as his present rewriting of Persius shows, 'quelli ch'anticamente poetaro'. He has also, like Statius, drunk fully from its 'cistern', imbibing the very essence of inspiration with the holy water of the Muses. He can, therefore, look at the living light and, albeit indirectly, express it in words. In the next movement of the passage the object itself of the epiphany, the 'second beauty' disclosed by the unveiling of Beatrice's mouth (136–8) as 'isplendor di viva luce etterna', is simultaneously reduced and dilated. For the heaven now extended over Dante, by harmonizing both with earthly paradise and with Beatrice's new 'bellezza' – with the supremely human and the incipiently divine – 'adumbrates' this splendour. The mysteriousness of line 144[61] constitutes an infallible signal of sublime tension, and this tension surfaces in 'adombra', a word that can mean 'overshadow', 'veil', 'foreshadow', 'represent', but which inevitably establishes an imaginative correspondence with the 'ombra' of Parnassus. Poetry and its objects have become such stuff as dreams are made on, and not even Dante can now treat shades as solid things.

The mirrored, glowing light of the beginning returns, then, at the end of the sequence, opening up in blinding splendour through the air. The seal of the sublime is, however, present once more. The word which indicates this full revelation, 'solvesti', is strung between two extremes: disclosure and dissolution. Thus, recognition goes beyond the boundary of human knowledge while remaining expressible by man. We are on the very threshold between these two poles. And there we are kept by the play of anagnorisis–revelation that takes place in the *Paradiso*. In the third cantica, we have to face the paradox that the higher Dante ascends through the heavens, the more human and at the same time more mysterious epiphany and knowledge become.

In *Paradiso* III, for instance, we meet with a transitional case. Piccarda Donati, Forese's sister, does not appear as a light, but still as a shade (34), although Dante's perception of her and her companions is envisaged, by means of five successive images, as something which stands on the very border between nature and myth, between reality and illusion, between 'sembianti' and their reflection in a mirror:

> Quali per vetri trasparenti e tersi,
>   o ver per acque nitide e tranquille,
>   non sì profonde che i fondi sien persi,
> tornan d'i' nostri visi le postille
>   debili sì, che perla in bianca fronte
>   non vien men forte a le nostre pupille;
> tali vid'io più facce a parlar pronte;
>   per ch'io dentro a l'error contrario corsi
>   a quel ch'accese amor tra l'omo e 'l fonte.   (10–18)

(As through smooth and transparent glass, or through clear and tranquil waters, yet not so deep that the bottom be lost, the outlines of our faces return so faint that a pearl on a white brow comes not less boldly to our eyes, so did I behold many a countenance eager to speak; wherefore I fell into the contrary error to that which kindled love between the man and the fountain.)

The 'contrary error' to that made by Narcissus is corrected by Beatrice who, smiling, points out that these are 'true substances' (29). Dante turns to the spirit who seems most eager to speak and asks her who she is. Piccarda then appeals to Dante's memory, says that her being more beautiful will not conceal her identity, and finally reveals her name:

I' fui nel mondo vergine sorella;
e se la mente tua ben sé riguarda,
non mi ti celerà l'esser più bella,
ma riconoscerai ch'i' son Piccarda   (46–9)

Once more, the mechanism of recognition is slowed down, and by the very words that produce the anagnorisis. Piccarda's speech hinges on her increased beauty and on the work of Dante's mind. Looking at itself (as if it were an unerring Narcissus), Dante's memory will re-cognize the lady. The pilgrim's reply underlines these ideas. There is, he says, 'something divine' in the spirits' wonderful aspect, and this 'transmutes' them from the images one might have had of them before. This is why Dante could not remember earlier; but now Piccarda's words help him to recall easily (58–63).

The faces of Hell were disfigured by dirt and sin. The visages of Heaven are metamorphosed by beauty. In Hell and Purgatory, Dante had to rely on his own eyes to recognize his interlocutors. Here, without self-revelation, memory is helpless: yet memory is present, and the verbal emphasis lies on the suffix 're' of 'ri-guarda', 'ri-conoscerai', 'rimembrar', 'raffigurar'. Human and divine meet in reflexive anamnesis.

By the time we reach King Charles Martel in *Paradiso* VIII, shades have definitively given way to lights,[62] and recognition is purely a question of photo- and logo-phany. When the spirits of the third Heaven, subject to the influence of Venus, mention Dante's own canzone, 'Voi che 'ntendendo 'l terzo ciel movete', the pilgrim fixes his eyes on Beatrice as if to have her approval, and then asks 'the light which had promised so much', 'Deh, chi siete?'. The soul's 'allegrezza' increases, and the voice answers:

La mia letizia mi ti tien celato
che mi raggia dintorno e mi nasconde
quasi animal di sua seta fasciato.   (52–4)

(My joy, which rays around me, holds me concealed from you and hides me like a creature swathed in its own silk.)

Charles Martel, whose name is nowhere explicitly mentioned in the canto, relies on Dante's (and our) knowledge of historical events in order to be identified. Above all, he appeals to Dante's 'love': 'You loved me much, and had much reason for it' (55). Earthly (indeed political) passion, and earthly history are the instruments by which man can know an entity whose radiating happiness keeps it concealed.

Beatrice (the constant authenticating device), light-revelation, and the human heart constitute the very coordinates of heavenly anagnorisis.

The final threshold in this process is reached with the Cacciaguida episode in *Paradiso* xv. Here, Dante suggests a comedy more sublime than ever before. Let us look at what Aristotle would have called the 'plot'. Dante and Beatrice have reached the fifth heaven, the heaven of Mars, where they meet the spirits of those who have fought for faith. The inexpressibility topos once more signals a key event in the poem (xiv, 130–9). Brought back to the scene, we are plunged in total silence and, as if we were watching the falling of a star on a summer night, one light, looking like a flame behind alabaster, glides down towards Dante.[63] The first surprise explodes here. For this sudden appearance is compared, with a leap back to Virgil, to the way in which Anchises' 'pious' shade 'offered' itself to Aeneas in *Aeneid* vi. Virgil's Anchises, however, held out his hands to his son. The as yet unknown Cacciaguida simply 'offers himself', as if he were the Host after Consecration, to Dante's sight. Furthermore, in his simile the poet goes as far as to insinuate a doubt concerning Virgil's authority.[64] Then, the spirit pronounces a solemn Latin sentence where Anchises' address to Julius Caesar and the Sibyl's words to Aeneas are transformed by Christian overtones:[65]

> O sanguis meus, o superinfusa
> gratia Dei, sicut tibi cui
> bis unquam celi ianua reclusa?　　　　　　　　(28–30)

(O blood of mine, O lavish grace of God! To whom was Heaven's gate ever twice opened, as to thee?)

Dante fixes his eyes on the light and as usual turns to Beatrice. He is 'stupefied', for in her eyes there burns such a smile that he thinks he is reaching the 'bottom' of his 'grace' and his 'paradise'.

Clearly, this is both a re-enactment and a transformation of the Statius–Virgil recognition scene in *Purgatorio* xxi. There, however, Dante's own smile constituted the very medium of anagnorisis. Here, Beatrice's laughter is beatifying, and Dante is caught between two mysteries ('e quinci e quindi'), the spirit's words and the lady's 'riso', which plunge him into stupor. Indeed, the way to full manifestation is barred and the climax delayed longer than ever before. This is not recognition, but the mysterious *apokalypsis* of God's voice to the prophet. The spirit addresses the pilgrim with necessarily obscure, incomprehensible words (37–42), and when, forty lines later, he comes

closer to self-revelation, he speaks to Dante as if he were the Voice
thundering over Jesus at the baptism on the Jordan:

> O fronda mia in che io compiacemmi
> pur aspettando, io fui la tua radice.   (88–9)[66]

(O my branch, in whom I took delight only expecting you, I was your root.)

With this 'root' Dante goes beyond Odysseus' recognition of his mother
and Aeneas' reunion with his father to reach an ancestor in whom
human and divine are inextricably mixed. Suddenly, we understand
why in the course of his journey Dante has never encountered his real
parents even though he shows us spirits eager to be reunited with their
mothers and fathers (*Paradiso* XIV, 64–6). With a gesture which is the
symptom both of delicate affection and psychological remotion, he
stays away from Alighiero and Bella, and replaces them with Virgil,
Brunetto, Guinizelli, Beatrice, and Cacciaguida:

> Voi siete il padre mio.   (XVI, 16)

Cacciaguida is a human and trans-human Father, the exact counterpart
of Brunetto (*Inferno* XV – *Paradiso* XV), the true, sublime counterpoint
of Ugolino. For Bernardus Silvestris Anchises represents, as we have
seen, the Creator.[67] Cacciaguida, born of Mary (XV, 133) and christened
in the Baptistry of Florence consecrated to John the Baptist, is Dante's
'creator'. For he embodies Dante's past, his roots in flesh and history
(XV, 91–148; XVI), and foretells his present (the exile: XVII, 46–93) and
his future, finally anointing him as the new prophet (XVII, 124–35).

The Cacciaguida episode is sublime, then, because by allusion and
polysemy it makes us see as it were a bridge between the human and the
divine, a threshold that opens up on to many different dimensions
(personal, historical, prophetic, poetic). Revelation and discovery of
these stupefy not only Dante, but also his readers.

The interplay between human and divine dominates the last two
great 'recognition' scenes of the *Paradiso*, Dante's encounters with St
John and St Bernard. In the eighth sphere, the lights of St Peter and St
James dance and sing with all the other spirits. Suddenly, one light
becomes so bright that, Dante says, 'if the constellation of Cancer had
such a crystal, winter would have a month consisting of only one day'
(XXV, 100–2). The new 'splendour' joins the other two as if it were a
maiden who enters the dance in honour of a bride. Fixing her eyes on it,
for once Beatrice does not delay revelation:

173

> Questi è colui che giacque sopra 'l petto
> del nostro pellicano, e questi fue
> di su la croce al grande officio eletto.   (xxv, 112–14)

(This is he who lay upon the breast of our Pelican, and this is he who was chosen from upon the Cross for the great office.)

The pilgrim might have been satisfied with this. But once more the poet manoeuvres him into a little comedy. Medieval legends based on a passage in John's Gospel (21. 20–3) maintained that the Beloved Disciple had ascended to Heaven in the flesh. Dante the pilgrim wants to ascertain whether the light that has now appeared contains a body. As so many times before in recognition scenes, he directs his eyes towards the spirit. But this is neither Brunetto nor Forese. Looking at the light of St John is like trying to behold the sun at the beginning of an eclipse: in order to see, one becomes blind (118–20). And John speaks to Dante:

> Perché t'abbagli
> per veder cosa che qui non ha loco?
> In terra è terra il mio corpo, e saragli
> tanto con li altri, che 'l numero nostro
> con l'etterno proposito s'agguagli.   (xxv, 122–6)

(Why do you dazzle yourself in order to see that which has here no place? On earth my body is earth, and there it shall be with the rest, until our number equals the eternal purpose.)

The comedy is over. As Statius learnt from Virgil that they were both but shades, so Dante discovers here that even the highest of the blessed are 'earth on earth'. It is not, however, this knowledge that stirs him profoundly. When he next turns to Beatrice, he can see nothing. And this blindness terrifies him (136–9; xxvi, 1). Revelation, knowledge, and blindness; stupor and terror: the divine and the human meet in sublime comedy.

When Bernard appears in canto xxxi, Beatrice disappears. Thus, the scene of *Purgatorio* xxx is re-enacted and transformed. While Virgil returns to Limbo, Beatrice ascends to her throne next to Rachel, and Dante can still see her. The spirit who suddenly materializes looks like an old man 'clad like the folk in glory', and his self-revelation is delayed by Dante, who raises his eyes towards Beatrice and thanks her. But when this revelation comes ('i' sono 'l suo fedel Bernardo', line 102), an extraordinary scene takes place in the pilgrim's heart. The last human anagnorisis of the poem fuses earthly and heavenly in a sublime amalgam. What Dante experiences when the old man reveals himself as St Bernard of Clairvaux at the very summit of Paradise is compared to the emotion felt by a pilgrim who comes to Rome from, say, Croatia to look at the 'Veronica', i.e. the true image ('vera icona') of Jesus' visage imprinted on a veil which a woman handed him to wipe the sweat off his face while he climbed the Calvary – a cloth that was exhibited in St Peter's at Rome every year.[68] Like the foreign pilgrim, whose 'old hunger' for the icon is not sated but who, when the relic is shown, exclaims in his thought, 'My Lord Jesus Christ, true God, was then your semblance like to this?', Dante gazes on the 'living charity' of him who 'in questo mondo, contemplando, gustò di quella pace'. Aware of the poet's intense scrutiny, Bernard interrupts this rapture with an exquisitely gentle, slightly jocose comment: My dear son, you cannot contemplate Heaven if you keep your eyes only down here at the bottom of it! Look up instead until you see 'the Queen to whom this realm is subject and devoted' (103–17).

Dante's 'hic et nunc', the specific moment of his journey when he recognizes St Bernard acquires in this passage a threefold historical dimension and prefigures the supreme stage of his beatific vision. Concentrated in three terzine, we have a vivid image of contemporary life – the pilgrim from Croatia looking at Veronica's veil – which sends us back to Christ's earthly features and simultaneously to the Saint who, *in this world*, tasted of that 'peace' (the ultimate bliss of Heaven) through contemplation. Dante's recognition of Bernard is like the pilgrim's recognition of Jesus' visage on the Veronica. But Dante himself, the spiritual pilgrim of the other world, will soon recognize 'our effigy', the image of the Son of Man, in God's essence (XXXIII, 127–32). Dante, who is entering the very last stage of his beatific vision, will soon fulfill within himself the 'taste' Bernard had of that peace in his mystical experiences on earth. In his surprise, moreover, the Croatian pilgrim expresses the unsoundable depth of the mystery of the Incarnation that Dante will try to describe in Canto XXXIII. In his thoughts, the historical, human 'semblance' of Jesus is superimposed onto the idea of the 'Lord' and the 'Dio verace'.

The complex presence in this passage of both projection of the earthly onto the eternal and reflection of the eternal into the earthly should not make us forget that this interplay is in a sense incidental – that in fact what Dante is describing is the climax of the surprise he felt when, instead of Beatrice, he found the old man at his side, and the wonder he now feels as a lifelong expectation (the 'antica fame') is finally fulfilled by the recognition of the 'senex' as Bernard of Clairvaux, the great saint of the twelfth century. This is a strong human emotion, heightened by intellectual awareness. Dante has studied Bernard's works and knows their importance for the culture of his time. His present emotion is similar to that he felt when he saw his first guide, Virgil, in the dark wood. At the end, we are brought back to the beginning. This movement which, as we shall see in a later chapter, is typical of the last cantos of the *Paradiso*, represents one more step towards sublimity. With it, Dante overcomes the initial 'faintness' of Virgil, his tragic return to the shadowy existence of Limbo, and at the same time points to the final cognitive stage of the poem: recognition of God.

7

His desir wol fle withouten wynges: Mary and love in fourteenth-century poetry

The medieval history of Marian devotion and theology is long and complex. Similarly varied and fascinating is the development that the figure of the Virgin undergoes in the visual arts. And a particularly important place is occupied in medieval devotional poetry by the eulogies of, and the prayers to the Virgin, the forms of which were described forty years ago by Erich Auerbach in a memorable article.[1]

The scope of this chapter is more limited. Its purpose is to examine the versions of Marian prayers left to us in lyrical and narrative poetry by four great fourteenth-century writers, Dante, Guillaume de Deguileville, Petrarch, and Chaucer. There are four basic reasons for doing this. In the first place, all four poets use prayers to the Virgin at crucial moments of their works. Secondly, the prayers by Dante and Deguileville directly influenced Chaucer. Thirdly, a comparative study of their contexts may tell us something about fourteenth-century changes in religious attitudes and above all about personal and narrative strategies, throwing some light on Chaucer's technique in the *Troilus* and the *Canterbury Tales*. Finally, we shall approach the problem of the sublime from a stylistic point of view.

The first stage of our story begins with Dante, whose decision to make St Bernard invoke the Virgin in canto XXXIII of *Paradiso* just before the poet-protagonist has the ultimate vision of God, responds to a precise poetic and religious logic. While contemplating the mystical rose and the 'general form of Paradise' in canto XXXI Dante turns around to ask Beatrice some questions as to which his mind is 'in suspense' (55–7). To his great surprise, instead of seeing Beatrice, he finds before him an old man, 'clad like the folk in glory'. He immediately asks him, 'Ov'è ella?', where is she? (64). And the 'tender father', whose eyes and cheeks are 'suffused with benign gladness'

(61–2), replies that Beatrice has urged him from his place to fulfill Dante's desire. She is now in her throne, 'in the circle which is third from the highest tier' (65–9), and Dante, without answering the old man, lifts up his eyes to behold his lady making a crown for herself as she reflects the eternal rays of God's light (70–2). The distance between the poet and Beatrice is infinite, but this makes no difference to Dante, for her image comes down unblurred by anything between (76–8). Dante fervently thanks her aloud for having saved and freed him, and prays to her now to loose his soul from his body (79–80). Distant as she seems, Beatrice smiles and looks on him and then turns again to the 'eternal fountain' (91–3). The holy elder who accompanies him invites the poet to fly with his eyes throughout the 'garden' of the Empyrean, and declares that the Queen of Heaven, for whom he himself is all afire with love, will grant them every grace, 'però ch'i' sono il suo fedel Bernardo', since he is her faithful Bernard (94–102).

I have examined the recognition scene that ensues in the preceding chapter. Here, what interests me is to point out that, like Virgil, Bernard is 'moved' to Dante's help by Beatrice, and becomes the poet's last guide. His function is precisely that of directing Dante's heart and mind towards Mary, the intermediary *par excellence* between man and God, that through her he may come closer to the Supreme Being and that she may obtain for him the grace of finally looking into God's essence. And this Bernard does three times, by inviting Dante to lift up his eyes to the Queen immediately after the poet recognizes him (XXXI, 115–17), by talking about her at the beginning of Canto XXXII and again asking the pilgrim to gaze into the face which alone can prepare him to see Christ (XXXII, 85–7), and finally by praying to her on his behalf, as a spokesman followed by his 'affection' (XXXII, 147–51; XXXIII, 1–39).

To these three invitations on Bernard's part correspond three successive stages of Dante's vision of the Virgin – what Chiappelli has called the 'polyptych of the Mother'.[2] We shall soon return to this stage and its implications. But first we must pause to glance briefly at the poetic logic which, together with theological reasons, rules the gradual focussing of Dante's attention on Mary. In the last cantos of the *Comedy* Dante passes from Beatrice's guidance to that of Bernard and, finally, simply follows Mary's gaze into the 'eternal light' (XXXIII, 43–8). Neither Beatrice nor Bernard are absent even from the last phases of this movement towards Mary and God. Indeed, Beatrice joins Bernard in his prayer to the Virgin (XXXIII, 38–9), and Bernard himself, after constantly urging Dante towards Mary and pronouncing his 'santa orazione', signs to him with a smile to look upward into God (XXXIII, 49–51). But there is no doubt that while Beatrice is now distant from a Dante who has pronounced a valediction towards her and while Bernard is only an instrument, the last stage of Dante's journey before the 'visio Dei' is dominated by the Virgin. Though she remains present, Beatrice has been replaced, or is being supplemented by Mary, the true 'donna' (XXXIII, 13) – Lady and Queen – of the highest Empyrean. The love incarnated by Beatrice, a love which, sprung on earth, partakes of Heaven as well, is now transcended by the Virgin's love (XXXIII, 7) before being sublimated and becoming one with 'l'amor che move il sole e l'altre stelle'.

This shift, theologically appropriate, has a deep *raison d'être* in the architectural fabric of the poem. In the thrones around and under Mary there shine, together with Eve, John the Baptist, St Peter and others, Beatrice and Lucy, who, as Bernard reminds Dante, 'moved [his] lady when [he] was bending [his] brows downward to [his] ruin' (XXXII, 137–8). What is recalled here is in fact the original impulse that sets the poem, and Dante's salvation, in motion. In *Inferno* II, when Dante seems on the point of giving up the journey that has been proposed to him as the only way of escaping from the dark wood, Virgil reveals why he has come to save him. In the course of this explanation (52–120) we learn that it was Mary herself who sent Lucy to Beatrice that she might help Dante (II, 94–108). Beatrice, in turn, asked Virgil to act as Dante's first guide (58–72; 115–20). Thus, the *Divine Comedy* presents a double movement – from Mary through Lucy and Beatrice to Virgil, and from Virgil to Beatrice, Bernard and Lucy, to Mary.

The Virgin is at the beginning and end, and, as has been shown by others, throughout the poem.[3] When, in *Purgatorio* V, Buonconte da Montefeltro arrives, after the battle of Campaldino, with a hole in his throat, spilling blood on the ground, where the Archiano flows into the Arno, he loses his sight and speech, but dies 'in the name of Mary', invoking her. And this 'small tear' of repentance, this final silent prayer to Mary in the hour of his death ('ora pro nobis peccatoribus nunc et in hora mortis nostrae', says the *Ave Maria*) saves Buonconte's soul.

The triumph of Mary, however, begins in *Paradiso* XXIII, when, in the eighth circle of Heaven, Dante's mind, 'made greater' than before, goes out of itself (43–5) in contemplating the light of Christ and the transfigured smile of Beatrice. There, in the 'beautiful garden' 'which blossoms beneath the rays of Jesus' is 'la rosa in che 'l verbo divino carne si fece' (73–4), as Beatrice tells Dante. And at the mention of her name the poet fixes his sight upon her 'fire'. The 'living star' is mirrored in his eyes, and Mary's apotheosis reaches its climax. A torch, the archangel Gabriel, descends through the heaven, forming a circle in the likeness of a crown that girds her and wheels about her. An ineffable melody surrounds 'il bel zaffiro del quale il ciel piú chiaro s'inzaffira'. Gabriel celebrates in his holy dance 'the supreme joy that breathes from out the womb which was the hostelry of our Desire', and circles around the Virgin until she follows her Son up to the highest sphere. All the other lights make Mary's name resound, while her 'crowned flame' mounts upward after her 'seed' – Christ. The blessed reach their lights upward, showing the love they bear to the Virgin, 'like an infant which, when it has taken the milk, stretches its arm toward its mother 'per l'animo che 'nfin di fuor s'infiamma' – the first of the three similes with the image of mother and child at their centre that Dante uses in the final section of the *Paradiso*.[4] The *Regina coeli* resounds as Mary finally ascends to the Empyrean and St Peter appears (58–139).

'Figurando il paradiso', the 'sacred poem' does indeed 'make a leap' (61–3) here. Anticipating the beatific vision of canto XXXIII,[5] it calls Mary 'stella' as in the litanies,[6] proclaims her superior to any other creature,[7] alludes to the Incarnation three times (73–4, 104–5, 119–20), and in short sets her at the centre of our attention by means of a holy pageant where elements of earthly ceremonial and liturgy, and mystical vision, are fused.

This scene is re-enacted and widened when Dante reaches the Empyrean, in the triptych I mentioned a while ago. In Canto XXXI, at the end of the recognition scene between Dante and Bernard, the play of light and fire which dominates the whole of the *Paradiso* is intensified by two similes that compare the splendour of Mary on the background of the general effulgence of the blessed to the fiery shining of the eastern sky at dawn:

> Io levai li occhi; e come da mattina
> la parte oriental de l'orizzonte
> soverchia quella dove 'l sol declina,
>
> cosí, quasi di valle andando a monte
> con li occhi, vidi parte ne lo stremo
> vincer di lume tutta l'altra fronte.
>
> E come quivi ove s'aspetta il temo
> che mal guidò Fetonte, più s'infiamma,

e quinci e quindi il lume si fa scemo,
  cosí quella pacifica oriafiamma
nel mezzo s'avvivava, e d'ogne parte
per igual modo allentava la fiamma   (118–29)

(I lifted up my eyes; and as at morning the eastern parts of the horizon outshine that where the sun declines, so, as if going with my eyes from valley to mountain-top I saw a part on the extreme verge surpass with its light all the rest of the rim. And as the point where we await the pole that Phaethon misguided is most aglow, and on this side and on that the light diminishes, so was that pacific oriflamme quickened in the middle, on either side in equal measure tempering its flame)

Mary is indeed 'stella matutina', but the magnificent articulation of the dawn image recalls other key moments of the poem – the beginning itself of the journey (*Inferno* I, 37–40), which is echoed, too, in that movement of the eyes from valley to mountain-top (*Inferno* I, 13–18); the arrival on the shores of Purgatory, when the 'bel pianeto che d'amar conforta faceva tutto rider l'oriente' (I, 19–20); and the appearance of Beatrice in the Earthly Paradise (*Purgatorio* XXX, 22–4).

  Here, more than a thousand feasting angels converge towards Mary with open wings and Dante sees the Virgin smile ineffably at their games and songs. The actual expression he uses – 'ridere una bellezza' (134) – is a contrapuntal reminiscence of *Purgatorio* I. It once more condenses human and divine and makes Mary's face radiate forth in and be mirrored by the eyes of all the saints. In the 'caldo suo calor' Dante's own gaze is now fixed, as if in anticipation of Bernard's praise of that warmth in *Paradiso* XXXIII (7–9).

  When canto XXXII begins, Bernard, the 'contemplante', becomes a 'doctor' – a 'magister' – and illustrates to his pupil the structure of the mystical rose, at the centre of which sits Mary, whose historical function of healer of the wound inflicted by Eve (who now shines at the Virgin's feet) is recalled at the opening of the canto (4–6). This historical function is sublimated and transposed onto eternity by the re-enacting of the Annunciation that constitutes the second scene of the triptych. Here, Gabriel descends before Mary and, spreading his wings, sings 'Ave Maria, gratia plena'. The whole blessed Court responds to the 'divina cantilena' (94–9). To contemplate the Virgin in this context means to become ready to see Christ, for hers is the face that most resembles His, and Bernard once more underlines the central importance of the Incarnation when he explains to Dante that it is Gabriel who 'looks into the eyes of our Queen', 'so enamoured that he seems afire'

(103–4), precisely because he it was 'who bore the palm down to Mary, when the Son of God willed to load Himself with the burden of our flesh' (112–14).

It is, then, in this context that Dante inserts the prayer to the Virgin of *Paradiso* XXXIII – as part of the innermost texture of the entire poem, as the last stage of the transformation of the protagonist's love, as a preparation for his supreme experience, the vision of God. Mary's triumphs are the last appearances of a human being, however now transfigured, in the poem, because Mary represents the point where human and divine have met in the flesh, changing the world's history. This is why she acquires more and more prominence, and why Bernard now addresses her.

This tie between history and eternity is the theme of Bernard's prayer. Its first part (lines 1–21), which constitutes a traditionally formal *elogium*, or praise of the Virgin, is an illustration of the history of man's salvation (lines 1–9), and a praise of Mary as intermediary between man and God, of her role for men on earth and for the blessed in Heaven (lines 10–21). The second section of Bernard's speech (lines 22–39) is his prayer on behalf of Dante and it recounts the story of Dante's own salvation from time to eternity. In the first nine lines of the prayer, history is seen and interpreted by a divine measure, as an element of an eternal plan. From line 10 to line 21 God's grace is shown as acting, through Mary's person, both in time, on earth, and beyond time, in Heaven. Finally, in the last section of the prayer, the history of man's salvation becomes the story of one man's salvation: the grace of God has, through Mary, acted upon Dante and brought him to Heaven. This grace is now invoked, through Mary ('per grazia', 25), so that Dante may be enabled to attain ultimate salvation, the contemplation of God with his own, human eyes.

What is presented to us in the first six lines of the canto is the historical side of God's incarnation: the meta-historical, eternal mystery of this Incarnation will be contemplated later in the canto (127–32). Mary is the human medium of man's salvation as fore-ordained by God: 'ab aeterno ordinata sum', as the Bible says.[8] Dante makes this explicit in the central line of the opening:

termine fisso d'etterno consiglio

Mary is the terminal point of eternal counsel, the goal in time of a plan conceived out of time. We have, then, in these two terzine, a straight line from Creation to Incarnation, from 'fattore', the Maker, through human nature ('umana natura', 4), to 'fattura', its making, a creature of flesh and blood, the Son of Man. Human nature was ennobled and ransomed through Mary, a virgin humble and therefore, according to the Gospels, exalted beyond all creatures ('umile e alta').[9] Upon Mary came the Holy Ghost, one of whose names, according to the theologians,[10] is *Amor*, Love. Hence, in Mary's womb was rekindled love:[11]

> nel ventre tuo si raccese l'amore.

Mary's womb was the key to God's love: Mary herself was, as Dante says in the *Purgatorio* (x, 41–2),

> quella
> ch'ad aprir l'alto amor volse la chiave.

Mary reopened God's love for man. But only through her own love and humility did God take flesh. Mary's acceptance of the Divine burden was man's supreme act of love. Thus Mary's womb was the meeting point of human and divine love.

Once the Incarnation took place, the way to God was open. In the third terzina of the canto we then have a straight line from Incarnation to beatitude in God, from history to eternity. God's love, rekindled in Mary's womb, makes it possible for men to raise themselves to Him and rest in the eternal peace of the mystical rose. The straight line, here, implies Christ's passion, crucifixion and resurrection, through which man was saved and shown the way past death to eternal life. From line 1 to line 9 the circle is then complete; from God to God, from the eternity of Creation through history to the eternity of beatitude:

> Vergine Madre, figlia del tuo figlio,
> umile e alta più che creatura,
> termine fisso d'etterno consiglio,
> tu se' colei che l'umana natura
> nobilitasti sì, che 'l suo fattore
> non disdegnò di farsi sua fattura.
> Nel ventre tuo si raccese l'amore,
> per lo cui caldo ne l'etterna pace
> così è germinato questo fiore.

(Virgin Mother, daughter of thy Son, humble and exalted more than any creature, fixed goal of the eternal counsel, thou art she who didst so ennoble human nature that its Maker did not disdain to become its creature. In thy womb was rekindled the love under whose warmth this flower in the eternal peace has thus enfolded.)

Until now Bernard has, in his *elogium*, praised Mary as the historical mediator between man and God: now, in lines 10–15, Mary's eternal function is celebrated. Torch of charity for those saved, for the blessed (10–11), and font of hope for those who are to be saved, for mortal men (11–12), Mary is the medium of God's grace:

> che qual vuol grazia e a te non ricorre,
> sua disianza vuol volar sanz'ali

The past tense used in the first eight lines of the canto is abandoned as soon as Bernard comes to the mystical flower of the Empyrean: the present is used afterwards, to indicate the ever-present role of Mary. The passage is smooth and takes place by association of ideas: the first movement ends with 'questo fiore', indicating the Empyrean; the second begins with 'qui', indicating the Empyrean again.

Bernard's praise now mounts in crescendo, pausing on Mary's own qualities: loving-kindness, mercy, pity, bounty. Mary is, then, the epitome of all creatures' goodness:

> in te s'aduna
> quantunque in creatura è di bontate.

At the same time, Bernard lays the ground for the request that forms the second part of the prayer. He reminds Mary that only through her can Dante obtain the final vision. Her qualities should prepare her to grant Dante his final request. In celebrating Mary's 'benignità' Bernard says that many times it freely anticipates the asking. This is not only true in general. It is particularly true for Dante, who, as we have seen, was saved by her intervention when he was lost in the dark wood of sin. She is the Grace at the beginning and end of Dante's journey.

This journey is now recalled by Bernard: from the 'infima lacuna dell'universo' to the Empyrean, Dante has seen the lives of the spirits one by one. He has come all the way from the river over which the sea has no boast of *Inferno* II to the river out of which issue living sparks, the Empyrean. It was the journey that Virgil had proposed to him, and Dante is now at the end of it. There is, in Bernard's words here (22–4), a heaviness, underlined by the enjambment and by the slow 'ad una ad una', which does not express tiredness, but all the weight of the experience conquered by Dante. It is of the whole journey, of all this experience that Mary – and we with her – are reminded. The entire poem is summed up before its end.

This recalling is, however, functional: it constitutes the proem to

184

Bernard's requests on behalf of Dante. Here, then, the praise becomes prayer, the *elogium, supplicatio*. Bernard's requests are basically two: the first, expressed in lines 22–33, regards Dante's immediate objective, the attainment of ultimate salvation with the vision of God; the second, expressed in lines 34–6, regards Dante's future, the stability of his 'affetti' after the beatific vision. Bernard's first request is, however, articulated in two moments, which are separated both formally and substantially. In the first, Bernard presents his request as a mere interpreter of Dante's own wishes: 'Or *questi* . . . supplica a te.' In the second, it is Bernard himself who prays to the Virgin, underlining his request with rhetorical emphasis: 'E *io* . . . tutti miei prieghi ti porgo, e priego che non sieno scarsi.' What Dante asks through Bernard is to receive, by divine grace, so much power that he can raise himself with his eyes to the 'ultima salute'. Through Bernard, Dante asks for the supreme Object. Bernard, in his own request, emphasizes the subject-ive means for the attainment of this Object. He asks Mary to disperse every cloud of Dante's mortality, so that the supreme joy may be disclosed to him. In other words, Bernard asks Mary to grant Dante the last *trasumanar*, the final stage of that passing beyond humanity which had begun in the first canto of *Paradiso*. Here we have the announce-ment of the central themes of canto XXXIII: the sight of the Object and the progressive passing beyond humanity of the seer, the subject. At the same time, both the subjective and objective aspects of the final goal are indicated by the two expressions, 'ultima salute' and 'sommo piacer'. God is, in Himself, both *salvatio* and *diligibile*;[12] yet ultimate salvation and supreme pleasure are Dante's own, subjective ends. 'Piacer', in particular, indicates the main dimension of Dante's feelings in canto XXXIII of *Paradiso*.[13]

Bernard's third request refers to Dante's future: this, too, is presented as the saint's own preoccupation ('Ancor ti prego'). What the last guide asks is that, after the overwhelming vision, Dante's 'affetti' may remain 'sani'. It is clear that Bernard refers to Dante's inclinations, which must be kept pure even after the vision in order for Dante to avoid sinning again. The vision in itself is no guarantee against a new fall. But 'affetti' has a wider meaning: it implies passion, feeling, state of mind, will. And 'sani' means not only 'pure', but also 'wholesome'. Bernard, then, asks Mary to grant Dante his integrity as man and poet after the beatific vision.

Finally, Bernard passes from indirect prayer to direct exhortation:

Vinca tua guardia i movimenti umani.

This line introduces the last stage of the prayer, which is now choral. It is not just Bernard and Dante, but also Beatrice and all the blessed who pray to Mary. 'Vedi', says Bernard to Mary, and indirectly we see the silent congregation clasp their hands. Not a word is spoken, but a gesture is glanced at – the hieratic gesture of medieval painting. The rest of the canto is silent, and we only follow sight: Mary's eyes fixed on Bernard (40–1), then on God (43–5) – only their movement meaning acceptance of the prayer and address to God for intercession. Bernard's eyes sign to Dante to look upward (40–50), but Dante's eyes are already fixed on God (50–4).

The first – and lasting – impression that this prayer makes on the reader and even more on the listener is that of a severity and solemnity behind which burns an extraordinary ardour. The antitheses of the first two lines – virgin, mother; daughter of thy Son, etc. – are based upon totally abstract, dogmatic definitions. It is on the intellectual level that we receive Bernard's message. In the third line – 'termine fisso d'etterno consiglio' – the antithesis is more subtle, for it rests on a less directly identifiable contrast of 'fixed goal' and 'eternal'. But the effect is, again, purely intellectual. There is no doubt that this is 'austere' poetry. Part of its appeal rests precisely on this. But there is more. In the first place we realize that these three lines constitute just an invocation. What Bernard accumulates here are four vocatives – and this, by itself, provides his opening words with great solemnity and majesty. To this we must add the effect of the rhetorical antitheses themselves, which produce vivacity within the severity. Finally, we must consider the internal, grammatical balancing out of these antitheses: the first is based on a contraposition of two nouns ('vergine' – 'madre'), the third of two adjectives ('umile' – 'alta'); the second results from a contrast between a noun in the vocative and a noun in the genitive ('figlia del tuo figlio'), accompanied by a possessive adjective ('tuo') which grammatically refers to the genitive but conceptually to the vocative; the fourth has the same structure of the second, with a noun in the vocative ('termine') and a noun in the genitive ('consiglio'), but the contraposition is based on the adjectives that accompany both ('fisso' – 'eterno'). The distribution is perfect. But this is not all. The third line ('termine fisso d'etterno consiglio') sums up the meaning of the first two: Mary is the fixed goal of eternal counsel inasmuch as she is virgin and mother, daughter of her Son, humble and exalted. At the same time she is these things, virgin and mother, daughter of her son, humble and exalted precisely because she is 'ordinata ab aeterno' to be the goal of a divine plan. When we add to all this the echoes of the Gospels, of the Old Testament, of Bernard's own sermons that Dante has adapted and condensed in these three lines, [14] we begin to understand the nature of this poetry. These lines have no halo of vagueness around them: the terms are very precise and imply well-defined concepts. But the reverberation they have on each other and their concentration in three lines produce an effect of extraordinary intensity. When the sentence, in the following three lines, is brought to completion, Bernard's thought widens into a slow circumlocution: two enjambments make it pause and revolve upon itself. The antithesis ('fattore' – 'fattura') is resolved through the verb ('non disdegnò di farsi'). The verb itself placates the tension: Dante does not simply say: 'the Maker made Himself its [human nature's] making'. Dante says: 'the Maker *did not disdain* to make Himself its making'. Yet, though more articulate than the preceding one, the phrase is no less compact. Its second section ('che 'l suo fattore . . .') is a consecutive clause dependent on the first part ('nobilitasti sì), and the two possessive adjectives ('suo' and 'sua'), which refer to the subject and the object of the consecutive clause, are tied up to the object ('umana natura') of the principal clause. In the principal clause the subject, the anaphorical 'tu', opens the sentence, thus emphasizing the person of the addressee; but then the object ('umana natura') precedes the verb, so that the stress falls on it. In the consecutive clause, the tension produced by this inversion disappears: Here, the sequence is the normal one – subject ('fattore'), verb ('non disdegnò di farsi'); predicate-object ('fattura').

The explosion of images and metaphors in the next terzina reveals, however, that the tension is stronger than ever:

> Nel ventre tuo si raccese l'amore
> per lo cui caldo nell'etterna pace
> così è germinato questo fiore.

The field is defined by the images of generation ('ventre' and 'germinato') and fire ('raccese' and 'caldo'). The interaction of these images makes us feel as if in Mary's womb an explosion has taken place, the heat of which arouses life and pervades the universe. It is as if we were witnessing the action of the sun through the millennia – its rekindling after ages of darkness and cold, its heat radiating through space and time and finally causing the flower to grow. The movement is indeed, as we have seen, through time: from Incarnation to beatitude. But the image suggests more. We do not merely have generation and fire: we also have 'eternal peace' and 'flower'. There is some kind of reverberation of the first line into the third, as if an analogy were implied – and 'così' might have a shade of the 'così' of similes. The analogy implied by this reverberation is between the rekindling of love in Mary's womb and the germinating, the blooming of the flower in the eternal peace: in this manner, the rekindling of love in a woman's womb acquires a shadow of vegetable life, and viceversa, the blooming of the flower becomes like an explosion of fire. Here again, Dante has adapted expressions derived from Church writers,[15] has perfected images which he had already used,[16] but he has inserted them in a wider, more compact context.

From this moment on, the image of fire and burning pervades this section of the canto: Mary is a noonday *torch* (10–11), Bernard *burns* for Dante's vision (28–9), Dante himself ends the *ardour* of his craving (48). When Bernard says, 'E io, che mai per mio veder non arsi', he makes explicit precisely that ardour which, as I have said, shows itself in the images that enlighten the austerity of his words: the torch of charity, the spring of hope, the flying without wings, the 'infima lacuna dell'universo', the cloud of mortality. One cannot fail to notice a particular flickering of the flame of emotion, for instance, when Dante mentions that 'infima lacuna dell'universo', by which, with remote detachment, he expresses all together the sensations of bottom, emptiness, lagoon and lake of Cocytus.[17] The ardour shows in the accumulation of abstract nouns which define the virtues of Mary, with the iteration of 'in te', in the repetition of 'prego' in lines 29–32; in the final, direct exhortation to the Virgin. It is the mixture of historical, dogmatic, figural, emotional and rhetorical elements[18] that determines the intensity of this ardour. It is this eloquence that became a model which, as we shall soon see, appealed to Petrarch and Chaucer, and much later to the poet of *Ash-Wednesday* (II, 25–47) and *The Dry Salvages* (IV):

> Repeat a prayer also on behalf of
> Women who have seen their sons or husbands
> Setting forth, and not returning:
> Figlia del tuo figlio,
> Queen of Heaven.

In short, in Bernard's prayer the medieval 'sermo humilis' is replaced by a new style, the 'sermo sublimis'.[19] Mary's eyes, those eyes 'beloved and reverenced by God', are fixed on the 'orator', thus showing 'how

greatly devout prayers please her' (40–2). Then, with a sudden, silent
shift, they turn to the Eternal Light (43–5). And this simple gesture
makes Dante approach the paroxysm of his desire ('l'ardor del desiderio
in me finii', 48). The language of earthly love becomes the language of
the beatific vision.

I shall return to this in the next chapter. Here, I shall pause to
consider how Dante's sublimity – and for the moment I am talking
about an elevated style employed to deal with 'high' topics – is new
even in Italian literature. If we compare the prayer to the Virgin in
Paradiso XXXIII to three of the *Laude* written a generation before by
Iacopone da Todi, we shall immediately see fundamental differences.
Iacopone exalts mystical folly and proclaims the ineffability of *extasis*,
but he deliberately rejects 'sublimity' and, following the radical
Franciscan interpretation of the Gospels' 'humble' and concise style,[20]
tackles his theme with passionate directness. In Laude 13, he addresses
the Virgin as 'noble Queen', but the secular language of courtliness he
seems to adopt is in fact subverted by the absence of any conceit. His
appeal comes as a desperate cry for help:

> O Regina cortese, eo so' a vvui venuto,
> c'al meo core feruto deiate medecare!
>
> Eo so' a vvui venuto com'omo desperato;
> perduto onn'altro adiuto, lo vostro m'è lassato;
> s'e' nne fusse privato, farìme consumare. (13, 1–5)

(O noble Queen, I have come to you that you may heal my wounded heart! I
have come to you as a man in despair. Having lost any other help, yours only is
left to me. If I were deprived of this, I would die.)

In Laude 32, Iacopone praises Mary by putting together a series of
traditional ideas. Thus, he celebrates her immaculate conception, her
virginity and humility, returning time and again to the paradoxes they
represent for the human mind ('it is above custom and reason to
conceive without corruption', 63–5), but finally concentrating on the
Mother's love for her Son. This is the image that carries him away in a
fit of mystical passion:

> O Maria, co' facivi,
> quanno tune 'l vidivi?
>
> Or co' non te morivi
> de l'amor affocata?

Co' non te consumavi,
quanno tu li sguardavi,

che Deo ce contemplavi
en quella carne velata?
. . .
O Madonna, quelli atti,
avivi en quelli fatti,

quelli 'nfocati tratti
la lengua m'ò mozzata.
. . .
O cor salamandrato
de viver sì enfocato,

co' non t'à consumato
la piena ennamorata?

(32, 95–102, 111–14, 119–22)

(O Mary, what did you do when you saw him? Didn't you die, burnt by love?
How didn't you consume yourself when you looked at him, contemplating
God in that veiled flesh? . . . O Lady, those living actions, that inflamed
countenance, have cut off my tongue . . . O heart salamandered by such fiery
living, how did such full love not consume you?)

Iacopone is not primitive. He knows how to use rhetoric, and in this
poem, for instance, he echoes Adam of St Victor.[21] But he deliberately
chooses the 'docta ignorantia', 'learned ignorance', as a religious and
stylistic programme. In his Letter to Cangrande (XIII, 10, 31), Dante says
that the language of the *Comedy* is 'remissus et humilis' (modest and
humble) because he uses the vernacular, 'in qua et muliercule
comunicant', in which little women also communicate. Yet no 'mulier-
cula' would have been able to understand fully and immediately the
subtleties of his Prayer to the Virgin in *Paradiso* XXXIII. On the
contrary, any popular audience, any churchgoer would be at home
with Iacopone's direct language. Every layman would be moved by the
famous Laude 70, where Iacopone stages with a perfect sense of drama
Jesus' Passion as witnessed by Mary, showing us all her pain and
despair. Iacopone's style is the true 'sermo humilis'. Dante's is a gradual
ascent towards a language where Biblical humbleness and classical
rhetoric merge in a new 'sermo sublimis'.

Though in a completely different manner, the prayer to the Virgin, if
not Mary herself, occupies an important place in the story of another

fourteenth-century pilgrimage, the *Pèlerinage de la Vie Humaine* of Guillaume de Deguileville, of which the author himself compiled two different versions, one dating back to 1331, and another to 1355. In both redactions, the story, narrated in purely allegorical terms, is represented by the earthly adventures of a man who, having seen the Heavenly Jerusalem in a vision, decides to undertake a pilgrimage thither. Helped by Grace Dieu in his many troubles, the pilgrim goes through life until Age and Sickness, the precursors of Death, warn him of his approach and, while Prayer comes as a guide, he finally wakes up.

It is impossible here to do justice to, or examine in detail, this monumental work.[22] Suffice it to say that while in our own century it has been taken as a paradigm of medieval allegorical fiction,[23] it seems to have been extremely popular throughout Europe from the fourteenth through the fifteenth down to the beginning of the seventeenth century. Starting in 1426, Lydgate translated and adapted the second, and longer, version into English, and it is his rendering that I shall use here.[24]

In this version we have three prayers to the Virgin. The first occurs rather early in the poem (after line 7188 in a total of 24,832), after the pilgrim's meeting with Lady Reason and Moses. Nature has a long argument with Grace Dieu over transubstantiation in the Eucharist, which she obviously cannot tolerate (how can bread and wine not remain bread and wine?), and resorts to her clerk Aristotle, who debates with, and is defeated by, Sapientia. At this point Grace Dieu hands the pilgrim a scroll which contains a Latin poem on the Trinity (*Pater, creator omnium*) and a longer hymn, in Latin, to the Virgin Mary (*Ave reclinatorium*). Here, the *elogium* celebrates the Mother of God as she who changed Eve's 'damnatorium' into joy (1–12), as the reference point for all men who are lost (13–24), the most splendid of stars, humble in prosperity and strong in adversity (25–36). Gradually, the images focus on Mary as the receptacle of the divine seed. Announced in stanza 8 ('Tu divine imaginis, Et eterni es luminis Beatum receptaculum', 88–90), this theme reaches its climax towards the end of the hymn, where the birth and death of Christ are linked to the Eucharist, and this in turn, through the image of the fruit, to Mary's womb and to her virginity, the 'flower' which she kept together with the 'fructus':

> Ventris tui in ortulo, Ornato flore primulo,
> Iste fructus colligitur; Sed, ut vultus in speculo
> Representatur oculo, Et speculum non leditur,

The Tragic and the Sublime in Medieval Literature

Sic dum a te recipitur, Dum manet; dum egreditur,
Hoc sit illeso claustrulo: Nulla via relinquitur,
Nil suspectum admittitur; Fructum habes cum flosculo.

(151–6, stanza 13)

(In the orchard of your womb, ornated by the first flower, this fruit is collected; but as a visage is represented to the eye in a mirror and the mirror is not affected by it, so when this fruit is received by you, it remains; when it comes out it does so through an untouched door: no way is abandoned, no suspicion is admitted; you have the fruit with the flower.)

There is no doubt that this is Grace Dieu's answer to Nature and Aristotle: the mysteries here concentrated in a few lines are indeed 'wonderful to nature, unteachable to art', and comprehensible only to faith (136–7, 144). And this is precisely the reason why this hymn is inserted here together with the *Pater, creator omnium*, where the Trinity is extolled.

The second prayer to the Virgin is part of a different context. When, after choosing the right path on the advice of Moral Virtue, the pilgrim is led astray by Youth, he meets Gluttony, Venus and Sloth, then Pride and Envy, and finally Wrath and Tribulation. Attacked by all these in turn, the protagonist defends himself by appealing to Mary (16275–16978).

As in Dante's case, though in a more pedantic manner, St Bernard is the intermediary. The *Pilgrimage* inserts here an English version of Bernard's homily 'De Laudibus Virginis Matris Super Verba Evangelii *Missus est angelus Gabriel*', making it end with a ballad on the Virgin.[25] Once more, the purpose of both is clear in the context of the narrative. Recourse to Mary saves man from sin and protects him in tribulation. With the magnificent rhetoric that characterizes his fervent prose, St Bernard expounds in his homily the Gospel of the Annunciation, beginning with Adam and Eve, explaining the Old Testament prophesies and figures of Mary, the paradoxes of the Incarnation, and the name of the Virgin. 'Maria' is 'Maris stella' for indeed her rays shine on the entire universe, her splendour pervades Heaven, penetrates Hell, and runs through the Earth inflaming human minds. The 'cohortatio ad cultum' follows this last eulogy. I quote a section of it from the original Latin to give an idea of the style which inspired Dante and countless other medieval authors:

Si insurgant venti *tentationum*, si incurras scopulos *tribulationum*: respice stellam, voca Mariam. Si jactaris superbiae undis, si ambitionis, si detractionis, si aemulationis; respice stellam, voca Mariam. Si iracundia, aut avaritia, aut carnis illecebra *naviculam* concusserit mentis; respice ad Mariam

(If the winds of temptation arise, if you stumble on the rocks of tribulation: look at the star, call Mary. If you are hurled by the waves of pride, of ambition, of detraction and emulation: look at the star, call Mary. If wrath, avarice, the allurements of the flesh strike the little boat of your mind: look at Mary)[26]

We shall soon see how the image of the sea prompts the pilgrim to pray to Mary once more. Here, it is evident that Bernard's exhortations fit the plight of the pilgrim attacked by various temptations (pride, envy, wrath, avarice and lust in the Homily's order) and above all faced by the 'rocks of tribulation'. It is Mary as 'Refuge in Tribulation' that the Ballad at the end of the prose tract invokes, making each of the four stanzas end with the word 'trybulacion'. Here is the third, where several of St Bernard's images recur:

> O holy Sterre / ffyx in stabylnesse,
> With-oute Eclypsyng / Or Mutabylyte,
> Ylyche Clere / shynyng in bryghtnesse,
> In whom the Sonne / sent ffro the deyete,
> lyste ffor to take / Oure humanyte,
> Off Mankynde / to make Redempcion,
> That thow shuldest / O maybe, O Moder ffre,
> Be Oure Reffuge / In trybulacion!   (16963–70, stanza 3)

The next prayer to the Virgin comes shortly afterwards (19791), as the pilgrim, having met Avarice and Heresy and talked to Satan, tries to swim across the sea because the devil blocks all other routes. This time, Mary's help is invoked with even greater urgency in a poem which, 276 lines long in the French original, has been reduced to 184 in the English translation. The surprise is that the English version is not by Lydgate, but by Chaucer, whom the monk of Bury acknowledges and celebrates before reverently quoting his *ABC*.

Here, we have an instance of the transformations that literary forms undergo in the Middle Ages. The *ABC*, itself but an example of the many 'Abecedaria' in honour of Mary such as those collected in the *Analecta Hymnica Medii Aevi*, is used by Deguileville as a lyrical utterance serving the purposes of a narrative. As in the two previous instances of prayers to the Virgin, the pilgrim invokes Mary as the only source of help in his distress:

> A toy du monde le refui,
> Vierge glorieuse, m'en fui

Tout confus, ne puis miex faire;
A toy me tien, a toy m'apuy.
Relieve moy, abatu suy:
Vaincu m'a mon aversaire.   (1–6)[27]

Elaborate as it is, the *elogium* that follows these lines is always also *supplicatio* – indeed in each stanza the last lines seem to focus on the protagonist's condition. Now, if the tradition recorded in Speght's edition of Chaucer is correct, the *ABC* was translated and adapted by the English poet 'at the request of Blanche, Duchess of Lancaster, as a prayer for her private use'.[28] In any case, Chaucer's *ABC* is a purely lyrical piece, and the transformations it has undergone in passing from French to English respond to this new purpose. Both Wolfgang Clemen and Patricia Kean remark that Chaucer's version shows 'a greater intensity conveyed by heightened expression and a strengthening and simplification of the thematic material'.[29] At the same time, the 'I' behind the urgency of the French *Pèlerinage* (and of Lydgate's *Pilgrimage*) has become impersonal. The *ABC* is a prayer that can be used by anyone – it is as if Dante's St Bernard had stopped at line 21 of his *elogium* and then attached to it a general request for help and mercy.

Moreover, if we look at the *ABC* in the light of Auerbach's distinction between dogmatic, historical, figural and emotional elements and their developments in medieval eulogies of the Virgin,[30] we immediately realize that not only is there no consecutive thread running through the poem',[31] but the dogmatic element is diluted throughout the composition, and only six stanzas out of twenty-three present either historical or figural ideas. Thus the sorrow of Mary under the cross is recalled at lines 81–2, but only to be appealed to, that the foe might not prevail against it and render vain what Christ and His mother 'have bought so deere'. The burning bush of Moses, 'signe' and 'figure' of Mary's 'unwemmed maidenhede' receiving the Holy Ghost (89–94) is evoked simply in order to be associated with the fire 'that in helle eternalli shal dure', from which Mary should defend us (95–6). The meditation on 'wherfore and whi the Holi Gost thee soughte, Whan Gabrielles vois cam to thin ere' (114–15) is abandoned after a few lines. Christ's Passion and the figure of Longinus (unnamed in Deguileville) are mentioned only to be contrasted to the sinner's falseness and unkindness (161–8). Isaac was the 'figure' of Jesus' sacrifice (169–72), but this is only the 'measure' of the mercy that is invoked (173–6). Zechariah's words (13.1), 'In that day there shall be a fountain opened to the house of David and to the inhabitants of Jerusalem for sin and uncleanness', generally applied to the blood of Christ as in Revelation

1.5, are here figurally related to the Virgin (177–8), but the rest of the last stanza draws from this the rather abrupt conclusion that 'nere thi tender herte, we were spilt' (180).[32] Chaucer does indeed, as Wolpers and Clemen have observed,[33] go beyond doctrinal limits, 'ascribing to the Virgin the epithet "Almighty" which is rightly applicable to none but God alone', and this 'in his very first address'; but the rest of his epithets concentrate on the idea of Mary as 'Queen' (24, 25, 77, 97, 121, 149) – 'glorious mayde and mooder' and 'temple devout' (49, 145) being the only two exceptions.

There are, however, at least two sections of the *ABC* where Chaucer goes far beyond the original of Deguileville. In stanzas 13 and 14 of his version, the 'N' and 'O' of the alphabet, Chaucer seems to explore the possibilities inherent in two different ways of dealing with the traditional Marian eulogy. In the first, after calling Mary 'advocat' according to the *Salve Regina*, he points to the fact that the Virgin helps men but 'for litel hire':

> We han noon oother melodye or glee
> Us to rejoyse in oure adversitee,
> Ne advocat noon that wole and dar so preye
> For us, and that for litel hire as yee
> That helpen for an Ave-Marie or tweye.   (100–4)

The last line of this passage (which is totally different in the French original) slightly jars with the solemn intonation of the rest of the poem and particularly with the rhetorical sweep of the next stanza. In fact, it is a brief experiment in poetic simplicity and candour, in the 'humble' style that will characterize some of the *Canterbury Tales*, namely the Prioress' portrait of the little child who, whenever he saw 'th'ymage Of Cristes mooder', used to kneel and 'seye His *Ave Marie*, as he goth by the weye' (VII, 507–8). The intonation suddenly reminds us of Buonconte da Montefeltro's end 'in the name of Mary' – the 'lacrimetta' that snatches his soul from the devil's hands.

The next lines, on the other hand, make use of a very different register. Here, the experiment is in the 'high' style of some traditional eulogies, where Auerbach's 'emotional' element is mixed with scriptural echoes ('ancilla Domini') and contrasts are established ('ancille'.– 'maistresse') to produce an invocation with the breath and vigour of those we shall hear in *Troilus*:

> O verrey light of eyen that ben blynde,
> O verrey lust of labour and distresse,
> O tresoreere of bountee to mankynde,

Thee whom God ches to mooder for humblesse!
From his ancille he made the maistresse
Of hevene and erthe, oure bille up for to beede.   (105–10)[34]

We will soon see where this kind of inspiration leads Chaucer once he comes into contact with Dante and can use the *elogium* to Mary in a narrative context. The *ABC*, a lyrical piece drawn from a French allegorical narrative and employed again in an English version, provides us with a good touchstone against which to measure Dante's use of Mary and of the Prayer to the Virgin in the story of his ascent to God. In both the *Divine Comedy* and the *Pèlerinage*, recourse to Mary takes place at crucial moments, when the protagonist is in need of help. There are, however, three basic differences between Dante and Deguileville-Lydgate. In the first place, Deguileville's presentation has the appearance of flat 'literariness': the prayers to Mary come on a scroll, or as a quotation of Bernard's sermon, or as an 'abecedarium'. The medium is a purely 'literal' use of literature on an allegorical background. What counts is the message. In Dante, as we have seen, all this becomes 'dramatic': Bernard is a character, Mary triumphs in Heaven in a continuous play of lights, the Annunciation is re-enacted, the images recall other key moments of the poem. The medium complements and enriches the message. Secondly, there are differences in the message itself. In the *Pèlerinage*, the first hymn to Mary is Grace Dieu's answer to the rationalistic speculations of Nature and Aristotle, but the other two prayers come from the soul of the pilgrim himself. In the *Divine Comedy*, Mary acts of her own accord when she sets in motion Lucy, Beatrice, and Virgil to save Dante:

Donna è gentil nel ciel che si compiange
di questo impedimento ov'io ti mando,
sí che duro giudicio là su frange

(In Heaven there is a gracious lady who has such pity of this impediment to which I send you that stern judgement is broken thereabove)

says Beatrice to Virgil (*Inferno* II, 94–6). Mary's pity of Dante's 'impediment' acts to 'break' the 'stern judgement' of God, according to which Dante would be condemned. And indeed Bernard confirms in his prayer to the Virgin in *Paradiso* XXXIII that her 'loving-kindness not only succours him who asks, but oftentimes freely foreruns the asking' (16–18). This Dantean Mary is in a way, as several early commentators pointed out,[35] the theological 'prevenient Grace'. Deguileville's pilgrim, and Chaucer's 'I' in the *ABC*, must *ask* for grace.[36] *Grace Dieu* does indeed appear at the beginning of the French poem, but she only points out to the protagonist the truth of transubstantiation by handing him a scroll with a hymn to Mary. Finally, when at the end of his journey Dante, through Bernard, implores Mary 'per grazia' (*Paradiso* XXXIII, 25), he does so in order to be granted enough 'virtue' as to be capable of gazing into God's own essence – a request which is far from the mind of Deguileville's and Lydgate's pilgrim as well as from the lips of Chaucer's praying 'I'. The dreamer of the *Pèlerinage* wakes up just before Death catches him. He prays to God, but never enters the Heavenly Jerusalem he saw at the beginning of his vision. What is possible in the world of Dante's poetry and theology is avoided, if not altogether impossible, in Deguileville's and Chaucer's. Nor, though he does contemplate the City of God, is the dreamer of *Pearl* allowed inside it. And the pilgrimage of *Piers Plowman* never ends.

The *ABC* is, as I hope to have shown, a lyric that represents the form in a state of transition.[37] Starting with a French 'abecedarium', Chaucer explores several ways of dealing with his subject – 'historical', 'figural', 'emotional', 'humble' and 'high' – but settles on none. In this sense, the *ABC* is completely different from Dante's prayer to the Virgin, in which all traditional forms are fused in a very tight whole by the control of a mature poet. The question we must ask ourselves now is, what does the greatest lyric poet of the fourteenth century do when he, too, writes his prayer to the Virgin?

In the *Canzoniere* such as we have it and such as he finally arranged it, Francis Petrarch, the 'lauriat poete' of the *Clerk's Tale*, placed *Vergine bella* at the very end, as the last of the 366 lyrics that make up the collection. This choice, together with that of *Voi ch'ascoltate* to introduce the 'rime sparse', reveals that Petrarch thought carefully about the 'frame' of the *Canzoniere*, and that this frame has a decidedly 'penitential' character. In the first sonnet the poet recalls the sighs he used to utter 'in his youthful error', asks for pity and forgiveness, and concludes with a confession:

> et del mio vaneggiar vergogna è 'l frutto,
> e 'l pentersi, e 'l conoscer chiaramente
> che quanto piace al mondo è breve sogno   (12–14)[38]

(the fruit of my raving is shame, and repentance, and the clear knowledge that what pleases in this world is a brief dream)

In the last canzone, he prays to Mary to help him now that death is near, and repeats his confession of sin, error and repentance. The love story of the *Canzoniere* – a spiritual autobiography that describes, in a non-organic, not rigidly structured manner, the inner experiences of the poet – is divided into two major sections, one 'in vita' and one 'in morte' of Laura. The second section opens with canzone CCLXIV, where the author's divided mind between love for Laura and love for God is the central theme, issuing in a declaration of impotence: 'et veggio 'l meglio, et al peggior m'appiglio' (I see the best, but hang on to the worst).[39] Though 'penitential' compositions are present in the first part of the *Canzoniere*[40] – thus showing that Petrarch's consciousness is fully alert throughout the collection and that religious impulses are strong even at the point of maximum infatuation with Laura[41] – a decisive turning point in this direction is represented by the last four poems of the second part. In sonnet CCCLXII, the poet asks God to be enabled to contemplate both His and transfigured Laura's face. In fact, what he presents to us here is a vision. Significantly, the poem begins with a flight image: Petrarch flies to heaven so often with his thoughts that it seems to him he is one of those who, having left their 'broken veil' (the body) on earth, possess their 'treasure' (God) in Paradise: one of the blessed. His heart often trembles with a 'sweet cold' as he hears Laura, for whom he loses all his hue in love, address him. 'My friend', she says, 'now I love and honour you, because you have changed your habits and your hair'. Then, she leads him to her Lord. The poet kneels and begs to be allowed to contemplate both visages. The answer (whether from Laura or from God Petrarch does not explicitly say) is the following: 'Your destiny has been fixed. If it is delayed twenty or thirty years, it will seem too long a time to you, but it will in fact be short'.

> Volo con l'ali de' pensieri al cielo
> sí spesse volte che quasi un di loro
> esser mi pare ch'àn ivi il suo thesoro,
> lasciando in terra lo squarciato velo.
>
> Talor mi trema 'l cor d'un dolce gelo
> udendo lei per ch'io mi discoloro
> dirmi: – Amico, or t'am'io et or t'onoro
> perch'à i costumi variati, e 'l pelo. –
>
> Menami al suo Signor: allor m'inchino,
> pregando humilemente che consenta
> ch'i' stia a veder et l'uno et l'altro volto.

Responde: – Egli è ben fermo il tuo destino;
et per tardar anchor vent'anni o trenta,
parrà a te troppo, et non fia però molto. –

This vision, together with that recounted in sonnet CCCII, is Petrarch's version of Dante's scenes on the summit of Mount Purgatory (the encounter with Beatrice) and in the final cantos of the *Paradiso*. The difference between the two does not lie in the contrast between Dante's certainty and Petrarch's uncertainty (the latter is after all assured that he will go to Heaven, although he has to wait for it), but in the different poetic method. Dante stretches words, outlines details, dramatizes the scene so as to attain the highest possible precision. Petrarch builds around his words an aura of indefiniteness. 'Squarciato velo', for instance, is both allusive and supremely delicate. Dante had used a similar expression ('mi squarciò 'l velo') in *Purgatorio* XXXII (71–2) to show how a sudden glow broke the veil of his dream. In *Inferno* XXXIII, as we have seen in chapter 2, Ugolino talks of the nightmare that broke for him the veil of the future. Petrarch employs 'squarciato velo' to indicate the body 'opened up' by death and out of which the soul issues to reach heaven. With 'squarciato' we seem to face a typically Dantean violence; we find ourselves before a re-enactment of the rending of the veil of the temple at the moment of Christ's death. 'Velo' complements 'squarciato', thus apparently increasing the tension; but in fact it calms it down. The earthly body is, after all, but an insubstantial veil. Paradoxically, the 'contemptus mundi' which the expression reveals is a 'veil' that hides the cruelty of death emerging from 'squarciato'. We are in the presence of a different type of stylistic sublimity – one that tries to harmonize differences in a perpetual oxymoron ('dolce gelo').

In sonnet CCCLXIII, Laura's death becomes the starting point of a return to God. Petrarch's contrapuntal, oxymoronic technique reaches another climax. Free from love – and this freedom is both bitter and sweet (11), with thoughts now incapable of daring flights, and feelings deprived of both warmth and coldness, hope and grief (6–8); tired of, and sated with living, the poet turns to the Lord he now adores and thanks. The opening of the sonnet presents a very different picture:

Morte à spento quel sol ch'abagliar suolmi,
e 'n tenebre son li occhi interi et saldi;
terra è quella ond'io ebbi et freddi et caldi;
spenti son i miei lauri, or querce et olmi

(Death has extinguished the sun that used to blind me, the wholesome and pure eyes are in darkness; she from whom I had both cold and warm is now earth; my laurels are now withered, nay, turned into oaks and elms)

The tragic (and tragic because perfectly balanced) oppositions of this first quatrain are slowly mitigated by the oxymora of the next seven lines, for while in the opening the poet describes the irremediable facts of Laura's death and of his own decay as a man and as a writer, immediately afterwards he turns to his inner reactions against these events; and his feelings are, as we have seen, contradictory. Inner tensions can, however, be placated. Thus, suspended as it were between death and love, pain and freedom, Petrarch finds peace in God.

The tiredness that dominates here, the sense of a soul exhausted, at the same time 'satio' and expiring, recurs in sonnet CCCLXIV ('Omai son stanco', line 5), but accompanied by a more active repentance. Reviewing the thirty-one years in which Love has kept him in the fire both during Laura's life and after her death (1–4), Petrarch reproaches himself for the 'error' which has almost completely extinguished in him any seed of virtue (5–7) and devoutly 'renders' his final years to God (7–8). He is now 'pentito et tristo' of the years he has spent as he should not have (9–11) and implores the Lord who has imprisoned him in his earthly gaol to free him and save him from Hell, for he knows his fault and does not excuse it (12–14).

In sonnet CCCLXV the invocation to the 'invisible, immortal King of Heaven' (6) is more pressing. It occupies three out of four stanzas, in which the poet, aware of his 'mali' which have now become 'indegni et empi', asks for help to his 'frail and erring' soul and for the divine grace that can compensate its defects (5–8). If he has lived in war and storms, may he at least die in peace and 'in porto' (9–11). And may God's hand help him in whatever life is left him, and in death (12–14). Once more, this prayer is preceded by a meditation on the past (1–4), on which Petrarch weeps now as he wasted it 'in loving a mortal thing' instead of lifting himself up in flight though he had 'wings' for it:

> I' vo piangendo i miei passati tempi
> i quai posi in amar cosa mortale,
> *senza levarmi a volo, abbiend'io l'ale,*
> per dar forse di me non bassi exempi. (1–4)

Here, the image of flying and wings, which I have stressed in quoting the passage, is used in a way fundamentally different from Dante's. There, in *Paradiso* XXXIII, the need to ask for Mary's help was expressed as a *sine qua non*: whosoever wants grace and does not pray to her will 'fly his desire without wings'. Here, Petrarch states that he did indeed have wings to attain the highest Good and thus make of himself an 'example', but he did not even attempt to fly. There, we see Dante in the supremely humble posture of one who has flown to the Heavens and implores for a final grace, the vision of God. Here, we see Petrarch regret never having left the earth and his love for 'cosa mortale', Laura.

What, in other words, we witness in these sonnets is the gradual maturing of a conversion the seeds of which are present from much earlier on in the *Canzoniere*,[42] but which is precipitated by the growing awareness of death's imminence and a sense of tiredness and dissatisfaction with life. Detachment from Laura, even as transfigured after her death,[43] becomes repentance from past errors and finally rejection of love for 'cosa mortale'. Hence, Petrarch turns to God and asks for peace.

It is this intensely, personally lived summing up and coming to an end of a whole experience of feelings and sufferings that *Vergine bella* retraces. And it is significant that after repeatedly invoking God in the last sonnets, the poet should turn to Mary – like Dante before the very end of his poem – for an *elogium* as well as a *supplicatio*. When the symbolic year of man's life indicated by the number of poems in the *Canzoniere* (366 minus the Prologue sonnet)[44] comes to an end, Petrarch replaces Laura with the Virgin.[45]

The construction of *Vergine bella* is highly elaborate. Carducci and Ferrari called it 'both canzone and lauda, both hymn and elegy', and added that

as hymn or lauda, it is objective and it sings the praises of the Virgin; as elegy or canzone, it is subjective and it describes the poet's feelings. Of the hymn, or Christian prayer and litany, it maintains the continuous invocation, 'Vergine', which is repeated at line 1 and line 9 of each stanza. It is a hymn especially in the first five stanzas (1–78): here, after the invocation and the proposition (1–8), come the prayers and the praises. The latter are mostly contained in the first eight lines of each stanza; in the following five, beginning with the apostrophe, 'Vergine', are contained the prayers – and these are general, that the Virgin may turn to him, obtain for him grace, peace, and good speed. In the second part, that is, in the last five stanzas and in the envoy (79–136), it is canzone and elegy. From line 79 to line 103 the poet confesses his vanity and earthly love, and prays to have rest to that passion which is still burning in him. In the remaining lines, he implores, as a Christian and a devout person, that he may have mercy, contrition, and a good death.[46]

The first thing one notices in reading *Vergine bella* after Dante's prayer or even Chaucer's *ABC* is that figural images have totally disappeared. There are only two 'historical' references, one to Christ's Passion (22–4), and one to Eve, whose 'pianto' the Virgin has turned into 'allegrezza' (36). The central 'theological' image is of course that of the Incarnation, which is repeated, with variations, at least once in each of the first six stanzas (6, 28, 30–2, 43, 56–8, 76–9). Scriptural, dogmatic, and liturgical definitions are present throughout,[47] often employed with that 'wit' which, according to Walter Ong, medieval writers use to describe the divine 'mystery'.[48] Thus, for instance, Mary is called 'virgo sapiens, et una de numero prudentum' (14–16), 'scutum' (17), and 'refugium peccatorum' (20). In the third stanza, which I here take as an example, the echoes of the liturgy and the play on mystery are as intense as in Dante. Petrarch begins by calling Mary 'pure and intact Virgin', and immediately adds 'noble daughter and mother of your issue', ending the invocation with the image of the Virgin as light of this world and ornament of Paradise. In the second section of the stanza Mary, now 'fenestra coeli' (31), 'blessed among women' (35), called 'beata' by all generations (38), and 'crowned' in Heaven (39), is implored for her Son's grace (37). Her Son, the Son of the highest Father (30), the Word Itself 'in extremis diebus' 'dwelt in her womb for our salvation' (32). 'Ab aeterno ordinata' (34), chosen among all other women (33–4), she turned Eve's tears into joy (36):

> Vergine pura, d'ogni parte intera,
> del tuo parto gentil figliuola et madre,
> ch'allumi questa vita, et l'altra adorni,
> per te il tuo figlio, et quel del sommo Padre,
> o fenestra del ciel lucente altera,
> venne a salvarne in su li extremi giorni;
> et fra tutti terreni altri soggiorni
> sola tu fosti electa,
> Vergine benedetta,
> ch 'l pianto d'Eva in allegrezza torni.
> Fammi, ché puoi, de la Sua gratia degno,
> senza fine o beata,
> già coronata   nel superno regno.

(Pure Virgin, whole in every part, daughter and mother of your noble Son, who give light to this life and adorn the other, through you, O shining, noble window of heaven, your Son, Son of the highest Father, came to save us in the last days of the world; and amongst all the other earthly dwellings you alone were chosen, blessed Virgin, who turn the tears of Eve to joy. Make me, for you can, worthy of His grace, O blessed without end, already crowned in the celestial kingdom.)[49]

Here, reminiscences from the Gospels, the antiphons of the Church, the hymns of Venantius Fortunatus and St John of Damascus, the prayer of *Paradiso* XXXIII,[50] are blended in a unique amalgam. Petrarch is adopting the elevated style, the new 'sermo sublimis', of Dante.

Elsewhere, what strikes the reader is the way in which the love images of the *Canzoniere* are applied in a totally religious sphere. When, opening the canzone, Petrarch calls Mary 'beautiful virgin', 'clothed with the sun', 'crowned with stars', he clearly adapts images from the Song of Songs (1.7) and the Apocalypse (12.1), but we cannot forget that throughout the *Canzoniere* Laura is presented as a sun surrounded by stars. Nor can we neglect the fact that the 'amor' which now prompts the poet to speak of the Virgin (4) and with which the Holy Ghost incarnated Himself in her womb (6) is a purely heavenly love, quite different from that which reigns elsewhere in the collection. Indeed, the very invocation for mercy here addressed to Mary is generally addressed to Laura, and the love and the faith towards Mary proclaimed in the first stanza (4, 8) are explicitly opposed to the faithful love for Laura recalled in the last (122).

This transformation of love language into the language of religion – a phenomenon which is common, in both directions, throughout the Middle Ages – culminates, through a revisitation of the poet's own past life and an examination of his present condition, in a rejection of Laura. A triple series of images, which becomes more intense in the second part, dominates in *Vergine bella*. The first focusses on the poet's 'error'. The 'cieco ardor' that 'burns' among 'stupid mortals' (20–1) is gradually transformed and finally seen as the poet's own 'dubio stato' (25). The 'secol pien d'errori oscuri et folti' (45) becomes a personal 'fallo' (62), a 'torta via' (65), an 'error' (111), a 'madness' (117). The 'war' of the first stanza (12) recurs as the terrible storm in which the poet finds himself alone, 'senza governo' (69–70), and as the 'affanno' which is the epitome of his life (84).

Death – the second series of images – is more and more impending. Coupled with Fortune as the ruler of the world's affliction in the second stanza (18), it is again viewed as a very personal fact – the poet's own 'ultime strida' (71), his 'last year' (88), his approaching death (91). From 'extremo passo' (107) to 'ultimo pianto' (115), to the very last day (131) death obsesses the writer. 'Conscience' and 'death' do indeed 'sting' him (134).

The images of 'earth' and 'earthliness' sum up this particular dimension. 'Earth', as opposed to Mary's 'Heaven', is the poet himself (13); 'earth' is Laura now dead (92), and 'poca mortal terra caduca' is even the Laura he loves with such wonderful faith (121). And he prays that his last tears may be devout, 'without earthly mud' (115–16).

Gradually, through this triple movement, there emerges a rejection of Laura. At first this happens implicitly, as the poet calls Mary *'vera beatrice'* (52). Earlier on in the *Canzoniere*, Laura had twice been given that very attribute of 'bringer of happiness' (LXXII, 37; CXCI, 7). Nor should we, in our context, forget the way in which Dante's 'Beatrice' is sublimated, left behind, and yet always present at the end of the *Divine Comedy*.[51]

Five stanzas later, the rejection of Laura is explicit. Petrarch now calls her 'Medusa' and says that she and his error made him a stone 'dripping with vain tears' (111–12). As Medusa, she had been enchanting earlier in the collection (CLXXIX, 10 and CXCVII, 6), but as 'a mere image of the love-obsession, almost without moral overtones'.[52] Here she is seen, because of the poet's own 'error', as bewitching, with a decidedly moral implication. Hence, the writer now views his entire life as the obsessive pursuit of 'mortal beauty, acts and words' (85–6). Stanza 7 is perhaps the most 'autobiographical' of *Vergine bella* and the one where Petrarch's examination of conscience and final repentance vibrate with the most intense emotion:

> Vergine, quante lagrime ò già sparte,
> quante lusinghe et quanti preghi indarno,
> pur per mia pena et per mio grave danno!
> Da poi ch'i' nacqui in su la riva d'Arno,
> cercando or questa et or quel'altra parte,
> non è stata mia vita altro ch'affanno.
> Mortal bellezza, atti et parole m'ànno.
> tutta ingombrata l'alma.
> Vergine sacra et alma,
> non tardar, ch'i' son forse a l'ultimo anno.
> I dí miei piú correnti che saetta
> fra miserie et peccati
> sonsen' andati,   et sol Morte n'aspetta.   (79–91)

(Virgin, how many tears have I scattered already, how many blandishments and how many prayers in vain, simply for my pain and my grave harm! Since I was born on the banks of the Arno, searching now one way now another, my life has been nothing but sorrow; mortal beauty, acts, and words have encumbered all my soul. Sacred and life-giving Virgin, do not delay, for I am perhaps in my final year: my days swifter than an arrow, have departed amidst wretchedness and sin, and death alone awaits us.)

The conversion prepared and asked for in the next two stanzas is so complete ('cangiati desiri', 130), that the poet declares that if he can leave his 'stato assai misero et vile' with Mary's help (124–5; the verb he uses, 'resurgo', has an obvious religious overtone), he will consecrate to her name his whole mind and art,

> et penseri e 'ngegno et stile,
> la lingua e 'l cor, le lagrime e i sospiri.   (127–8)

Thus, with a 'retraction' which seems to be much more final than the one Chaucer apparently added at the end of the *Canterbury Tales*, Petrarch ends his poem. When, in the envoy, he asks the Virgin to recommend him to her Son, 'true man and true God', that He may welcome his 'spirto ultimo' 'in peace' (135–7), we realize that we have gone through the whole of a man's experience, the whole of his 'guerra' to be ready, with him, for ultimate 'pace'. The 'biographical' elements implicit in the image of Dante who has seen the 'spiritual lives one by one', or in that of Deguileville's 'pilgrimage of the life of man', are here completely personalized. Dante's example is obviously present, even determining, in Petrarch's mind, to the point of making him conclude the *Canzoniere* with a Prayer to the Virgin after the 'Pater' of sonnet LXII and the implorations to God in sonnets CCCLXIV–V. But Petrarch's Prayer to the Virgin – and he must have invoked her often since in his will he mentions a picture of the Madonna he had at home and which he believed to be Giotto's work – is not, like Dante's, the prologue to a beatific vision,[53] nor merely, like the pilgrim's of Deguileville's poem, an imploration of help in a moment of crisis and temptation. It is a poet's searching review of his entire life, a surrendering of himself to God's hands,[54] a deliberate, artistic decision to end the *Canzoniere* with Buonconte da Montefeltro's last cry to Mary.

We have already seen how our fourth and latest author, Chaucer, transforms the Prayer to the Virgin inserted in a narrative context into a 'private' lyric. Chaucer's Marian 'poems' and his personal devotion to the Virgin must have been well known. In his *Regement of Princes*, Hoccleve mentions the 'many lines' his 'master' wrote in honour of

Mary 'wyth lovyng herte' and calls Chaucer the Virgin's 'servaunt' (4985–91). Did Hoccleve know more 'lyrical' pieces by Chaucer on Mary than have come down to us? Or did he count the Prologues to the Prioress' and the Second Nun's Tales simply as 'lines' in honour of the Virgin? In other words, would these, together with the *ABC*, be taken as lyrical Prayers, isolated from their narrative contexts? Now that we have studied Petrarch's *Vergine bella*, it will be enough to set Chaucer's *ABC* against it to see how 'impersonal' the English translation of Deguileville's Prayer is when compared to the intensely autobiographical poem that concludes the *Canzoniere*. What I propose to do now is to examine Chaucer's other Marian 'lyrics' not as such, but as parts of narratives – to study what happens to the Prayer to the Virgin when it is taken out of a narrative context to be employed in another narrative. For this is precisely what occurs, and on three different occasions, when Chaucer handles Dante's Prayer.

Let us begin, then, with *Troilus and Criseyde*.[55] Book III of the poem celebrates, after a splendid invocation–hymn to Venus by the poet, Troilus' supreme bliss – his conquest of Criseyde and the consummation of their love. In the course of this celebration, Troilus himself pronounces two hymns to Love, one during his night in Criseyde's bed, and one at the end of the Book in the presence of Pandarus. In the first (1254–74) he salutes Love, Venus and Imeneus (1254–60), who have 'brought [him] fro cares colde', and then turns to Love himself:

> Benigne Love, thow holy bond of thynges,
> Whoso wol grace, and list the nought honouren,
> Lo, his desir wol fle withouten wynges;
> For noldestow of bownte hem socouren
> That serven best and most alwey labouren,
> Yet were al lost, that dar I wel seyn, certes,
> But if thi grace passed oure desertes.
>
> And for thow me, that koude leest disserve
> Of hem that noumbred ben unto thi grace,
> Hast holpen, ther I likly was to sterve,
> And me bistowed in so heigh a place
> That thilke boundes may no blisse pace,
> I kan namore; but laude and reverence
> Be to thy bounte and thyn excellence!   (III, 1261–74)

The second and third line of the first stanza are a translation of lines 13–15 of Dante's Prayer to the Virgin:

Donna, se' tanto grande e tanto vali,
che qual vuol grazia e a te non ricorre
sua disianza vuol volar sanz'ali.

Troilus is calling the God of Love the unique medium of grace as Dante
and St Bernard had done with Mary. He is using a religious image of
divine grace in a secular context. This is not, in itself, surprising in a
medieval poem. But the shift of emphasis in these stanzas makes us
pause. In the first, Troilus thanks Venus, Love and Hymen for having
done *him* a service. In the third, he gives 'laude and reverence' to the
'bounte' and 'excellence' of Love, who has granted *him* 'grace', helped
him as he 'likly was to sterve', and allowed him to have the secular
equivalent of a beatific vision, bestowing him 'in so heigh a place That
thilke boundes may no blisse pace'. In the second stanza, the
meditation is more general: '*whoso* wol grace', '*hem* socouren', '*oure*
desertes'.

Now, what causes Troilus' *elogium* of Love is not the vision of Mary's
triumph in the Empyrean, but the view, and the fondling of, and the
delight in, a rather different 'hevene':

Hire armes smale, hire streghte bak and softe,
Hire sydes longe, flesshly, smothe, and white
He gan to stroke, and good thrift bad ful ofte
Hire snowissh throte, hire brestes rounde and lite.
Thus in this hevene he gan hym to delite,
And therwithal a thousand tyme hire kiste,
That what to don, for joie unnethe he wiste.   (III, 1247-53)

And at the end of his hymn Troilus does not direct his gaze into God,
but kisses Criseyde again (1275-6). The contrast with Dante's experience seems deliberate, as the quotation from *Paradiso* XXXIII and
the allusions to Heaven, grace, bliss, to the very passing from 'cares
colde' and death to the 'heigh place' – from Inferno to Paradise – would
indicate.

Yet there is in Troilus, as well as in his narrator, a complementary
movement. Both celebrate here the sublimation of love as emotional
and sexual experience in a kind of ecstasy, of supreme rapture (*raptus*
was the word theologians used to describe Paul's vision of God in II
Corinthians 12, and hence the state a man must necessarily be in to
obtain a beatific vision):

For out of wo in blisse now they flete.   (1221)

207

But this experience acquires a higher status once Troilus starts meditating on it. When, in his hymn, he passes from his own concerns in the first stanza to general considerations in the second, the Love which he had already called 'Charite' (1254) becomes 'benigne Love' and above all 'holy bond of thynges' (1261). The Narrator had anticipated this in his Prologue to the third Book, describing the universal power of the 'blisful light', 'of which the bemes clere – Adorneth al the thridde heven faire'. God Himself, he said there, loves:

> In hevene and helle, in erthe and salte see
> Is felt thi myght, if that I wel descerne,
> As man, brid, best, fissh, herbe, and grene tree
> Thee fele in tymes with vapour eterne.
> God loveth, and to love wol nought werne,
> And in this world no lyves creature
> Withouten love is worth, or may endure. (III, 8–14)

The last three lines of this stanza, be it noted, have only a partial precedent in Boccaccio's original (*Filostrato* III, 74–79), where the *gods* ('iddii', 74, 7) accompany men and the animal and vegetable kingdoms in 'feeling' the might of Venus, and where *God* as agent of love is totally absent. Troilus will return to this idea of cosmic love in his hymn at the end of Book III, which is totally detached from contingent concerns. There, the splendid Boethian mould of the four stanzas containing Troilus' song is Chaucer's closest equivalent to Dante's 'amor che move il sole e l'altre stelle':[56]

> Love, that of erthe and se hath governaunce,
> Love, that his hestes hath in hevenes hye,
> Love, that with an holsom alliaunce . . .
> . . .
> So wolde God, that auctour is of kynde,
> That with his bond Love of his vertu liste
> To cerclen hertes alle and faste bynde,
> That from his bond no wight the wey out wiste (III, 1744–68)

Troilus' use of some lines from St Bernard's Prayer to the Virgin responds, then, to the deeper logic of Chaucer's poem. It is part of a wider pattern in which human, sexual love is seen as a manifestation of the love that governs the whole universe. But it is also a double-edged image. Troilus may, in his meditation, come closer to the world of the spirit – does indeed seem to fly 'his desir' *with* 'wynges' to the 'grace' of the 'holy bond of thynges' – but he begins by stroking Criseyde's body and ends by kissing her. His flight ultimately is 'withouten wynges', for the object through which Troilus wants and seems to attain cosmic love is decidedly earthly.[57] Like Petrarch in his adoration of Laura, Troilus has forgotten love *for* God.[58] In this he is of course justified, as he is supposed to be, after all, a pagan, though one who mentions *God*.[59] But the narrator who extols Troilus' love and the cosmic might of Venus cannot adhere to 'oblivio Dei' for long. In the Prologue to Book III he declares, 'God loveth, and to love wol nought werne', but this is only one side of the coin. 'L'amor che move il sole e l'altre stelle', the last line of the *Divine Comedy*, is only the subject in a sentence where Dante's desire and will are the object. Like a wheel that is evenly moved, these are now revolved by the love which moves the sun and the other stars. Dante's desire and will become part of the same movement which involves the universe and which proceeds from God's love. This, however, is possible only because Dante's love for God has led him to conform to God's love for him and the world.[60] And I suspect that the reason why Chaucer does not use the last line of *Paradiso* XXXIII in the third Book of *Troilus* (in spite of the fact that it would apparently fit very well with Troilus' second hymn to Love and would come naturally to a poet who had employed lines from that canto earlier on) is precisely his awareness of the context in which that verse is inserted.

For the author of *Troilus* knows very well what the place of love for God should be. At the end of his 'litel bok', after paying homage to poetic tradition and placing himself within it, and after recommending that no one 'myswrite' and 'mysmetre' his poem (V, 1786–99), Chaucer relates his hero's death in a single stanza, which shows how un-Iliadic his book has been. The 'wrath' of Troilus (a deliberate take-off of the *Iliad*'s first line, which Chaucer knew from Latin 'florilegia') is 'despitously' abated by the 'fierse Achille' (Achilles' 'wrath', indeed!) in one single line (1800–6). Then, following Boccaccio's Arcita,[61] Troilus' ghost ascends to the eighth sphere, where it contemplates the 'erratik sterres, herkenyng armonye With sownes ful of hevenyssh melodie' (1807–13). Immediately afterwards, the soul of the Trojan hero turns its gaze downwards, where he beholds 'this litel spot of erthe' and consequently despises 'this wrecched world' (1814–20).

This ascension corresponds to Dante's arrival into the *eighth* sphere when, prompted by Beatrice, he casts his eyes through the heavens he has passed and down to 'this globe', now such, he says, that he smiled at its paltry semblance (*Paradiso* XXII, 133–8, 139–53). It is Dante's last glance at Earth. In the following canto, he witnesses the triumph of Christ and Mary which I discussed at the beginning of this chapter.

Troilus, instead, looks intently at the spot where he was slain and laughs at the grief of those who weep over his death (1821–22). His soul had, a moment before, 'held al vanite – To respect of the pleyn felicite – That is in hevene above'. It now condemns

> al oure werk that foloweth so
> The blynde lust, the which that may nat laste,
> And sholden al oure herte on heven caste. (1823–5)

The great love of Book III has become but an aspect of the '*blynde* lust' which cannot last long though it dominates 'oure werk'.

Troilus' soul is spared further recantation. While realizing how 'pleyn' is the happiness of the 'hevene above', the immortal essence of Troilus proceeds, as Mercury guides it, to a dwelling which, like the Boccaccio of the *Teseida*, Chaucer leaves mysterious (1826–7). The Stoic end of Troilus is, however, insufficient for his creator. Speaking now in the first person, and prompted by Boccaccio (*Filostrato* VIII, 28), he launches into a melancholy consideration of Troilus' love story:

> Swich fyn hath, lo, this Troilus for love!
> . . .
> Swich fyn his lust (1828–31)

Then, once more following Boccaccio (*Filostrato* VIII, 29, 1–5), but boldly abandoning his source after two lines, Chaucer appeals to the 'yonge, fresshe folkes' 'in which that love up groweth' and invites them to cast their hearts to that God who has made them in His image (1835–41). And it is here that the correspondence between the love of God for man and that which man ought to bear to God is finally preached in purely Christian terms and opposed to 'feynede loves':

> And *loveth* hym the which that right for *love*
> Upon a crois, oure soules for to beye,
> First starf, and roos, and sit in hevene above;
> For he nyl falsen no wight, dar I seye,
> That wol his herte al holly on hym leye.
> And syn he best to *love* is, and most meke,
> What nedeth *feynede loves* for to seke? (1842–8)

Hence, the poet now looks with disdain at the 'corsed olde rites' of pagans, the 'wrecched appetites' of this world, the 'fyn and guerdoun' one gains in serving the rabble of heathen deities, the 'forme' itself 'of

olde clerkis speche In poetrie' (1849–55). Recommending his book to
his friends Gower and Strode (1856–9), he turns 'to that sothefast Crist'
who, as he has just said and repeats here, died on the cross (1860,
1842–4) for *love*. With all his heart, he ends his poem, like Petrarch his
Canzoniere, with a prayer – one to the Lord in the Trinity as celebrated
by Dante in *Paradiso* xiv, but one in which the last line, with a final
twist on the original, and repeating once more the word 'love', sends
back to us an echo of the Prayer to the Virgin:[62]

> Thow oon, and two, and thre, eterne on lyve,
> That regnest ay in thre, and two, and oon,
> Uncircumscript, and al maist circumscrive,
> Us from visible and invisible foon
> Defende, and to thy mercy, everichon,
> So make us, Jesus, for thi mercy digne,
> *For love of mayde and moder thyn benigne.*

The way in which Dante's Prayer to the Virgin and the lines from
Paradiso xiv are used in the *Troilus* corresponds, then, to a precise,
'ideal' as well as narrative strategy. In Book iii, a few lines from Dante's
Marian eulogy are inserted into a paean that celebrates the power of
sexual attraction and fulfilment as an aspect of cosmic love. Although
the use of sacred images in courtly poetry and viceversa is fairly
common in the Middle Ages, here it reaches a startling climax. Yet the
context in which this image is employed is somewhat ambiguous. And
it is this ambiguity that the poet brings out fully in the epilogue, where,
again by means of Dantean lines, he points out the importance in a
Christian context of man's love for God and God's love for man.

Finally, one understands why Chaucer calls this poem a 'little
tragedy' and places it, though with a gesture of humility, in the shade
of great classical 'poesye'. *Troilus* is a tragedy not only because of the
hero's earthly adventures in love, melancholy, and death (as we have
seen in chapter 3), but also because, as Dante puts it following Horace's
Ars Poetica, 'sometimes even Comedy raises her voice' to reach the
style of tragedy, which speaks 'elate et sublime', in an exalted and
sublime manner.[63]

The other occasions on which Chaucer uses Dante's prayer to the Virgin
are very different. In the Prologues to the Prioress's and the Second
Nun's stories such as we read them in Fragments vii and viii of the
Canterbury Tales,[64] the Invocation to Mary has a more straightforward

function. When, after the Shipman, the Prioress is invited to tell a tale, she begins by invoking the Lord[65] and talking about the way His name is celebrated by 'men of dignitee' as well as by 'the mouth of children' (453–9). It is, therefore, 'in laude' of God and Mary that she will do her 'labour' 'to telle a storie' (460–6). At this point, the Prioress inserts her Prayer to the Virgin, which occupies three stanzas (467–87). The first two are an *elogium*, the third a *supplicatio*. But in the last line of the first and third stanzas the speaker invokes Mary's help in her narrative enterprise:

> Help me to telle it in thy reverence!
> Gydeth my song that I shal of yow seye.

The Prioress, then, announces the theme and the purpose of her tale, which is about and for Mary. The Virgin represents, however, the epitome of divine mystery, as the first stanza makes absolutely clear:

> O mooder Mayde, O mayde Mooder free!
> O bussh unbrent, brennynge in Moyses sighte,
> That ravyshedest doun fro the Deitee,
> Thurgh thyn humblesse, the Goost that in th'alighte,
> Of whos vertu, whan he thyn herte lighte,
> Conceyved was the Fadres sapience,
> Help me to telle it in thy reverence!   (467–73)

Here, especially if compared to the *ABC*, the language is rich, compressed, figural as well as dogmatic. The Dantean lesson has been learnt to perfection.[66] And to Dante the Prioress turns in her second stanza, where the Virgin's virtues are celebrated in the inexpressibility topos (476), and prevenient grace is evoked (477–8) to recall precisely the function that the Prayer to the Virgin had in *Paradiso* XXXIII – that of obtaining, through Mary, the 'lyght' by which man is guided unto her Son (479–80):

> Lady, thy bountee, thy magnificence,
> Thy vertu and thy grete humylitee
> Ther may no tonge expresse in no science;
> For somtyme, Lady, er men praye to thee,
> Thou goost biforn of thy benygnytee,
> And getest us the lyght, of thy preyere,
> To gyden us unto thy Sone so deere.   (474–80)

In the final stanza of the Prologue the Prioress turns to her own lack of 'konnyng' and incapacity to express herself:

> My konnyng is so wayk, O blisful Queene,
> For to declare thy grete worthynesse
> That I ne may the weighte nat susteene;
> But as a child of twelf month oold, or lesse,
> That kan unnethes any word expresse,
> Right so fare I, and therfore I yow preye,
> Gydeth my song that I shal of yow seye.   (481–7)

Dante complains about this very incapacity three times in *Paradiso* XXXIII (55–7, 106–8, 121–3), and he once asks the 'somma luce' to make his tongue so powerful that he may leave at least a spark of Its glory to people in the future (67–72). And the child imagery associated with the vision of the supreme mysteries (*Paradiso* XXIII, 121–6, and XXX, 82–7) is here employed to describe Dante's 'corta favella' before he plunges into the three gyres of the Trinity:

> Omai sarà più corta mia favella,
> · pur a quel ch'io ricordo, che d'un fante
> che bagni ancor la lingua a la mammella.   (XXXIII, 106–8)

(Now will my speech fall more short, even in respect to that which I remember, than that of an infant who still bathes his tongue at the breast.)

It will not therefore seem farfetched to suggest that the idea of making his Prioress illustrate her inability to express herself by means of the image of the little child may have come to Chaucer from Dante's supreme canto, to be appropriately associated with the story of a boy. The tale's teller is indeed like a baby, smaller even than her protagonist, and incapable of speaking. He, the little child of her story, will sing, and in Latin, to the greater glory of Mary and God.

The story that the Prioress proceeds to tell after this invocation is not a beatific vision, but a miracle of the Virgin. But a literal comparison with Dante's final canto is misleading. The *Prioress's Tale* and the *Second Nun's Tale* represent the only examples of religious narrative and the only two celebrations of human love for God in a fully Christian sense in the *Canterbury Tales*. In these two stories, the human logic and motivations which rule the world of the other tales seem to be suspended. Nor is the way chosen by Chaucer to show how man can reach God negative, as happens in the *Parson's Tale*, which purports to point out to the other pilgrims the way 'of thilke parfit glorious pilgrymage – That highte Jerusalem celestial' but does so by means of a sermon on *penitence*. The Parson tells us what we should *not* do and what we ought to repent of if we want to attain the heavenly Jerusalem.

The Prioress and the Second Nun tell us what some people are capable of doing for love of God.

In both cases, this love culminates in martyrdom. Chaucer, who seems incapable of the philosophical and mystical *élan* necessary to a beatific vision and who makes final his decision against it in the *House of Fame*,[67] is, like Petrarch, prepared to renounce human for divine love. He does so in the final stanzas of *Troilus*. In the tales of the Prioress and the Second Nun, he goes beyond this. Here, he does not simply pray. In the *Prioress's Tale* he recounts the story of a child who, in love with Marian songs, is murdered and hidden away by the Jews of his town. When his mother, a widow also devoted to Mary, looks for him in the Jewish ghetto, the boy, though 'with throte ykorven', starts singing *Alma redemptoris*. While the Jews are killed in an awful pogrom, the child is brought on a bier before the high altar and, blessed with holy water, once more sings the Marian antiphon. The abbot then asks him to explain why he can sing though his throat has been cut. And the boy declares that the law of nature (650) is suspended in him because Jesus 'wil that his glorie laste and be in mynde' (653).

But it is his devotion to Mary – that very devotion with which the Prioress had invoked the Virgin in her Prologue – that has produced the miracle, as the child himself proclaims:

> This welle of mercy, Cristes mooder sweete,
> I loved alwey, as after my konnynge;
> And whan that I my lyf sholde forlete,
> To me she cam, and bad me for to synge
> This anthem verraily in my deyynge,
> As ye han herd, and whan that I hadde songe,
> Me thoughte she leyde a greyn upon my tonge.
>
> Wherfore I synge, and synge moot certeyn,
> in honour of that blisful Mayden free
> Til fro my tonge of taken is the greyn;
> And after that thus seyde she to me:
> 'My litel child, now wol I fecche thee,
> Whan that the greyn is fro thy tonge ytake.
> Be nat agast; I wol thee nat forsake'.   (656–69)

The logic of these two stanzas corresponds to that of the Prioress's Prologue, down to the 'konnynge' of the second line, which recalls the 'konnyng' of line 481.

The *exemplum* of Chaucer's 'litel clergeon' is an extreme, though one that a modern poet like Geoffrey Hill can still understand if, addressing Our Lady of Chartres, he writes: 'Child-saints rejoice you, small immaculate souls'.[68] Chaucer's protagonist is a seven-year-old who is taught devotion to Mary (505–12) and learns the first verse of *Alma redemptoris* though he does not understand Latin (523–4). He asks an older boy to explain the meaning to him, then learns all of it off by heart, and sings it on his way to school and back. The portrait we have of him in the Prioress's words centres on his simplicity, single-minded determination, devotion, and innocence.[69] He illustrates perfectly Jesus' preaching in the Gospel:

And Jesus called a little child unto him, and set him in the midst of them, and said, Verily I say unto you, Except ye be converted, and become as little children, ye shall not enter into the kingdom of heaven. Whosoever therefore shall humble himself as this little child, the same is the greatest in the kingdom of heaven. And whoso shall receive one such little child in my name receiveth me.[70]   (Matthew 18. 2–5)

And indeed the human punishment of the Jewish murderers does not simply respond to the *lex talionis* proclaimed by the provost, 'Yvele shal have that yvele wol deserve' (632),[71] but also to the warning Jesus gives to those who harm his 'parvuli':

But whoso shall offend one of these little ones which believe in me, it were better for him that a millstone were hanged about his neck, and that he were drowned in the depth of the sea.   (Matthew 18. 6)

The Prioress's little child 'is' Christ in the same manner as the little child received in Jesus' name 'is' Jesus in the Gospel. And the *Tale* widens and deepens this dimension by making its protagonist appear as an heir of Abel, one of the Holy Innocents of Herod's massacre, a follower of the Lamb,[72] a St Nicholas (513–15), and a Hugh of Lincoln (684–5). From Genesis to the Gospels, to the Apocalypse and to saints' legends, Chaucer's 'parvulus' is innocence and martyrdom, in and out of time. The subject of the Prioress's Tale may seem less exalted than Dante's beatific vision, but it is absolutely central to Christianity, for it is no less than the condition upon which man can gain entrance into the kingdom of Heaven visited by Dante and shut off for the jeweller of *Pearl* and to Deguileville's pilgrim: 'Except ye be converted, and become as *little children*, ye shall not enter into the kingdom of heaven'. It is therefore appropriate that its teller should invoke Mary's help in a high-sounding Prayer to the Virgin, and that its audience should be left marvellously 'sobre' at the end (691–2).

The new 'sermo sublimis' of the Invocation prefaces a story the subject of which is 'humble' precisely in the evangelical sense. And the style with which Chaucer has the Prioress recount the story is the 'sermo humilis' that leads the 'poor in spirit' to an understanding of the highest mysteries. Let us, with Erich Auerbach, read Augustine:

> Holy Writ, adapting itself to *babes* ('parvulis'), has not been afraid to use expressions taken from any kind of thing, from which, as though drawing food from it, our understanding may rise gradually to things lofty and sublime ('ad divina atque sublimia').[73]

Similarly, if not more appropriate, is the 'Invocacio ad Mariam' in the Second Nun's Prologue. Here, the speaker is particularly close to Dante, whose St Bernard is evoked in the second line of the Invocation (30) and whose *elogium* is adapted fairly faithfully:[74]

> Thow Mayde and Mooder, doghter of thy Sone,
> Thow welle of mercy, synful soules cure,
> In whom that God for bountee chees to wone,
> Thow humble, and heigh over every creature,
> Thow nobledest so ferforth oure nature,
> That no desdeyn the Makere hadde of kynde
> His Sone in blood and flessh to clothe and wynde.
>
> Withinne the cloistre blisful of thy sydis
> Took mannes shap the eterneel love and pees,
> That of the tryne compas lord and gyde is,
> Whom erthe and see and hevene out of relees
> Ay heryen; and thou, Virgine wemmelees,
> Baar of thy body – and dweltest mayden pure –
> The Creatour of every creature.
>
> Assembled is in thee magnificence
> With mercy, goodnesse, and with swich pitee
> That thou, that art the sonne of excellence
> Nat oonly helpest hem that preyen thee,
> But often tyme, of thy benygnytee
> Ful frely, er that men thyn help biseche,
> Thou goost biforn and art hir lyves leche.   (36–56)

Once more, the comparison with Chaucer's own *ABC* shows how Dante's model prompts the English author to treat the eulogy in a highly rhetorical manner, interweaving sources[75] and images and producing a compact lyrical piece. As examples, I would point to at least two sets of lines. In the first, Chaucer takes Dante's

Tu se' colei che l'umana natura
nobilitasti sí, che 'l suo fattore
non disdegnò di farsi sua fattura

and, translating the first line and a half, enlarges on the rest, rendering 'fattore' with 'the Makere . . . of kynde' and loosening 'fattura' into 'his Sone in blood and flesh to clothe and wynde'. Thus, Dante's 'audacia' is lessened and made plain, and a new rhetorical pattern is found. The concept is taken up again in the following stanza, where the mystery of the Incarnation is dwelt upon at greater length and inserted into a cosmic background (43–7), the paradox of maternity in virginity being repeated together with that of the 'Creatour of every creature' borne by a human 'body' (47–9).

In the second set of lines, Chaucer keeps an eye on Dante, but alters the ideas and their sequence, integrating them with images taken from elsewhere. Thus, 'nel ventre tuo' is amplified into 'withinne the cloistre blisful of thy sydis' by the introduction of the traditional 'claustrum' image. 'Raccese', which in Dante represents the first image of fire and warmth and implies a re-vival of God's love for man after the Fall, is replaced by the much plainer 'took mannes shap'. The 'germinating flower' of Dante's ninth line is eliminated. 'Amore' and 'etterna pace' are kept, but not in Dante's highly elaborate sequence, where 'amore' means God's love and the Holy Ghost as subject, and 'etterna pace' indicates the place where the protagonist now finds himself – the Empyrean – as well as the 'aeterna pax' to which all beings tend with their desire (*Paradiso* III, 85–7). In Chaucer, 'the eterneel love and pees' are, together, the cumulative subject of the Incarnation, of 'took mannes shap'. They are God, whose power is described in the following line, 'that of the tryne compas lord and gyde is'. Here, 'tryne compas' means the threefold world of earth, sea and heaven evoked immediately afterwards, but the suggestion of the triple circle of the Trinity such as described by Dante towards the end of *Paradiso* XXXIII may also be present.[76] In any case, the image seems to suggest a reflection on the tripartite nature of the visible universe of the trinitarian nature of the Deity.

In other words, what we have in the first four stanzas of the 'Invocacio ad Mariam' is a solemn evocation of the supreme mysteries in the form of an *elogium*. The *supplicatio* comes in the next three stanzas (57–77), where the speaker asks Mary for mercy and help as a human being steeped in sin (58, 62, 71–4) and as the singer of St Cecilia's life. In fact, consideration for the task of 'enditing' a sacred subject opens and closes the 'Invocacio' (29–35 and 78–84). At the beginning, inspiration is asked of Mary as the Muse of this particular tale. At the end, the humility formula sends the audience back to the source, Jacopo da Varazze's *Legenda Aurea*. The composition and telling of the story are given a theological justification. As 'feith', says the narrator, 'is deed withouten werkis', 'wit and space' 'for to werken' are implored of Mary so as to obtain salvation from Hell (64–6). But the 'work' the speaker means is not just the 'opera' in general without which, as James' Epistle proclaims (2. 17 and 20), 'faith is dead, being alone': it is also the narrator's present 'werk' (77 and 84).

The *Second Nun's Tale* is presented to us, then, as the religious opposite of *Troilus and Criseyde*. Mary replaces the Muses and the Furies. The author appeals to his authority's 'wordes and sentence', and trusts his 'werk' to the audience's 'amende'. In Book III of *Troilus*, as we have seen, Venus and Love are celebrated as the supreme powers of earth, sea, and heaven (8 and 1744–5). In the Prologue to the *Second Nun's Tale* 'erthe and see and hevene' 'ay heryen' the 'eterneel love and pees', God, the true 'lord and gyde' of 'the tryne compas'. A direct line seems to link the Epilogue of *Troilus*, with its Dantean prayer to the Trinity and the Love of the Virgin Mother, to the Dantean Prologue to the *Second Nun's Tale*. Nor is it perhaps without significance that in neither the Prioress' nor the Second Nun's Prologues do we find any trace of Troilus' perversion of the Dantean 'sua disianza vuol volar sanz'ali'. It looks as if, having given Dante's 'disianza' the erotic connotation of 'desir' in the *Troilus*, Chaucer decided to avoid this image in a 'sacred' context. Though on both occasions he translates the terzina that immediately follows those two lines (*Paradiso* XXXIII, 16–18; *Prioress's Tale*, 477–8; *Second Nun's Tale*, 52–6), reproducing the concept of prevenient grace, he eliminates the splendid 'flying without wings' which is the epitome of Troilus' adventure in life *and* death.

That the enterprise to which Chaucer is now setting hand in the *Second Nun's Tale* is intended to be an exalted one is confirmed also by his reproduction of the 'Interpretacio nominis Cecilie quam ponuit Frater Jacobus Januensis in Legenda'. The fivefold etymology of 'Cecilia' makes the protagonist of the story a mirror of Heaven on earth and an intermediary between them. Cecilia is 'hevenes lilie' but also 'the wey to blynde'. She is 'hevene' and 'Lia', that is, 'in figurynge', 'thoght of hoolynesse' and active life. She is 'wantynge of blyndnesse' 'for hir grete light Of sapience, and for hire thewes clere'. She is, finally, 'hevene' and 'leos', 'the hevene of peple', 'ensample of goode and wise werkes alle' (85–105). In the last two stanzas of the 'Interpretacio', Chaucer enlarges upon his source and alters its conceptual sequence[77] to make the name of the saint acquire a cosmic and celestial dimension (107–8, 114–15). Cecilia, already the epitome of 'chastnesse of virginitee', 'honestee', 'conscience', 'good fame', 'good techynge', the contemplative and active lives, 'sapience' and 'goode and wise werkes', becomes now 'of feith the magnanymyte', 'the cleernesse hool of sapience', and 'sondry werkes, brighte of excellence'. Thus, *spiritualiter* ('goostly'), she is the heaven in which the sun, the moon and the stars are visible (106–12). And like heaven, she has roundness and wholeness, the swiftness in movement of the Primum Mobile, and the 'brennynge', the *ardor* of the Empyrean (113–18).[78]

The 'lyf of Seinte Cecile' *is*, then, a beatific vision *sui generis*,[79] appropriately prefaced by a Prayer to the Virgin. Chaucer not only loved the intense lyricism of the Dantean eulogy, but also understood its narrative, poetic, and theological function. For what follows in the tale is, as in the Prioress', an extreme story of devotion to Christ and to the ideal of chastity and 'maydenhede'. Cecilia is going to be married to Valerian. She does not refuse marriage, but asks that she may keep virginity in it – a totally 'unnatural' request, which hardly agrees with the Church's matrimonial doctrine. But the laws of nature are suspended in this tale as they are in the Prioress', and to an even greater extent. Here, the supernatural is present not only in the miracle of Cecilia surviving and preaching for three days though 'with her nekke ykorven' – as the Prioress' little child sings 'with throte ykorven' – but also in the various visions that mark the most important stages of the story and point to the ultimate vision of God.

When Cecilia tells her husband she has an angel for lover and entreats him to 'gye' her 'in clene love', she adds that if he will do so, the angel will show him 'his joye and his brightnesse' (161). Later, when Valerian, until now 'a fiers leoun', becomes a 'lomb' before Pope Urban, an old man 'clad in white clothes cleere' and with 'a book with lettre of gold in honde' appears to him. This 'senex', so similar to Dante's St Bernard, is none other than St Paul who, instead of showing truth and pointing to Death in a 'negative' parable like the Old Man of the *Pardoner's Tale*, announces the mystery of God *aureis litteris*:

Unus Dominus, una fides, unum baptisma. Unus Deus et pater omnium, qui est super omnes et per omnia et in omnibus nobis.   (Ephesians 4. 5–6)

> O Lord, o feith, o God, withouten mo,
> O Cristendom, and Fader of alle also,
> Aboven alle and over alle everywhere. (207–9)

And as soon as the newly christened Valerian arrives at home, he sees Cecilia's angel with two crowns, of roses and lilies (symbols of martyrdom and purity),[80] which he says he has brought 'fro paradys' and will never rot or lose their perfume. Valerian's brother, Tiburce, smells this scent when he reaches the couple but cannot see the crowns. The 'swete smel' operates in him a wonderful metamorphosis: 'hath chaunged me al in another kynde' (252). Cecilia leads the two men 'to blisse above' (281), as before the angel had promised her and Valerian the 'palm of martirdom' and participation in God's 'blisful feste' (240–1).

Truth, then, is what man beholds when he is ready for conversion. When Tiburce asks Valerian whether what he has said about the existence of the two crowns was 'in soothnesse' or heard 'in dreem', Valerian answers with a phrase that announces a total revolution of natural law:

> 'In dremes', quod Valerian, 'han we be
> Unto this tyme, brother myn, ywis.
> But now at erst in trouthe oure dwellyng is'. (262–4)

In truth, be it noted, not 'in reality'. For this 'truth' is the subject of Paul's Epistle to the Ephesians, where the Apostle advocates 'the perfecting of the saints', 'the work of the ministry', 'the edifying of the body of Christ', 'till we all come in the unity of the faith, and of the knowledge of the Son of God, unto a perfect man, unto the measure of the stature of the fulness of Christ' and, 'speaking the truth in love, may grow up into him in all things, which is the head, even Christ' (4. 12–15). Putting off the 'old man' and putting on the 'new man' (4. 22–24), the Christian must not walk 'as other Gentiles walk, in the vanity of their mind, having the understanding darkened, being alienated from the life of God through the ignorance that is in them, because of the blindness of their heart' (4. 17–18).

The story of Cecilia, Valerian and Tiburce is an illustration of these words. Cecilia shows Tiburce, and will later tell Almachius, that 'alle ydoles nys but a thyng in veyn' – that the heathen, gentile religion is dumb and deaf, the pagan gods but stones, and whoever believes in them is blind (284–91, 498–511). The Second Nun's Tale brings to completion Chaucer's detachment from the 'payens corsed olde rites', from the 'rascaille' of Jove, Apollo and Mars announced at the end of *Troilus*. It makes man's love for Christ finally correspond to Christ's love for man.[81] In the *Troilus* epilogue, as we have seen, the narrator invites the 'yonge, fresshe folkes' to love Him, 'the which that right for love Upon a crois, oure soules for to beye, First starf, and roos, and sit in hevene above'. But Cecilia's whole life is devoted to this love – 'for his love that dyde upon a tree' (138) – and her 'lover' is an angel, as the initially and understandably incredulous Tiburce, threatening her with a truly Sicilian 'delitto d'onore', must come to realise.

Hence, the 'truth' of the *Second Nun's Tale* is that of life after death, of the Trinity, of the Redemption, which Cecilia expounds to Tiburce (320–48). The ultimate truth is that 'corone of lif that may nat faille' which will receive the martyrs after death, their souls reaching the 'Kyng of grace' – Maximus' vision of their ascent, their 'gliding' to Heaven 'with aungels ful of cleernesse and of light' (402–3).

The itinerary of Valerian, Tiburce and Maximus thus faithfully reproduces an 'itinerarium perfectionis' of conversion, martyrdom, and elevation to God's presence. The 'cleernesse' and the 'light' of Maximus' vision are the nearest Chaucer comes to Dante's beatific vision, and the closest to it he is prepared to take us in the *Canterbury Tales*. The Second Nun's story is Chaucer's 'litel', divine 'comedye'.

The action of St Paul's Christian people 'speaking the truth in love' does however also have a paramount 'earthly' consequence. Initiated by Cecilia and then pursued by Valerian, Tiburce, Maximus, and other 'ministres' of Almachius (410–20), this is the spreading of Christianity through martyrdom, the gradual building of the primitive Church in history. And it is precisely this 'increase of the body unto the *edifying* of itself in love' (Ephesians 4. 16), this growth of the *ecclesia*, that Cecilia fittingly wants to be commemorated 'perpetuelly' after her death by the *building* of a church. Her house becomes the basilica of St Cecilia in Rome,

> In which, into this day, in noble wyse,
> Men doon to Crist and to his seint servyse.

Thus the *Second Nun's Tale*, which is prefaced by an Invocation where the new 'sermo sublimis' is once more recreated, and which is narrated with a keen sense of pathos – on the threshold, as it were, between the humble and the exalted – ends in Rome, where the earthly and the heavenly met throughout the Middle Ages:

Coelum luminibus tantis et Roma refulgent;
hos coelo genuit et sibi terra viros

(The heaven and Rome shine with so many lights; the earth generated them for heaven and for itself – as heroes)[82]

The coming together of earth and heaven, of humble and sublime, is one of the messages of the *Canterbury Tales* which we tend to forget. But, whenever the *Second Nun's Tale* became part of that collection of stories, it was clearly meant to take its place with the *Prioress's Tale* in an ideal pair of hagiographic visions of central Christians truths, as Petrarch's 'penitential' sonnets and *Vergine bella* are meant to have a special position in the *Canzoniere*.

The movement which started in *Troilus* now comes to completion. The presence of Dante's *Paradiso*, and in particular of his Prayer to the Virgin, accompanies its salient stages. Thus, to study the forms and functions of the *Invocacio ad Mariam* in fourteenth-century poetry means to become aware of different approaches to religion as well as to lyric and narrative. In Dante, the *elogium* is the prologue to a beatific vision: it brings him back to Mary before plunging him into God. By adopting a 'high' language, he prepares us for sublimity. Petrarch retraces Dante's steps, shifting the emphasis on to a more personal, intimate, 'autobiographical' intonation: his elevated style is the result of different factors. The *supplicatio* becomes an invocation in the crises of human life and a private prayer 'in the hour of our death'. Such it remains in the allegory of Deguileville's *Pèlerinage*. In Chaucer's hands, everything changes. The *ABC* is still uncertain, suspended between the old and the new style. But the poet of *Troilus* knows how to use Dante's *Paradiso* to celebrate both human and divine love. His craft in the high style is perfect. Yet Chaucer does not forget the original function of the Prayer, that of a 'prologue'. Two of his Canterbury pilgrims use it almost as if it were a poetic-religious manifesto, a 'sublime' overture to stories, both humble and exalted, of martyrdom, miracle, and ascent to Heaven. And this, after all, is the function of the angel's 'Hail Mary' in Luke's Gospel. With it, Gabriel announces in a high-sounding eulogy a tale 'humilis' and 'sublimis' – the story of a child who grows into a man who performs miracles, suffers martyrdom, and is finally carried up into heaven.

8

The Sibyl's leaves: Reading *Paradiso*
XXXIII

In canto XXXIII of *Paradiso* the solitary voice of an old man, St Bernard, fills the Empyrean and the entire universe. His words, however, end about one third of the way through the canto. Then, silence falls over the heavens and Dante, the man whose questioning had resounded through Hell, Purgatory, and Paradise, is left mute and alone with his God. It is the presence and the quality of the human voice that define the structure and the atmosphere of canto XXXIII. In the first thirty-nine lines it is Bernard who speaks, praising Mary and praying to her. In the second part of the canto, the drama as such, as action, is over. For the first time in the poem Dante has no interlocutor except his own memory and the supreme Light that his memory and his pen are trying to recreate for us.

In the preceding chapter, I have examined Bernard's prayer as an example of the new style, the 'sermo sublimis', that Dante inaugurates with it. Here, I would like to read the second and longer section of *Paradiso* XXXIII paying attention to Dante's own voice, to the theological and poetic problems that the ultimate vision sets the thinker and writer. We shall see that in both areas these problems produce almost unbearable tensions, which the imagery of the canto reflects and overcomes. By studying the final struggle of the *Paradiso* I shall, then, pave the way to a closer examination of Dante's sublimity – no longer as a mere stylistic feature, but as the poetics of the entire third cantica – in my last chapter.

After responding to Bernard's prayer by fixing her eyes on him, Mary turns them to God, and Bernard himself motions Dante to raise his gaze. The pilgrim, however, has already done so. He is looking into God's light. Dante had already glanced at it from far away: in the ninth heaven God had appeared to him as a mathematical point radiating such light that it blinds the eye (XXVIII, 16–21). Dante has come closer and closer to this point and can now, in canto XXXIII, look into it and distinguish its form, content, colours, and images. Here, in the Empyrean, he fixes his eyes on the light which has blinded him before and which must now be even stronger. Theologically, this is possible. That the vision of the divine essence must be the *sine qua non* of the ultimate and perfect beatitude had been considered by Thomas Aquinas as both an article of faith[1] and a conclusion that could be reached by reason.[2] Thomas had also asked himself whether *delectatio* (joy, pleasure) was more important, in beatitude, than vision. He had answered that a cause is greater than its effects and since vision is the cause of *delectatio*, 'vision is more important than pleasure'.[3] Vision is a function of the intellect, and delight of the will: an act of the intellect precedes that of the will.

Dante had accepted this position and, through Beatrice, made clear that the basis of celestial beatitude lies in the vision of God, not in love, which is an effect of vision (XXVIII, 109–11). So far, both Thomas and Dante have been concerned with the vision of God as reserved to the blessed. For them, this vision is possible and indeed necessary. But on exceptional occasions living men, too, can see God in His essence. It is to this end that they are granted a form of rapture called *raptus*. When man's mind, to whose dignity, because he was made in God's image, appertains to be elevated 'ad divina', is raised by a gift of grace to the vision of God, not against nature but 'above the faculty of nature', we can speak of *raptus*.[4] 'Rapture', says Thomas, 'is in some way proper to prophecy';[5] but prophecy is not just the foreknowledge of future events: since the gift of prophecy is granted 'through divine light', and since by divine light everything, both human and divine, can be known, 'prophetic revelation extends to everything', for instance to the excellence of God and of the angels.[6] Prophecy and *raptus* are not permanent states; they are both transitory, 'in the mode of a transient passion'.[7] Only the blessed can see the divine essence 'per modum formae immanentis': the light which allows them to behold God is a permanent and perfect form.[8] This, however, is the only difference between the vision of God which the blessed have and that which a living man can be granted in prophecy or *raptus*. Both the prophet and the man in the highest form of rapture[9] see God's essence, not a similitude. Since, however, God transcends the created intellect of man, the creature needs a special gift of grace in order to contemplate its Creator's essence: the *lumen gloriae*. The 'light of glory' is a supernatural disposition of the created intellect, a disposition determined by

God's grace and by which the 'intellectual virtue' of the creature is augmented so that it might be able to see God's essence.[10]

As far as Thomas Aquinas is concerned, the *lumen gloriae*, the *raptus*, and the vision of God's essence have been granted to only two men while still alive: Moses and St Paul. Scholars have underlined that Dante's ascent through Paradise follows the example of St Paul's rapture as related by the Apostle in the Second Letter to the Corinthians (12. 2–4):[11]

I knew a man in Christ above fourteen years ago, (whether in the body, I cannot tell; or whether out of the body, I cannot tell: God knoweth;) such an one caught up to the third heaven. And I knew such a man, (whether in the body, or out of the body, I cannot tell: God knoweth;) How that he was caught up into paradise, and heard unspeakable words, which it is not lawful for a man to utter.

Various passages and allusions in the *Comedy* itself support this interpretation.[12] Thus, Dante's vision of God in the last three cantos of *Paradiso*, and particularly in canto XXXIII, is the fruit of a *raptus* similar to that of the Apostle of the Gentiles.[13]

We must not, however, neglect the *prophetic* nature of Dante's beatific vision and indeed of his whole journey. Dante presents himself to us, through the words of his characters and his guides, as the foreteller of future events,[14] And, commenting on the end of the *Paradiso* in the Letter to Cangrande (XIII, 90), the poet implicitly draws a parallel between the final lines of his poem and the 'visio Iohannis', the Book of Revelation. In canto XXXIII of *Paradiso*, then, Dante appears to us as a St Paul and as a prophet: he has finally realized fully those potentialities of his nature which we can see displayed throughout the *Comedy*.

Dante himself had presented his final vision as a consequence of *raptus*. In *Paradiso* XXX, when the pilgrim reaches the Empyrean, a light as bright as that of lightening suddenly shines around him, leaving him swathed in such a web of its glow that he can see nothing (49–51). This, as Beatrice immediately explains, is done by God, who receives into Himself with such light 'per far disposto a sua fiamma il candelo', to fit the candle to its flame. When Dante hears these words, he understands that he is surmounting his own power and that he has acquired a new sight, such that he can now behold the brightest light (55–60). This 'novella vista' explains why Dante, who was blinded by the 'point' of light in canto XXVIII, can now behold the river of light (xxx, 61–81). Yet his sight is not powerful enough, or, as Beatrice tells him: 'non hai viste ancor tanto superbe'. It is here that the 'light of glory' intervenes and grants Dante the vision of the mystical rose:

> Lume è là su che visibile face
> lo creatore a quella creatura
> che solo in lui vedere ha la sua pace.   (xxx, 100–2)

(A Light is thereabove which makes the Creator visible to every creature that has his peace only in beholding Him.)

Finally, Dante's sight does not lose itself in the breadth and height of the rose, but grasps the scope and nature 'of this joyance'. It is the movement of this sublimated sight that we follow in canto XXXIII from the moment Bernard ceases to speak:

> ché la mia vista, venendo sincera,
> e più e più intrava per lo raggio
> de l'alta luce che da sé è vera.   (XXXIII, 52–4)

(for my sight, becoming pure, was entering more and more through the beam of the lofty Light which in Itself is true.)

The whole of canto XXXIII is dominated by verbs and nouns which belong to the sphere of 'seeing', and we can follow the movement of this canto by tracing the various stages and changes which these words undergo. We must, however, introduce here a triple distinction. The nouns that Dante uses to indicate this 'seeing' are basically three: *vista*, *veduta*, and *visione*. They outline three dimensions of 'seeing'. For instance, the *veduta* of line 84 refers to the organ of sight, the 'virtú visiva' of Dante himself. The *vista* of line 136 refers to what was seen by Dante, whereas the *vista* of line 112 is, again, Dante's own organ of sight. Finally, the *visione* of line 62 alludes to a vision which is both present and past. This vision, says Dante, is fading here and now, as he writes ('cessa', 61); yet it is a vision that began a long time ago, for, within the poet's heart, there still drops the sweetness that was born ('nacque', 63) of it. This vision must be the mystical one, the *raptus* which Dante had or pretended to have had at one point of his mortal and poetic life. These three dimensions can then be called *subjective* (he who saw), *objective* (what was seen), and *mystical*.

The first, the subjective one, that of Dante's sight, brings the pilgrim, four times and in each instance by two parallel stages, to join his *vista* with the Object:

1 Dante's sight penetrates deeper and deeper into God:

> (a) ché la mia vista, venendo sincera,
>   e più e più intrava per lo raggio
>   de l'alta luce che da sé è vera.   (52–4)

(for my sight, becoming pure, was entering more and more through the beam of the lofty Light which in Itself is true.)

> (b) Così la mente mia, tutta sospesa,
>   mirava fissa, immobile e attenta,
>   e sempre di mirar faceasi accesa.   (97–9)

(Thus my mind, all rapt, was gazing, fixed, motionless and intent, ever enkindled by its gazing.)

2 Dante cannot turn away from the Object:

> (a) Io credo, per l'acume ch'io soffersi
>   del vivo raggio, ch'i' sarei smarrito,
>   se li occhi miei da lui fossero aversi.   (76–8)

(I believe that, because of the keenness of the living ray which I endured, I should have been lost if my eyes had been turned from it.)

> (b) A quella luce cotal si diventa,
>   che volgersi da lei per altro aspetto
>   è impossibil che mai si consenta   (100–2)

(In that Light one becomes such that it is impossible he should ever consent to turn himself from it for other sight.)

3 Dante sustains the brilliance of the light more and more:

> (a) E' mi ricorda ch'io fui più ardito
>   per questo a sostener   (79–80)

(I remember that on this account I was the bolder to sustain it)

> (b) ma per la vista che s'avvalorava
>   in me guardando   (112–13)

(but through my sight, which was growing strong in me as I looked)

4 Dante joins his seeing with the Infinite Goodness and consumes and completes his sight in It, by thrusting his face into It. Later, this is repeated with the thrusting of Dante's sight into the circle of the Incarnation:

> (a)   tanto ch'i' giunsi
>   l'aspetto mio col valore infinito.
>   Oh abbondante grazia ond'io presunsi
>   ficcar lo viso per la luce etterna,
>   tanto che la veduta vi consunsi!   (80–4)

227

(until I united my gaze with the Infinite Goodness. O abounding grace whereby I presumed to fix my look through the Eternal Light so far that all my sight was spent therein!)

> (b) per che 'l mio viso in lei tutto era messo. (132)
>
> (wherefore my sight was entirely set upon it.)

The second dimension, that of the Object, passes through three stages: (1) manifestation of God as the Pure Act which contains in Its unity and simplicity all the elements that constitute the universe (85–90); (2) manifestation of the Trinity as three circles of three colours and of the same extent; the first and second are reflected in each other as if it were in a rainbow; the third is like fire (115–20); (3) manifestation of the Incarnation as a circle in which appears the image of man (127–31).

The third dimension, that of *visione*, is suspended between past and present, between memory and words. St Paul, Dante's precursor and prototype, had said that he was caught up into Paradise and heard unspeakable words, which it is not lawful for a man to utter. Dante had echoed the Apostle right at the beginning of the *Paradiso*, saying he had been in the heaven that 'most receives of His light' and had seen 'things which whoso descends from up there has neither the knowledge nor the power to relate' (I, 4–6), explaining why:[15] 'because, as it draws near to its desire, our intellect enters so deep that memory cannot go back upon the track' (I, 7–9). In canto XXXIII, Dante has reached precisely that heaven which most receives of God's light, the Empyrean, and his problem is therefore that of calling his vision back to his memory and of putting it into words. The third dimension, that of *visione*, covers Dante's three statements on the impossibility of remembering, speaking, and thinking:

(1) sight is greater than speech, and memory fails with language:

> Da quinci innanzi il mio veder fu maggio
> che 'l parlar mostra, ch'a tal vista cede,
> e cede la memoria a tanto oltraggio. (55–7)

(Thenceforward my vision was greater than speech can show, which fails at such a sight, and at such excess memory fails.)

(2) Dante's language is more inadequate than baby talk:

> Omai sarà più corta mia favella,
> pur a quel ch'io ricordo, che d'un fante
> che bagni ancor la lingua a la mammella. (106–8)

228

(Now will my speech fall more short, even in respect to that which I remember, than that of an infant who still bathes his tongue at the breast.)

(3) speech is scant and feeble to the conception; the conception, to what the poet saw, is not enough to say, 'little'. With speech, thought fails, too:

> Oh quanto è corto il dire e come fioco
> al mio concetto! e questo, a quel ch'i' vidi,
> è tanto, che non basta a dicer 'poco'.   (121–3)

Against these three utterances of impotence stand Dante's three apostrophes to God: (1) as light, that He may re-lend to his mind a little of his appearance, and give the poet's tongue enough power (67–75); (2) as grace (82–4); (3) again as light (124–6). Above all, against the three statements of impotence stand the three passages where Dante tends to overcome the problem: (1) Not all of his vision has vanished, but *almost* all (61), and it still drops some sweetness in his heart (62–3). (2) In the first invocation to the supreme Light, Dante asks God Himself to grant him memory and speech so that he may leave at least a 'gleam' of the divine glory to posterity. It is as if Dante, who has already been granted the *lumen gloriae* necessary for contemplation, asked for a smaller light, a gleam of glory ('una *favilla* sol *de la* tua *gloria*'), the spark of the poet. Indeed he maintains that through his remembrance and language the glory of God will be better known (73–5). He celebrates poetry while stating the impossibility of making poetry. (3) Dante declares that, in using a certain expression ('la forma universal di questo nodo'), he feels his joy expand:

> La forma universal di questo nodo
> credo ch'i' vidi, perché più di largo,
> dicendo questo, mi sento ch'i' godo.   (91–3)

(The universal form of this knot I believe that I saw, because, in telling this, I feel my joy increase.)

What Dante tells us here is, however, not only that the use of this expression procures him a greater joy, but also that the telling of his vision gives him pleasure: 'dicendo questo' does not refer only to the 'universal form', but also to 'I believe that I saw'. Dante rejoices in saying: this is why, 'perché', he believes that he has seen the 'forma universal'. Dante is a poet who believes in that vision because he can tell of it and delight in telling. This may seem paradoxical, but the poet has already told us so. In *Paradiso* XXXI, when he describes – and the similarity of the expression is striking – 'la forma general di paradiso' (the general form of Paradise), Dante explains that he feels like the pilgrim who, as he gazes around in the church, 'draws fresh life of his vow' and already hopes *to tell* 'how it is placed' (43–8). *Perché più di largo, dicendo questo, mi sento ch'i' godo* is Dante's most direct statement of his passion for poetry. It justifies the entire canto XXXIII.

Four times, each by two similar successive stages, has Dante thrust his eyes into God's essence. He has cried out his inability to remember and to speak three times. Three times he has addressed God and described Him. He has, finally, proclaimed the subjective, emotional reason for his telling of the ineffable vision. But we cannot abandon the problem of how a poet can translate such a vision into language. The question had been examined by Dionysius the Areopagite in his *De Divinis Nominibus*, and, amongst others, by Thomas Aquinas in his commentary on the pseudo-Dionysian work. The solutions pointed out by Dionysius and Thomas are three. First, God can be named *per remotionem*, that is to say by denying that He can be named. For instance, Scripture makes Him say: 'I am That I am.'[16] Second, God can be named *per intelligibiles processiones* (by intelligible procedures), that is to say by going back from material effects to their causes. As God is the principle of everything, all causes will be found in Him, and thus all their names can be attributed to Him.[17] Third, God can be named *per sensibiles similitudines* (by sensible, perceptible likeness), that is by giving Him attributes of material objects, for instance fire, light, and crowns. This is the way in which prophets and 'Magistri' described Him, having been illuminated in 'imaginative visions'.[18] A good example of the latter two methods is offered by Dionysius and Thomas when they discuss the name 'lumen' (light), as applied to God. Both Dionysius and Thomas distinguish two ways of attributing this name to God. One is by considering Him as 'intelligible light', because, as Dionysius says, the supreme Good

fills all supracelestial intelligences with an intelligible light, as It expels all ignorance and error from those souls into which It penetrates, gives them Its holy light, and opens up the eyes of their intelligence, closed by heavy darkness, cleaning them of the dirt of ignorance;[19]

or, as Thomas comments, 'inasmuch as He is the ray and source of every intellectual light', 'the first principle of light and that which shines over and above everything' (331). In other words, God is called *lumen intelligibile* because He is the first Intellect, the supreme Truth, the Light that dispels obscurity from the mind of all creatures. On the other hand, God is also called *lumen sensibile*. Indeed, as Thomas observes, 'the name of solar light is metaphorically attributed to God' (304). He explains why in the following manner:

As the things mentioned above receive being and well-being from divine Goodness, so the ray of the sun, considered in itself, comes from God's goodness and is as it were an image, i.e. an expressed likeness of divine Goodness. Hence the Good itself, God, is praised with the name of solar light ('solaris luminis') because divine Goodness is manifested in it as an archetype ('archetypum'), the principal figure or exemplar in the imprinted image ('principalis figura vel principale exemplar in impressa imagine'). Malachi (4.2): 'But unto you that fear my name shall the Sun of righteousness arise.'[20]

This definition of God as 'sensible light' is an example of the third way of naming Him, *per sensibiles similitudines*. Dionysius and Thomas recognize this themselves.[21]

Dante cannot limit himself to proclaiming God ineffable: he must somehow describe Him. He will therefore leave aside the first method and rely on the other two. Only once in the entire canto XXXIII of *Paradiso* does Dante actually name God as such, when Mary's eyes turn on Bernard:

Li occhi da Dio diletti e venerati   (40)

In all other cases except one he applies to Him the name, *lumen*: 'etterno lume' (43), 'alta luce' (54), 'somma luce' (66), 'luce etterna' (83), 'quella luce' (100), 'vivo lume' (110), 'alto lume' (116), 'luce etterna' (124), 'lume reflesso' (128). The light which dominates in the canto is a complex one. When Dante calls God 'the lofty Light which in Itself is true' (54), he clearly implies the *lumen intelligibile*. But when he describes the three circles of three colours and of the same extent with which the 'alto lume' of the Trinity manifests itself to him, the light acquires the connotations of *lumen sensibile*. This ambiguity indicates that a double process takes place in *Paradiso* XXXIII: on the one hand, Dante defines God 'by intelligible procedures'. Following the philosophers (in particular Aristotle, Dionysius, and Thomas), and imitating Scripture, Dante gives us, in the course of canto XXXIII, several definitions of God *per intelligibiles processiones*: all, except one, are accompanied by the term 'light'. Dante, then, calls God 'first and supreme Truth':[22]

alta luce che da sé è vera   (54)

Light of the world (*Lux mundi*):[23]

O somma luce che tanto ti levi
da' concetti mortali (67–8)

(O Light Supreme that art so far uplifted above mortal conceiving)

Infinite Virtue (*Virtus Infinita*):[24]

valore infinito (81)

Supreme Good (*Summum Bonum*):[25]

però che 'l ben, ch'è del volere obietto,
tutto s'accoglie in lei, e fuor di quella
è defettivo ciò ch'è lì perfetto (103–5)

(for the good, which is the object of the will, is all gathered in it, and outside of it that is defective which is perfect there)

Supreme Being (*Summum Ens*):[26]

O luce etterna che sola in te sidi (124)

(O Light Eternal, who alone abidest in Thyself)

the Intellect that understands and loves Itself (*Intellectus intelligens et amans Seipsum*):[27]

O luce etterna che sola in te sidi,
sola t'intendi, e da te intelletta
e intendente te ami e arridi! (124–6)

(O Light Eternal, who alone abidest in Thyself, alone knowest Thyself, and, known to Thyself and knowing, lovest and smilest on Thyself!)

Dante, however, cannot simply pour out philosophical or theological definitions. He must describe God. Therefore, he must resort to the language of similitude. His final solution is metaphorical discourse. Although not very clearly, and indeed in such manner that modern scholars are still debating its true meaning,[28] Dante points it out himself in his Letter to Cangrande by referring to the way in which Plato spoke of his 'myths', the verisimilitudes expressed by metaphors.[29] But Dante presents himself throughout the *Paradiso* as a prophet, as the writer of a sort of Holy Scripture. Now, in Quaestio 12 of the *Prima Pars* of his *Summa Theologiae* Thomas Aquinas explains how God can be known by man. In the third article of this Quaestio, Thomas sets out to prove that God can be seen only by the intellect, but not by the senses or by imagination. At the end of the article there is a passage worth quoting:[30]

God's essence is not seen in a vision of the imagination ('visione imaginaria'): in such a vision, a form takes shape in the imagination, and this form represents God as if it were through a likeness ('secundum aliquem modum similitudinis'), as when in Holy Writ things divine ('divina') are described metaphorically by means of sensible things ('per res sensibiles').

Dante's vision in the *raptus* is an intellectual one: the fact that 'vista' becomes 'mente' in line 97 of our canto is significant enough. But 'mente' also means 'memory', and the 'visione' that Dante tries to recreate in the present, the vision which, in his own words, *is* fading away, must be a reconstruction of the imagination and must be expressed *per res sensibiles*, or else it would be impossible to communicate it to the reader. The past rapture engaged the intellect. The present description must employ *sensibiles similitudines*. This is why Dante distinguishes between 'vista' and 'visione': the 'veduta' (what was seen) can then be described by metaphors which represent God 'secundum aliquem modum similitudinis' like Holy Writ.

The entire canto XXXIII is an explosion of metaphors which, as we have seen in the preceding chapter, begins with Bernard's prayer to the Virgin. In the second part of the canto metaphors and images become more frequent: they refine and sum up the imagery which, derived from Scripture or from the classics through medieval tradition, had been used throughout the *Paradiso*, throughout the *Comedy*, and in Dante's earlier works. Indeed, the two central movements of the canto, that of sight and that of vision, have their two poles in the similes of lines 58–66 and 133–8, two explosions of metaphors *par excellence*. The pattern which these two similes follow is the same. In both the poet begins by stating his inability, to remember in the first, to understand in the second:

> Qual è colui che sognando vede,
> che dopo 'l sogno la passione impressa
> rimane, e l'altro a la mente non riede   (58–60)

(As is he who dreaming sees, and after the dream the passion remains imprinted and the rest returns not to the mind)

> Qual è 'l geomètra che tutto s'affige
> per misurar lo cerchio, e non ritrova,
> pensando, quel principio ond'elli indige,
> tal era io a quella vista nova:
> veder voleva come si convenne

233

l'imago al cerchio e come vi s'indova
ma non eran da ciò le proprie penne (133–9)

(As is the geometer who wholly applies himself to measure the circle, and finds not, in pondering, the principle of which he is in need, such was I at that new sight. I wished to see how the image conformed to the circle and how it has its place therein; but my own wings were not sufficient for that)

In both, however, the poet ends by saying that he has achieved something:

cotal son io, ché *quasi* tutta cessa
mia visione, *e ancor mi distilla*
nel core il dolce che nacque da essa. (61–3)

(such am I, for my vision almost wholly fades away, yet does the sweetness that was born of it still drop within my heart.)

se non che la mia mente fu percossa
da un fulgore in che sua voglia venne. (140–1)

(save that my mind was smitten by a flash wherein its wish came to it.)

What we have here is, then, an illustration of the two struggles that Dante engages in in *Paradiso* XXXIII: in the first case, to bring his vision back to memory and language; in the second, to thrust his intellect fully into God's essence. The words used in the first simile are 'sogno', 'passione', 'mente', 'core', 'dolce', 'neve', 'sol', 'vento', 'foglie', 'sentenza' – the words of the sensible world. The second simile is an austere block which uses austere words: 'geomètra', 'cerchio', 'principio', 'vista nova', 'imago'. The sphere of geometry is the world of the intellect. That Dante has reached the highest tension in both cases is shown by his use of precious, rare, or even newly coined words: 'distilla', 'disigilla', 'indige', 'indova'.[31] It is shown also by all the echoes that we hear in these five terzinas.

If we look, first, at lines 58–66, we shall remember that the simile of the forgotten vision had already been used by Dante in canto XXIII of *Paradiso* to show how he could not describe Beatrice's smile. Indeed the problem of oblivion and inadequate language was at the centre of that passage as now it is at the centre of canto XXXIII:[32]

Io era come quei che si risente
di visione oblita e che s'ingegna
indarno di ridurlasi a la mente (49–51)

(I was as one that wakes from a forgotten dream, and who strives in vain to bring it back to mind)

When we read this, however, we realize that although the images of *Paradiso* XXIII and XXXIII are similar, the way in which they are conveyed is different. The simile of canto XXXIII takes up two terzinas instead of one and is much more articulate: it brings in the image of the dreamer, which is absent in canto XXIII; it introduces the idea of the 'imprinted passion'; and it develops into two separate parts, 'la passione impressa rimane' and 'l'altro a la mente non riede', the short 'visione oblita' of canto XXIII. This vision itself is articulated in two movements, its fading away on the one hand, and its lasting sweetness on the other. When, after this, Dante adds two more similes, the impression we receive is of a tension that, after mounting to its highest pitch, subsides in two final waves. For the vision, already dream-like, is like snow dissolving in the sun, like the light leaves of the Sibyl dispersed by the wind. Now, the image of the melting snow had already been used by Dante in *Purgatorio* XXX (85–90). There, it was employed to illustrate Dante's feelings when the angels pitied the pilgrim reproached by the newly appeared Beatrice. On the Apennines, snow freezes when it is blown and packed by Slavonian winds; then, when earth breathes again, it melts and 'trickles through itself' 'so that it seems a fire that melts a candle'. Thus Dante had been unable at first to sigh or weep; then, hearing the angels' song, the ice that was bound tight around his heart, 'became breath and water, and with anguish poured from (his) breast through (his) mouth and eyes'. The return of the beloved was a moment of supreme emotion. The vision of God fading away and Dante's struggle to retain it is another such moment. And here its illustration is purified to the bone. We do not have the double movement of *Purgatorio* XXX, but only one verse, 'così la neve al sol si disigilla' (thus is the snow unsealed by the sun), with just two elemental objects, the snow and the sun, and the untranslatable, new verb, 'disigilla'. If memory is for Dante the wax on which the seal leaves its imprint ('la passione impressa rimane'),[33] here the seal itself is finally 'unsealed', at once opened up in revelation and dissolved. As the image fades with the vision, the evocation is total.

Then the third simile appears:

> così al vento ne le foglie levi
> si perdea la sentenza di Sibilla. (65–6)

(thus in the wind, on the light leaves, the Sibyl's oracle was lost.)

The intonation is amazingly similar to that of the preceding line. The melting of the snow is a fact of natural life that Dante had almost certainly witnessed. It is a natural event made precious and unique by 'disigilla'. The dispersing of the Sibyl's leaves is presented in the same manner: 'così', 'così'. It is the memory of something concrete, made precious by 'levi' and 'si perdea'. It is as if Dante had been present at the fact itself. What amazes us here is the naturalness with which he speaks of something that he could never have witnessed with his own eyes. Dante evokes here, as later with the image of Neptune and the shadow of the Argo, a whole world of remote, Mediterranean, mythological past. And this past he recreates out of the words of another poet, his beloved master, Virgil, who is thus spiritually present to the very end of the *Comedy*. It was Virgil who, in Book III of the *Aeneid*, had described how the Sibyl let her leaves be dispersed by the wind.[34] Dante, then, recreates an image which another poet had laboured on, and presents this image as an event he himself has witnessed. The poet being Virgil, and the relation of Dante to Virgil being what it is, this is hardly surprising. But the power of evocation that it makes us feel in Dante's poetry is enormous: when poetry is about to fail together with language and thought, Dante sails through thirteen centuries of written word, of Western tradition, and rewrites – in the final revolution of intertextuality – an ancient poem to signify the end of poetry.

For the expression 'sentenza di Sibilla' recalls both the activity of writing ('foglie' – 'fogli') and that of prophesying, of which the oracle of the Sibyl is a classical, pagan example.[35] When we remember that in canto XXXIII Dante presents himself as a prophet and a poet who writes metaphorically like a prophet, we understand that this is not just a triple simile, but a metaphorical construction with several layers. Let us turn to the image of the dreamer. There, the vision of God was presented as the vision of dream, which, when it ceases, leaves only an impression and a lasting sweetness. Dante had already used this image in the *Convivio* when, talking about things which our intellect cannot look at, such as God, eternity, and prime matter, he had said that no one can come close to their knowledge 'but as it were in a dream'.[36] The divinatory value of dreams for all things divine was admitted by Thomas Aquinas who, in that same Quaestio 12 where he discussed how God is known by us, had said:[37]

The more our soul abstracts itself from corporal things, the more it becomes capable of comprehending intellectual matters. Hence divine revelations and the foreseeing of the future are better perceived in dreams and in alienations from bodily senses.

236

This theory of the 'divinatio per somnium' was, as Bruno Nardi has shown, common in the Middle Ages, which inherited it from Neoplatonism and from Arab philosophy.[38] In both the *Convivio* and the *Comedy* there is evidence that Dante accepted this theory.[39] It is interesting to note that in the passage quoted above Thomas Aquinas puts together dreams, revelations of things divine, and the foreseeing of the future; for this is what Dante does too, when in the three terzinas with which I am now concerned, he mentions the dreamer, the vision of God, and the Sibyl.

What, then, we have discovered is that these nine lines are not merely a very effective illustration of Dante's trouble with his memory and his language, but also an allusion to a particular way of seeing God (the dream-vision of the prophet) and of describing Him (like the Sibyl on her leaves). This double effect is achieved by superimposing three spheres of reference: the dream, the natural phenomenon (sun and snow), the mythological event mediated through a poet, Virgil – or, to put it in more general terms, by combining the philosophical dimension with the enchanted contemplation of nature and the absorption of classical poetry.

When I said that the other metaphorical pole of canto XXXIII, the two terzinas of the geometer's simile, is an austere block of austere images, I was really contraposing it to the triple simile of the dreamer, the snow, and the Sibyl's leaves. The latter is the field of passion and sweetness, of the present struggle of the poet; the former is the field of the intellect which fixes totally on its Object. Confronted with the mystery of the Incarnation, Dante does not limit himself to the description of the human effigy that he sees in the circle of reflected light, the second person of the Trinity. He stresses the moment of his struggle to understand ('veder *volea*'). It is this that makes these lines a sort of epitome of the *Divine Comedy* and of Dante's entire career. Here we understand what it means to write 'intellectual' or 'philosophical' poetry, for this is the supreme effort of the 'mind in love'.[40]

Dante had already set the contemplation of this mystery as the ultimate goal of desire, of man, of his own journey. In *Paradiso* II, he had written that his penetrating with his body into the sphere of the Moon was like the presence of human and divine nature in the person of Christ, and that the former should increase his desire to see the latter, the mystery of Incarnation. In this passage, Dante shows the conviction that the supreme mysteries cannot be demonstrated, but can only be known as evident by themselves, like the axioms man believes in without proving them (II, 40–5).[41] In canto XXXIII Dante tries precisely to see the mystery as if it were in a scientific demonstration. He is like the geometer, and geometry is the demonstrative science *par excellence*. What Dante tries to do is to see *how*, 'come si convenne l'imago al cerchio e come vi s'indova'. The contrast between these two passages reveals Dante's intellectual ardour and his passion for understanding. To the last minute, and although he is *a priori* aware of the vanity of his effort, Dante tries to understand. Geometry is the science which proceeds by demonstrations, and hence the ultimate effort of understanding is compared to the activity of the geometer, whose intentness is underlined by 'tutto s'affige' and 'pensando'.

Yet of all the truths of geometry, two, its beginning and its end, as Dante had said in the *Convivio*,[42] cannot be demonstrated: the point, which is not measurable, and the circle, which cannot be squared. Indeed the latter, the squaring of the circle, constitutes for Dante the paradigm of the impossibility of man's understanding everything. 'There are many things', he says in the *Monarchia*,[43] 'of which we are ignorant, and on which we do not dispute; for instance, the geometer does not know how to square the circle, but does not dispute thereon'. The squaring of the circle is an insoluble problem, and one which the Middle Ages associated with the mystery of Incarnation. In his *Rhythmus de Incarnatione*, as Peter Dronke has pointed out,[44] Alain de Lille introduces the image of the geometer who fails at squaring the circle. Once more, then, Dante sums up in *Paradiso* XXXIII the problems he has discussed in the *Comedy* and in his earlier work; once more, he 'transumes' the images used by medieval tradition. There is, however, more to this simile than one notices at first. If, as Dante says in the *Convivio*, the point and the circle are the beginning and end of geometry, both the point and the circle are, in the *Comedy*, images of God: the point is the radiating point of *Paradiso* XXVIII (16–21), and the circle is the 'cerchio' of *Paradiso* XXXIII (138) – the beginning and end of the beatific vision. Geometry becomes the austere, tense metaphor of the final stages of Dante's ascent (from the point to the circle), and indeed of his whole journey, from the 'punto' at which Dante abandons the way of truth in the first canto of *Inferno* (11), to the circle of God, through the circles of Hell, Purgatory, and Paradise. Furthermore, the point constitutes one pole of canto XXXIII, and the circle represents the other: for the point is the 'punto' of an oblivion greater than that which twenty-five centuries have laid over the enterprise of the Argonauts (94–6), and the circle is the circle where high phantasy fails. At the 'point' vision vanishes; on the circle the intellect no longer functions.

Finally, the effigy that Dante sees in the circle of reflected light is the human one. Later in the same simile (138) the poet uses for it the Latin word, 'imago'. This of course has another meaning as well. In the First Letter to the Corinthians (11.7), St Paul maintains that man 'is the image and glory of God'; and Thomas Aquinas says that the Latin Doctors of the Church hold the second person of the Trinity, the Son, to be 'a perfect image of the Father'.[45] Dante is talking about the human nature of the second person of the Trinity and using the very word, 'imago', which is applied by the theologians to both man and the Son of God who became Son of Man. The perspective becomes deeper, and the metaphor more Scriptural. At the end of his poem Dante joins together Genesis, where God makes him in His image, and the Incarnation, where God becomes man.

That we are reaching the heart of the matter is confirmed by another explosion of metaphors and images in the second section of canto XXXIII, the passage where Dante describes the idea of the universe as contained in God's eternal light:

> Nel suo profondo vidi che s'interna,
>   legato con amore in un volume,
>   ciò che per l'universo si squaderna:
> sustanze e accidenti e lor costume
>   quasi conflati insieme, per tal modo
>   che ciò ch'i' dico è un semplice lume.
> La forma universal di questo nodo
>   credo ch'i' vidi, perché più di largo,
>   dicendo questo, mi sento ch'i' godo.   (85–93)

(In its depth I saw ingathered, bound by love in one single volume, that which is dispersed in leaves throughout the universe: substances and accidents and their relations, as though fused together in such a way that what I tell is but a simple light. The universal form of this knot I believe that I saw, because, in telling this, I feel my joy increase.)

Language is still very precious: 'squaderna' and 'conflati' are used here for the first and only time in the *Comedy*, and 's'interna' is merely at its third occurrence. The preciousness of the language points to more than one dimension and to several echoes. First of all, we have the image of the volume which binds with love all that is scattered in quires or in leaves through the universe. This, as Curtius noted, relies on the book imagery that medieval tradition and Dante himself had inherited from the classics and the Bible.[46] Dante's volume is the book 'in which all is contained' of the *Dies Irae*, Isaiah's scroll of Heaven,[47] the scroll rolled together of Revelation (6. 14), the book written within and without (i.e. the wisdom of God and the earthly world), of Ezekiel and St Bonaventure,[48] the 'liber vitae' analysed by Thomas Aquinas.[49] And the love by which this book is bound is the love of God or, more particularly, the Holy Ghost, Whom theologians called 'Amor'.[50] Throughout the universe, the book becomes its quires: the substances, the accidents, and their relations, which in God's volume are fused together as 'forma universal', become the 'contingenze' of the material world. What Dante contemplates in this 'knot' is the pure Act. He had already been shown, and by no less a man than Thomas Aquinas himself, how, to use Bruno Nardi's expression,[51] the One becomes the many. In the Neoplatonic exposition of a scholastic Dante had been told in *Paradiso* XIII (52–66) that God the Lord begets in love (the Holy Ghost) the Idea (the Word, His Son), and that this Idea which is pure Act becomes, through the nine Intelligences, potencies, and finally contingencies.[52] At the end of his journey Dante contemplates the pure act as it stands still in eternity, containing in its depth the elements that constitute the universe. The language of the philosophers, of the theologians, and of the prophets is the language of the poet.

The image of the volume and its quires or leaves rests on the material experience of the intellectual, who is used to turning the pages of books or, perhaps, to unfoldding ancient scrolls. The image, however, is only one illustration of how all that is scattered throughout the universe finds its unity in God. The content of this unity, and, by implication, the universe itself are expressed by abstract words, *substantiae, accidentia, habitus* – in short, the words of Aristotle and Scholasticism. In a supreme effort of concentration Dante, prompted by his whole cultural background, makes the decisive choice: by using categories, which do not describe physical elements but indicate the fundamental formalities of being in the decreasing order implied by Aristotle, he sums up the entire universe and the Divine Unity.

These lines bear a striking resemblance to a passage of Thomas Aquinas' commentary on the pseudo-Dionysian *De Divinis Nominibus*:[53]

After showing that all which exists in the universe comes from God, here Dionysius intends to show that all things in the universe (*universaliter*) are in Him . . . In the first place he says that being in itself (*per se esse*) does not only proceed from God's goodness but is in it, as God's participation and all the principles of existing things and all things that exist: substances as well as accidents and everything that in some way is contained in the notion of being (*tam substantiae quam accidentia et omnia quocunque modo continentur sub esse*), like imperfect beings such as potential ones, or movement, or others of this kind. And that no one may believe that these are in God as they are in themselves, Dionysius excludes it with reason. For in itself everything produced by a cause is finite, whereas in God it is infinite because in Him it constitutes the divine essence itself. Hence Dionysius says, *et hoc incomprehensibiliter* (and this in an incomprehensible manner). Again, all things produced by a cause have in themselves opposition and diversity (*oppositionem . . . et diversitatem*), whereas in God they are joined together (*coniunguntur simul*). And hence he says: *et coniuncte* (in conjoined fashion). Finally, all such things have multiplicity in themselves, but in God they are one (*in seipsis habent multitudinem, in Deo autem sunt unum*).

Poetry shows us the *cosmos* in its ontological roots. At this point, the word 'volume', accompanied by the 'un' which underlines the unity of the many in the One, acquires its other meaning, that of 'mass'. To it is opposed the looseness of the material world. The force that keeps the elements of the universe together is described by the verb, 'legato', to which corresponds 'nodo' in the conclusive definition. The effect of this tie is shown in the expression, 'quasi conflati insieme', where 'quasi' denotes both Dante's effort in looking for the right word and his awareness that the phenomenon he is describing remains in any case a mystery: *incomprehensibiliter*, as Dionysius says. 'Conflati insieme' implies a particular kind of fusion. 'Conflare' is used by the Vulgate to indicate the melting of metals for the making of idols, and in this sense it implies a dense, fluid mass.[54] Here, for instance, is Deutero–Isaiah contrasting the absolute transcendence of Jahweh with the casting of statues:

To whom then will ye liken God? or what likeness ('imaginem') will ye compare unto him? The workman melteth a graven image ('numquid sculptile conflavit faber') . . . Have ye not understood from the foundations of the earth? . . . It is he . . . that stretcheth out the heavens as a curtain, and spreadeth them out as a tent to dwell in.   (Isaiah 40. 18–22)

God cannot be 'conflated'. He it is who extends and expands (in the Vulgate, 'extendit' and 'expandit'), who actively 'squaderna' the universe. But Dante will indeed compare a likeness unto Him – the image of a book. He is a long way from the 'volume' of Virgil which he recalled in *Inferno* I (84) and with which his journey began. Now, he faces the supreme Book and dares to look into it, to read it. To paraphrase

Hans Blumenberg's title, Dante proclaims the 'Lesbarkeit Gottes', the 'readability' of God.

Both the Vulgate and the classics use 'conflare' in the sense of kindling, implying 'blowing' ('flatus'). Finally, Latin writers employ 'conflare' to indicate composing and creating, especially of things which, being many, are composed into a single unity.[55] In his description of the beauty of the *cosmos* in the *De Natura Deorum* Cicero, for instance, says that 'the sea itself, yearning for the earth, sports against her shores in such a fashion that the two elements appear to be fused into one' ('ut una ex duabus naturis conflata videatur; II xxxix 100). Dante's 'conflati', then, confirms on the one hand the sense of 'mass' that 'volume' has introduced; on the other, it suggests that aspect of 'blowing' which is associated with the divine activity of creation and the fusion of the many into the one: the breathing of the Spirit, *Amor*. The 'forma' of line 91 brings us back to the philosophical language of the preceding verses and to its theological overtones. 'Forma' defines the unchanging element, the 'essence' of the knot seen by Dante, and at the same time it alludes to the divine Idea that shines throughout the universe as explained in *Paradiso* XIII: in other words, to the Logos, the Son.

The imagery of these two terzinas is among the most dense of the entire canto, and perhaps of the whole *Comedy*. With the metaphor of the book we are given a material *similitudo* of the ineffable mystery. As, earlier on, between the 'imprinted passion' and the leaves of the Sibyl, so here a contrast is set forth between 'profondo' and 's'interna' on the one hand and 'si squaderna' on the other. The light leaves of the Sibyl get lost in the wind, the divine book opens out in the leaves of the universe. After deconstructing his own memory, Dante reconstructs it with the world, for he is seeing and telling it all. Yet the reader is forced to follow both the penetration and the spreading out, both the unity of God and the looseness of the universe. The three categories that describe the Pure Act and the physical world (substances, accidents, and their relations) are fused and scattered away in centripetal and centrifugal movements which are watched at one and the same instant. The iteration of *e*'s in line 88 ('sustanze e accidenti e lor costume') widens, in successive waves, our wonder at being plunged into this heart of All-that-is, with its systole and diastole, by a language which has overcome the barriers of material similitude.

And the tensions of language are there, at the centre of the poet's awareness: his impotence ('che ciò ch'i' dico è un semplice lume') finds a counterpart in his joy ('perché più di largo, dicendo questo, mi sento ch'i' godo'). The reader, however, will immediately connect the 'simple light' of line 90 with the 'spark' of God's glory that Dante begged of the supreme Light earlier in the canto. That 'favilla' has already become a 'lume', and if the two words, linked by the addition of 'merely' ('sol', 'semplice') undoubtedly mean 'a mere gleam', we shall not forget that 'lume' is predicated of God, and specifically of the One and Triune appearance (110 and 116) throughout *Paradiso* XXXIII. Is Dante suggesting, then, that his poetry ('ciò ch'i' dico') is 'like' that Light which, for Dionysius, represents Supreme Beauty?[56] Only a complex and oblique answer is possible.

On the one hand, God's light is called 'somma' and the 'lume' of the Trinity accompanied by the adjectives 'vivo' and 'alto', whereas Dante's words are but 'un semplice lume'. Thus, his poetry is but a remote reflection of the divine light, a product of what Dionysius and Thomas call the 'effusions' ('traditiones') of God's *claritas* and *pulchritudo*.[57] On the other hand, 'semplice' is an ambiguous word, and its ambiguity is present in this very canto. When Dante describes the Trinity, he begins by saying that its 'semblance' was one and unchangeable: in that 'vivo lume' there lay no more than 'un semplice sembiante' (109). Between 'semplice lume' and 'semplice sembiante' (followed by 'lume') there is an unmistakable echo. Is the 'lume' of Dante's words as 'simplex' as this? The possibility is there; the question has been, and had to be asked, as a test of the tensions that dominate *Paradiso* XXXIII. Whether as reflection or as 'likeness' of God's beauty, no small claim is made here for Dante's poetry. The whisper that suggests it *sottovoce* as something which *is* ('ciò ch'i' dico è un semplice lume') becomes, immediately afterwards, the full voice of the poet as subject. For when 'la forma universal di questo nodo' sums up the mysterious essence, echoing the philosophical intonation of line 88, and 'nodo' returns to the bound volume of line 85, the speaker does not hesitate to proclaim his own delight in thus speaking:

> perché più di largo,
> dicendo questo, mi sento ch'i' godo.

The next explosion of images of canto XXXIII operates at a different level of resonance:

> Un punto solo m'è maggior letargo
> che venticinque secoli a la 'mpresa
> che fé Nettuno ammirar l'ombra d'Argo.

Così la mente mia, tutta sospesa,
mirava fissa, immobile e attenta,
e sempre di mirar faceasi accesa. (94–9)

(A single moment makes for me greater oblivion than five and twenty centuries have wrought upon the enterprise that made Neptune wonder at the shadow of the Argo. Thus my mind, all rapt, was gazing, fixed, motionless and intent, ever enkindled by its gazing.)

I shall discuss this passage at greater length in the last chapter of the present volume. A few considerations, however, must be made here. The key words of the two terzinas are 'letargo', 'ombra', and 'mirrar'. For the moment, let us take 'letargo' at its face value, that of oblivion. Dante tells us that he is now in a state of lethargy, of sleep and forgetfulness, and this once more underlines the dream-like quality of the remembrance of the supreme vision which Dante has anticipated in an earlier simile ('Qual è colui che sognando vede'). Lethargy is, however, like sleep, a transitional state, from which the poet wakes with just an 'impression' of his 'passion'. Lethargy then indicates one moment ('un punto'), as well as the nature of the entire vision.

In projecting this image back through time to the enterprise of the Argonauts, Dante gives his vision a mythological dimension. Once more, he brings us back, as with the simile of the Sibyl, to the remote past of Mediterranean myth, which constitutes one of the imaginative fields of his journey, and particularly of his ascent through Paradise. The long 'cammin' of the *Comedy* begins with Dante's partial identification with Aeneas, who visited the world of the dead. But Aeneas is now a long way back. The Trojan hero asked the Sibyl to speak her prophecies to him rather than trust them to the leaves that might be dispersed by the wind (*Aeneid* VI, 74–6). At this point, Dante has no such hope: his vision is vanishing like the Sibyl's leaves. At the beginning of the *Paradiso*, however, Dante does not invoke a human prophet, but Apollo himself, the divine 'virtue' of the Logos (I, 13–36). And he envisages his own enterprise, as we shall see in the last chapter, no longer as that of Aeneas, but as that of the Argonauts (II, 16–18). This enterprise is both the journey itself and the retelling of it. Poetry, then, is the creation and the performance of myth. The shadow of the Argo is the last re-enactment of this process. As Patrick Boyde has shown,[58] Dante is 'philomythes': a poet in love with myth and at the same time a philosopher. Both the former and the latter share the feeling of admiration; both wonder at the mysteries of the universe and thus try, each in his own fashion, to acquire knowledge. Hence in *Paradiso* XXXIII the 'myth' of Neptune gazing at the ship of the Argonauts is coupled with 'mirare' and 'ammirare'.

What Neptune wonders at is the *shadow* of the ship, Argo. I shall return to the implications of this expression in the next chapter. Here, let us note how the power of the image rests on the aerial, volatile quality of the word, 'ombra', which casts a shade of remoteness, transience, and insubstantiality on the whole vision. One is reminded of Plato's cave, where the prisoners can see only their own shadows projected by the fire onto the wall.[59] Dante keeps returning to the snow melting in the sun, to the light leaves of the Sibyl dispersed by the wind. The two passages are indeed echoes of the same emotion. What they evoke is a vision melting into thin air. Language itself will then acquire this insubstantial quality: it will be a speech 'corto' and above all 'fioco' (121), a word which suggests both the acoustic effect of a murmur and the visual impression of a shadow.[60] The language of poetry becomes the baseless fabric of the vision.

With Dante, however, even this leaves a rack behind. The three circles of the Trinity must be gazed at and described. Another explosion of images takes place:

> Ne la profonda e chiara sussistenza
> de l'alto lume parvermi tre giri
> di tre colori e d'una contenenza;
> e l'un da l'altro come iri da iri
> parea reflesso, e 'l terzo parea foco
> che quinci e quindi igualmente si spiri.   (115–20)

(Within the profound and shining subsistence of the lofty Light appeared to me three circles of three colours and one magnitude; and one seemed reflected by the other, as rainbow by rainbow, and the third seemed fire breathed forth equally from the one and the other.)

Here, the tension begins with the very first line. The substance of the Supreme Light looks both deep and transparent, bottomless and clear. As we shall see, Dante opposes depth and clarity in *Paradiso* III (11–12) and XIX (58–63). In the latter he in fact contrasts the depth of divine Justice with the human eye, which cannot see through to Its bottom *because* of Its 'esser profondo'. In *Paradiso* XXXIII, however, we are not looking at the ocean: the sea has now been left behind, in the remote depths from which Neptune beholds the shadow of the Argo. We are contemplating the *substance* of divine Light, and as earlier on Dante saw the essence of God and of the universe ingathered in His depth, so now the luminous 'sussistenza' is simultaneously deep and clear.

The opposed movements of canto XXXIII emerge, then, once more: implosion and explosion, immersion and surfacing, splendour and reflection. Here, the tension mounts through the repetition and opposition of numbers ('tre giri', 'tre colori', 'una contenenza', 'l'un da l'altro', 'il terzo'). The three sentences follow on the heels of each other: the two e's prepare an effect of accumulation and crescendo. Dante himself has introduced this stage of his vision in a highly dramatic fashion:

> ma per la vista che s'avvalorava
> in me guardando, una sola parvenza,
> mutandom'io, a me si travagliava. (112–14)

(but through my sight, which was growing strong in me as I looked, one sole appearance, even as I changed, was altering itself to me.)

The broken, contorted syntax underlines the effort of the poet, the last line indicates the painful transformation of subject and Object, the final clause climaxes (because of its position) in a feeling of relief, which is, however, immediately cut off by the meaning of the words as they sink into the reader's consciousness. 'A me si travagliava' becomes the emblem of Dante's situation in *Paradiso* XXXIII, of the philosopher who strives to see the essence of the Pure Act, of the geometer who wants to square the circle, of the man who struggles to contemplate God Triune. It becomes the key expression to understand how God can 'travagliarsi', manifest Himself to the changing eyes of the pilgrim.

The imagery with which Dante describes the Trinity echoes, as elsewhere in this last canto, other passages of the *Paradiso*;[61] with the three circles, it evokes the circular nature of the universe, the circles in which it is organized: the Trinity, Paradise, Purgatory, and Hell. Once more, we find an allusion to philosophical definitions, 'sussistenza' being the correct one for all things which exist in themselves and therefore *par excellence* for God. Yet this imagery also corresponds to the doctrine of the Church: in the Creed, the Son is 'light from light', the Holy Ghost 'proceeds from the Father and the Son'. In Acts 2.3 the Spirit is the fire that sat upon the Apostles on the day of Pentecost. The voice of the prophets is also heard: the third Person of the Trinity is like the 'appearance of fire' of Ezekiel's vision; the rainbow that provides a similitude for the reflection of the first two circles is 'the appearance of the bow that is in the cloud in the day of rain', which, in Ezekiel's words, is 'the appearance of the likeness of the glory of the Lord'. And the circles echo the 'circuitus' and the 'gyrus' of Ezekiel's 'appearance of the brightness'.[62] To describe the Trinity, Dante adopts prophetic language: he prefers the image of the circles to the symbol of the triangle which Western theology applies to this supreme of mysteries. Once more, this is a decisive choice – and one which might have been influenced by the *Liber Figurarum* of a man whom Dante considered a modern prophet, the Calabrian abbot Gioacchino da Fiore.[63]

Dante's representation of the Trinity remains, however, mysterious, as the poet meant it to be: one can explain the significance of each separate image theologically – the reflection, the proceeding of the third circle from the first two like fire[64] – and indeed see it in agreement with the orthodox doctrine of the Church. But the effect of the whole is that of a vortex in which rainbow-like halos pervade a circular structure and in which a fire-red breath dominates.[65] Earlier Dante chose book imagery and the universalizing categories of the philosophers to show us the mystery of God Who contains in Himself the whole *cosmos*. Now he relies on the pictorial quality of prophetic language to tell us that the mystery of the Trinity . . . cannot be translated into images.

What must be stressed is that these two descriptions have several elements in common: both hide theological definitions, contain images, produce a whole which cannot be reduced to an exact formula, but which generates a profound elation. Both are built on the base of a crescendo, in both there is a tension between expansion and penetration, that is, between the 'internarsi' and the 'squadernarsi' in the first, between the deep reflection of the first two circles and the blowing away of fire in the second. In both the powerful imprint of God's Spirit, of His breath, is left in our imagination – blowing into Himself the scattered leaves of the universe ('conflati'), and breathing forth His Love like fire ('si spira').

The circle becomes the dominant image of *Paradiso* XXXIII: the Incarnation, as we have seen, is represented as the human image mysteriously contained in the circle of reflected light, the second of the Trinity;[66] and finally Dante himself becomes, in the last metaphorical flicker of the canto, a circle, a wheel moved with even motion by the Love that moves the sun and the other stars:

> A l'alta fantasia qui mancò possa;
> ma già volgeva il mio disio e 'l *velle*,

sì come rota ch'igualmente è mossa,
l'amor che move il sole e l'altre stelle.   (142–5)

(Here power failed the lofty phantasy; but already my desire and my will were revolved, like a wheel that is evenly moved, by the Love which moves the sun and the other stars.)

It is to the end of the *Comedy* that we must now turn. A final struggle precedes, as we have seen, the moment of fulfilment. The geometer who has built with precision the architecture of his poem now fails to square the circle of the Incarnation. The 'new sight' is impenetrable. The pilgrim who, asking for grace, had obtained from Mary 'wings' with which to 'fly his desire' ('his desir wol fle withouten wynges') now finds that his own wings are inadequate for the last flight (139). Dante's Ulysses turned the oars of his ship into wings with which he madly flew towards darkness and shipwreck (*Inferno* XXVI, 125); Dante humbly recognizes that man's intellect cannot comprehend the mystery, that human pen[67] cannot describe it:

ma non eran da ciò le proprie penne.

A last *lumen gloriae*, however, strikes him – a 'fulgore' which, irradiated by God, shines now in his mind's desire (140–1).[68] And with this lightning ('folgore') and glow ('fulgore'), the light of the canto comes to an end. Here, high phantasy, the power by which the intellect represents what it sees, fails altogether, and desire and will are revolved like a wheel by God.

Love is clearly the central word in the final lines of the *Comedy*. It is the love which has inspired cantos XVII and XVIII of the *Purgatorio* and the love which moves the universe, the love of all created beings for the unmoved mover who moves by being loved, and the love of God, the cosmic force. It is the love, as Peter Dronke puts it, of both the Boethian and the Aristotelian traditions.[69] It is the love which, as Dante says at the beginning of our canto, was enkindled in Mary's womb, where the loves of man and God meet. Now, Dante's love and God's love meet in Dante's desire and will. Hence Dante himself is revolving like a wheel in a uniform motion, like the angels, like the first heaven: the 'circular and uniform motion which', according to the philosophers, 'indicates perfect concord of the human with the divine will'.[70] With the failing of phantasy Dante's voice becomes a heavy sigh of relief and peace. And a slow, solemn turning around of the phrase, with the object at the beginning, the simile in the middle, and the subject at the end, terminates the *Paradiso* and the *Comedy* with the three primeval words: love, sun, and stars. The circle seems to be complete.

At the beginning of his journey, in the first canto of the *Inferno*, Dante, lost at the foot of the 'dilettoso colle' and hindered by the leopard, had looked up in the light of the rising sun. There, he had used an image which echoes in the last one of the *Paradiso*:

> Temp'era dal principio del mattino,
> e 'l sol montava 'n su con quelle stelle
> ch'eran con lui quando l'amor divino
> mosse di prima quelle cose belle   (37–40)

(It was the beginning of the morning, and the sun was mounting with the stars that were with it when Divine Love first set those beautiful things in motion)

Here, at the beginning of the poem, only the sun, the stars, and the 'cose belle' are moved by divine love. There, at the end of his ascent, Dante, too, is moved by love. Dante's pilgrimage is from isolation to participation. The man separated from God and therefore from the universe becomes a part of the whole. In the first canto of the *Inferno*, divine love moved the universe in a remote past ('mosse'). The enchanted moment of Creation, the first motion of beauty had been lost by Dante, who could only look at it with melancholic longing. There, at the end of *Paradiso*, love moves the sun, the stars, and Dante himself in the present of eternity. Dante has become one of the 'cose belle', Creation continues.

Our 'sense of an ending' is fully satisfied. Yet even here, in this final peace, Dante does not give up his 'poetics of the struggle'. For the poem does not rest; it ends with movement, as if it did not want to end. Revolving in its wheel-like fashion, the *Comedy* seems to return to its beginning, to the first canto of the *Inferno*. The circle cannot be squared, its motion can hardly be halted. As T.S. Eliot puts it in the poem that comes closest in theme and ambition to the *Divine Comedy* among those which have attempted this feat,[71]

> What we call the beginning is often the end
> And to make an end is to make a beginning.

9

L'acqua che ritorna equale: Dante's sublime

In this chapter I intend to ignore the dimensions of style and genre within which the Middle Ages usually consider the problem of the sublime (for example, Dante says that comedy speaks 'remisse et humiliter', tragedy 'elate et sublime').[1] I will only touch upon Auerbach's stimulating treatment of the 'sermo humilis' which, born with the Latin translation of the Bible, dominates medieval literature and is transformed by Dante into a new sublimity.[2] Finally, I will leave aside Contini's conception of the central function memory has in our 'aesthetic' reception of the *Comedy* – and hence the idea of the poem's 'memorable quality' which would fit in well with a passage in chapter 7 of Longinus' *Peri Hypsous*.[3] What, on the other hand, I would like to do is to read Dante's poetry in the light of classical and modern responses to the sublime and ask whether there is, in that sense, any 'sublimity' in the *Divine Comedy*. In order to do this, I shall choose a series of images through which the Dantean sublime takes form, for us who come after Milton and the romantics, in a way which is at once problematical and explosive. In the second part of this chapter, I shall therefore examine exclusively the *Paradiso* and, within it, only the image of the sea, a dimension with which this earthly and earthy poet must not have been very familiar and which is nevertheless constantly present in his work, as if it were a 'horizon growing clearer', an ever fleeing and ever recaptured 'tremolar de la marina'.[4]

The reasons why I have chosen the image of the sea are two. In the first place, one of the most important examples of Longinus' sublime is Homer's simile of the divine steeds that leap 'as far as a man can see with his eyes into the hazy distance as he sits upon a mountain-peak and gazes over the wine-dark sea'[5] – an instance of 'supreme grandeur' conveyed by the sense of 'cosmic distances' which the passage suggests. It is this dimension of the sublime that Romanticism fully exploits, and Leopardi's 'L'infinito' constitutes one of its highest expressions:

> Sempre caro mi fu quest'ermo colle,
> e questa siepe, che da tanta parte
> dell'ultimo orizzonte il guardo esclude.
> Ma sedendo e mirando, interminati
> spazi di là da quella, e sovrumani
> silenzi, e profondissima quiete
> io nel pensier mi fingo; ove per poco
> il cor non si spaura. E come il vento
> odo stormir tra queste piante, io quello
> infinito silenzio a questa voce
> vo comparando: e mi sovvien l'eterno,
> e le morte stagioni, e la presente
> e viva, e il suon di lei. Cosí tra questa
> immensità s'annega il pensier mio:
> e il naufragar m'è dolce in questo mare.

> (They were always friends, this hill where no one comes
> And this hedge here, that from so large a part
> Of the ultimate horizon shuts out the eye.
> Sitting in contemplation, I form unbounded
> Distances on the other side, silences
> Past man, and deepest calm. Then my heart comes
> Close to taking fright; and, as the breeze
> Rustles among the leaves, I keep comparing
> That infinite silence to this small voice: recall
> Eternity, and the seasons that are gone,
> And the living present one, the sound of it.
> And so my thought founders, lost in this
> Immensity; and it seems to me a gentle thing
> To suffer shipwreck in this pacific ocean.)[6]

Secondly, the image of the sea allows me to go back, although indirectly, to the Middle Ages. Speaking with his usual elegance and clarity of the medieval universe, C.S. Lewis maintained that 'while unimaginably large', it 'was also unambiguously finite'.[7] 'To look out on the night sky with modern eyes is like looking out over a sea that fades away into mist . . . to look up at the towering medieval universe is much more like looking at a great building.' He added that 'the "space" of modern astronomy may arouse terror, or bewilderment or vague reverie' – in aesthetic terms, the sense of the sublime. 'The spheres of the old present us with an object in which the mind can rest, overwhelming in its greatness but satisfying in its harmony' – in other words, what eighteenth-century theorists would call 'the beautiful'. 'That', Lewis concluded, 'is the sense in which our universe is romantic, and theirs was classical.'[8] Turning to Dante, Lewis observed that at first glance one might expect him to strike the note 'of the pathless, the baffling, and the utterly alien' – Pascal's terror at 'le silence éternel de ces espaces infinis'. In fact, wrote Lewis, Dante 'is like a man being conducted through an immense cathedral, not like one lost in a shoreless sea'.[9]

In short, Lewis denied that the Middle Ages, and Dante in particular, had any sense of the sublime such as Longinus had sketched and such as European culture developed from the eighteenth century onwards.[10] It is significant that Lewis himself used the image of the sea twice in order to give an emblematic representation of the infinite and of our emotional reaction towards it. Lewis, of course, was perfectly right: in the Middle Ages, the feeling aroused by contemplation of the physical universe was not one of a shoreless ocean fading away into mist. However, Lewis also made two mistakes. In the first place, he neglected a beautiful passage of the *Convivio* where Dante does not of course mention the sublime, but where the feeling of awe he describes comes very close to it:

Chè lo stupore è uno stordimento d'animo per grandi e maravigliose cose vedere o udire o per alcuno modo sentire: che, in quanto paiono grandi, fanno reverente a sè quelli che le sente; in quanto paiono mirabili, fanno voglioso di sapere di quelle.

(For Awe is a certain bewilderment of the mind at seeing or hearing great and wonderful things, or feeling them in some way. These, in so far as they are great, make him who feels them reverent towards them: in so far as they appear wonderful, they make him who feels them desirous of knowing them.)[11]

Dante's conception is clearly inspired by Aristotle's *Metaphysics* and particularly by the notion it proposes of the human being who, by means of wonder, passes from ignorance to love of knowledge (*philosophia*) or of 'myths' (*philo-mythia*), and hence to poetry of the 'first things'.[12] But the expression, 'stordimento d'animo' (literally, the mind's 'stupefaction' or 'daze') is stronger than anything Aristotle ever used, and in reading it one is reminded of Longinus' coupling of the marvellous (*to thaumasion*) with *ekplēxis*, the shock of amazement it produces.[13] It is, then, in this sphere of 'stupore' at seeing, hearing or *feeling* great and wonderful things, of the 'reverence' and 'ardour for knowledge' which they produce that we must look to find Dante's sense of the sublime, and to it I will return later on in this chapter. For the moment, let me go back to C.S. Lewis and to what I consider his second mistake. The medieval universe is undoubtedly finite, but above, beyond and, mentally, within it, there is God, who is certainly not finite. In contemplating the infinite beauty of God the Middle Ages came close to what Edgar De Bruyne has called 'Romanticism'.[14] 'Est igitur in Deo *altitudo* terribilis, *pulcritudo* mirabilis, *dulcedo* desiderabilis', writes St Bonaventure:[15] there is in God a terrible sublimity, a wonderful beauty, a desirable sweetness. Here is a more eloquent passage from Richard of St Victor:

The human soul is drawn above itself by the greatness of wonder when, irradiated by divine light and suspended in the admiration of the supreme beauty, it is so strongly struck that it is shaken to the very foundations of its being. Then, as happens with the flash of lightning, through scorn of itself it is thrown down from unseen beauty to the lowest things. The more deeply hurled down, the higher and more quickly it beats back through yearning for the supreme things and, ravished above itself, is elevated to things sublime ('tanto sublimius, tanto celerius per summorum desiderium reverberata, et super semetipsam rapta, in sublimia elevatur').[16]

In the *Paradiso* Dante journeys towards God and, by way of imagery, within God. And this voyage is continuously presented as one that takes place on the sea. Moreover, Dante invites us to embark with him upon a sailing that will open up infinite vistas of the Godhead and of the poetry which describes it. Before doing so, however, we must have reliable charts and understand the coordinates of Dante's writings.

The first appearance of the sea image in his works occurs in a famous sonnet addressed to Guido Cavalcanti where the poet expresses his wish to be placed by magic in a little boat together with his friends and fellow poets of the Dolce Stil Nuovo, Guido himself and Lapo Gianni. The voyage would have no specific destination but, 'whatever the wind', simply follow the three men's 'voler'. A good wizard would then add their three ladies as company, and all would be perfect happiness. The enchanted aura of the composition is enhanced by the oblique reference to Merlin (the 'buono incantatore') and to his magic boat. There is even the possibility that Dante may have had in mind the boat on which Tristan and Isolde cross the Irish Sea and, by drinking the filtre, fall in love with each other:[17]

> Guido, i' vorrei che tu e Lapo ed io
> fossimo presi per incantamento

> e messi in un vasel, ch'ad ogni vento
> per mare andasse al voler vostro e mio,
>
> sì che fortuna od altro tempo rio
> non ci potesse dare impedimento,
> anzi, vivendo sempre in un talento,
> di stare insieme crescesse 'l disio.
>
> E monna Vanna e monna Lagia poi
> con quella ch'è sul numer de le trenta
> con noi ponesse il buono incantatore:
>
> e quivi ragionar sempre d'amore,
> e ciascuna di lor fosse contenta,
> sì come i' credo che saremmo noi.

(Guido, I wish that you and Lapo and I could be taken by magic and placed in a boat that, whatever the wind, was carried over the sea wherever you and I chose to go, unhindered by tempest or any foul weather – our desire to be together in fact always increasing, living as we would in unceasing harmony.

And with this, that the good wizard should give us for company lady Vanna and lady Lagia and her who stands on number thirty, there to talk always of love; and that each of them should be happy, as I'm sure we would be.)[18]

The purpose of this dreamlike sailing is clear – to be together 'in one desire' and 'to talk always of love', in other words to further deepen the experience, cultural and poetic as well as existential, of the Stil Nuovo circle. The sea is a true 'mare amoroso'.[19]

Later in the *Rime*, in a sonnet addressed to another love poet, Cino da Pistoia, both the craft and its course have significantly changed – the 'vasel' has become a 'nave', a true ship, which will from now on sail 'further from the shore'.[20] Dante announces he has abandoned 'these our rhymes' – love poetry in the 'dolce stil' – and signals the beginning of a new major phase, the philosophically inspired lyric of *rectitudo*:

> Io mi credea del tutto esser partito
> da queste nostre rime, messer Cino,
> ché si conviene omai altro cammino
> a la mia nave più lungi dal lito

(I thought, messer Cino, that I had quite abandoned this poetry of ours; for now my ship must hold a different course, being further from the shore)[21]

Further from the shore, there lies the ocean, and in the *Convivio* this image surfaces punctually at the beginning (I ix 7), where the treatise itself is called a 'pelago' or open sea. At the opening of Book II, the metaphor is fully fledged. Here, the author's itinerary is envisaged as that of a ship crossing the deep from one harbour to another:

lo tempo chiama e domanda la mia nave uscir di porto; per che, dirizzato l'artimone de la ragione a l'òra del mio desiderio, entro in pelago con isperanza di dolce cammino e di salutevole porto e laudabile ne la fine de la mia cena.

(II i 3–6)

(the season calls and requires my ship to leave harbour. Wherefore, with the mainsail of reason adjusted to the breeze of my desire I launch on the deep, with hope of pleasant voyage and of wholesome and commendable harbour at the end of my repast.)

The image of a voyage across the ocean – not merely the sea – points to the difficulty of the enterprise. Dante is writing a moral and philosophical commentary to his own poetic compositions and claims to be offering it to mankind as a 'banquet' of true science and wisdom (I i 8–12). He opens his treatise fittingly with a solemn quotation from the very beginning of Aristotle's *Metaphysics*, the 'First Philosophy': 'all men naturally desire to know'. There is also, more boldly, both in the structure and images Dante uses a conscious echo of Acts 27. 40:

And when they had taken up the anchors, they committed themselves unto the sea, and loosed the rudder bands, hoisted up the mainsail to the wind ('levato artemone, secundum aurae flatum'), and made toward shore.

Dante implicitly compares his voyage to no less a feat than Paul's fateful journey towards Rome. Yet, following the traditional topos, Dante wishes for his ship a 'wholesome and commendable harbour', a precise destination which is the conclusion of his work and the end of the banquet. The sailing of the *Convivio* is presented then as extremely daring, but not as an endless journey. The perspective of the infinite is missing. On the level of his own individual existence Dante sees himself, here and now, as 'a ship without sail and without rudder, wafted to diverse havens and inlets and shores by the parching wind which woful poverty exhales' (I iii 5), but human life as such appears to him as a great sea through which body and soul sail towards definite ports – those, respectively, of natural death and of God.[22]

In chapter XXVIII of *Convivio* IV, where Dante illustrates the fourth age of man, 'senio' or decrepitude, three great waves of imagery break and dissolve, as it were, upon entering the harbour (the word 'porto' is itself repeated eight times in the first half of the chapter). In this last age the noble soul 'returns to God as to that haven whence she set forth when she came to enter on the sea of this life' and 'blesses the journey which she has finished, because it has been straight and good, and free from bitterness of storm'. For us, 'natural death' is, as Cicero says in his *De Senectute*, 'a haven . . . and resting-place after a long voyage'. When the good sailor draws near to the harbour, he 'lets down his sails, and enters it gently with slight headway on'. We too 'ought to let down the sails of our worldly pursuits . . . so that we may come to that haven with all composure and with all peace' (2–3).

Here, the image changes: death appears in its double perspective, as end of earthly life and beginning of the otherwordly. The apple detaches itself from the bough, the traveller reaches the gate of his city after a long journey and is met by its inhabitants. An aura of peace and hope dominates the scene:

And our own nature gives us a good lesson in gentleness, in so far as there is in such death no pain, nor bitterness; but as a ripe apple lightly and without violence detaches itself from its bough, so our soul severs itself without suffering from the body where it has dwelt. Wherefore Aristotle in his book *On Youth and Old Age* says that 'death is without sadness when it takes place in old age'. And just as a man who comes off a long journey, before he enters the gate of his own city, is met by her citizens, so the noble soul is met (as it should be) by the citizens of the life immortal. (4–5)

The passage ends with another great wave of *repetitio*:

Rendesi dunque a Dio la nobile anima in questa etade, e attende lo fine di questa vita con molto desiderio e uscir le pare de l'albergo e ritornare ne la propria mansione, uscir le pare di cammino e tornare in cittade, uscir le pare di mare e tornare a porto.   (IV xxviii 7)

(The noble soul therefore gives herself up to God at this age and awaits the end of this life with much longing; she seems to herself to be departing from an inn and returning to her own mansion; to be coming off her journey and returning to the city; to be leaving the ocean and returning to port.)

Then, Dante rails at those who 'run into this port with sails full set' and therefore founder right at the end of their journey. By contrast, he praises Lancelot and Guido da Montefeltro who 'in their extreme age' 'surrendered themselves to religion' (8). Finally, in order to explain why the soul blesses the time gone by, he sets before us a comparison. The soul behaves 'like the good merchant, who, when he comes near to port balances his profits and says, "If I had not journeyed by such a road, I should not have this treasure, nor should I have aught

wherewith to enjoy myself in my city to which I am drawing nigh";
and therefore he blesses the journey he has made' (12).

There clearly is no tragic tension in this passage. In the *Inferno*, by
contrast, Guido da Montefeltro reaches that part of his life 'in which
everyone should lower his sails and coil up his ropes', but, after
repenting, gives fraudulent advice to the pope, and the devil snatches
his soul from St Francis.[23] Ulysses, who launches on his 'foolhardy
flight' in old age, is shipwrecked just as he sights the 'new land'.[24] The
possibility that human life may have a tragic destiny is recalled by
Thomas Aquinas in the *Paradiso*:

> e legno vidi già dritto e veloce
> correr lo mar per tutto suo cammino,
> perire al fine a l'intrar de la foce.   (XIII, 136–8)

(And I have seen ere now a ship fare straight and swift over the sea through all
her course, and perish at the last as she entered harbour.)

In our first chapter we have seen how in Chaucer's *Pardoner's Tale* the
Old Man's 'life of dying' is tragically uncanny. In the *Convivio*, the old
man's death is a perfectly peaceful, natural end. At the same time, we
get no sense of the infinite. The perspective is almost physically limited
by the walls of the city, by the harbour to which the merchant comes.
The picture is extraordinarily evocative, but fully harmonious. By
means of the rhythm itself of the sentences and through the succession
of images Dante builds an aura of supreme serenity and plenitude. In
this harmony everything falls into place easily and lightly like a ripe
apple dropping from the bough. This is an organized loveliness that
does not upset us in any way, it is, in terms of a later aesthetic, not the
sublime, but the beautiful.

Things are not so simple in the *Divine Comedy*, where the images of
the sea and of sea journeys are repeatedly used throughout the poem on
different levels and where they outline a complex net of multiple routes
which contain both the extremes of tragic tension and its denouement.
For instance, in *Paradiso* XXVI Dante declares to St John that his moral
voyage in the poem – and his whole life – consists in his having passed
'dal mar de l'amor torto . . . del diritto a la riva' (from the sea of
perverse love to the shore of right love), that is, from earthly passions to
the ardour of charity and the love of God.[25] Thus, at the beginning of
his adventure we find Dante 'su la fiumana ove 'l mar non ha vanto' (the
flood over which the sea has no vaunt) where death assails him[26] – the

death of sin but also what Montale called the tragic 'fiumara del vivere', the torrent of living.[27] At the end, in the Empyrean, Dante sees a 'fiumana' of lights which, as soon as his eyes 'drink' of it, becomes 'round'. The 'lumen gloriae' strikes him; truth, heretofore veiled, is now resplendent; and the river is transformed into 'so wide a circle that the circumference would be too large a girdle for the sun',[28] in other words, into the Ocean of God which 'inghirlanda', encircles not only, as it does in the common medieval conception, the Earth, but the entire universe.[29] In the first canto of the *Comedy* Dante turns back 'to gaze upon the pass that never left anyone alive'. Having, like Aeneas and St Paul, and unlike Ulysses, escaped from the shipwreck, he is

> come quei che con lena affannata,
> uscito fuor del pelago a la riva,
> si volge a l'acqua perigliosa e guata   (*Inferno* I, 22–4)

(as he who with laboring breath has escaped from the deep to the shore [and] turns to look back on the dangerous waters)

Dante's image of shipwreck was familiar to him from the Church fathers, who used the phrase 'tabula secunda post naufragium'[30] – that is, the plank to which the soul clings, the penitential acts of repentance and conversion – to indicate man's salvation after the original sin. Dante begins his voyage with just that image, a voyage towards the 'desert shore' near the sea that surrounds Mount Purgatory, where Virgil, instructed by Cato, cleanses the pilgrim and girds him 'with a smooth rush' as if for a new baptism:[31] a 'penitential' journey which will end only at the top of that mountain, in the Earthly Paradise, where Dante repents, confesses, and is immersed in the Lethe and where he finally drinks of the Eunoe's 'most holy waves' becoming 'pure and ready to rise to the stars'.[32]

Before these rituals are completed, the protagonist looks upon Lethe, only three paces wide, as if it were the Hellespont of Xerxes and Leander, because it does not 'open up' for him.[33] And his feeling here reminds us that the entire *Divine Comedy* is presented as a re-enactment and, in a figural sense, a fulfilment of Exodus,[34] the crucial moments of which are "l mar fuggir, quando Dio volse' and 'Iordan vòlto retrorso' – the fleeing, the opening up, of the Red Sea, and the turning back of the Jordan at God's will.[35] Dante, as Beatrice declares to St James in the *Paradiso*, has been allowed 'to come from Egypt to Jerusalem, that he may see'.[36]

These itineraries trace a series of dizzy vistas, of perspectives that keep changing in physical, metaphorical, mythic, and allegorical width and depth. The reader keeps meeting and crossing in different ways and in different vessels the polysemic rivers, the seas and the oceans of the *Comedy*. Meanings and contexts change so rapidly that they make us start. Surprise and awe shock us into an awareness of the power of Dante's sublime.

I shall give two different examples of this, one centred on thematic accumulation, the other on the effect produced by a sequence of images. In canto I of *Purgatorio*, Virgil and Dante come to the shore of the island. It is a shore that, as Dante says, recalling the tragic story of his Ulysses, 'mai non vide navicar sue acque – omo, che di tornar sia poscia esperto' (never saw any man navigate its waters who afterwards had experience of return). But it is a shore which an extraordinary, non-human ship is able to reach. Steered and propelled by an angel, this is the boat that collects at the Tiber's mouth the souls destined to purification and salvation. Unlike Ulysses' and Dante's, it needs no oars and no sail, but only the angel's wings (II, 32–3). A 'vasello snelletto e leggero' (41), it moves so swiftly that no human flight can equal its speed (18). Surrounded by a white halo which will turn out to be the angel's wings (22–4), it hovers above the water without cleaving the waves (42), but spreading through the air a solemn melody: in short, it is a ship that 'cantando varca', that goes beyond – singing.[37] The song is Psalm 113, 'In exitu Israel de Aegypto', which celebrates the events of Exodus and which in ancient times used to be sung when the body of a dead man was brought to consecrated ground 'as if to indicate . . . the mystical journey of the Christian, prefigured by the Jews, towards the heavenly Jerusalem'.[38] The Psalm itself is crucial to Dante's own interpretation of Scripture and of poetry in general as well as of his poems in particular.[39] In both the *Convivio* and the Letter to Cangrande, although with differences that have kept scholars busy for decades, Dante uses it as an example of 'polysemic' writing, that is to say, of a text which can be interpreted according to its multiple meanings – literal, allegorical, moral, and anagogic. In the *Comedy* as a whole, the singing of that Psalm constitutes a sort of anticipated celebration of Dante's journey, a true 'exodus'. In the present circumstances, it fits the plight of both the souls destined to Purgatory and of Dante the pilgrim, who has been symbolically 'cleansed' by Virgil and will be 'absolved' at the end of his ascent. But if we are to believe what Charon shouts to Dante in *Inferno* III, the 'real' Dante seems to think that he, too, will go to Purgatory after death. He too, we must assume, will sing that Psalm.

In other words, we are reading one of the most dense and central scenes of the *Divine Comedy*. While the poet announces that the 'little ship' of his 'genius' hoists her sails 'to course over better waters' (I, 1–3), in the fiction Dante the character, unlike Ulysses, arrives at that shore of Purgatory which he will reach after death. And from the sea, on a boat that sails in song, the souls who in the fiction are destined to Purgatory draw near, singing the Psalm of Exodus which, in Dante's own exegesis, means all of this. The sea that appears before us is in sum before and after, outside and inside, here and elsewhere – truly endless.

In the Old Testament, the book of a nation that was not much at home with sailing, the 'waters' and the sea always signal crucial moments, from the Creation to the Flood, from the parting of the Red Sea to Jonah's adventure. Furthermore, there is no better image of human life in the whole of Scripture than that proposed by Psalm 106, which medieval interpreters see, 'morally', as a picture of the 'speculative' man's experience.[40] Dante must have considered it as a 'figure' of his own human and poetic experience:

They that go down to the sea in ships, that do business in great waters;
These see the works of the Lord, and his wonders in the deep.
For he commandeth, and raiseth the stormy wind, which lifteth up the waves thereof.
They mount up to the heaven, they go down again to the depths: their soul is melted because of trouble.
They reel to and fro, and stagger like a drunken man, and are at their wits' end.
Then they cry unto the Lord in their trouble, and he bringeth them out of their distresses.
He maketh the storm a calm, so that the waves thereof are still.
Then are they glad because they be quiet; so he bringeth them unto their desired haven. (23–30)

The New Testament adds to all this Paul's journey across the Mediterranean and Jesus' mysterious walking on the sea towards his disciples' ship, 'tossed with waves'.[41] It is in that episode that Peter, recognizing his Master, walks on the water to reach him. Dante recalls that supreme (although in fact double-edged) instance of faith in *Paradiso* XXIV, where Beatrice addresses St Peter himself:

tenta costui di punti lievi e gravi,
come ti piace, intorno de la fede,
per la qual tu su per lo mare andavi. (37–9)

(test this man on points light and grave, as pleases you, concerning the Faith by which you did walk upon the sea.)

The *Divine Comedy* goes through all the most important stages of the Bible's sea imagery.[42] It builds on it to outline its own polysemy and opens up astonishing views of time and space.

My second example is of a different nature. In his journey Dante crosses the 'abyss', the 'cruel sea' of Hell.[43] When he and Virgil emerge from it onto the island of Purgatory, they see the shore and the reflection of the dawn light upon the water. The 'tremolar de la marina' (I, 117) is the first, remote and insubstantial, appearance of the new sea, trembling like a mirage in the eyes of the beholders. It has the same primordial, cosmic appeal of Lucretius' 'rident aequora ponti' and of its source in Aeschylus – 'the infinite smile of the waves of the sea'.[44] Now, it is typical of Dante's suggestive and indirect method – of the meticulous precision with which he discloses infinite horizons within iron borders – to evoke by metaphor or simile the two opposite poles of a situation. In doing so, he establishes a link between extremes and outlines a perspective with broad and vague contours, leaving an empty width which we must ourselves fill with our imagination. In a way, we are thus forced to give form to our own sense of the sublime. At the opening of *Purgatorio* VIII the day which began in the first canto comes to an end – it seems, as Dante says, 'to die'. The sun sets. In the simile that specifies the time, we find ourselves with the sailors, a full day's journey from home, when their hearts are full of longing:

> Era già l'ora che volge il disio
> ai navicanti e 'ntenerisce il core
> lo dì c'han detto ai dolci amici addio　　　　　　　　　(1–3)

(It was now the hour that turns back the longing of seafaring folk and melts their heart the day they have bidden sweet friends farewell)

The sea is not in sight, but it is – we know – all around us. And the echo suddenly resounds in our mind: from dawn to sunset, from the shore to midsea. This must be the same water that trembled under the rising sun. How infinitely distant, how palpably close it is!

The sailing, then, goes on, 'to course over better waters', urging the bark 'with sail and oars',[45] stopping a while 'as a ship that arrives at the shore',[46] and further on 'as a ship driven by fair wind',[47] until the imaginary navigation of the *Purgatorio* finds an extraordinary landfall on the shores of another sea. When Dante enters the 'divine forest' of Earthly Paradise (the exact counterpart of the 'selva selvaggia' at the beginning of the poem), he hears the birds sing 'with full joy' in the first breeze of morning. These 'rhymes' are accompanied by the rustling of the leaves, 'such as gathers from branch to branch through the pine forest on Chiassi's shore when Aeolus lets forth Sirocco',

> tal qual di ramo in ramo si raccoglie
> per la pineta in su 'l lito di Chiassi,
> quand'Eolo scilocco fuor discioglie.　(XXVIII, 19–21)

With this sudden, dizzying projection of a personal and earthly experience onto the level of the edenic, with this letting forth and melting ('discioglie') of myth into wind, we reach another 'lito' and another 'marina', on the shore of the Adriatic, near Ravenna, where Dante lived and where the forest of Classe still lies. Dante's 'little ship' has sailed a long way indeed – in imaginative terms, from the desert shore of mount Purgatory to the enchanted beach of a real place that has become Paradise. It is from here, it would seem, that the navigation of the *Paradiso* will begin. And, following Dante's sea voyage, we start shivering, we feel the 'frisson' of sublimity:

> What seas what shores what grey rocks and what islands
> What water lapping the bow[48]

As soon as we begin reading the *Paradiso*, however, we realize that there is a qualitative and quantitative leap in Dante's use of the sea image. The very first thing that happens to the pilgrim in his ascent through heaven is that he 'passes beyond humanity' by gazing at Beatrice's eyes, which are in turn 'intent upon the eternal sphere'.[49] This 'trasumanar', as the poet calls it with a daring neologism, is a first step in the long journey to God, which requires that the human being be gradually transformed by divine grace (the 'lumen gloriae') so that he may acquire greater faculties and thus be enabled to contemplate the Divinity. And in the *Paradiso*, each of these 'steps' of illumination and transformation will be accompanied by the sea image.

Human words, Dante says in canto I, cannot express the change of man into a higher, 'divine' being. The journey through God's own kingdom is ineffable both 'a parte obiecti' (Dante has seen 'such things unveiled as neither – mind can mirror now nor mouth express') and 'a parte subiecti'. It is, however, significant that, even before pronouncing this sentence ('trasumanar significar *per verba* non si poria') which appears to condemn poetry to silence before the supreme mysteries, Dante has recourse to an 'essemplo', an example from classical poetry:

> Nel suo aspetto tal dentro mi fei,
> qual si fé Glauco nel gustar de l'erba

> che 'l fé consorto in mar de li altri dèi.

> (Gazing at her then I changed within me,
>   and became like Glaucus, when he tasted
>   grass that made him the sea-gods' kin.)[50]

Glaucus' metamorphosis is much more than 'a sea-change into something rich and strange'. Tasting the miraculous weed, Ovid's fisherman suddenly feels a yearning to abandon the earth and plunges into the sea.[51] Here, the divinities 'purge' his 'mortal nature away' by means of a 'magic song nine times repeated', to wash all evil from him, and then bathe his body in a hundred streams. The last thing he remembers – the rest is inexpressible – is how the rivers poured from every side upon his head. The closing in of the waters over Glaucus is a baptismal drowning,[52] the exact opposite of the fate of Dante's Ulysses:

> totaque vertuntur supra caput aequora nostrum
> 'nfin che 'l mar fu sovra noi richiuso[53]

The sea condemns Ulysses forever, the sea welcomes Glaucus as a god, the sea changes Dante. The abyss that separates myth from experience is bridged by a breathtaking leap of the imagination, which gives expression to the ineffable by recourse to intertextuality.

It will be surprising then to find that the sea image dominates the *Paradiso*. Immediately after Dante's allusion to his total immersion in the divine 'mare', Beatrice herself picks up the metaphor and moves it onto a purely metaphysical plane in her speech on the order of the universe. Here, all 'natures', both those which lack intelligence and those that have intellect and love, whether they be near or far from their Origin,

> si muovono a diversi porti
> per lo gran mar de l'essere   (I, 112–13)

(move to different ports over the great sea of being)[54]

The extreme teleological tension that dominates the cosmos of the *Divine Comedy* is finally uncovered, and the harbour is once more part of Dante's imagery. As the final destination of every creature that sails on the ontological ocean, the port Dante envisages in this passage is both a divine and a natural goal, for the 'ordine' of which Beatrice speaks is a 'form' that 'makes the universe similar to God' and the 'footprint' of that 'eternal Good' 'to Whom, as end, that order moves'.[55]

In the address to the readers that opens canto II[56] we would therefore expect Dante to invite us, following the traditional topos he had employed in the *Convivio*, to sail with him towards that haven. Instead he offers us something much more challenging. Dante goes back to the metaphor of the sea journey he had employed at the beginning of the *Purgatorio* but deepens, amplifies, and strengthens it: *now there is no port*. In fact, we find ourselves in a very peculiar situation. We are in midsea, far from land. Dante asks the readers who sail in a 'little boat' to 'turn back to the shore again' without venturing out onto the 'pelago', the ocean, because if they lost him they would go astray. We are, as it were, at the Pillars of Hercules, which separate the Mediterranean from the Atlantic. The fact is that the poet's 'legno', his ship, 'cantando varca' – singing makes her way 'beyond'. 'The water I take', he proclaims, 'was never coursed before'. Apollo, the Spirit invoked in the first canto, already guides him, all the nine Muses point out to him the Bears, and Minerva herself (divine Wisdom) 'spira', breathes on his sail and inspires his song. Only those of us, therefore, who have lifted up our necks in good time to the bread of angels, i.e. to true wisdom, are invited to launch our craft on the salt and bottomless sea ('alto sale'), following close in the poet's wake 'dinanzi a l'acqua che ritorna equale', ahead of the point where the water, smoothing, becomes everywhere the same. We will, Dante adds, experience 'wonder' far greater than that known by the glorious heroes who sailed to Colchis (the Argonauts, the first navigators ever) when they saw Jason set his hand to the plough:

> O voi che siete in piccioletta barca,
>> desiderosi d'ascoltar, seguiti
>> dietro al mio legno che cantando varca,
> tornate a riveder li vostri liti:
>> non vi mettete in pelago, ché forse,
>> perdendo me, rimarreste smarriti.
> L'acqua ch'io prendo già mai non si corse;
>> Minerva spira, e conducemi Appollo,
>> e nove Muse mi dimostran l'Orse.
> Voialtri pochi che drizzaste il collo
>> per tempo al pan de li angeli, del quale
>> vivesi qui ma non sen vien satollo,
> metter potete ben per l'alto sale
>> vostro navigio, servando mio solco
>> dinanzi a l'acqua che ritorna equale.
> Que' glorïosi che passaro al Colco
>> non s'ammiraron come voi farete,
>> quando Iasón vider fatto bifolco.   (II, 1–18)

A first disquieting aspect of this 'exordium' is that it contains two lines which seem to open and close the voyage within a very short space:

> l'acqua ch'io prendo già mai non si corse
> dinanzi a l'acqua che ritorna equale

The contrast between the first and the second verse is very strong, and it is impossible not to notice that the latter closes the sailing only by as it were freezing it in midsea. Furthermore, the sense one gets from line 3 ('dietro al mio legno che cantando varca') is that of a going 'beyond' into infinity. In this context, the image of the water that becomes everywhere the same shows us the present ending of something which is presented as endless. It catches the instant which immediately follows, and will forever follow, the moment when the ship ploughs the waves. The tension between the final peace it intimates and the infinite perspective it opens up is what differentiates this from a very similar image in T.S. Eliot's *Four Quartets*. In *The Dry Salvages*, time and human life are represented by the river and the sea, the former biological and cyclical, the latter 'all about us', a 'meaningless perpetual flux'.[57] In the third movement Eliot concentrates on the relationship between past, present, and future, and employs the image of the passengers who, when the train starts, settle 'to fruit, periodicals and business letters'. The past seems to have vanished ('those who saw them off have left the platform') and the travellers relax 'to the sleepy rhythm of a hundred hours', in a present open to the future. Eliot, however, warns them:

> Fare forward, travellers! not escaping from the past
> Into different lives, or into any future;
> You are not the same people who left that station
> Or who will arrive at any terminus,
> While the narrowing rails slide together behind you;
> And on the deck of the drumming liner
> Watching the furrow that widens behind you,
> You shall not think 'the past is finished'
> Or 'the future is before us'.   (14–22)[58]

We move from the train to the ship, and Dante's image is split into two complementary ones, the rails that slide together and the furrow that widens. Both are merely apparent signs of the end of the past, of its closing down on the one hand, of its opening up *ad infinitum* on the other. In fact, these are illusions: the rails remain separate and the furrow in the water eventually disappears – 'l'acqua . . . ritorna equale'. It is precisely the contrast between appearance and reality that interests Eliot. 'Here between the hither and the farther shore', he writes, 'time is withdrawn'. We only 'think' that we are voyaging. The real destination is here, in 'the sphere of being' on which our mind may be intent 'at the time of death' ('And the time of death is every moment').[59] In Dante, the contrast is between opposite aspects of something which is claimed as real in its entirety – the going beyond, the launching of the craft onto unknown seas, the water becoming everywhere the same.

If it were not for these tensions, the experience line 15 describes would be perfectly normal. However big, no ship, not even the fleet of three boats (a sort of Niña, Pinta, and Santa Maria *avant la lettre*) that Dante imagines here, leaves an everlasting wake. 'Solomon' already knew it:

Like a ship that cuts through heaving waves – leaving no trace to show where it has passed, no wake from its keel in the waves[60]

The Book of Wisdom applies the image to the life of the godless, who leave behind no trace of themselves: 'scarcely born, [they] disappear'. On the other hand, Hippolytus maintains that as a ship that crosses the *pelagos* leaves behind neither trace nor way, so does the Church. 'She sails through this world as on a sea, but she has left her earthly hope back on land, because her life is already anchored in Heaven.'[61]

Wisdom and Hippolytus use the same image. The former, however, employs it to underline the transience of everything human, the latter to suggest that true Christian life consists in relinquishing the world, in leaving the earth because the real 'harbour' has already been prepared in Heaven. Both elements are present in *Paradiso* II, but whereas the abandonment of everything earthly agrees with Dante's situation, at this point an evocation of the passing of all things startles us. The poet has just proudly proclaimed that the waters he takes have never been coursed before. Now he seems to tell us that after his and our sailing everything becomes the same as if nothing had happened – that the experience of the *Paradiso* is as transient as a ship that leaves no trace behind.

Our uneasiness before all this increases when we consider that the first five terzinas of *Paradiso* II contain distinct echoes of an episode in *Inferno* XXVI which torments Dante throughout the *Comedy*.[62] No one can forget the 'legno' and the 'deep open sea' of Ulysses, the old man who turns 'his stern to the morning' in the Mediterranean and sails towards the darkness of night 'beyond the sun', towards 'the world that has no people' until, within sight of the mountain of Purgatory, the sea closes in on him. No one can fail to compare Ulysses' 'mad flight' to Dante's ascent through Heaven, and Ulysses' 'varco folle', the 'mad passage' which the pilgrim contemplates from the height of the eighth sphere,[63] to Dante's ship which 'cantando varca'.[64]

In Western culture, the enterprise of Dante's Ulysses becomes a paradigm of what Leopardi will ironically call the 'magnificent and progressive destinies of the human race'[65] to the point of being identified as the model of Columbus' voyage.[66] But it also becomes one of the archetypes of man's primeval and ever-recurring transgression.[67] 'Now', writes Melville superimposing the time of the Flood and the fall of Milton's angels[68] on the shipwreck of Dante's Ulysses, 'Now small fowls flew screaming over the yet yawning gulf; a sullen white surf beat against its steep sides; then all collapsed, and the great shroud of the sea rolled on as it rolled five thousand years ago'.[69] *Moby Dick* represents that phase of modernity in which the tragic is recreated as sublime. *Inferno* XXVI is tragic *tout court*. If Ulysses' ''nfin che 'l mar fu sovra noi richiuso' is the climactic seal of that tragedy, Dante's 'acqua che ritorna equale' constitutes its fleeting echo, its mysterious, sublime counterpoint.

And the 'stupore' of our initial *Convivio* passage is fittingly evoked at this point: the readers' amazement will be greater now than the wonder the Argonauts felt when they saw Jason turn to the plough. Our minds begin to be bewildered as we see, hear, and feel the great and wonderful things the poet writes.[70]

It may be opportune then, to ask ourselves which waters are now coursed by Dante, the new Ulysses, the primeval Argonaut, the transhumanized Glaucus. The simple answer is, the waters of Paradise and of the *Paradiso*; but what sort of waters are they? On the one hand they are the celestial, divine waters 'above the firmament'[71] and the seas of mysticism. Hugh of St Victor, for example, maintains that 'transnavigare extra mundum' (to sail beyond and out of the world) means 'seipsum transire' and 'ascendere in Deum', to transcend oneself and ascend to God. For John of Damascus and Thomas Aquinas, God Himself is the 'infinite and indeterminate *pelagos* of essence', the 'ocean of substance'.[72] On the other hand Dante's sailing is, according to the traditional topos, his poetic enterprise, the navigation of writing.[73] And finally, we must remember that medieval writers, from Jerome to Ambrose, from Gregory the Great to Honorius, from Hrabanus

Maurus[74] to Dante's contemporary, Iacopo Passavanti,[75] consider the Bible as an unfathomable abyss, an immense sea, an ocean of mystery. In his homilies on Genesis, Origen writes a sentence which is in fact very close to the opening of *Paradiso* II:

As great fear and awe pervade the mind of someone who enters the sea carried in a small boat because he has trusted his little raft to such immense billows . . . so we also fare because we dare to enter such vast ocean of mysteries[76]

In other words, at the beginning of the *Paradiso* Dante is about to launch his craft on to just such a sea, a voyage which produces a dramatic tension. It is this tension that is revealed by 'l'acqua ch'io prendo giá mai non si corse' and its opposite, 'l'acqua che ritorna equale'. The former dissolves and at once crystallizes into the murmured cry of the latter. To navigate the waters above the firmament and simultaneously describe this journey with human words as a 'scriba Dei', a writer inspired by God,[77] in sum, to write another Scripture is, as Dante will soon tell us, no 'pareggio da picciola barca', no voyage for a little boat. The flight of the angel's singing vessel in *Purgatorio* II, which leaves no trace on the water because it does not touch it, represents the unattainable term of comparison for Dante's own enterprise in the *Paradiso*.

Let me now examine the various levels of God's sea on which the poet's sailing takes place in the third cantica. No harbour is in sight, no port is reached at the end. The will of God is 'that *sea* to which all moves, both what It creates and what nature makes' (III, 86–7) – a goal, but one that has no boundary in either width or depth. The 'eternal counsel', or 'statute', is seen as an abyss,[78] His grace is 'a fountain so deep that never did creature thrust eye down to its first wave'.[79] And the culminating point of this imagery is reached when the Eagle speaks of Eternal Justice:

> Però ne la giustizia sempiterna
> la vista che riceve il vostro mondo,
> com'occhio per lo mare, entro s'interna;
> che, ben che da la proda veggia il fondo,
> in pelago nol vede; e nondimeno
> èli, ma cela lui l'esser profondo.   (XIX, 58–63)

(Therefore the sight that is granted to your world penetrates within the Eternal Justice as the eye into the sea; which, though from the shore it can see the bottom, in the open sea it sees it not, and none the less it is there, but the depth conceals it.)

Dante's pronouncement goes much further than the Psalmist's 'thy judgments are a great deep' (35. 7). His text is both perfectly mimetic and full of tension.[80] For if this is 'the greatest single assertion in the *Divine Comedy* of God's transcendence',[81] the effect it produces on us rests on the absolute naturalness of the image: the bottom of the sea can be perceived near the shore, but depth itself conceals it in midocean. The supreme Good 'non ha fine', 'has no limit and measures Itself by Itself' (XIX, 51), but the infinity of this perspective is determined only by our being finite. The eye that tries to penetrate into the abyss is human understanding, which is limited to the shoal but – and here the contrast becomes dramatic – knows there is a principle that lies well beyond appearances. Man's mind is aware that the bottom exists, but it is intrinsically incapable of reaching it because the bottom is hidden by its depth.

There is perhaps no better way of describing this effect than to employ the words with which Dante himself recounts the appearance and disappearance of Piccarda Donati in *Paradiso* III (10–13 and 122–3):

> Quali per vetri trasparenti e tersi,
>   o ver per acque nitide e tranquille,
>   non sì profonde che i fondi sien persi,
>   tornan d'i nostri visi le postille

(As through smooth and transparent glass, or through clear and tranquil waters, yet not so deep that the bottom be lost, the outlines of our faces return)

> e cantando vanio
>   come per acqua cupa cosa grave.

(and, singing, [she] vanished, as through deep water some heavy thing.)

The sailing that Dante implicitly outlines in the passage on Eternal Justice of *Paradiso* XIX moves from the shore to midsea (once more no harbour is in sight), from 'clear and tranquil' to 'deep water'. In our metaphorical use of the image, the 'cosa grave', the heavy thing would be our own intellect, which sinks away towards the bottom lost in the depths.

We are on the plane of theology, but gnoseological problems inevitably surface. And in fact Dante conceives man's search for truth as a sailing of the same kind, a 'fishing' that starts from the shore and moves to an immense sea.[82] Those who undertake this enterprise without having 'the art' necessary for it, Thomas Aquinas proclaims in *Paradiso* XIII (121–3), leave home in vain for they return poorer than they were at the outset. Yet we learn from Dante's own lips that, though 'our intellect can never be wholly satisfied unless that Truth shine on it beyond which no truth has range', we can indeed reach that 'vero', for our intellect

> Posasi in esso, come fera in lustra,
> tosto che giunto l'ha; e giugner puollo:
> se non, ciascun disio sarebbe *frustra*. (*Paradiso* IV, 127–9)

(Therein it rests, as a wild beast in his lair, so soon as it has reached it; and reach it it can, else every desire would be in vain.)

Provided it is performed 'with art', the fishing for truth has a goal to which we can come gradually, by reason. Because of man's natural desire to know, doubt 'springs up like a shoot at the foot of the truth'. This is what 'al sommo pinge noi di collo in collo', what urges us to the summit from height to height. We can climb to the very peak – a harbour, it seems, will appear at the end of our voyage.[83]

These then are the tensions that make the unprecedented navigation of the *Paradiso* a dramatic one: between passing 'beyond' and reaching port, between fishing and returning, navigating and shipwreck,[84] surface and bottom, shore and midsea. There is a crucial moment when these tensions are once more crystallized in the image of the poet's sailing. After trying to look at the effulgence of the sun (Christ) Dante's mind, shattered as if by lightning,[85] becomes 'greater' and 'goes out of itself'. This is a second illumination, a higher 'trasumanar' which enables the pilgrim to sustain Beatrice's smile. As he does ever more often in this cantica, the poet resorts to the ineffability topos[86] and refrains from describing this new wonder: 'and so', he writes, 'depicting Paradise, the sacred poem must needs make a leap, even as one who finds his way cut off'. The theme is 'ponderous' and the shoulders on which it is loaded are only mortal:

> non è pareggio da picciola barca
> quel che fendendo va l'ardita prora,
> né da nocchier ch'a sé medesmo parca. (XXIII, 67–9)

(It is no voyage for a little bark, this which my daring prow cleaves as it goes, nor for a pilot who would spare himself.)

The great ship appears once more. Undoubtedly it now embodies the 'sacred poem', the new Scripture. But the helmsman who steers it is burdened with fatigue, the pilgrim must continuously fight 'the battle of the feeble brows' (XXIII, 78), the poet must increasingly bear his 'sustained attack on the inarticulate'.[87] Will his be, as he announces in canto I, but an 'ombra', a shadow of the blessed kingdom? What is certain is that his prow cannot fly above, but must still *cleave* the waves.

Let us then see what happens when this pilot, who soon hereafter declares that he will catch the fleece of the Argonauts with his 'sacred poem to which both heaven and earth have set their hands' (xxv, 1–9) – when this writer who almost presents himself as the Writer – faces the supreme Author, the Creator, and the instant itself of Creation. Without hesitating, Longinus proclaimed the primal 'Fiat lux' of the Bible 'sublime'.[88] Confronted with it, Augustine, who theorized on the relationship between the 'sermo humilis' of Scripture and the sublimity of its mysteries, sighed his 'horror'.[89] Dante rewrites Genesis, mimics the Bible, recounts with an impudent mixture of philosophy and myth how God created the angels, 'primary matter', and the heavens.[90] Let us read the beginning of his account with attention, wonder, and horror:

> Non per aver a sé di bene acquisto,
>   ch'esser non può, ma perché suo splendore
>   potesse, risplendendo, dir '*Subsisto*,'
> in sua etternità di tempo fore,
>   fuor d'ogne altro comprender, come i piacque,
>   s'aperse in nuovi amor l'etterno amore.
> Né prima quasi torpente si giacque;
>   ché né prima né poscia procedette
>   lo discorrer di Dio sovra quest' acque.   (XXIX, 13–21)

(Not for gain of good unto Himself, which cannot be, but that His splendor might, in resplendence, say, '*Subsisto* – in His eternity beyond time, beyond every other bound, as it pleased Him, the Eternal Love opened into new loves. Nor before, as if inert, did He lie, for neither before nor after did the moving of God upon these waters proceed.)

It would not be opportune to comment here on each of these nine extraordinary lines nor on the eighteen that follow them and which are as powerful. I will examine only line 21, 'lo discorrer di Dio sovra quest'acque', where our image recurs once more. This line is Dante's translation of Genesis 1. 2c, in the Vulgate 'et Spiritus Dei ferebatur super aquas'. The Latin Bible in turn reproduces the Hebrew 'rūaḥ ʾelōhīm merahepetʿal-penē ha majim'. As each of these words can be interpreted in at least three radically different manners, exegesis and poetry have busied themselves for hundreds of years with this verse.[91] Milton, for instance, the highest exponent of modern religious sublimity, adopts a reading that entirely differs from Dante's. Here is the invocation to the Spirit in Book I of *Paradise Lost*:

> thou from the first
> Wast present, and with mighty wings outspread
> Dove-like sat'st brooding on the vast abyss
> And madest it pregnant (19–22)

In translating the Biblical expression from the Vulgate, Dante introduces three basic changes. In the first place, he qualifies the waters as 'these'. Following a tradition which had become increasingly common in the thirteenth century, he sees them as the waters 'above the firmament', namely those of the ninth transparent heaven above the stars, the 'caelum crystallinum' or 'aqueum' which is later identified as the 'Primum Mobile'.[92] He and Beatrice now find themselves on the same primordial 'waters' over which the 'rūaḥ ʾelōhīm' had moved before the beginning of time. This is the 'sea' that the pilgrim crosses now.

Secondly, Dante boldly cuts through centuries of controversy over the expression 'Spiritus Dei' (which can mean 'dreadful wind', 'terrible storm', 'breath' or 'Spirit' of God), quite simply attributing the action to God Himself. Finally, Dante eliminates the neutral 'ferebatur' of the Vulgate, rejects the 'incubabat' and the 'fovebat' (the brooding and incubating) that underlie Milton's rendering, neglects the 'volitabat' and the 'irruebat' (the fluttering and rushing) of other interpretations, and chooses a word both powerful and delicate, 'discorrer'. This may go back to Ovid ('ipse deus velox discurrere gaudet in altis montibus'),[93] but its meaning is closer to that of 'perlabitur', the word Virgil employs to recount how Neptune smoothed out the sea by skimming the waves with the light wheels of his chariot ('rotis summas levibus perlabitur undas').[94] Furthermore, classical and medieval Latin apply 'discurrere' to the mind's 'branching out' and a speaker's 'ranging over something'. The former agrees with the unfolding of the Eternal Love into new loves which constitutes the Dantean climax of God's Neoplatonic creation of the angels. The latter would obliquely refer to the action of God's word, which is fundamental in Genesis ('Let there be light') but notably absent, except for its reflection in the angels' '*Subsisto*', from Dante's account. Finally, in the *Convivio* (III vii 3) Dante quotes the *Liber de causis* (Prop. 20) to maintain that 'the Primal Goodness sends His bounties upon all things with a single diffusion'. Here, he significantly replaces the Latin 'influxio' with *discorrimento*.

Once more, God 'descends' into all creatures by this constant 'discorrer'.

In the Vulgate, God's Spirit 'is borne' or 'proceeds' ('ferebatur') over the waters. A medieval tradition embodied by Augustine, Peter Lombard, and Thomas Aquinas interprets this as the 'voluntas artificis quae superfertur materiae quam vult formare', the will of the maker which goes over the matter he wants to shape.[95] Hence what Dante, who certainly knew this interpretation, indicates with his line is the action by which the supreme Artifex–Artisan–Artist prepares Himself to give form to formless matter, to the 'res fabricandae' or things that are to be forged.

Dante rewrites Genesis as 'scriba Dei', as a 'sacred' writer. As he declares in the following canto, he is now beyond the theme of both comic and tragic poet; he is an 'artist' who is reaching 'l'ultimo suo', his utmost (XXX, 22–33). At precisely this moment, he sets up a decisive comparison between his writing and the writing of God. The latter is an effortless, sovereign moving *over* the primordial waters, the former crosses the very same sea but must *cleave* the waves and take into account that, 'as the material is deaf to respond, often form does not correspond to the intention of the art' (I, 127–9). Whereas God's 'discorrer' is followed by His 'Fiat lux' and His division of the waters from the waters, after the 'correr' of Dante who recounts that 'discorrer' . . . the water becomes everywhere the same: 'l'acqua ritorna equale'.

The sublime that Dante makes us feel in the *Paradiso* is a complex phenomenon. On the one hand, by launching on the endless ocean he recreates with the words of an inspired poet the sublimity of the Bible such as Longinus had envisaged it. On the other, prompting the bewilderment and terror that constitute the main symptoms of the modern 'sense of the sublime', he makes us emotionally conscious of this infinity by showing us the continuous tensions inherent in man's sailing over a non-human abyss, by setting what is limited but potentially boundless against what is 'fuor d'ogne comprender':[96] by freezing the ship in midsea and making the water – that water – turn smooth after his vessel. Dante places himself on an ever-shifting border, at a 'varco' that constantly moves further towards the horizon. The distinctive sign of his sublimity is the poetics that force us to catch and follow his ever-repeated 'varcare' or going beyond, and to 'wonder' at his determination to sing that 'passage' at all costs.

Proverbial wisdom maintained that amongst the four things one could not know was 'the way of a ship in the midst of the sea' (Proverbs 30. 19). Dante tries to understand and to describe it. The Psalmist proclaimed, 'Deep calleth unto deep at the noise of thy [God's] waterspouts: all thy waves and thy billows are gone over me.'[97] Dante is fully aware of the abyss, but he does not let himself be submerged.

In fact Dante can be seen as standing halfway between these 'sublime' pronouncements of the Old Testament and the new road of modern European poetry. Petrarch, for instance, swims in a sea that has neither bottom nor shore, ploughs waves, builds on sand, and writes in wind but a 'breve stilla d'infiniti abissi', a small drop in an infinite abyss.[98] But what he conveys with these images is the feeling of his own interior inadequacy as a man and a love poet. With him, infinity has moved within the human soul. In the same subjective vein, Wordsworth considers the face of Newton's statue as

> The marble index of a mind for ever
> Voyaging through strange seas of Thought, alone.[99]

Again, it is Leopardi's 'pensiero' that drowns in the immensity of his own fantasy, and for him foundering in that sea is a pleasure. For Dante, as we have seen, shipwreck is the quintessence of man's tragedy. The voyaging 'alone' of Newton's mind would have appeared to him far too similar to the sailing of his Ulysses. For him, the infinite abyss cannot stand for any Laura, nor indeed for Beatrice. In the *Comedy* the adjective 'infinito' is predicated of God alone. Above all, Dante never 'abandons' himself to the infinite. He reaches the point of *joining* his gaze with the Infinite Goodness and of having his desire and will moved by the supreme Love (XXXIII, 80–1 and 143–5), but the tension between finite and infinite, between what is knowable and must be known and what is unknowable, between the ineffable and what can and must be expressed, is present to the very end of the *Paradiso*. Dante stands on the borderline, on a perpetual *limen*.

It is this tension that makes articulate his 'attack on the inarticulate'. His 'wrestling match' (the 'aringo' of *Paradiso* I, 18) is a true battle. And like all epic contests, in order to be sung it requires the sublime manner. Hegel maintained that 'the sublime in general is the attempt to express the infinite, without finding in the sphere of phenomena an object which proves adequate for this representation'.[100] This definition may seem appropriate to Dante's *Paradiso*, but I hope that the present essay will have proved that it is not. Through the stratifications and tensions that Dante builds in it, the sea image I have examined constitutes precisely the 'object' Hegel sought. With it, in his own special manner, Dante has found the equivalent of the Homeric simile which Longinus considers a supreme example of the sublime.

I offer here a last magnificent piece of evidence. When, in the last canto of the poem, between three definitive (*sic!*) proclamations of ineffability, Dante describes what is concentrated within the depths of the Eternal Light, of the Infinite Itself, the ship, abysmally remote, appears again:

> Un punto solo m'è maggior letargo
> che venticinque secoli a la 'mpresa
> che fé Nettuno ammirar l'ombra d'Argo.
> Così la mente mia, tutta sospesa,
> mirava fissa, immobile e attenta,
> e sempre di mirar faceasi accesa.   (XXXIII, 94–9)

(A single moment makes for me greater oblivion than five and twenty centuries have wrought upon the enterprise that made Neptune wonder at the shadow of the Argo. Thus my mind, all rapt, was gazing, fixed, motionless and intent, ever enkindled by its gazing.)

The mystery, the 'secrecy' which has shrouded the first of these two terzinas for the following six (if not for twenty-five) centuries undoubtedly accounts for a great part of the fascination it exerts on us. I shall, however, try to explain the reason for its appeal. In these six lines Dante sets up an implicit comparison between the present of his remembering and writing and the past of his vision ('un punto solo m'è' – 'così la mente mia mirava') as well as between Neptune's admiration and the fixed, rapt gazing ('mirare') of the pilgrim's mind into the divine substance. He declares that one point alone of that vision is for him now, as he writes, greater oblivion than twenty-five centuries have been for the enterprise that made Neptune wonder at the shadow of the Argo. On the other hand, he maintains that as the 'point' is now greater 'letargo' for him, so his mind looked, then, motionless and intent, into God. In short, he at once denies and asserts something while disclosing an immense abyss of time.

How can a 'point' be greater than twenty-five centuries, which in Dante's eyes must have constituted almost the entire length of human history?[101] It can because, as scholars have discovered, it means 'eternity', because it is the 'punto a cui tutti li tempi son presenti', the Point to which all times are present.[102] Furthermore, between time, 'letargo', and 'point' there is a mysterious connection which has already been foreshadowed in canto XXXII, when St Bernard told Dante,

> Ma perché 'l *tempo* fugge che t'*assonna*,
>   qui farem *punto*   (139–40; italics mine)[103]

(But because the time flies that brings sleep upon you, we will stop here)

'In its punctual deflection and reduction towards eternity', writes Gianfranco Contini, 'time implies sleep and oblivion.'[104]

But how can one reconcile the present 'letargo' with the stupefied, self-regenerating attention of the past, and with the memory of the Argonauts' enterprise which is still vivid after twenty-five centuries? The fact is that 'letargo' means a very precise illness, 'oblivio', but because it denotes that illness it also alludes to the symptoms that accompany it: and these are delirium, stupor, 'Entrückung', rapture.[105] 'Where the disease of lethargy', writes Peter Dronke, 'suspends the mind and makes the patient gaze in a fixed, immobile fashion, so Dante's lethargy too has these effects – in precisely the opposite sense . . . "Thus did my mind, entirely suspended, gaze fixed, immobile and intent".'[106] Negative and positive, past and present are joined because Dante finds himself 'là 've s'appunta ogne *ubi* e ogne *quando*', where all space and all time have their 'point', are centred.[107]

Thus the present lethargy of the poet, Neptune's admiration, and Dante's 'mirare' become a series each term of which sheds light on, and is reflected and amplified by the other. We are witnessing the supreme instant of wonder, where the echo of the *Convivio*'s 'stordimento d'animo' is magnified to the furthermost limit. The mechanism itself of the 'stupor' such as outlined in the treatise is reproduced here. Dante's mind is 'all suspended'. This is the moment of desire, expectation, and 'suspense', when the emptiness cries out to be filled up – the moment of ad-miration. There follows the fixed, immobile, intent gazing, which fills up the gap. Then, in the last stage, desire burns again out of fulfilment itself. This is the ardour to 'mirare', to know, which 'wonderful things' produce, according to the *Convivio*, in the state of 'stupore'. And Dante's wonder is aroused precisely by the 'principia rerum' that Aristotle and Thomas Aquinas consider as the primary objects of attention for the philosopher and the Ur-poet. The pilgrim is now gazing at the 'universal form' of the 'knot' in whose depth is 'ingathered, bound by love in one single volume, that which is dispersed in leaves throughout the universe'.

Admiration is a state of mind of the subject at the moment of vision.

Immediately afterwards it is reverberated in the subjective 'letargo' of the writer. Finally, it enters the sphere of the receiver through the image of Neptune admiring in the remoteness of time. Indirectly, the dimension of poetry surfaces from this complex play. For the enterprise of the Argonauts that prompts Neptune's admiration is Dante's own in the *Paradiso*, as he has intimated at the beginning:

> Que' gloriosi che passaro al Colco
> non s'ammiraron come voi farete,
> quando Iasón vider fatto bifolco.　　　(II, 16–18)

Held together by wonder, this is the enterprise of Dante's journey, of his recounting it, and of our reading it.[108] And the 'point', which in the *Comedy* always 'wins or goes beyond, responding to the subject's supreme risk or test',[109] no longer appears as a mere spatial or temporal entity, but acquires a 'thematic', poetic notation as well:

> Da questo *passo* vinto mi concedo
> più che già mai da *punto di suo tema*
> soprato fosse comico o tragedo (XXX, 22–4; italics mine)

(At this pass I concede myself defeated more than ever comic or tragic poet was defeated by a point in his theme)

Thus the Argo, with which the *Paradiso* had started, returns at the end. Once more, it is the ship that, like Dante's, 'first ploughed an unknown sea'.[110] But it has also become the 'holy' 'vessel of light' of tradition,[111] the 'heavenly ship' represented by the constellation, Argo. Perhaps this ship is now, finally, sailing *over* ('discorrer') the waters above the firmament:

> Insequitur labens per caeli lumina Navis
> . . .
> totaque iam supera fulgens prolabitur Argo

(The Ship follows, skimming through the lights of the sky . . . all shining, the Argo skims over the celestial region)[112]

Here, finally, is 'the other Argo' prophesied by Virgil for the new golden age.[113] It has not reached port, but is still in midocean, 'in the stillness Between two waves of the sea',[114] suspended upon the waters from the depths of which Neptune's wonder rises in contemplation.

We have thus looked at the sea of Dante's journey to God from the surface ('l'acqua ch'io prendo', 'l'acqua che ritorna equale'). We have tried to penetrate down into its unfathomable abyss ('cela lui l'esser profondo'). Now, Neptune gazes from the bottom up towards the surface, and Ovid's 'mirantibus aequoris undis'[115] sinks, like Adrian Leverkühn's sphere, down into the 'ocean of all the worlds'.[116] From there, the Argo appears only as a shadow passing on the waves. The word, 'ombra', is the same that Dante had employed in *Paradiso* I while asking of Apollo (the divine Power of the Word) that He may grant the poet strength and speech enough to express the 'shadow of the blessed realm' imprinted in his mind. That 'ombra' indicates the mental image, the memory of Heaven that Dante carries with him when he 'descends' back to Earth after his journey, when, that is, he again sees 'through a glass, darkly'. The Argo is not just the ship of myth. However obliquely, it alludes to the vessel of Dante pilgrim and poet sailing through God's ocean. It is this ship that has now become a shadow, for this is the price one must pay to express what is ineffable and the prize one gets for doing so. By fading away at their own boundary human words can, in the present wondering oblivion, try to tell that which man 'neither can nor knows how to relate'.[117] The 'ombra' of the Argo now embodies the 'ombra' of Parnassus, under which poets grow 'pale'.[118] It is not by chance that the words of our terzina become a mystery, that Dante stretches them, as we have seen, to their utmost limit. The shadow of the Argo is the last echo of the water that turns smooth again – the light whisper of Dante's sublimity at its definitive 'passage beyond'.

Notes

I THE OLD MAN AND THE EARTH: ALTERITY AND OTHERNESS OF A MEDIEVAL STORY

1 The concepts to which I refer here have been expounded by H.R. Jauss in his famous essay 'Alterität und Modernität der mittelalterlichen Literatur', now in his collection, which bears the same title (Munich, 1977), pp. 9–47. An English translation of that essay by T. Bahti was published in *New Literary History*, 10 (1979), 181–229. In the same issue, see J.A. Burrow, 'The Alterity of Medieval Literature', pp. 385–90. *The Discarded Image: An Introduction to Medieval and Renaissance Literature* is the title of a fundamental book by C.S. Lewis (Cambridge, 1964) to which Jauss refers.

2 In this sense, I use the expression with the meaning most recently given to it by J.-P. Vernant, *La mort dans les yeux* (Paris, 1985).

3 The edition of Hemingway's novella I use here is the Penguin one (Harmondsworth, 1966). This quotation pp. 5–6.

4 D. Pearsall, 'The Canterbury Tales' in W.F. Bolton, ed., *The Middle Ages* (London, 1970), p. 177.

5 See note 1 above.

6 D. Pearsall, 'Chaucer's Pardoner: The Death of a Salesman', *Chaucer Review*, XVII (1983), 358–65. On the *Pardoner's Tale* in general, see D.R. Faulkner, ed., *Twentieth-Century Interpretations of the Pardoner's Tale* (Englewood Cliffs, N.J., 1973); A.C. Spearing's introduction to his edition of the Tale (Cambridge, 1965); R.P. Miller, 'Chaucer's Pardoner, the Scriptural Eunuch, and the *Pardoner's Tale*', now in R. Schoeck and J. Taylor, eds., *Chaucer Criticism*, vol. I (Notre Dame, 1960), pp. 221–44; W.B.J. Owen, 'The Old Man in *The Pardoner's Tale*', now in E. Wagenknecht, ed., *Chaucer* (London, 1960), pp. 159–65; F. Tupper, *The Pardoner's Tale* in W.F. Bryan and G. Dempster, eds., *Sources and Analogues of Chaucer's Canterbury Tales* (Chicago, 1941), pp. 415–38; D. Pearsall, *The Canterbury Tales* (London, 1985), pp. 91–104. See also the references in *The Riverside Chaucer*, general editor L.D. Benson (Boston,

3rd edn, 1987), pp. 907–10. My own analysis of the Tale and of the old man's episode in *English Medieval Narrative in the 13th and 14th Centuries* (Cambridge, 1982), pp. 260–5, is the point of departure for the present essay, where I reproduce a few sentences from that earlier work.

7 *Measure for Measure*, III. i. 11–13: 'Merely, thou art Death's fool; – For him thou labour'st by thy flight to shun, – And yet run'st toward him still.'

8 See the references to Ronsard's *Derniers vers* in P. Ariés, *L'homme devant la mort* (Paris, 1977), II, iii and notes therein. For Michault Taillevent, see below, p. 17. On the theme of death, see also P. Tristram, *Figures of Life and Death in Medieval English Literature* (London, 1976); R. Woolf, *The English Religious Lyric in the Middle Ages* (Oxford, 1968), pp. 67–113, 309–55; D. Gray, *Themes and Images in the Medieval English Religious Lyric* (London, 1972), pp. 176–220; S. Wenzel, 'Pestilence and Middle English Literature: Friar John Grimestone's Poems on Death' in *The Black Death*, ed. D. Williman (Binghamton, N.Y., 1982), pp. 131–59.

9 *As You Like It*, II. vii, 163–6. And cf. Milton, *Paradise Lost*, XI, 535–46.

10 See E. Deschamps, 'Ballade des signes de la mort', in *Anthologie poétique française, Moyen Âge*, 2, ed. A. Mary (Paris, 1967), pp. 151–2, and for instance lines 11–15: 'Convoiteus suis, blans et chanus, – Eschars, courroceux; j'adevine – Ce qui n'est pas, et loe plus – Le temps passé que la doctrine – Du tems present; mon corps se mine.'

11 Fable 78 in E. Chambry's edition (Paris, 1967), p. 37. On this fable and its implications see the splendid essay by H. Blumenberg, 'Nachdenklichkeit', *Deutsche Akademie für Sprache und Dichtung, Jahrbuch* 1980, pp. 57–61; and, for analogues, J. Bolte and G. Polivka, *Anmerkungen zu den Kinder-und Hausmärchen der Brüder Grimm* (Leipzig, 1913–31), No. 177, pp. 294–5. One could of course interpret the 'burden' (*phortion*) which Aesop's old man bears and of which he asks Death to relieve him as meaning 'life' with all its miseries, but the moral of the fable such as we have it is that every man is *philozōos*, a lover of life.

12 See references in the Riverside Chaucer, p. 905, and Skeat's edition of Chaucer's *Complete Works* (Oxford, 2nd edn, 1899), vol. v, p. 287. The relevant lines of Maximian's first Elegy, 223–8, are as follows: 'hinc est quod baculo, incumbens ruitura senectus – assiduo pigram verbere pulsat humum. – et numerosa movens certo vestigia plausu – talia rugato creditur ore loqui: – "suscipe me, genetrix, nati miserere laborum: – membra peto gremia fessa fouere tuo"'. For Middle English equivalents, see Riverside Chaucer, p. 909, note to 727–36.

13 *De Consolatione Philosophiae* I, m. 1; in Chaucer's *Boece*: 'For eelde is comyn unwarly uppon me, hasted by the harmes that I have, and sorwe hath comandid his age to ben in me. Heeris hore arn schad overtymeliche upon myn heved, and the slakke skyn trembleth of myn emptid body. Thilke deth of men is weleful that ne comyth noght in yeeris that ben swete, but

cometh to wrecches often yclepid. Allas! allas! with how deef an ere deth, cruwel, turneth awey fro wrecches, and nayteth to closen wepynge eien.'

14 Lines 743–4: Leviticus 19. 32: 'Thou shalt rise up before the hoary head, and honour the face of the old man, and fear thy God.' Lines 745–7: Matthew 7. 12: 'Therefore all things whatsoever ye would that men should do to you, do ye even so to them.'

15 N.C. Habel, *The Book of Job: A Commentary* (London, 1985), p. 111.

16 Text in J.B. Pritchard, ed., *Ancient Near Eastern Texts Relating to the Old Testament* (Princeton, 3rd rev. edn, 1969), pp. 405–7.

17 For which see G. Ravasi, *Giobbe* (Rome, 2nd edn, 1984), pp. 170–80 and references therein.

18 Job 3. 11

19 Job 3. 23: 'Viro cuius abscondita est via Et circumdedit eum Deus tenebris?'

20 Gregory the Great, *Moralia in Iob*, *Patrologia Latina* 75–76; and see Ravasi, pp. 175–6.

21 In the Vulgate, the sequence of three accusatives in Job 3. 21–2 is highly evocative: *mortem, thesaurum, sepulchrum*.

22 Pearsall, 'Chaucer's Pardoner: The Death of a Salesman', p. 363. The reference is to Romans 7. 24, translated in the *Parson's Tale* (I, 344) as 'Allas, I caytyf man! who shall delivere me from the prisoun of my caytyf body?'

23 Because, in a sense, it has itself become a feature of 'alterity' in Jauss' meaning of the word.

24 *Purgatorio* XXXIII, 54.

25 Pierre de Nesson, 'Paraphrase sur Job' in *Anthologie poétique française, Moyen Âge*, 2, p. 183, lines 13–15.

26 In the Hebrew original, the play is different but equally, if not more, effective: the 'grave' at the end of Job 3. 22 is *qéver*, the 'man' at the beginning of 3. 23 is *géver*. 'Womb and 'tomb' are an assonance: *réhem, qéver*. See R. Alter, *The Art of Biblical Poetry* (New York, 1985), pp. 78–82.

27 Quoted by P. Dronke, *Dante and Medieval Latin Traditions* (Cambridge, 1986), p. 17.

28 Quoted by Dronke, *Dante*, p. 25.

29 The equivalence between the treasure and death can be found in the analogues. In two different *exempla*, 'vere non est aliud thezaurus nisi periculum et mors', 'illud aurum mors fuit' (*Sources and Analogues*, pp. 420, 423). In the Italian *Rappresentazione di Sant'Antonio* Tagliagambe says the hermit is mad to call 'death' what (the gold) is 'life' (*Sources and Analogues*, p. 424).

30 Matthew 13. 10–13.

31 By S. Battaglia, 'Dall'esempio alla novella', now in his *La coscienza letteraria del medioevo* (Naples, 1965), pp. 532–47. For definitions and

analyses of the Gospel parables, see the classic works of C.H. Dodd, *The Parables of the Kingdom* (London, rev. edn, 1961) and J. Jeremias, *The Parables of Jesus*, English trans. (London, 3rd rev. edn, 1972); and the essays by J. Drury, 'Origins of Mark's Parables', and B. Harrison, 'Parables and Transcendence' in M. Wadsworth, ed., *Ways of Reading the Bible* (Sussex, 1981), pp. 171–89 and 190–212.

32 Mark 4. 11–12.

33 On this, see P.C. Bori, *L'interpretazione infinita: l'ermeneutica cristiana antica e le sue trasformazioni* (Bologna, 1987).

34 F. Kermode, *The Genesis of Secrecy: On the Interpretation of Narrative* (Cambridge, Mass.–London, 1979), especially pp. 23–47, on which I obviously draw for my argument.

35 *King Lear*, IV. i. 72–7 and IV. vi. 34–41.

36 *King Lear*, V. iii. 304–10.

37 T.S. Eliot, 'Gerontion' (*Poems – 1920*), 16 and 59. For line 59 interpreters quote J.H. Newman's sermon on 'Divine Calls', but Jaques' words in *As You Like It*, II. vii. 166 quoted above may also be relevant. The epigraph for 'Gerontion' is taken from *Measure for Measure*, III. i. 32–4 (and see note 7 above).

38 Coleridge, *The Rime of the Ancient Mariner*, III, 193–4.

39 Michault Taillevent, 'Le pauvre vieux', from *Le Passe-Temps Michault*, in *Anthologie poétique française, Moyen Âge*, 2, p. 232.

40 *Canzoniere* XVI. The 'Veronica' is the image (the 'true icon') of Jesus' visage kept in St Peter's, Rome.

41 G. Leopardi, *Canti*, ed. N. Gallo and C. Gàrboli (Turin, 1962), p. 190, lines 21–38 (and see notes there for references to the *Zibaldone*). Translation by G.R. Kay, *The Penguin Book of Italian Verse* (Harmondsworth, 1958), p. 280. Later in the 'Canto' (65 ff.) Leopardi focusses on *dying*: 'che sia questo *morir*, questo supremo – scolorar del sembiante'.

42 Battaglia, *La coscienza*, p. 545.

43 Chaucer, *The Pardoner's Tale*, eds. N. Coghill and C. Tolkien (London, 1958), p. 37.

44 *Knight's Tale*, 2743–58 and 2798–806.

45 F.W.J. Schelling, *Sämmtliche Werke*, 2, II (Stuttgart–Augsburg, 1857), *Philosophie der Mythologie*, 28, p. 649.

46 Johannes von Saaz, *Der Ackermann aus Böhmen*, ed. G. Jungbluth (Heidelberg, 1969), 16, 11–15. The *Ackermann* is attributed to Johannes von Tepl (mid-fourteenth century – 1414). On this topic, see J.O. Fichte, 'Der Ackermann aus Böhmen: "Experience" Becomes Art – A Poetic Response to Death' in P. Boitani and A. Torti, eds., *Intellectuals and Writers in Fourteenth-Century Europe* (Tübingen–Cambridge, 1986), pp. 178–90.

47 S. Freud, 'The Uncanny' in *An Infantile Neurosis and Other Works*, vol. XVII of *The Standard Edition of the Complete Psychological Works of Sigmund*

Freud, trans. and general editor, J. Strachey (London, 1955); the quotations in this paragraph come from pp. 238, 241, 241–2. And cf. R. Gill, 'Jung's Archetype of the Wise Old Man in Poems by Chaucer, Wordsworth, and Browning', *Journal of Evolutionary Psychology* 2 (1981), 18–32.

48 A comparison with another 'old man' in Chaucer's works will prove that what is said here about 'uncanniness' in the *Pardoner's Tale* may enable us to explain our reaction to the story. In the *Second Nun's Tale* an old man appears, 'clad in white clothes cleere' and holding in his hands a book 'with lettre of gold', to Valerian. There is no doubt that here, too, we have a 'supernatural presence gliding into our experience'. It is, however, easy to discover this old man's identity or at least to understand his function: if he is not St Paul himself, the message he presents is certainly Pauline (Ephesians 4. 5–6). While the figure may belong to the sphere of 'otherness', no hermeneutic uncertainty or multiplicity is produced by his appearance. In this case, furthermore, Chaucer's presentation is totally direct. Finally, the sudden materializing of the old man in the *Second Nun's Tale*, while understandably frightening for Valerian, cannot be considered uncanny in either Schelling's or Freud's sense. Being described as (and because it is) a miracle, it cannot be something that should have remained secret, nor something that can be repressed by our psyche. It remains, of course, a mysterious phenomenon, but one which Christians would be prepared to accept unhesitatingly, and the purpose of which would be fully clear in the context. And see chapter 7 in this volume, *His desir wol fle withouten wynges*, pp. 219–20 below.

If it were not for its lack of uncanniness, the closest post-medieval, English equivalent of Chaucer's old man would be found in Ellice Hopkins' 'Life In Death' (which can be read in *The Penguin Book of Victorian Verse*, ed. G. MacBeth, 1969, pp. 274–6), where the 'I' sets out to seek Death but, though catching 'his image faint and far', can never see his face because every image of death is also one of life. In the last stanza the poet tells us she is always finding 'the downward swing,/ Decay' (a parallel to the old man's vanishing flesh), but, as she grasps 'the flying skirts of Death', he turns and, 'beaming fair', reveals 'the radiant face of Life'. The only radiance in Chaucer's story comes, as we have seen, from the gold.

49 It may be interesting to note that for a modern critic such as Harold Bloom 'uncanny' seems to be the equivalent of 'sublime'. See, for instance, his 'Freud and the Sublime: a Catastrophe Theory of Creativity' in *Agon* (New York, 1982), pp. 91–118. Bloom develops Freudian categories, but the equivalence between what frightens (what evokes death) and the sublime is already present in Edmund Burke's *Philosophical Enquiry into the Origin of our Ideas of the Sublime and Beautiful*, IV, i–v. The unbearable contrast I see represented by the old man is what makes me prefer the notion of the tragic.

2 TWO VERSIONS OF TRAGEDY: UGOLINO AND HUGELYN

1 Statius, *Thebaid* VIII, 739–62.
2 See A. Pézard, 'Le chant XXXIII de l'Enfer' in *Letture dell'Inferno* of the *Lectura Dantis Internazionale* (Milan, 1963), pp. 343–96.
3 *Aeneid* II, 3 and 11.
4 See G. Barberi Squarotti, 'L'orazione del Conte Ugolino', *Letture Classensi*, IV (Ravenna, 1973), pp. 147–82; and E. Bigi, 'Carratteri e funzione della retorica nella *Divina Commedia*', *Letture Classensi*, IV, pp. 185–203, and particularly 200–1.
5 G. Villani, *Cronica* (Florence, 1845), vol. I, p. 450.
6 P. Villari, ed., *Cronica Fiorentina compilata nel sec. XIII* in *I primi due secoli della storia di Firenze*, vol. I (Florence, 1898), p. 250.
7 As there are in many medieval narratives. And see W.W. Ryding, *Structure in Medieval Narrative* (The Hague–Paris, 1971); and E. Vinaver, *The Rise of Romance* (Oxford, 1971), pp. 68–98.
8 Like those of Francesca, Ulysses, and Guido da Montefeltro. And see Aristotle, *Poetics* 23, 1459a 15 ff.
9 Seamus Heaney, *Field Work* (London, 1979), p. 63.
10 Description of their feelings is limited to the 'tristi' of line 64.
11 Significantly, Dante shifts the emphasis, underlining the children's role and their innocence, in the invective against Pisa at the end of the episode.
12 For this concept, see M.W. Bloomfield, 'Authenticating Realism and the Realism of Chaucer', *Thought*, 39 (1964) 335–58.
13 With an ellipsis, i.e. the omission of part of the story (Ugolino's own treasons), for which see Barberi Squarotti, quoted in n. 4 above.
14 See M. Shapiro, 'Addendum: Christological Language in *Inferno* XXXIII', *Dante Studies*, 94 (1976) 141–2, who rightly quotes John 13. 13. My interpretation differs from hers.
15 Matthew 7. 7–9; Luke 11. 9–11, first pointed out by R. Hollander, '*Inferno* XXXIII, 37–74: Ugolino's Importunity', *Speculum*, 59 (1984), 549–55. Hollander convincingly argues that the parable of the importunate friend (Luke 11. 5–13), preceded by the Lord's prayer in the Gospel account (Luke 11. 1–4) lies behind Dante's text: 'If a son shall ask bread of any of you that is a father, will he give him a stone?' (11). J. Jeremias, *The Parables of Jesus*, 3rd rev. edn (London, 1972), pp. 158–9, stresses the fact that the story is meant to illustrate God's readiness to hearken to the cry of the needy and come to their help. God is a 'giving' Father.
16 For references, see E. Pasquini, s.v. 'cieco' in *Enciclopedia Dantesca*, I (Rome, 1970), p. 998.
17 Deuteronomy 28, 28–29 (in the Vulgate: 'Percutiat te Dominus amentia et caecitate ac *furore mentis*, et palpes in meridie sicut palpare solet caecus in tenebris, et non dirigas vias tuas'), and Isaiah 59, 9–10.

18 See V. Russo, 'Il "dolore" del Conte Ugolino', now in his *Sussidi di esegesi dantesca* (Naples, 1967), pp. 147–81.

19 Russo, 'Il "dolore"', p. 179.

20 For which see F. De Sanctis, 'Il Canto XXXIII dell' *Inferno*', now in G. Getto, ed., *Letture Dantesche* (Florence, 1964), pp. 629–49; and F. D'Ovidio, 'Il vero tradimento del Conte Ugolino' in his *Studi sulla Divina Commedia* (Caserta, 1931); 'L'episodio di Ugolino', 'Le ultime parole di Ugolino', 'L'Ugolino del De Sanctis', all in his *Nuovi studi danteschi* (Naples, 1932). Cf. V. Russo in *Sussidi di esegesi dantesca*, pp. 152–3 and n. 1.

21 See Singleton in his commentary to *Inferno* XXXIII, 69 (1970); J. Freccero, 'Bestial Sign and Bread of Angels: *Inferno* XXXII and XXXIII', now in his *Dante: The Poetics of Conversion* (Cambridge, Mass., and London, 1986), ed. R. Jacoff, pp. 152–66.

22 See N. Frye, *Anatomy of Criticism* (Princeton, 1957), p. 148; and Freccero, 'Bestial Sign', pp. 164–5.

23 See Villari, *Cronica Fiorentina*, p. 251; and L. Scarabelli, ed., *Commedia di Dante degli Allagherii col commento di Jacopo della Lana* (Bologna, 1866), p. 501; D'Ovidio, *Nuovi studi danteschi*, vol. 1, pp. 51–96.

24 The series of hunger, mouth, and biting images is obviously relevant here. See J.L. Borges, *Nueve ensayos dantescos* (Madrid, 1983), pp. 105–11.

25 See G. Contini, 'Filologia ed esegesi dantesca', now in his *Un'idea di Dante* (Turin, 1976), pp. 125–8.

26 Contini, 'Filologia', p. 125.

27 We may compare the ground, 'my moodres gate', in the Old Man episode of the *Pardoner's Tale*. He begs the earth, 'Leeve mooder, leet me in!'

28 And see R. Kirkpatrick, *Dante's 'Inferno': Difficulty and Dead Poetry* (Cambridge, 1987), pp. 363–432.

29 See n. 3 above; Hollander, '*Inferno* XXXIII', pp. 549–50. For this and the following classical references, see U. Bosco, s.v. 'Ugolino' in *Enciclopedia Dantesca* V (Rome, 1976), p. 799.

30 *Aeneid* XII, 883–4; and see also *Aeneid* IV, 26 and X, 675–6.

31 Seneca, *Thyestes*, 1006–9; and see Contini, 'Filologia', p. 126.

32 Seneca, *Oedipus*, 868 ff.

33 Ovid, *Metamorphoses* VI, 277–8.

34 See n. 1 above.

35 *Thebaid* VIII, 756.

36 A model for which may be Lucan, *Pharsalia* VIII, 823–30.

37 The *locus classicus* is Horace, *Ars poetica*, 394–6, but it may be opportune here to recall *Thebaid* X, 873–7 and (in particular) I, 9–10. It should be noted that Amphion married Niobe.

38 Letter to Cangrande, *Epistole* XIII, 10. 29: 'Tragoedia in principio est admirabilis et quieta, in fine seu exitu est fetida et horribilis.' The *Inferno* itself is the first part – 'horribilis et fetida' – of the *Comedy* (Letter to Cangrande 10, 31).

39 It will be obvious that on this point I do not agree with Kirkpatrick, *Dante's Inferno'*, p. 366: nor with J. Tambling, *Dante and Difference: Writing in the 'Commedia'* (Cambridge, 1988), pp. 67–95.

40 Aristotle's comment in the *Poetics* 7, 1451a 9 ff. may be appropriate: 'For had it been the rule for a hundred tragedies to compete together, the performance would have been regulated by the water-clock' (S.H. Butcher's translation in his *Aristotle's Theory of Poetry and Fine Art* (London, 1911), p. 33.

41 See R.E. Kaske, 'The Knight's Interruption of the Monk's Tale', *English Literary History*, 24 (1957) 249–68).

42 In spite of what Troilus himself says at IV, 260–80, and particularly 270–3.

43 On this aspect, see J.D. Burnley, *Chaucer's Language and the Philosophers' Tradition* (Cambridge–Totowa, N.J., 1979), pp. 11–43.

44 And see D. Pearsall, *The Canterbury Tales* (London, 1985), pp. 279–85; and the classic P.G. Ruggiers, 'Notes Towards a Theory of Tragedy in Chaucer', now in W. Erzgräber, ed., *Geoffrey Chaucer* (Darmstadt, 1983), pp. 396–408.

45 *De Casibus Virorum Illustrium* VIII vi 14, ed. P.G. Ricci and V. Zaccaria (Milan, 1983), p. 682.

46 And see P. Godman, 'Chaucer and Boccaccio's Latin Works' in P. Boitani, ed., *Chaucer and the Italian Trecento* (Cambridge, 2nd edn, 1985), pp. 269–95.

47 2 Maccabees 9. 9: 'And so the ungodly man's body swarmed with worms, and while he was still living in anguish and pain, his flesh rotted away, and because of his stench the whole army felt revulsion at his decay.' See also 9. 10. Translation from *The Oxford Annotated Bible with the Apocrypha*, ed. H.G. May and B.M. Metzger (New York, 1965), Apocrypha, p. 280.

48 This is to be found again in one stanza of the Caesar account (2679–86) and at the opening of the second part of a stanza in the story of Samson (2075–8).

49 See A. Brusendorff, *The Chaucer Tradition* (Milford, 1925), p. 489; and M. Praz, 'L'influsso italiano' in his edition of *The Canterbury Tales* (Bari, 1961), p. 84.

50 In the Caesar story 'Brutus Cassius' or 'false Brutus and his othere foon' would belong to *Giudecca*.

51 G. Steiner, *The Death of Tragedy* (London, 1961), pp. 12–13.

52 The model is clearly Boccaccio's *De Casibus*, which proceeds 'a mundi primordio in nostrum usque evum' (Zaccaria, p. 10). The order of the *Monk's Tale* may have been the same: see D.K. Fry, 'The Ending of *The Monk's Tale*', *Journal of English and Germanic Philology*, 71 (1972) 355–68. This would support my idea that the Hugelyn story is meant to represent the climax of the Monk's sequence.

53 See E. Raimondi, 'Una tragedia del Trecento', now in his *Metafora e storia*

(Turin, 1970). pp. 147–62; and R. Haas, 'Chaucer's *Monk's Tale*: An Ingenious Criticism of Early Humanist Conceptions of Tragedy', *Humanistica Lovaniensia*, 36 (1987) 44–70, and references therein.

54 *De Casibus*, Prohemium 6; v x 28; v xii 12–13; v iv 1; and see Zaccaria's Introduction, pp. xxxiii–xxxvii. On Fortune, see the classic H.R. Patch, *The Goddess Fortuna in Mediaeval Literature* (London, 1967 reprint); and K. Reichert, *Fortuna oder die Beständigkeit des Wechsels* (Frankfurt, 1985).

55 The idea of inserting Ugolino into the Fortune scheme may have come from Boccaccio's *De Casibus* IX xx, where he appears 'lamenting in tears the cruelty of his fellow citizens and the hunger of which he had died".

56 See Praz, 'L'influsso italiano', pp. 79–80.

57 See J. Mann, 'Parents and Children in the "Canterbury Tales"' in P. Boitani and A. Torti, eds., *Literature in Fourteenth-Century England* (Tübingen–Cambridge, 1983), p. 166 and, for a comparison with Griselda, pp. 180–1.

58 Mann, 'Parents and Children', pp. 166–7.

59 See R. Girard, *Job, the Victim of his People*, trans. Y. Freccero (London, 1987), pp. 3–18.

60 Quoted by H. Schless, 'Transformations: Chaucer's Use of Italian' in D. Brewer, ed., *Geoffrey Chaucer* (London, 1974), p. 223.

61 See L. Pareyson, 'La sofferenza inutile in Dostoevskij', *Giornale di metafisica*, 4 (1982) 123–70.

62 See T. Spencer, 'The Story of Ugolino in Dante and Chaucer', *Speculum*, 9 (1934) 295–301; Praz, 'L'influsso italiano', pp. 80–3; Schless, 'Transformations', pp. 220–3. I include myself in this category.

63 Goethe, *Tasso* v. v. 3426–9.

64 Sophocles, *Oedipus Rex*, 1307–11; *Philoctetes*, 278.

65 I am obviously using H. Bloom, *A Map of Misreading* (Oxford, 1975).

66 Once more H. Bloom, *The Anxiety of Influence* (Oxford, 1973).

67 *Troilus and Criseyde* III, 491–9; and see J.A. Burrow, *Ricardian Poetry* (London, 1971), p. 69–78.

68 *Poetics* 14, 1453b 22–6 (S.H. Butcher's translation, p. 51). For the observations in the last few paragraphs I would like to acknowledge my debt to Winthrop Wetherbee, who set me thinking about these problems in a new way during a lecture he gave in Rome in November, 1987. I am aware that he may not agree with all I say.

3 O QUIKE DETH: LOVE, MELANCHOLY, AND THE DIVIDED SELF

1 All quotations from Petrarch's *Canzoniere* are from G. Contini's edition, Turin, 1964.

2 Translation by M. Bishop, *Petrarch and his World* (London, 1963), p. 154. Other translations from Petrarch, unless otherwise specified, are mine.

3 L. Forster, *The Icy Fire; Five Studies in European Petrarchism* (Cambridge, 1969), p. 6.
4 *Ibid., Icy Fire*, p. 5.
5 *Ibid., Icy Fire*, p. 6.
6 For which see P. Dronke, *Medieval Latin and the Rise of European Love-Lyric*, 2nd edn (Oxford, 1968), p. 599; and E. Wind, *Pagan Mysteries in the Renaissance*, rev. edn (New York–London, 1968), p. 161.
7 K. Foster, *Petrarch. Poet and Humanist* (Edinburgh, 1984), p. 78.
8 *Ibid., Petrarch*, p. 78.
9 Sonnet CCCLXIII. The translation is R.M. Durlings, from his edition of *Petrarch's Lyric Poems* (Cambridge, Mass., 1976).
10 Text and translation are from K. Foster and P. Boyde, eds., *Dante's Lyric Poetry*, I (Oxford, 1967), pp. 48–9. The sonnet is part (8–9) of chapter xiii of the *Vita Nuova*. The *incipit* derives from Peire Vidal's 'Tuiz mei cossir son d'amor et de chan'. See also Dante Alighieri, *Vita Nuova*, ed. D. De Robertis (Milan–Naples,1980), pp. 86–8, notes and references therein.
11 P. Boyde, *Dante's Style in his Lyric Poetry* (Cambridge, 1971), p. 242.
12 M. Pazzaglia in *Enciclopedia Dantesca* V (Rome, 1976), p. 761; and see K. Foster and P. Boyde, eds., *Dante's Lyric Poetry*, II (Oxford, 1967), pp. 71–2, 77–9.
13 Pazzaglia, *ibid.*
14 *Ibid.*, p. 761.
15 *Filostrato*, IV, 70, 1–2.
16 R. Amaturo, *Petrarca* (Bari, 1980), p. 302.
17 No. 26 in Thomas Wyatt, *Collected Poems*, ed. J. Daalder (Oxford, 1975), p. 24.
18 *Don Quijote* (Madrid, 1971), Part II, p. 227. Translation by S. Putnam, *Don Quixote* (London, 1953), vol. II, p. 760 (Part II, chapter 38). Italics mine. French, Italian and English Petrarchists do not seem to catch the moral import of some of the compositions in Petrarch's *Canzoniere*. The situation seems to be different in Spain, where Garcilaso de la Vega portrays love as a self-destructive state of contrary passions, an 'expense of spirit in a waste of shame'. In the Second Eclogue, he depicts it as a maddening experience, literally deranging the shepherd Albanio and depriving him of rational self-control. Here, Garcilaso pastoralizes the theme of 'loco amor', morally and tragically treated by Fernando de Rojas in *La Celestina*. Garcilaso himself greatly influenced Herrera and Quevedo.
19 G. Contini, ed., *Poeti del Duecento*, I (Milan–Naples, 1960), p. 885.
20 Dronke, *Medieval Latin*, I, pp. 25–6.
21 Wind, *Pagan Mysteries*, p. 161; and see F. Wessel, *Probleme der Metaphorik und die Minnemetaphorik in Gottfrieds von Strassburg 'Tristan und Isolde'* (Munich, 1984), pp. 401–11.

22 Plato, *Philebus* 46b 6–9; the translation is B. Jowett's in his edition of *The Dialogues of Plato*, vol. III (Oxford, 1953), p. 604.

23 *Philebus* 47e 1–3; Jowett, p. 606.

24 *Secretum*, in *Francesco Petrarca. Prose*, G. Martellotti, P.G. Ricci, E. Carrara, E. Bianchi, eds. (Milan–Naples, 1955), p. 106.

25 Foster, *Petrarch*, p. 172.

26 S. Wenzel, *The Sin of Sloth. Acedia in Medieval Thought and Literature* (Chapel Hill, N.C., 1960), p. 159; and see E. Loos, 'Die Hauptsünde der acedia in Dantes *Commedia* und in Petrarcas *Secretum*' in F. Schalk, ed., *Petrarca 1304–1374: Beiträge zu Werk und Wirkung* (Frankfurt am Main, 1975); H. Baron, *Petrarch's Secretum* (Cambridge, Mass., 1985), pp. 215–18.

27 Wenzel, p. 159.

28 *Ibid.*, p. 162.

29 G.E. Lessing, *Briefe die neueste Literatur betreffend*, letter 332, in F. Budde and W. Riezler, eds., *Lessings Werke*, vol. IV (Berlin, n.d.), p. 273.

30 R. Klibansky, E. Panofsky, F. Saxl, *Saturn and Melancholy. Studies in the History of Natural Philosophy Religion and Art* (London, 1964), Part III, chapter 2; and see S. Wenzel, 'Petrarch's *Accidia*', *Studies in the Renaissance*, 8 (1960), 36–48.

31 See *Secretum*, pp. 106 ff.

32 See G. Agamben, *Stanze. La parola e il fantasma nella cultura occidentale*, 2nd edn (Turin, 1977), pp. 18–23.

33 *Knight's Tale*, 1372–6.

34 F. Rico, *Vida u Obra de Petrarca. I, Lectura del Secretum* (Padua, 1974), pp. 205–6.

35 *Ibid.*, *Lectura*, pp. 203–4.

36 *Ibid.*, *Lectura*, pp. 204–5. For the contrary view see U. Bosco, *Francesco Petrarca*, 3rd edn (Bari, 1965), pp. 95–8.

37 I mention just two examples in Canzone LXXI, 97, and sonnet CLXXIII, with the two motifs of 'dolce et amar' and 'lieti e tristi'.

38 Foster, *Petrarch*, p. 65.

39 *Ibid.*

40 *Hamlet*, II. ii, 295 ff.

41 *Troilus and Criseyde* V, 360, 622, 1216, 1646. E.T. Donaldson has spoken of Troilus' paralysis and inaction: see his 'Chaucer and the Elusion of Clarity', *Essays and Studies*, n.s. 25 (1972), 33–4.

42 Notice the connection between melancholy and dreams. Later (623), the connection is between melancholy and 'fantasie'.

43 It is particularly interesting to note that in his 'translation' of the passage Wordsworth replaced Chaucer's lines with 'All which he of himself conceited wholly – Out of his weakness and his melancholy', where the

second part of the sentence is a definite echo of *Hamlet*, II. ii. 638. See Wordsworth's *Poetical Works*, ed. E. de Selincourt, vol. IV (Oxford, 1966 reprint), p. 231.

44 *Filostrato*, I, 37, 4. On the 'mirror of the mind' see S.L. Clark and J.N. Wasserman, 'The Heart in *Troilus and Criseyde*: the Eye of the Breast, The Mirror of the Mind, The Jewel in Its Setting', *Chaucer Review*, 18 (1984), 316–28.

45 E.H. Wilkins, 'Cantus Troili', *Journal of English Literary History*, 16 (1949), 167–73; P. Thomson, 'The "Canticus Troili": Chaucer and Petrarch', *Comparative Literature*, 11 (1959), 313–28.

46 This is just possible in Italian and may even have been at the back of Petrarch's mind. If he had wished to be absolutely clear he could have written 'Se non è amor' without affecting the rhythm of his line.

47 For analogues and possible sources of this passage see B.A. Windeatt's edition of *Troilus and Criseyde* (London–New York, 1984), p. 127.

48 *Philebus* 48a 5–6 and 50b 1–4; Jowett's translation, pp. 606 and 609.

4 SUNSET, FLOWERS, AND LEAVES: TRADITION AND TRAGIC IMAGES

1 *Goethes Natur-Wissenschaftliche Schriften*, ed. G. Ipsen, vol. I (Leipzig, n.d.), p. 9 (Journal von Tiefurt. 1782, 32. Stück).

2 I would take as models the works, both theoretical (*Paradigmen zu einer Metaphorologie* (Bonn, 1960)) and applied (*Schiffbruch mit Zuschauer. Paradigmen einer Daseinsmetapher; Die Lesbarkeit der Welt; Die Sorge geht über den Fluss* (Frankfurt, 1979; 1981; 1987)) of Hans Blumenberg; and those of Friedrich Ohly, particularly *Diamant und Bocksblut. Zur Traditions- und Auslegungsgeschichte eines Naturvorgangs von der Antike bis in die Moderne* (Berlin, 1976) and many of the *Schriften zur mittelalterlichen Bedeutungsforschung* (Darmstadt, 2nd edn, 1983), which are the best studies of this kind after those of Ernst Robert Curtius.

3 H. Bloom, *The Breaking of the Vessels* (Chicago–London, 1982), pp. 74–5.

4 On the sunset and night images, see P. Boyde, *Night Thoughts on Italian Poetry and Art* (Cambridge, 1985).

5 *King Lear*, III. iv. 5 and 12.

6 Text edited by E. Paratore (Fondazione Lorenzo Valla, Milan, 1978–83) in six volumes, as throughout this chapter. The translation is Dryden's. On Dante's use of Virgil, see R. Hollander, *Il Virgilio Dantesco: Tragedia nella "Commedia"* (Florence, 1983), and, on this passage, R. Kirkpatrick, *Dante's 'Inferno': Difficulty and Dead Poetry* (Cambridge, 1987), pp. 47–9; pp. 54–6 for the 'fioretti' simile.

7 The text on which I have based my translation is that edited by C. Gallavotti, *Saffo e Alceo*, vol. I (3rd rev. edn, Naples, 1962), p. 139. And cf. Antonio Machado's 'Noche de verano' for a modern version.

8 The translation is mine, based on the text in E. Diehl, *Anthologia Lyrica Graeca* (Leipzig, 3rd edn, 1949–52). On this edition, unless otherwise specified, I base all my translations from Greek lyric poetry in this chapter.

9 In *Iliad* II, 1–2 the opposition is between Zeus, awake through the night, and all the other gods and warriors: 'nature' plays no part in the image.

10 Statius doubles the opposition: the night is quiet, but the storm is beginning; Polynices is brave, but also tormented by fear and uncertainty.

11 K. Foster and P. Boyde, eds., *Dante's Lyric Poetry*, vol. II, Commentary (Oxford, 1967), p. 259. And see P. Boyde, *Dante's Style in His Lyric Poetry* (Cambridge, 1971), pp. 296–9, and references therein.

12 'De ramis cadunt folia' in F.J.E. Raby, ed., *The Oxford Book of Medieval Latin Verse* (Oxford, 1959), pp. 353–4. And see P. Dronke, *Medieval Latin and the Rise of the European Love-Lyric*, vol. I (Oxford, 2nd edn, 1968), pp. 288–91.

13 The translation from Petrarch (*Canzoniere*, ed. G. Contini, Turin, 1964) is mine. On classical reminiscences in this poem, see the commentary by G. Carducci and S. Ferrari in their edition of *Le Rime* (Florence, 1978 edn), *ad loc.* Cf. also *Canzoniere* CLXIV. In 'Abendphantasie', a poem written between 1797 and 1799, Hölderlin still uses the same imagery and opposition.

14 For the initial image, see what Leopardi himself says about Homer's simile in *Iliad* VIII, 555–60; quoted by N. Gallo and C. Gàrboli in their edition of Leopardi's *Canti* (Turin, 1962), p. 110. Classical echoes are also pointed out in their commentary. The translation is mine.

15 And see *Zibaldone*, 718–19, 5 March 1821, quoted in *Canti*, p. 85.

16 See D. Comparetti, *Virgilio nel Medio Evo* (Florence, 2nd edn, 1943), vol. I, pp. 247–8; and A. Scaglione, 'Imagery and Thematic Patterns in *Paradiso* XXIII' in T.G. Bergin, ed., *From Time to Eternity* (New Haven–London, 1967), pp. 137–72.

17 In his own notes Eliot refers to the Fragment of Sappho quoted above (see n. 7), saying his notation 'may not appear as exact' as her lines. His passage also contains an echo of R.L. Stevenson's 'Requiem': 'home is the sailor, home from sea'.

18 On which see A.M. Chiavacci Leonardi, *Lettura del Paradiso Dantesco* (Florence, 1963), pp. 39–40.

19 See A.M. Chiavacci Leonardi, *La guerra de la pietate. Saggio per una interpretazione dell'Inferno di Dante* (Naples, 1979).

20 There are two key sunset–evening scenes in Chaucer's *Troilus*. The first, more elaborate one (II, 904–10) follows Antigone's song and precedes Criseyde's dream. It is a moment of great lyrical intensity (without an equivalent in the *Filostrato*) that marks the beginning of Criseyde's love (899–903) and culminates in a splendid line ('And white thynges wexen dymme and donne', for which Robinson quotes, without much reason,

Paradiso, XXII, 93) and the nightingale's song (918–22). The second (v, 1142 ff.) frames the scene of Troilus and Pandarus vainly waiting on the walls of Troy for Criseyde's return. Chaucer underlines the passing of time, from morning (1107–13) to noon and evening (1142), without actually describing sunset. Boccaccio emphasizes the change of light in his fuller image (*Filostrato*, VII, 9, 4–5; and see VII, 6, 1).

21 In the *Parliament of Fowls*, the progress of our three images is rather different from that I outline in the present paper. From the sunset of lines 85–91 we pass to the flowers (186) and the leaves (202) of the Park of Love–Garden of Eden. Both are sempiternal (173). We encounter another sunset in the Temple of Venus (226, with fully erotic connotations), but, coming out of it, the dreamer contemplates Nature herself 'upon an hil of floures' (302; on this image, see G.D. Economou, *The Goddess Natura in Medieval Literature*, Cambridge, Mass., 1972). I have discussed the significance of this movement in my *English Medieval Narrative in the 13th and 14th Centuries* (Cambridge, 2nd edn, 1986), pp. 168–83. The best treatment of the Nature theme in the *Parliament* is still J.A.W. Bennett's in his *The Parlement of Foules. An Interpretation* (Oxford, 1957).

22 Caesari Heisterbacensis *Dialogus Miraculorum*, ed. J. Strange, vol. II (Cologne–Bonn–Brussels, 1851), p. 266; trans. H. Von E. Scott and C.C. Swinton Bland (London, 1929), II, p. 231.

23 See also *Paradise Lost*, IX, 48 ff., where Satan renews his attack on man – the decisive and successful one – in the twilight after sunset; and cf. IV, 589 ff., the picture of prelapsarian man at one with nature and God in the quiet of night. And cf. M. Lermontov's 'Night II'.

24 U. Foscolo, 'Alla Sera', *Opere* (Milan, 1966), p. 12. And cf. T. Tjutčev's 'Autumn Evening' and 'Sacred Night'.

25 Baudelaire, *Les Épaves* in *Les Fleurs du Mal et autres poèmes* (Paris, 1964), p. 158. And cf. J.R. Jiménez's 'Ponientes'.

26 G. Trakl, *Dichtungen*, ed. K. Röck (Salzburg, 1938) in *Im Dorf*. Sunset and evening are favourite themes of Trakl's, who devotes several poems to them. And cf. A. Machado's 'Hacia un ocaso radiante'.

27 Where, however, the final wish is that our 'joy' may 'go down' in the 'seriousness of life' like the sun and die, like the sun, 'a beautiful death'.

28 F. Nietzsche, *Also sprach Zarathustra*, eds. G. Colli and M. Montinari (Berlin, 1968), pp. 5–6; trans R.J. Hollingdale (Harmondsworth, 1961), p. 39.

29 Nietzsche, *Zarathustra*, pp. 245 and 273; trans. pp. 216 and 238, 336.

30 Thomas Mann, *Doktor Faustus* (Frankfurt, 1982), ch. 34, pp. 356, 358; English trans. by H.T. Lowe-Porter (New York, 1971), pp. 355, 358.

31 Thomas Mann, *Die Entstehung des Doktor Faustus. Roman eines Romanes* (Frankfurt, 1984), pp. 96, 109, 160.

32 The flowers surrounding Beatrice are anticipated by those of the Earthly

Paradise in *Purgatorio* XXVII, 99 and 134; XXVIII, 55–6. Chaucer will remember them in the *Parliament*, 186.

33 On the frailty of Dante's 'fioretti', see A. Momigliano's comment in *La Divina Commedia con i commenti di T.Casini/S.A. Barbi e A. Momigliano*, ed. F. Mazzoni, vol. I (*Inferno*) (Florence,1972), p. 37; and R. Roedel, '"Quali i fioretti . . ."' Canto II' in *Lectura Dantis. Letture e Saggi* (Bellinzona, 1965), pp. 93–109.

34 Albertano da Brescia, *Dilezione*, quoted by M. Barbi in his *Problemi di Critica Dantesca* (Prima Serie, 1893–1918, Florence, 1975), p. 203; 'volgarmente si dice: ciò che nieve chiude sole apre'.

35 St Bonaventure ('Sicut rosa per frigus noctis clausa, solis ardore surgente, tota aperitur . . . Ita flos coeli') and Albert the Great's *De Vegetalibus* and *Meteorum* are referred to by F. Mazzoni, *Saggio di un Nuovo Commento alla Divina Commedia* (Forence, 1967), pp. 307–8.

36 *The Poetry of William VII, Count of Poitiers, IX Duke of Aquitaine*, ed. and trans. G.A. Bond (New York–London, 1982), pp. 36–7.

37 See E. Sanguineti, *Tre studi Danteschi* (Florence, 1961), pp. 16–17.

38 Poliziano, *Stanze*, II, 38, 6.

39 Tasso, *Gerusalemme Liberata* IV, 75; translation mine, from L. Caretti's edition (Bari, 1963).

40 Manzoni, *Adelchi* IV, Coro 'Sparsa le trecce morbide', 61–84; *Opere* (Milan–Naples, 1953), p. 296; translation mine.

41 Seamus Heaney, *Station Island* (London, 1984), 'Station Island' VI, p. 76.

42 And by Spenser, who combines two images from Chaucer's *Troilus* in the *Faerie Queene* IV, xii, 34; 'As withered weed through cruell winters time, – That feels the warmth of sunny beames reflection, – Liftes vp his head, that did before decline – And gins to spread his leafe before the faire sunshine' (ed. T. Roche, New Haven–London, 1981, p. 721). And see n. 49 below for references in Chaucer.

43 See H. Bloom, 'Freud's Concepts of Defense and the Poetic Will' in *The Literary Freud: Mechanisms of Defense and the Poetic Will*, ed. J.H. Smith (New Haven, 1980), pp. 1–28; p. 1.

44 The text of *Filostrato* and *Teseida* used here and in the following paragraphs is that edited by V. Branca (*Filostrato*) and A. Limentani (*Teseida*), in *Tutte le Opere di G. Boccaccio*, gen. ed. V. Branca, Vol. II (Milan, 1964). It should be pointed out that Chaucer eliminates this simile from his reworking of the *Teseida* in the *Knight's Tale*.

45 Dryden's translation.

46 Pope's translation.

47 Text in *Catullo, Le Poesie*, ed. F. Della Corte (Fondazione Lorenzo Valla, Milan, 2nd edn, 1984). On this image, see A. Rutgers van der Loeff, 'Het sterven van de rode bloem', *Hermeneus* 24 (1952) 41–65.

48 Sappho, fr. 105, 4–6 (Gallavotti, n. 7 above, p. 129), certainly imitated by Catullus in 62, 39–45.

49 Cf. *Filostrato*, III, 12. For correspondences and differences between Boccaccio and Chaucer in the use of these images, see H.W. Sams, 'The Dual Time-Scheme in Chaucer's *Troilus*', now in R.J. Schoeck and J. Taylor, eds., *Chaucer Criticism*, vol. II (Notre Dame–London, 1961), pp. 180–5. Spenser obviously combines *Troilus* II, 967–70 with III, 351–4 in the *Faerie Queene* IV, xii, 34. One should remember that the *Natureingang* at the opening of the *Canterbury Tales* (*General Prologue*, 1–11) shows us man in full harmony with nature.

50 W. Wetherbee, *Chaucer and the Poets. An Essay on Troilus and Criseyde* (Ithaca–London, 1984), p. 174.

51 J. Norton-Smith, *Geoffrey Chaucer* (London, 1974), p. 202. His and Wetherbee's analyses of the passage are the best I know.

52 There is no precedent in the *Filostrato*. On this line, see E.T. Donaldson, 'The Ending of "Troilus"', now in his *Speaking of Chaucer* (London, 1970), p. 98; on the passage, A.C. Spearing, *Readings in Medieval Poetry* (Cambridge, 1987), pp. 107–33.

53 *Georgics* II, 80–2: 'nec longum tempus, et ingens – exiit ad caelum ramis felicibus arbos – miratastque novas frondes et non sua poma'. After the grafting, the tree 'wonders' at the new branches and at the fruit which does not belong to it. On Dante's passage, see C.S. Lewis, 'Dante's Similes' and 'Imagery in the Last Eleven Cantos of Dante's "Comedy"' in his *Studies in Medieval and Renaissance Literature* (Cambridge, 1966), pp. 64–93; p. 67; on Dante's similes and metaphors in general, see A. Pagliaro's entry, 'similitudine' in *Enciclopedia Dantesca* V (Rome, 1976), pp. 253–9; E.N. Girardi, 'Le similitudini nella "Divina Commedia"' in *Nuovi studi su Dante* (Milan, 1987), pp. 117–42; and F. Tateo's entry, 'metafora' in *Enciclopedia Dantesca* III (Rome, 1971), pp. 926–32.

54 See Singleton's commentary, vol. I, ii, p. 55.

55 *Odyssey* XXII, 383–7 (trans. Lattimore, New York, 1965). And see Aeschylus, *Persae*, 424–6.

56 *Odyssey* XXII, 468–70.

57 *Odyssey* XXIV, 6–8.

58 For the Greeks, bats were birds. On this simile, see A. Heubeck's commentary *ad loc.* in *Omero, Odissea*, vol. VI (Fondazione Lorenzo Valla, Milan, 1986), p. 333. On dead heroes as birds, see E. Rohde, *Psyche. Seelencult und Unsterblichkeitsglaube der Griechen* (Freiburg i. Br., 1890–4), II, ii, 4 and notes therein.

59 W. Stevens, *The Rock* II, 'The Poem as Icon': 'The fiction of the leaves is the icon – Of the poem'. See H. Bloom, *A Map of Misreading* (Oxford, 1975), p. 135; *Breaking of the Vessels*, p. 95.

60 *Iliad* II, 468 (leaves in spring, coupled with bird image (cranes, for which see *Iliad* III, 1–6, and which, through *Aeneid* X, 264 and *Thebaid* V, 13, will reach *Inferno* V, 40–9); *Iliad* II, 800; *Odyssey* IX, 51. For other references, see *Enciclopedia Virgiliana*, II (Rome, 1985), p. 958, and bibliography therein.

61 Bacchylides 33 (v), 63–7; translation mine.
62 *Iliad* VI, 146–9. Homer's four lines become six in Pope's translation.
63 Fr. 29 D; translation mine.
64 Aristophanes, *The Birds*, 685–8, trans. B.B. Rogers (Loeb).
65 Fr. 2D; translation mine.
66 'Hesiod', *Shield*, 249 ff. The bird-like form of the *Kēres*, common in Greek iconography, is noteworthy in our context.
67 *Metamorphoses* XV, 199–236.
68 Translation from the Jerusalem Bible.
69 Helped, perhaps, by Ecclesiastes I. 4: 'One generation passeth away, and another generation cometh.'
70 *Paradise Lost* I, 302–3.
71 Bloom, *Map of Misreading*, p. 137. Italics mine.
72 Goethe, *Poetische Werke, Romane und Erzählungen* I (Berlin, 1961), p. 196 (Am 4. September).
73 *Christabel*, 48–52.
74 *Triumph of Life*, 41–52. Note Shelley's use of the Dantean terza rima.
75 W. Whitman, 'Here the Frailest Leaves of Me' in *Leaves of Grass*; T. Tjutčev, 'Leaves'; C. von Brentano, 'Es ist ein Schnitter, der heisst Tod', 'Wie so leis die Blätter wehn'; Baudelaire, 'Chant d'automne' in *Les Fleurs du Mal* (here, it is the wood that falls); Verlane, 'Chanson d'automne' in *Poèmes Saturniens*; Apollinaire, 'Rhénane d'automne' in *Alcools*; Yeats, 'The Falling of the Leaves' in *Crossways*; Jiménez, 'Canción de otoño' and 'Otoño'; Ungaretti, 'Soldati' in *L'allegria*: Frost, 'Gathering Leaves', 'Leaves Compared with Flowers', 'Leaf Treader', 'November'. This is obviously just a selection of passages and authors. For me, the most effective are the poems by Tjutčev, Apollinaire, and Ungaretti.
76 'In Act II of *Waiting for Godot* Estragon and Vladimir engage in a lyrical dialogue concerning "all the dead voices". Vladimir suggests that the dead voices make a noise like wings, like sand, like feathers, like ashes, but each time Estragon replies: "Like leaves"': Bloom, *Breaking of the Vessels*, p. 98. The poem by Lorca, 'Otra canción: otoño' goes back to 1919.
77 W.H. Auden, *Selected Poetry*, 2nd edn (New York, 1971), pp. 23–4.
78 W. Stevens, 'The Course of a Particular' in *The Palm at the End of the Mind*, ed. H. Stevens (New York, 1972), p. 367. Bloom, *Breaking of the Vessels*, p. 98, rightly compares this to Stevens' earlier 'An Ordinary Evening in New Haven'.
79 R.M. Rilke, *Ausgewählte Werke*, I, *Gedichte* (Leipzig, 1938), pp. 88–9; trans. mine.
80 *Ibid., Gedichte*, p. 114.
81 *Ibid., Gedichte*, p. 114; translation by A.E. Fleming, in R.M. Rilke, *Selected Poems* (St Petersburg, Florida, 1983), p. 15. I have modified the translation of lines 4 and 8–9. See also Rilke's *Die Sonette an Orpheus* I, xiv; II, xiv.
82 *Ars Poetica*, 60–2: 'ut silvae foliis pronos mutantur in annos, – prima

cadunt; ita verborum vetus interit aetas, – et iuvenum ritu florent modo nata vigentque'. And see T.M. Greene, *The Light in Troy* (New Haven–London, 1982), pp. 4–5, 13–14.

83 Shelley's own note to the 'Ode'.

84 *Paradiso* XVIII, 30; XXX, 117; XXXI, 11; XXXII, 15 and 25.

85 J. Ruskin, *Modern Painters*, III, pt. 4, 1856, conveniently reprinted in *English Critical Essays, Nineteenth Century*, ed. E.D. Jones (London, 1947), pp. 323–40; pp. 327–8.

86 See n. 53 above.

5 A SPARK OF LOVE: MEDIEVAL RECOGNITIONS

1 The edition I have used of the *Hildebrandslied* is that contained in *Die deutsche Literatur, I: Mittelalter I*, ed. H.J. Koch (Stuttgart, 1976), pp. 94–9. The translations are mine.

2 *Poetics*, chapters 11, 14, 16. For the scheme of anagnorisis, knowledge, and the elements of tragedy, see Aristote, *La Poétique*, ed. R. Dupont-Roc and J. Lallot (Paris, 1980), pp. 270–7, and V. Goldschmidt, *Temps physique et temps tragique chez Aristote* (Paris, 1982), pp. 294–7. An important book by Terence Cave, *Recognitions: A Study in Poetics* (Oxford, 1988), deals with my theme though not with medieval scenes.

3 Philo, 'De Migratione Abrahami' (Loeb edn, vol. IV), 1–12, 192, 195.

4 G.J. Botterwerk, s.v. *jada'* in *Theologisches Wörterbuch zum Alten Testament* (Zurich, 1973), 503.

5 Matthew 16. 13–17.

6 In *The Genesis of Secrecy* (Cambridge, Mass. – London, 1979), pp. 84–95, and in 'John' in R. Alter and F. Kermode, eds., *The Literary Guide to the Bible* (Cambridge, Mass., 1987), pp. 459–65.

7 *The Chester Mystery Cycle*, R.M. Lumiansky and D. Mills, eds., vol. I (London, 1974, E.E.T.S. S.S. 3), p. 274.

8 Gregory, *Hom. in Evangelia* II, xxvi, in *Patrologia Latina* 76, 1201–2; John Chrysostom, *In Hebr.*, 21, 2, in *Patrologia Graeca* 63, 151; both are also quoted by Peter Lombard, *Sententiae* III, Dist. xxiii–iv (Grottaferrata, Rome, vol. II, 1981), pp. 145–9.

9 *Sermones*, 145 A (Madrid, 1983), p. 327.

10 F.G. Klopstock, *Der Messias*, in *Werke in einem Band* (Munich–Vienna, 1982), XIII, 124, p. 519.

11 F.M. Dostoyevsky, *Bratia Karamazovi* (Leningrad, 1976), pp. 69–85; English trans. by D. Magarshack (Harmondsworth, 1958), vol. II, pp. 746–65.

12 Luke 24. 39: 'Behold my hands and my feet, that it is I myself: handle me, and see; for a spirit hath not flesh and bones, as ye see me have.'

13 'Epistula Apostolorum' in E. Hennecke, *New Testament Apocrypha*, ed. W.

Schneemelcher, English trans. edited by R. McL. Wilson, vol. I (London, 1963), p. 197.

14 *Piers Plowman* is quoted from the edition by W.W. Skeat (London, 1961).

15 M.E. Goldsmith, *The Figure of Piers Plowman* (Cambridge, 1981), pp. 11–19.

16 O. Pächt, *The Rise of Pictorial Narrative in Twelfth-Century England* (Oxford, 1962), pp. 39–45.

17 *Chester Mystery Cycle*, p. 367.

18 *The Towneley Plays* (London, 1897, E.E.T.S. E.S. 71), p. 352.

19 *The York Plays*, ed. R. Beadle (London, 1982), pp. 366–72.

20 *Towneley Plays*, pp. 344–51.

21 'Acts of Pilate' in *New Testament Apocrypha*, p. 466.

22 'Revelation of John', in *The Ante-Nicene Fathers*, eds. A. Roberts and J. Donaldson, VIII (Grand Rapids, Michigan, 1951), p. 583.

23 S. Anastasii Sinaite *Quaestiones*, 91, in *Patrologia Graeca* 89, 721–5.

24 See, for all, Peter Lombard, *Sententiae* IV, Dist. 1, 3 ff. and references therein; Thomas Aquinas, *De Veritate* XIX, 1–2.

25 *De Genesi ad Litteram* VIII, 5, 9 (Madrid, 1969), p. 776.

26 Grégoire le Grand, *Dialogues* IV, 34, 5 (Paris, 1980), vol. III, p. 116.

27 *Dialogues* IV, 34, p. 114. And see A.M. Chiavacci Leonardi, 'Il tema della resurrezione nel "Paradiso"' in *Dante e la Bibbia*, ed. G. Barblan (Florence, 1988), p. 262.

28 *Recognitions of Clement*, in *Ante-Nicene Fathers* VIII, pp. 77–211.

29 *Recognitions of Clement*, p. 191.

30 Euripides, *Helen*, 560.

31 *Libro de la infancia y muerte de Jesús*, ed. M. Alvar (Madrid, 1965), 213–36; and see pp. 88–98.

32 On which see the splendid book by F. Ohly, *Der Verfluchte und der Erwählte. Vom Leben mit der Schuld* (Rheinisch–Westfälische Akademie der Wissenschaften, Vorträge G 207, 1976), pp. 36–42, 65–97.

33 Text in A.V.C. Schmidt and N. Jacobs, eds., *Medieval English Romances*, vol. II (London, 1980), pp. 57–88. I prefer the spelling 'Degaré, to 'Degarré'.

34 Text in Hartmann von Aue, *Gregorius*, ed. H. Paul (Tübingen, 1984), translations mine.

35 T. Mann, *Doktor Faustus*, ch. 31 (Frankfurt, 1982), p. 316.

36 T. Mann, *Der Erwählte* (Frankfurt, 1984), English trans. By H.T. Lowe-Porter as *The Holy Sinner* (Harmondsworth, 1961).

37 *Jokes and their Relation to the Unconscious*, in vol. VIII of *The Standard Edition of the Complete Psychological Works of Sigmund Freud*, trans. and general editor J. Strachey (London, 1960), pp. 120–2.

38 See *Joseph in Aegypten* (Frankfurt, 1981), 4, pp. 614–16; English trans. by H.T. Lowe-Porter in *Joseph and His Brothers* (Harmondsworth, 1978),

pp. 550–3. And cf. Mann's lecture on Freud in *Adel des Geistes* (Stockholm, 1945), p. 590; English trans. by H.T. Lowe-Porter in *Essays of Three Decades* (London, n.d.), p. 421.

39 Wolfram von Eschenbach, *Parzival*, ed. A. Leitzmann, 3 vols. (Tübingen, 1961–5). I am deeply indebted here to D.H. Green's treatment of the theme in his *The Art of Recognition in Wolfram's Parzival* (Cambridge, 1982).

40 Here, I differ from the opinion of J.A.W. Bennett, 'Henryson's *Testament*: a Flawed Masterpiece', now in his *The Humane Medievalist*, ed. P. Boitani (Rome, 1982), pp. 89–103, p. 100. The edition of the *Testament* from which I quote is Charles Elliott's of the *Poems* (Oxford, 1974).

41 See M.W. Stearns, *Robert Henryson* (New York, 1949), pp. 98–105.

42 Plato, *Theaetetus* 193 b-c; translation mine.

43 Bennett, 'Henryson's *Testament*', p. 100.

44 *The Works of Sir Thomas Malory*, ed. E. Vinaver, 2nd edn (Oxford, 1967), vol. II, pp. 501–2.

45 It may be interesting to note that in an Irish composition which may go back to the thirteenth century, the 'Recognition of Ulysses', the supreme anagnorisis of Western literature, that between Penelope and her husband, is effected by his *dog*. After offering the queen many 'credentials' consisting of 'their secrets and their talks together and their hidden thoughts' and of several 'signs', Ulysses is finally recognized by the dog which, on hearing the sound of his master's voice, tugs its chain knocking its four guards flat, jumps at Ulysses' breast and licks his face. The passage is printed by R.T. Meyer in *Merugud Uilixi maic Leirtis* (Dublin, 1958), p. 8, and translated by K.H. Jackson in *A Celtic Miscellany* (Harmondsworth, 1971), pp. 57–8.

46 G. Steiner, *Antigones* (Oxford, 1984), p. 16. The translation from Wagner's *Tristan* below is Steiner's.

47 Wagner, *Tristan* 2. 2, end.

48 *Sir Orfeo*, ed. A.J. Bliss (Oxford, 1954), 319–30. And see Vinaver's notes to Malory's passage quoted above, III, pp. 1471–4.

6 I KNOW THE SIGNS OF THE ANCIENT FLAME: DANTE'S RECOGNITIONS

1 For the meanings of 'fioco' and 'lungo silenzio', see A. Pagliaro, *Ulisse* (Messina–Florence), pp. 25 ff.

2 *European Literature and the Latin Middle Ages*, trans. W.R. Trask (London, 1953), p. 358.

3 See V. Goldschmidt, *Temps physique et temps tragique chez Aristote* (Paris, 1982), pp. 294–7.

4 Proust quotes the episode of Odysseus and his mother during the great recognition scene of the 'Matinée at the Guermantes' in *Le Temps retrouvé*, *A la Recherche du temps perdu* III, ed. P. Clarac and A. Ferré (Paris, 1954),

p. 942. Joyce transforms the theme in the Hades episode of his *Ulysses*.

5 W.F. Otto, *Theophania* (Frankfurt, 2nd edn, 1979), p. 52.

6 See J.B. Friedman, *Orpheus in the Middle Ages* (Cambridge, Mass., 1970).

7 *Commentum Bernardi Silvestris super sex libros Eneidos Virgilii*, ed. G. Riedel (Greifswald, 1924), pp. 51–2.

8 *Convivio* II i 13, trans. W.W. Jackson (Oxford, 1909); and see Aristotle, *Physics* I, 1, 184a 16.

9 See B. Nardi, *Dante e la cultura medievale* (Bari, 1942), pp. 100–47; and the entries 'conoscere', 'intelletto', 'intelletto possibile', 'intenzione', 'memoria', 'mente' in the *Enciclopedia Dantesca*.

10 *Purgatorio* II, 79, and XXV, 79–108; and see E. Gilson, *Dante et Béatrice* (Paris, 1974), pp. 23–65.

11 *Studi su Dante*, Italian trans. (Milan, 3rd edn, 1971), p. 122.

12 On which see A. Tartaro, *Letture dantesche* (Rome, 1980), pp. 2–5.

13 *Inferno* II, 4–5; and see A.M. Chiavacci Leonardi, *La guerra della pietate* (Naples, 1979).

14 *La naissance du Purgatoire* (Paris, 1981), pp. 9–27.

15 For a comparison between the Brunetto and Forese scenes, see V. Russo, *Il romanzo teologico* (Naples, 1984), pp. 131–2.

16 *Aeneid* VI, 268–72; Dryden's translation.

17 *Aeneid* VI, 451–4; Dryden's translation.

18 *Convivio* III viii 7–8; and see also 10. For Dante's conception of the process of sight, see *Convivio* III ix 6–16.

19 On this episode, see J.H. Whitfield, 'Dante and Statius: Purgatorio XXI–XXII' in D. Nolan, ed., *Dante Soundings* (Dublin, 1981), pp. 113–29.

20 See Isidore, *Differentiarum Libri* I, 89 (Migne, *Patrologia Latina* 83, 20): 'Inter *cognitionem* et *agnitionem* quidam sic distinguunt, quod cognitio eorum sit quae ante non scivimus, et ea postea scire permittitur, agnitio vero eorum quae prius scientes, deinceps scire desivimus, eorumque postea recordamur.' See also Jerome, *Comm. in Ep. and Ephes.* I, i (15–18) in Migne, *Patrologia Latina*, 26, 489; and above all Servius' definitions in his commentary on the *Aeneid* III, 351 and VIII, 155.

21 *Aristoteles Latinus* XXXIII, *De Arte Poetica*, ed. L. Minio-Paluello (Brussels–Paris, 1968), p. 14: 'Anagnorisis autem, sicut et nomen significat, ex ignorantia in notitiam transmutatio'.

22 The first of whom, with Linus, Dante finds in the Castle of Limbo: *Inferno* IV, 140–1.

23 Luke 24. 36.

24 *Little Gidding* II, i.

25 Matthew 27. 51–2, explicitly recalled in *Inferno* XII, 34–45.

26 Luke 2. 8–14.

27 Luke 24. 13 ff.

28 Luke 24. 36; and cf. *Purgatorio* XXI, 13.

29 I use F. Fergusson's partition in *Dante's Drama of the Mind* (Princeton, 2nd printing, 1968), pp. 115–24, although it will be evident that I do not agree with everything he says.

30 XX, 145–51; XXI, 1–6 and 37–9.

31 For this problem, see P. Boyde, *Dante Philomythes and Philosopher* (Cambridge, 1981), pp. 90–5, and particularly 93–4.

32 The first being in *Purgatorio* IV, 122 at Belacqua's laziness.

33 *Vita Nuova* XXV, 2; *Epistole* XIII, 74.

34 The 'corruscazione' of *Convivio* III viii 11 is the exact equivalent of 'lampeggiar' in *Purgatorio* XXI, 114.

35 *Convivio* III viii 11.

36 On this problem, see F. Kermode, 'Recognition and Deception', now in his *The Art of Telling* (Cambridge, Mass., 1983), pp. 92–113.

37 *Poetics* 4, 1448b 4–19.

38 S. Freud, *Jokes and Their Relation to the Unconscious* in *Standard Edition*, general editor J. Strachey, VIII (London, 1960), p. 121; and see *Gesammelte Werke* VI (London, 1940), pp. 135–6.

39 Revelation 19. 10, from which the gesture and Virgil's first words derive.

40 Psalm 118 (119). 130: 'Declaratio sermonum tuorum illuminat, Et intellectum dat parvulis.'

41 J.L. Borges, 'El encuentro en un sueño' in his *Nueve ensayos dantescos* (Madrid, 1983), pp. 150–1.

42 See J. Petrie, 'Dante's Virgil: Purgatorio XXX' in *Dante Soundings*, pp. 130–45.

43 XXX, 11: Song 4.8; 19: Matthew 21. 9; 21: *Aeneid* VI, 883.

44 Probably inspired by *Metamorphoses* VI, 47–9.

45 I quote from T.S. Eliot's translation in his *Dante* (London, 1965 edn.), p. 43, which is a modified version of the Temple Classics translation.

46 See *Vita Nuova* II, 3 and III, 1. On this aspect of the *Vita Nuova* and the problem of recognition, see A.C. Charity, 'T.S. Eliot: The Dantean Recognitions' in A.D. Moody, ed., *The Waste Land in Different Voices* (London, 1974), pp. 117–56.

47 *Purgatorio* XXX, 115; XXXI, 34–6 and 49–54.

48 *War and Peace* IV, III, 15.

49 M. Proust, *Remembrance of Things Past*, III, *Time Regained*, trans. C.K. Scott Moncrieff, T. Kilmartin, A. Mayor (Harmondsworth, 1983), p. 982.

50 *Vita Nuova* II, 4–7 and XIV, 4; and see XXIV, 1–3 and 7–8, where an 'earthquake' in Dante's heart announces one of Beatrice's appearances.

51 Borges, 'Encuentro', p. 152.

52 And see s.v. 'virtù' in *Enciclopedia Dantesca* V (Rome, 1976), pp. 1055–7.

53 Singleton II, p. 739.

54 I quote from M. Andrew and R. Waldron, eds., *The Poems of the Pearl Manuscript* (London, 1978).

55 *Aeneid* IV, 23, already imitated by Ovid, *Amores* II i 8.
56 *Purgatorio* XXI, 95, 'divina fiamma'; *Inferno* XXVI, 85.
57 *Phèdre* I.iii. 125.
58 W.B. Yeats, 'Ego Dominus Tuus'.
59 Trans. C.H. Sisson (London–Sydney, 1981).
60 Persius, *Satires*, Prologue and v, 62. See E. Paratore, *Tradizione e struttura in Dante* (Florence, 1968), 37, 87, 211; and s.v. 'Persio' in *Enciclopedia Dantesca* IV (Rome, 1977), pp. 434–5; F. Mazzoni, 'Il canto XXXI del Purgatorio' in *Lectura Dantis Scaligera* (Florence, 1965), pp. 94–5.
61 For different interpretations of this line, see the commentary by T. Casini and S.A. Barbi in Dante Alighieri, *La Divina Commedia. Purgatorio* (Florence, 1973), p. 730.
62 On which see Gilson, *Dante et Béatrice*, pp. 23–65; G. Getto, 'Poesia e teologia nel Paradiso di Dante' in *Aspetti della poesia di Dante* (Florence, 1966), pp. 193–235; A. Mellone, s.v. 'luce' in *Enciclopedia Dantesca* III (Rome, 1971), pp. 706–13.
63 For this image, see *Aeneid* II, 693–4; *Pharsalia* V, 560–4; Nahum 2. 4.
64 See R. Hollander, *Il Virgilio Dantesco* (Florence, 1983), pp. 134–7.
65 *Aeneid* VI, 835 and 133–5; and see G. Brugnoli, s.v. 'superinfusa' in *Enciclopedia Dantesca* V (Rome, 1976), pp. 459–60 for Biblical and Christian overtones.
66 Matthew 3. 17.
67 *Commentum*, p. 52.
68 As we have seen in chapter I, this image will be picked up by Petrarch in the *Canzoniere* XVI, and employed there in a different light.

7 HIS DESIR WOL FLE WITHOUTEN WYNGES: MARY AND LOVE IN
FOURTEENTH-CENTURY POETRY

1 E. Auerbach, 'Dante's Prayer to the Virgin (*Par.* XXXIII) and Earlier Eulogies', *Romance Philology* 3 (1949), 1–26.
2 F. Chiappelli, 'La struttura figurativa del "Paradiso"', now in his *Il legame musaico* (Rome, 1984), pp. 126–8.
3 See M. Apollonio, s.v. 'Maria Vergine' in *Enciclopedia Dantesca* III (Rome, 1971), pp. 835–9.
4 The other two are *Paradiso* XXX, 82–4, and XXXIII, 107–8.
5 See *Paradiso* XXIII, 49–51, and XXXIII, 58–63.
6 *Paradiso* XXIII, 92. Mary is called 'stella matutina' and 'maris stella'.
7 *Paradiso* XXIII, 93; and cp. XXXIII, 1–6.
8 Proverbs 8. 22–30.
9 Matthew 23. 12; and, for Mary, Luke 1. 46–49.
10 See, for instance, Thomas Aquinas, *Summa Theologiae* I, q. 37, a. 1.
11 And see *Convivio* IV v 3.

12 See S. Thomae Aquinatis *In Librum Beati Dionysii De Divinis Nominibus Expositio* (Turin–Rome, 1950) I, lectio iii, 98.

13 See 'dolce' and 'godo' later in the canto (63, 93), and, on the latter, chapter 8 below.

14 For these, see the comments on the canto by modern editors, in particular those by Scartazzini–Vandelli, Casini–Barbi, and Sapegno.

15 For lines 7–9 see Ambrose, *De iust. Virg.* 91, and Bernard, *Serm. in adv. Dom.* II, 4.

16 See *Paradiso* XXII, 47–8.

17 'Infima' indicates the bottom; 'lacuna' = 'emptiness'; 'lacuna' = 'laguna' (lagoon), hence the lake of Cocytus at the bottom of Hell and, as we have seen in chapter 2 above, of the entire universe.

18 For a thorough analysis of these, see Auerbach, 'Dante's Prayer', and M. Fubini, *Due studi danteschi* (Florence, 1951), pp. 63–82.

19 For these concepts, see E. Auerbach, '*Sermo Humilis*' and '*Camilla, or, The Rebirth of the Sublime*' in his *Literary Language and Its Public in Late Latin Antiquity and in the Middle Ages*, trans. R. Manheim (New York, 1965), pp. 27–81 and 183–233; and P. Dronke, 'Medieval Rhetoric', now in his *The Medieval Poet and His World* (Rome, 1984), pp. 7–38.

20 Matthew 5. 37 and 12. 36; cp. *Laude*, ed. F. Mancini (Bari, 1977, from which I take all my quotations), 65, 1–12; 7, 87–90; 40, 9–12.

21 See *Laude*, p. xiv, n. 2.

22 Editions of the *Pèlerinage*: first version, ed. J.J. Sturzinger (Roxburghe Club, 1893); second version, eds. B. and J. Petit (Paris, c. 1500); ed. A. Verard (Paris, 1511). An English prose translation of the first version was edited by W.A. Wright for the Roxburghe Club in 1869.

23 R. Tuve, *Allegorical Imagery* (Princeton, 1966), pp. 145–218. Tuve writes about the first, more compact and artistically more balanced version, where I have been able to find only one prayer to the Virgin, the original of Chaucer's *ABC*.

24 The edition of Lydgate's *Pilgrimage* is by F.J. Furnivall and K.B. Locock, EETS ES 77, 83, 92 (London, 1899–1904).

25 Sancti Bernardi *Opera Omnia*, ed. J. Mabillon (Paris, 1690), III, 732–55. The prayer to the Virgin, which in Verard's edition is given in Latin, replaces a short prayer to God in the first redaction of the *Pèlerinage*. In Petit's French edition the prose is absent and we have 113 French lines ('Et que me vint a remembrance', printed also in Part III of the EETS edition of Lydgate, ES 92, pp. 684–5), which use various passages from St Bernard.

26 Bernard, *Opera* III, 743. Italics mine.

27 The French original of the *ABC* is printed also by W.W. Skeat in his *Complete Works of Geoffrey Chaucer* (London, 1963 reprint) I, pp. 261–71.

28 Robinson, p. 520; and see *Riverside Chaucer*, p. 1076.

29 W.H. Clemen, *Chaucer's Early Poetry* (London, 1963), pp. 175–9, at p. 175;

P.M. Kean, *Chaucer and the Making of English Poetry*, II (London, 1972), pp. 193–6. See also A. David, 'An ABC to the Style of the Prioress' in M.J. Carruthers and E.D. Kirk, eds., *Acts of Interpretation: The Text in Its Contexts, 700–1600* (Norman, Oklahoma, 1982), pp. 147–57.

30 For which see Auerbach, 'Dante's Prayer'.

31 Kean, *Chaucer*, p. 193.

32 The French is simpler but more effective: 'Fontaine patent te nomme – Pour laver pecheur homme: – ... Moy laver veillez entendre, – Moy garder et moy deffendre' (268–75; Skeat).

33 Clemen, pp. 176–7 (the following quotation is from this text). And see T. Wolpers, 'Geschichte der englischen Marienlyrik im Mittelalter', *Anglia*, 69 (1950), p. 29.

34 The French (Skeat, 157–68) is clearly the source here, but Chaucer has expanded, straightened out, and heightened it.

35 For references see the Scartazzini–Vandelli commentary (Milan, 1965), p. 17, n. 94. On 'prevenient grace' see, for instance, Thomas Aquinas, *Summa Theologiae* 1.2, q. 111, 3.

36 The idea of prevenient grace may be hinted at in *ABC* 66–8, and in the French original (Skeat, 97–102).

37 Important studies on the Middle English lyric and on the theme of the Virgin are R. Woolf, *The English Religious Lyric in the Middle Ages* (Oxford, 1968), pp. 114–58 and 274–308; and D. Gray, *Themes and Images in the Medieval English Religious Lyric* (London–Boston, 1972), pp. 75–121.

38 I use G. Contini's edition of the *Canzoniere* (Turin, 1979 reprint).

39 Derived from Ovid, *Metamorphoses* VII, 20–1.

40 For instance LXII, *Padre del ciel*; LXXX, *Chi è fermato*; LXXXI, *Io son sí stanco*; CXLII, *A la dolce ombra*.

41 The fact that Petrarch organized the *Canzoniere* – that we do not have in it a mere chronological–autobiographical sequence, but a conscious artistic construction – indicates that he deliberately chose to present himself in this manner. On the problem of the 'making' of the *Canzoniere*, see now K. Foster, *Petrarch: Poet and Humanist* (Edinburgh, 1984), pp. 92–105, and references therein.

42 And in *Secretum* III. See Foster, *Petrarch*, p. 42, on the relationship between *Canzoniere*, *Secretum*, and *Triumphus Eternitatis*.

43 In the so-called 'apparition' poems, for which see Foster, *Petrarch*, pp. 80–7.

44 See Foster, *Petrarch*, p. 96, pp. 198–9, n. 91 for references.

45 On the Mary–Laura contrast, see N. Iliescu, *Il Canzoniere petrarchesco e Sant'Agostino* (Rome, 1962), pp. 90–1; B. Martinelli, *Petrarca e il Ventoso* (Bari, 1977), pp. 225–39.

46 F. Petrarca, *Le Rime*, ed. G. Carducci and S. Ferrari (Florence, 1978 edn.), p. 511.

47 For a complete survey of these, see the notes in Carducci–Ferrari, pp. 512–21.

48 W.J. Ong, 'Wit and Mystery: A Revaluation in Medieval Latin Hymnody', *Speculum*, 22 (1947), 310–41.

49 Translations of *Vergine bella* are from S. Minta, *Petrarch and Petrarchism* (Manchester, 1980), pp. 96–9.

50 See Carducci–Ferrari, pp. 513–15.

51 For this, and the Dantean overtones and implications of Petrarch's 'Beatrice', see K. Foster, 'Beatrice or Medusa: the Penitential Element in Petrarch's "Canzoniere"' in C.P. Brand, K. Foster, U. Limentani, eds., *Italian Studies Presented to E.R. Vincent* (Cambridge, 1962), pp. 41–3.

52 Foster, 'Beatrice or Medusa', pp. 52–3.

53 Petrarch's version of the beatific vision, with Laura now triumphing in the world after resurrection, takes place in the last poem he wrote, the *Triumphus Eternitatis*, for a comparison of which with *Vergine bella* see Foster, 'Beatrice or Medusa', pp. 53–5, and now his *Petrarch*, pp. 42–3.

54 Compare lines 135–7 of *Vergine bella* with Luke's 'Father, into thy hands I commend my spirit' (23. 46).

55 I leave aside the problem of the chronology of Chaucer's poems. What interests me here is not in what order the *Troilus* and the Prologues to the Prioress's and Second Nun's *Tales* were composed, but what use Chaucer makes in them of the Prayer to the Virgin such as he read in *Paradiso* XXXIII.

56 On which see P. Dronke, 'L'amor che move il sole e l'altre stelle', now in his *The Medieval Poet*, pp. 439–75, and particularly 470–5.

57 The best pages I know on this passage have been written by W. Wetherbee, *Chaucer and the Poets: An Essay on Troilus and Criseyde* (Ithaca–London, 1984), pp. 80–3, 109–10.

58 Foster, *Petrarch*, pp. 74–5.

59 And see A. Minnis, *Chaucer and Pagan Antiquity* (Cambridge, 1982), pp. 61–107.

60 And see K. Foster, *The Two Dantes* (London, 1977), pp. 37–55.

61 *Teseida* XI, 1–3, in turn following the *Somnium Scipionis* in Cicero, *De re publica* I, 7, 11, and the ascent of Pompey's soul in Lucan's *Pharsalia* IX, 1–18.

62 The first two lines are translated from *Paradiso* XIV, 28–30. In the last line the poet asks mercy of Christ *for love* of his Mother. In Dante's prayer, Bernard asks Mary to help Dante see God. He calls her 'Vergine madre' (1), recalls Jesus' love (7) and her benignity (16, the line after those Chaucer uses in *Troilus* III, 1262–3).

63 *Epistole* XIII, 10, 30 (in *Opere Minori* II (Milan–Naples, 1979), p. 618); and cf. *Ars Poetica*, 93–8.

64 Here, I am not concerned with the problem of the composition of the

Canterbury Tales, and in particular with whether the *Second Nun's Tale* was written for that collection or earlier and independently of it. For references, see the *Riverside Chaucer*, pp. 942–3. It has also been suggested that Chaucer used in the Prioress' Prologue his own translation of Dante's Prayer such as we now read in the Prologue to the *Second Nun's Tale*: see R.A. Pratt, 'Chaucer Borrowing from Himself', *Modern Language Quarterly*, 7 (1946), 259–64.

65 The invocation is derived from Psalm 8. 1–2.

66 And see Kean, *Chaucer*, pp. 195–6.

67 *House of Fame*, 972–92.

68 G. Hill, *Collected Poems* (Harmondsworth, 1985), p. 178.

69 He is called 'innocent' three times (538, 566, 635) and celebrated as one of the Innocent at line 608. See *Riverside Chaucer*, pp. 915–16, notes to 579 ff.

70 Cf. Mark 10. 13–16.

71 For which see *Riverside Chaucer*, p. 916.

72 Line 578 is a reminiscence of Genesis 4. 10 (where God reproaches Cain for the murder of Abel); in line 574 the Jews are called 'cursed folk of Herodes al newe', and the 'innocentz' are celebrated in line 608. The massacre is recalled at line 627, where the child's mother is seen as 'newe Rachel' with an echo of Matthew 2. 18 (itself a 'figura' from Jeremiah 31. 15). The image of the Lamb taken from Revelation 14. 3–5 is elaborated upon in lines 579–85 (for which see references in the *Riverside Chaucer*, p. 915, note to 580–5).

73 Auerbach, 'Sermo Humilis', p. 49, quoting Augustine, *De Trinitate* I, 1.

74 The best comparative examination of the two passages is to be found in H. Schless, *Chaucer and Dante; A Revaluation* (Norman, Oklahoma, 1984), pp. 214–17.

75 On these, see *Riverside Chaucer*, p. 942.

76 In this case the 'eterneel love and pees' (i.e. God, called both 'Amor' and 'Pax' by for instance Pseudo-Dionysius in *De Divinis Nominibus* IV, lectio IX, 160, and IV, lectio XVII, 207) would be 'lord and gyde' of the Trinity – a theologically daring concept. Robinson, p. 757, quotes a hymn by Venantius Fortunatus in which the 'trina machina' represents the threefold universe.

77 Compare Jacopo's text in W.F. Bryan and G. Dempster, eds., *Sources and Analogues of Chaucer's Canterbury Tales* (Chicago, 1941), p. 671.

78 See Robinson, p. 757, note to 114; and cf. *Riverside Chaucer*, p. 944.

79 In her *The Structure of the Canterbury Tales* (London, 1983), Helen Cooper maintains that Chaucer's work 'barely touches on such ultimate religious experience as the beatific vision (the Second Nun's Tale comes closest)', p. 72. Cooper's statement and her analysis later of the *Second Nun's Tale* (pp. 188–95) are among the best I have read, and in what follows I am deeply indebted to her. On the iconographic background, see V.A. Kolve,

'Chaucer's *Second Nun's Tale* and the Iconography of Saint Cecilia' in D.M. Rose, ed., *New Perspectives in Chaucer Criticism* (Norman, Oklahoma, 1981), pp. 137–74.

80 For this, see *Riverside Chaucer*, p. 945, note to 221.

81 It may then be possible to conclude that the 'lyf of Seint Cecile' stems from the same kind of inspiration that dictated the epilogue of *Troilus*. The image of Chaucer that emerges from a comparison between the pagan and secular poet on the one hand and that of the religious writer on the other may suggest something like 'The Two Chaucers' as the title of a book, resembling Kenelm Foster's *The Two Dantes*.

82 Alexander Neckam, *De laudibus divinae sapientiae* (ed. Th. Wright, London, 1863), 492–3, at the beginning of his list of Roman martyrs which includes Caecilia, 'coeli lilia', 'coelica virgo'.

8 THE SIBYL'S LEAVES: READING *PARADISO* XXXIII

1 *Summa Theologiae*, Supplementum, q. 92, a. 1.

2 *Summa Theologiae* I, II, q. 3, a. 8.

3 *Summa Theologiae* I, II, q. 4, a. 2.

4 *Summa Theologiae* II, II, q. 175, a. 1.

5 *Summa Theologiae* II, II, q. 175, a. 3.

6 *Summa Theologiae* II, II, q. 171, a. 3.

7 *Summa Theologiae* II, II, q. 171, a. 2; and q. 175, a. 3.

8 *Summa Theologiae* II, II, q. 171, a. 2.

9 For Thomas there are three degrees of *raptus*: contemplation of the divine truth 'per similitudines quasdam imaginarias', 'per intelligibiles effectus', and 'in sua essentia'. The first occurred with St Peter's ecstasy, the second with David, the third with St Paul and Moses. See *Summa Theologiae* II, II, q. 175, a. 3. For a full account of traditional doctrine on the beatific vision, see H.F. Dondaine, 'L'objet et le "medium" de la vision béatifique chez les théologiens du XIIIe siècle', *Recherches de Théologie Ancienne et Mediévale* 19 (1952), 60–130.

10 *Summa Theologiae* I, q. 12, a. 5.

11 see J.A. Mazzeo, *Structure and Thought in the Paradiso* (Ithaca, N.Y., 1958), pp. 84–110; K. Foster, 'Dante's Vision of God', now in his *The Two Dantes* (London, 1977), pp. 66–85.

12 *Inferno* I, 118–22; II, 10–42; *Paradiso* I, 73–5; XXVI, 10–12; XXX, 49–51.

13 Both Benvenuto da Imola and Jacopo della Lana, two of the early commentators of the *Comedy*, had already realized that Dante's vision can be called a *raptus*. Jacopo explicitly refers the reader to Thomas Aquinas. See Benvenuto da Imola, *Comentum* V, eds. G.W. Vernon and J.P. Lacaita (Florence, 1887), p. 515; *Comedia di D.A. col Commento di Jacopo della Lana*, ed. L. Scarabelli (Bologna, 1866), p. 501.

14 See B. Nardi, 'Dante Profeta' in his *Dante e la cultura medievale* (Bari, 1941), pp. 258–334; and R. Morghen, *Dante Profeta* (Milan, 1983).
15 And see fuller explanation in the Letter to Cangrande, XIII, 78.
16 Exodus 3. 14. See S. Thomae Aquinatis *In Librum Beati Dionysii De Divinis Nominibus* (Turin–Rome, 1950) I, lectio III, 83 (23).
17 Thomas, *In Librum*, 85–101.
18 Thomas, *In Librum*, 102.
19 Thomas, *In Librum*, IV, lectio IV, 126–8.
20 Thomas, *In Librum*, IV, lectio III, 306.
21 Thomas, *In Librum*, IV, lectio IV, 125 and 322.
22 'Summa et prima veritas': *Summa Theologiae* I, q. 16, a. 5.
23 John 8. 12; Thomas, *In Librum* IV, lectio IV, 325.
24 Thomas, *In Librum*, VIII, lectio I, 750. This is the only definition that Dante does not tie to light. Another may be the 'fine di tutt'i desii' of line 46, for which cp. Thomas' 'ultimus finis humanae vitae' in *Summa Theologiae* II, II, q. 122, a. 2.
25 Thomas, *In Librum* IV, lectio I, 269; and *Metaphysicorum Aristotelis Expositio* V, lectio XVIII, 1040.
26 Thomas, *In Librum* V, lectio I, 633 and 636.
27 Thomas, *Metaphysicorum* XII, lectio VIII, 2542–4. To all these definitions may be added that of *Perfectum* (*Paradiso* XXXIII, 104–5), for which see Thomas, *In Librum* XIII, lectio I, 957–68.
28 See, for instance, B. Nardi, 'I sensi delle Scritture' in his *Nel Mondo di Dante* (Rome, 1944), pp. 55–61; Charles Singleton, *Commedia: Elements of Structure* (Cambridge, Mass., 1954), pp. 84–94; J.A. Mazzeo, *Structure and Thought*, pp. 25–49.
29 *Epistole* XIII, 83–4.
30 *Summa Theologiae* I, q. 12, a. 3, ad 4.
31 'Distilla' is used only four times in the *Comedy*; 'disigilla', 'indige', and 'indova' only here.
32 See *Paradiso* XXIII, 55–63.
33 *Convivio* I viii 12; *Purgatorio* XXXIII, 79–81, etc. see A. Maierù s.v. 'memoria' in *Enciclopedia Dantesca* III (Rome, 1971), pp. 890–1; and P. Boyde, *Dante Philomythes* (Cambridge, 1981), pp. 224–9 and references therein.
34 *Aeneid* III, 441–52; VI, 74–5.
35 See Isidore, *Etymologiae* VIII viii. Isidore calls 'vates' both the Sibyls and the Prophets of the Old Testament (*Etymologiae* VII viii). Later medieval examples are quoted by P. Dronke, *Fabula* (Leiden–Cologne, 1974), pp. 61–5, 120–2. And see A. Cutler, 'Octavian and the Sibyl in Christian Hands', *Vergilius*, 11 (1965), 22–32.
36 *Convivio* III xv 6.
37 *Summa Theologiae* I, q. 12, a. 11, resp.

38 B. Nardi, 'Il sogno divinatorio' in his *Saggi di filosofia dantesca* (Florence, 2nd. edn, 1967), pp. 55–8.

39 *Ibid.*, pp. 55–8.

40 See K. Foster, 'The Mind in Love: Dante's Philosophy' in J. Freccero, ed., *Dante* (Englewood Cliffs, N.J., 1965), pp. 43–60.

41 See *Purgatorio* XVIII, 40–60; *Paradiso* II, 44–5; and Nardi, *Dante e la cultura medievale*, pp. 125–6, for references to Aristotle.

42 *Convivio* II xiii 26–7.

43 *Monarchia* III iii 2.

44 Dronke, *Fabula*, pp. 152–3, n. 1.

45 *Summa Theologiae* I, q. 35, a. 2, ad 3.

46 E.R. Curtius, *European Literature and the Latin Middle Ages*, trans. W. Trask (London, 1953), pp. 326–32; and see G. Josipovici, *The World and the Book* (London, 2nd edn, 1979), in particular pp. 25–51; H. Blumenberg, *Die Lesbarkeit der Welt* (Frankfurt, 1981), in particular ch. 3.

47 Isaiah 34. 4.

48 Ezekiel 2, 9–10: 'and when I looked, behold, an hand was sent unto me; and, lo, a roll of a book was therein; And he spread it before me; and it was written within and without.' Note the movement in the two verses: the roll is spread (in the Vulgate, 'involutus liber' and 'expandit'). Bonaventure, *Breviloquium* II, 11, 2: the book written within is the eternal art and wisdom of God; the book written without is the 'sensible world'. For Bonaventure, Christ embodies both books.

49 *Summa Theologiae* I, q. 24, 'De libro vitae'.

50 *Ibid.*, I. 37.

51 B. Nardi, 'La dottrina dell'Empireo' in his *Saggi di filosofia dantesca*, in particular pp. 212–14.

52 See Boyde, *Dante Philomythes*, pp. 265–9.

53 Thomas, *In Librum* V, lectio I, 640–1; and see 648. Note Thomas' mention of *substantiae* and *accidentia*. The words *diversitatem, multitudinem*, and *oppositionem* would correspond to Dante's 'si squaderna'; *universaliter* to 'per l'universo'; *coniunguntur simul* to 'conflati insieme'; *unum* to 'un volume'.

54 See, for example, Isaiah 40. 19, 44. 10; Jeremiah 6. 29, 7. 20, 10. 14; Ezekiel 22. 20, 22. 21, 24. 11.

55 For the meanings of 'conflare' and the relevant examples, see Aeg. Forcellini *Totius Latinitatis Lexicon* (Prato, 1871), s.v.

56 See *De Divinis Nominibus* (Thomas, *In Librum*) IV, lectio V, 135, 339–40; and U. Eco, *Il problema estetico in Tommaso d'Aquino* (Milan, 2nd edn, 1970), pp. 132–53.

57 See *Paradiso* VII, 64–9; and Boethius, *De Consolatione Philosophiae* III, m. 9, 6–9.

58 *Dante Philomythes*, pp. 47–51.

59 *Republic* 514a–518b.

60 See the analysis of 'fioco' in *Inferno* I, 63 by A. Pagliaro, *Ulisse* (Messina–Florence, 1967) I, pp. 25–43; and *Enciclopedia Dantesca* II (Rome, 1970), s.v. 'fioco'.

61 Cp. *Paradiso* X, 2–3; XII, 10–21; XIII, 55–7.

62 Ezekiel I. 27–8; and see P.M.J. McNair, 'Dante's Vision of God: an Exposition of Paradiso XXXIII' in *Essays in Honour of J.H. Whitfield* (London, 1975), pp. 25–6.

63 *Paradiso* XII, 139–41. See P. Tondelli, *Il 'Libro delle Figure' dell'Abate Gioacchino da Fiore* (Turin, 2nd edn, 1953) I, pp. 171–80, 221–4, 378–81. Manuscripts of the *Liber* have a splendid illustration of the figure of the Trinity, in which the three great circles with equal circumference intersect each other. Each circle has a different colour and the name of the divine Person inscribed at the top – the third circle, that of the Holy Ghost, being red like fire. Dante does not accept Gioacchino's heretical thought on the Trinity, but he may be relying on the figure itself. Illustrations from the MS of the *Liber* in the Episcopal Seminary at Reggio Emilia and from MS 255 at Corpus Christi College, Oxford, are reproduced in *Il 'Libro'*, II, Tables XIa and XIb. The only other example surviving in Italy of an illustration of the Trinity as three circles (but concentric and all blue, though of different gradations) is in the Baptistry at Albenga (fifth or sixth century), influenced by Byzantine art. The three circles of Albenga have Christ's monogram at the centre, repeated three times, and show some sort of reflection of haloes and of the letters Alpha and Omega. See P. Toesca, *Il Medioevo*, I (Turin, 1965), pp. 218–19. Mosaics such as those in the apses of S. Clemente, Rome, and many other churches in Italy have three concentric circles of different colours.

64 And note the verb used by Dante, 'si spira', which contains an allusion to the meaning of 'breath', 'pneuma', of 'Spiritus'.

65 The image of fire is the last one in the two terzinas, and 'si spira' is the final word: both come at the climactic end of a crescendo.

66 Here Dante may have been inspired by the images of the Saviour (Pantocrator, Judge, etc.) inscribed in a circle, which often appeared at the centre of mosaics in the apse of early Italian churches influenced by Byzantine art, one example of which existed in S. Apollinare in Classe at Ravenna.

67 'Penne' = 'wings' and 'pens'; and see *Purgatorio* XXIV, 58.

68 See Thomas, *In Librum*, 135 and 340. Both the Latin translation of Dionysius and Thomas use 'fulgor' to show how God transmits beauty to His creatures.

69 P. Dronke, 'L'amor che move il sole e l'altre stelle', now in his *The Medieval Poet and His World* (Rome, 1984), pp. 439–75.

70 B. Nardi, 'Sì come rota ch'igualmente è mossa' in his *Nel Mondo di Dante*, p. 349.

71 *Little Gidding* V, 1–2.

9 L'ACQUA CHE RITORNA EQUALE: DANTE'S SUBLIME

1 See the Letter to Cangrande (*Ep.* XIII, 30; and cp. 28–32). Compare *De Vulgari Eloquentia* II iv 7–11. The *Comedy* is called 'comedìa' in *Inferno* XVI, 128 and XXI, 2, whereas Virgil's *Aeneid* is defined as 'alta tragedìa' in *Inferno* XX, 113. However, the *Inferno* itself is also called 'prima canzon' (XX, 3), the *Purgatorio* 'cantica seconda' (XXXIII, 140), and the *Paradiso*, as we shall see, 'poema sacro'. For a writer like Dante these are not merely casual definitions. On this, see V. Russo, *Il romanzo teologico* (Naples, 1984), pp. 13–30 and references therein.

2 E. Auerbach, 'Sermo Humilis' and 'Camilla, or, the Rebirth of the Sublime' in his *Literary Language and its Public in Late Latin Antiquity and in the Middle Ages*, trans. R. Manheim (New York, 1965), pp. 25–66 and 183–233. But see also P. Dronke, 'Medieval Rhetoric', now in his *The Medieval Poet and His World* (Rome, 1984), pp. 7–38; A.M. Chiavacci Leonardi, *Lettura del Paradiso Dantesco* (Florence, 1963), pp. 23–60.

3 G. Contini, 'Un'interpretazione di Dante', now in his *Un-Idea di Dante* (Turin, 2nd edn 1976), pp. 69–111. And see the *Peri Hypsous* 7, 3–4.

4 In his *Dante and Medieval Latin Traditions* (Cambridge, 1986), pp. 20–3, P. Dronke offers a first survey of the sea image in the *Comedy*. See also the important suggestions made by J. Pépin in the entry on 'allegory' in *Enciclopedia Dantesca* I (Rome, 1970), p. 165. The expressions I quote are Dante's own: *Paradiso* XIV, 69; *Purgatorio* I, 115.

5 *Iliad* V, 770–2; and see *Peri Hypsous* 9, 5; trans. T.S. Dorsch, *Classical Literary Criticism* (Harmondsworth, 1965), p. 110.

6 G. Leopardi, *Canti*, ed. N. Gallo and C. Gàrboli (Turin, 1962). For Leopardi's observations on the sublime, see p. 105, notes. The English translation I use here is by A. Fowler in *Leopardi: A Scottis Quair* (Edinburgh, 1987), p. 21.

7 C.S. Lewis, *The Discarded Image* (Cambridge, 1964), p. 99.

8 *Ibid.*, p. 99.

9 *Ibid.*, p. 99–100.

10 Essential references are S.H. Monk, *The Sublime: A Study of Critical Theories in XVIII-Century England* (Ann Arbor, 2nd edn 1961); T.E.B. Wood, *The Word 'Sublime' and Its Contexts, 1650–1760* (The Hague–Paris, 1972); T.A. Litman, *Le Sublime en France (1660–1714)* (Paris, 1971); D.B. Morris, *The Religious Sublime* (Lexington, 1972); M. Hope Nicolson, *Mountain Gloom and Mountain Glory* (Ithaca, 1959); T. Weiskel, *The Romantic Sublime* (Baltimore–London, 1978); the essays collected in *New Literary History*, 16 (1985), 2; and those edited by V. Fortunati and G. Franci in *Studi di estetica*, 12 (1984), 1–2; *Il Sublime*.

11 *Convivio* IV XXV 5. All quotations from, and references to the *Convivio* are to the edition by G. Busnelli and G. Vandelli, 2nd edn by A.E. Quaglio (Florence, 1968). The translations are by W.W. Jackson, *Dante's Convivio*

(Oxford, 1909). See now the edition by C. Vasoli and D. De Robertis, *Opere Minori* I ii (Milan–Naples, 1988).

12 *Metaphysics* I, 982b 11–19; and cf. Thomas Aquinas, *In Duodecim Libros Metaphysicorum Expositio* (Turin–Rome, 2nd edn 1971), L. I, 1. iii, 55, p. 18; D. Poirion, 'Théorie et pratique du style au Moyen Age le sublime et la merveille', *Revue d'histoire litteraire de la France*, I (1986) 15 ff.

13 *Peri Hypsous* I, 4.

14 E. De Bruyne, *The Esthetics of the Middle Ages*, trans. E.B. Hennessy (New York, 1969), pp. 125–30. For a more extensive discussion, see De Bruyne's *Études d'esthétique médiévale*, especially vol. III (Bruges, 1946). St Bonaventure is examined on pp. 191–9.

15 The phrase I quote is from the *Opusculum I De Triplici Via* 7, 12 (S. Bonaventurae *Opera Omnia* VIII (Quaracchi, 1898), p. 17); but see also Bonaventure's commentary on the *Sententiae* II, art. I, Quaest. III (*Opera Omnia* II, p. 887). *Terror, wonder* and *desire* are significant in our context.

16 *Benjamin Major* V, v; *Patrologia Latina* 196, 174. And see S. Battaglia, *Esemplarità e Antagonismo nel Pensiero di Dante* (Naples, 1975), I, pp. 224–5.

17 See G. Contini's commentary to this sonnet in his edition of the *Rime*, Dante Alighieri, *Opere Minori*, I, i, ed. D. De Robertis and G. Contini (Milan–Naples, 1984), pp. 324–5.

18 The edition and translation I use here is *Dante's Lyric Poetry*, by K. Foster and P. Boyde (Oxford, 1967), I, pp. 30–1.

19 See Contini's commentary, p. 324. For the sea image, see also *Il fiore* CXCIX, 6–7; XXXIII; CCXXVIII; *Detto d'amore*, 114–18.

20 A good analysis of this theme is now to be found in R. Mercuri, 'Genesi della tradizione letteraria italiana in Dante, Petrarca e Boccaccio' in *Letteratura Italiana* (general editor A. Asor Rosa), *Storia e geografia I. L'età medievale* (Turin, 1987), pp. 287–9.

21 *Dante's Lyric Poetry*, I, pp. 202–3; and see Commentary II, pp. 328–9.

22 For different uses of the sea image, see *Convivio* IV iv 5, and *Monarchia* III xv 11.

23 *Inferno* XXVII, 61–129, and particularly 79–81.

24 *Inferno* XXVI, 90–142.

25 *Paradiso* XXVI, 62–3.

26 *Inferno* II, 107–8. For the various interpretations of this phrase, see F. Mazzoni, *Saggio di un nuovo commento alla 'Divina Commedia'* (Florence, 1967), pp. 294–303, and the references therein.

27 E. Montale, *Ossi di Seppia* (Milan, 1948), p. 90 ('Ho sostato talvolta', 23–4).

28 *Paradiso* XXX, 61–105.

29 See Hrabanus Maurus, *De Universo* XI, ii–vi, in *Patrologia Latina*, 111, 311–12. And cf. *Paradiso* IX, 84; 'fuor di quel mar che la terra inghirlanda'. See also *Paradiso* XII, 49–51.

30 *Inferno* I, 22–7; and see H. Rahner, 'Der Schiffbruch und die Planke des Heils', now in his *Symbole der Kirche* (Salzburg, 1964), pp. 432–72; and J. Freccero, 'The Prologue Scene', now in his *Dante: The Poetics of Conversion* (Cambridge, Mass., 1986), pp. 1–28.

31 *Purgatorio* I, 115–29.

32 *Purgatorio* XXXI, 94–105; and XXXIII, 136–45.

33 *Purgatorio* XXVIII, 70–5.

34 For this, see C.S. Singleton, 'In Exitu Israel de Aegypto', *78th Annual Report of the Dante Society of America* (1960), reprinted in J. Freccero, ed., *Dante* (Englewood Cliffs, N.J., 1965), pp. 102–21; and P. Armour, 'The Theme of Exodus in the First two Cantos of the Purgatorio' in D. Nolan, ed., *Dante Soundings* (Dublin, 1981), pp. 59–99.

35 *Paradiso* XXII, 95 and 94.

36 *Paradiso* XXV, 55–6.

37 The expression, as we shall soon see, is Dante's own in *Paradiso* II, 3.

38 See s.v. 'In Exitu Israel' in *Enciclopedia Dantesca* III (Rome, 1971), p. 421. The Psalm is no. 113 in the Vulgate, 114 in King James.

39 See *Convivio* II i 7, and Letter to Cangrande XIII, 21. For discussion of these passages, see *Enciclopedia Dantesca* III, s.v.; Singleton, 'In Exitu'; A.C. Charity, *Events and their Afterlife* (Cambridge, 1966), pp. 198–226.

40 See the *Textus Biblie cum Glossa Ordinaria, Nicolai de Lyra Postilla*, etc. (Basle, 1509), 247 v.

41 Matthew 14. 22–36.

42 See references in notes 35 and 36 above. Noah is mentioned in *Inferno* IV, 56, and the Flood recalled in *Paradiso* XII, 17.

43 Hell is called 'abisso' several times: *Inferno* IV, 8, 24; XI, 5; XXXIV, 100; *Purgatorio* I, 46. For a splendid reading of the sea image and its meaning in the *Purgatorio*, see E. Raimondi, 'Rito e storia nel I Canto del *Purgatorio*', now in his *Metafora e storia* (Turin, 1977), pp. 65–94.

44 Lucretius, *De rerum natura* I, 8; Aeschylus, *Promētheus Desmōtēs*, 89–90.

45 *Purgatorio* XII, 4–7.

46 *Purgatorio* XVII, 78.

47 *Purgatorio* XXIV, 3.

48 T.S. Eliot, 'Marina', 1–2.

49 *Paradiso* I, 67–72. And see R. Hollander, *Allegory in Dante's Commedia* (Princeton, 1969), pp. 216–20.

50 The translation of *Paradiso* I used here is by K. Foster, *The Life of the Spirit*, 10 (1955), 180–4.

51 *Metamorphoses* XIII, 898–968.

52 Before Hollander, *Allegory*, pp. 216–20, the *Ovide Moralisé* XIII, 4489–608 interprets Glaucus as the Saviour.

53 *Metamorphoses* XIII, 955; *Inferno* XXVI, 142. Dante cannot have failed to notice that Book XIII of the *Metamorphoses* begins with Ulysses and ends with Glaucus.

54 I return here to Singleton's translation. And see n. 72 below for God as the ocean of being in John of Damascus and Thomas Aquinas.

55 *Paradiso* I, 103–8.

56 See E. Auerbach, 'Dante's Addresses to the Reader', *Romance Philology* 7 (1954), 268–78; and R. Hollander, 'The Invocations of the *Commedia*', now in his *Studies in Dante* (Ravenna, 1980), pp. 31–8.

57 H. Gardner, *The Art of T.S. Eliot* (London, 3rd edn 1964), p. 171.

58 It may be worth recalling that in the first draft of the *Waste Land* (later corrected and revised by Ezra Pound) the Phoenician sailor (in the final version named 'Phlebas') leaves towards his 'Death by Water' sailing beyond the Dry Salvages. In the draft, that section of the poem is inspired by Dante's Ulysses. See T.S. Eliot, *The Waste Land*, ed. V. Eliot (New York, 1971), p. 55, v. 16, and pp. 128–9. In the *Four Quartets* the Dry Salvages are also the place where 'the voiceless wailing' resounds 'to the drift of the sea and the drifting wreckage' (II, 21–4). From the *Waste Land* to *The Dry Salvages* Eliot seems bent on outlining an itinerary which resembles Dante's from Ulysses to the Argonauts.

59 *The Dry Salvages* III, 23–47.

60 Wisdom 5. 10 (trans. Jerusalem Bible). Benvenuto is the first to note the parallel in his *Comentum* IV (Florence, 1887), p. 339.

61 Hippolytus, *Fragmenta XXIII in Prov. 30. 19*, in *Die griechische christlichen Schriftsteller. Hyppolitus Werke* I, 2, p. 165. see Rahner, *Symbole*, p. 564, and for the sea and navigation images, pp. 239–431. G. Stabile has examined this passage with fundamental results in his 'Navigazione celeste e simbolismo lunare in "Paradiso" II', *Studi Medievali*, 3rd series, 21 (1980) 97–140. I am much indebted to this essay and to its author, with whom I have often discussed the themes of the present chapter. For other references to the sea image, see K. Manger, *Das 'Narrenschiff'* (Darmstadt, 1983); H.S. and I. Daemmrich, *Themes & Motifs in Western Literature* (Tübingen, 1987), s.v. 'sea' and 'ship', and relevant bibliography.

62 *Inferno* XXVI; *Purgatorio* I, 130–2; XIX, 19–24; *Paradiso* XXV, 49–50; XXVII, 82–3. See A.M. Chiavacci Leonardi, 'The New Ulysses' in P. Boitani and A. Torti, eds., *Intellectuals and Writers in Fourteenth-Century Europe* (Tübingen–Cambridge, 1986), pp. 120–37.

63 *Paradiso* XXVII, 82–3. For the importance of 'varcare' and 'varco' see the relevant entries in *Enciclopedia Dantesca* V (Rome, 1976).

64 See M. Corti, 'Le metafore della navigazione, del volo e della lingua di fuoco nell'episodio di Ulisse' in the *Miscellanea di Studi in onore di Aurelio Roncaglia* (Modena, 1989), and L. Battaglia Ricci, *Dante e la tradizione letteraria medievale* (Pisa, 1983), pp. 161–84.

65 Leopardi, 'La ginestra', 50–1.

66 See E. Bloch, 'Odysseus Did Not Die in Ithaca' in *Homer*, eds. G. Steiner and R. Fagles (Englewood Cliffs, N.J., 1962), pp. 81–5. I would add

Petrarch, *Familiares* IX, 13, 24 ff.; Pulci, *Morgante* XXV, cxxx; Ariosto, *Orlando Furioso* XV, xxi–xxvii; and above all Tasso, *Gerusalemme Liberata* XV, 24–32. Tennyson in his 'Ulysses', Pascoli in 'Ultimo Viaggio' (*Poemi Conviviali*), and D'Annunzio, *Laus vitae* xvii ('L'eroe senza compagno') and iv; *Maia* 31–3 move in this direction and go much further than Dante in their exaltation of Ulysses.

67 For this different tradition I would choose Petrarch, *Triunphus Fame* II, 17–18 (Petrarch identifies with Ulysses in *Familiares* I, 1, 21); Boccaccio, *Amorosa Visione* XXVII, 86–7; Melville, quoted below, n. 69; Eliot, quoted above, n. 58. On the development of Ulysses' figure see W.B. Stanford, *The Ulysses Theme* (Ann Arbor, 2nd edn 1968); Rahner, *Symbole*, pp. 239–71; H. Blumenberg, *Arbeit am Mythos*, 4th edn (Frankfurt, 1986), pp. 86–98. To these should be added G. Padoan, 'Ulisse "fandi fictor" e le vie della sapienza', now in his *Il pio Enea, l'empio Ulisse* (Ravenna, 1977), pp. 170–204; and J.A. Scott, *Dante Magnanimo* (Florence, 1977); for modern poetry, W. Stevens, 'The Sail of Ulysses' in *The Palm at the End of the Mind*, ed. H. Stevens (New York, 1972), pp. 388–93. The bibliography on Dante's Ulysses is so extensive that I refer the reader to the relevant entry in the *Enciclopedia Dantesca* V; to G. Mazzotta, *Dante, Poet of the Desert* (Princeton, 1979), pp. 66–106; M. Corti, *Dante a un nuovo crocevia* (Florence, 1981), pp. 85–97; R. Mercuri, *Semantica di Gerione* (Rome, 1983); A.A. Iannucci, *Forma ed Evento nella Divina Commedia* (Rome, 1984), pp. 147–88; and to the literature mentioned in these works.

68 Milton, *Paradise Lost* VI, 874–6.

69 H. Melville, *Moby Dick*, chapter 135 (Harmondworth, 1972), p. 685.

70 For the image of writing as ploughing (Dante is here the ploughing Jason), see E.R. Curtius, *European Literature and the Latin Middle Ages*, trans. W.R. Trask (London, 1953), pp. 313–14.

71 See Stabile, 'Navigazione', p. 108, n. 16.

72 Hugh of St Victor, *De Vanitate Mundi* II, in *Patrologia Latina* 176, 715 A/B; John of Damascus, *De Fide Orthodoxa* I, 1, 9, in *Patrologia Graeca* 94, 836 (cf. Gregory of Nazianzus, *Oratio* 38, 7 in *Patrologia Graeca* 36, 317); Thomas, *Summa Theologiae* I, q. 13, a. 11; and cf. *Paradiso* I, 113.

73 For this, see Curtius, *European Literature*, pp. 128–34.

74 For references to these, see H. De Lubac, *Exégèse Médiévale*, I, i (Paris, 1979), pp. 119–20 and notes. Jerome, *Comm. in Ezechielem* XII, xl, in *Patrologia Latina*, 25, 369D, should be added.

75 Iacopo Passavanti's *Specchio di penitenza* is quoted by Busnelli and Vandelli in their edition of the *Convivio*, p. 59, n. 4.

76 Origene, *Homélies sur la Genèse* (Paris, 1976), IX, 1, p. 236.

77 The two *loci classici* in the *Comedy* are *Purgatorio* XXIV, 52–4, and *Paradiso* XXVI, 16–18, both oblique proclamations, as R. Hollander rightly maintains in 'Dante Theologus–Poeta', now in his *Studies in Dante* (Ravenna, 1980). See also A. Jacomuzzi, *L'imago al cerchio: Invenzione e*

visione nella Divina Commedia (Milan, 1968), p. 65; G. R. Sarolli, 'Dante "scriba Dei"', *Convivium*, 31 (1963) 385–422, 513–44, 641–71; C. Mésoniat, *Poetica Theologia* (Rome, 1984), and several of the essays collected in *Dante e la Bibbia*, ed. G. Barblan (Florence, 1988), in particular G. Mazzotta's 'Teologia ed esegesi biblica', pp. 95–112; L. Battaglia Ricci's 'Scrittura sacra e "Sacrato Poema"', pp. 295–321; and G. Contini's statement, p. 17.

78 *Paradiso* VII, 94–5; XXI, 94–5; and see *Purgatorio* VI, 121–2.

79 *Paradiso* XX, 119–20; and see *Purgatorio* VIII, 98–9.

80 One should note that Dante opens this canto with a particularly bold proclamation: 'E quel che mi convien ritrar testeso, – non portò vove mai, né scrisse incostro, – né fu per fantasia già mai compreso' (7–9). On *Paradiso* XIX–XX see now the subtle observations by R. Kirkpatrick, *Dante's Inferno: Difficulty and Dead Poetry* (Cambridge, 1987), pp. 12–26; and Russo, *Il romanzo teologico*, pp. 145–70.

81 K. Foster, 'The Son's Eagle: *Paradiso* XIX' in his *The Two Dantes* (London, 1977), p. 146.

82 *Paradiso* XIII, 121–3: 'Vie più che 'ndarno da riva si parte, – perché non torna tal qual e' si move, – chi pesca per lo vero e non ha l'arte'.

83 See the fundamental and beautiful essay by K. Foster, 'The Mind in Love: Dante's Philosophy' in J. Freccero, ed., *Dante*, pp. 43–60.

84 The image of shipwreck as a possibility in human fate is presented, as we have seen, by Thomas Aquinas in *Paradiso* XIII, 136–8.

85 There is a striking parallel between this and the passage of Richard of St Victor quoted above, n. 16. see M. Colombo, *Dai mistici a Dante: il Linguaggio dell'ineffabilità* (Florence, 1987), pp. 68–71.

86 On which see L. Tonelli, *Dante e la poesia dell'ineffabile* (Florence, 1934); Jacomuzzi, *L'imago al cerchio*; Colombo, *Dai mistici a Dante*; R. Kirkpatrick, *Dante's Paradiso and the Limitations of Modern Criticism* (Cambridge, 1978), pp. 54–61.

87 Foster, 'The Mind in Love', p. 52.

88 *Peri Hypsous* 9, 9–10.

89 *Confessiones* XII, xiv, 17: 'Mira profunditas eloquiorum tuorum . . . Horror est intendere in eam, horror honoris et tremor amoris.'

90 See Boyde, *Dante Philomythes*, pp. 235–47.

91 Their historical development has been exhaustively studied by K. Smorońksi, 'Et Spiritus Dei Ferebatur Super Aquas: Inquisitio Historico-Exegetica in Interpretationem Textus Gen. 1. 2c', *Biblica* 6 (1925) 140—56, 275—93, 361–95. And see J. Daniélou, *The Theology of Jewish Christianity*, trans. J.A. Baker (London–Philadelphia, 1964), pp. 109–11.

92 B. Nardi, 'Lo discorrer de Dio sovra quest'acque' in his *Nel Mondo di Dante* (Rome, 1944), pp. 307–13. See also J. Pépin, *Théologie Cosmique et Théologie Chrétienne* (Paris, 1964), pp. 390–422.

93 *Fasti* II, 285–6. The subject is Pan.

94 *Aeneid* I, 147.
95 Ausgustine, *De Genesi contra Manichaeos* I, vii, 12; Peter Lombard, *Sententiae* II, xii, c. 3; Thomas Aquinas, *Summa Theologiae* I, q. 66, 1 ad 2.
96 *Paradiso* XXIX, 17.
97 Vulgate 41, 8; King James 42. 7.
98 *Canzoniere* 212, 3–4; 339, 9–11. Petrarch also uses the sea image to represent human life in *Canzoniere* 80; 272, 12–14; 189; 235, 5–8; 333, 5–6; and, with a different meaning, in 323, 13 ff.; 237; 132, 10 ff.; 177, 7–8; 277, 7. And see Mercuri, 'Genesi della tradizione', pp. 357–76.
99 1850 *Prelude* III, 62–3. And see now A. Corbin's important *Le territoire du vide: l'Occident et le désir du rivage 1750–1840* (Paris, 1988).
100 G. W. F. Hegel, *Aesthetics*, trans. T.M. Knox, vol. I (Oxford, 1975), p. 363 (II, ii).
101 See F. Tateo, *Questioni di Poetica Dantesca* (Bari, 1972), pp. 203–16.
102 *Paradiso* XVII, 17–18. See P. Dronke, 'Boethius, Alanus and Dante', now in his *Medieval Poet*, pp. 431–8.
103 See Singleton's commentary *ad loc.*, III, pp. 554–6.
104 G. Contini, 'Il canto XXVIII del "Paradiso"', now in his *Un'idea*, pp. 205–6; and see L. Pertile, '*Paradiso*, XXXIII: l'estremo oltraggio', *Filologia e Critica* 6 (1981), 1–21.
105 Dronke, 'Boethius', and references therein.
106 Dronke, 'Boethius', p. 435.
107 *Paradiso* XXIX, 12 (the beginning of Beatrice's speech on Creation).
108 Hollander, *Allegory*, p. 230.
109 Contini, 'Il canto XXVIII', p. 206.
110 *Metamorphoses* VI, 721; and see Hollander, *Allegory*, pp. 217–22.
111 Rahner, *Symbole*, pp. 314–15, 345, 370, 451, and references therein.
112 Cicero, *Aratea* 390 and 396. The latter is quoted by Hyginus, *Fabulae* XIV, 33.
113 *Eclogues* IV, 34. And see the magisterial essay by E.R. Curtius, 'The Ship of the Argonauts' in his *Essays on European Literature*, trans. M. Kowal (Princeton, 1973), pp. 465–96. Dante seems to suggest that the new Argo prophesied by Virgil is his ship.
114 Eliot, *Little Gidding*, when, at the end, fire and rose become one; v, 37–8.
115 *Amores* II, xi, 1. The image refers to the Argo.
116 T. Mann, *Doktor Faustus* (Frankfurt, 1982 edn.), pp. 265 ff. Mann uses F.G. Klopstock's 'Die Frühlingsfeier' ('Nicht in den Ozean der Welten alle') and changes its meaning. For the 'Tropfen am Eimer' which Mann's Adrian employs to begin his exploration of the 'ocean of all the worlds', see Isaiah 40. 15; Ecclesiasticus 18. 8; Wisdom 11. 23. And cf. J.W. Goethe, *Die Leiden des jungen Werther*, I, Am 16. Juni (Munich, 1985 edn, p.27).
117 *Paradiso* I, 6; and cf. II Corinthians 12. 3–4.
118 *Purgatorio* XXXI, 139–41.

Index

Index

Index

Index

Index

Index

Index

Index

Index

Index

Index

Index

Index

Index

Here Piero Boitani explores the areas of the tragic and the sublime in medieval literature by asking what medieval texts mean to modern readers. Professor Boitani, who has written widely on medieval and comparative literature, studies tragic and sublime tensions in stories and scenes recounted by such major poets as Dante, Chaucer and Petrarch, as well as themes shared by writers and philosophers and traditional poetic images. The result is a remarkable volume of studies in comparative European literature, which takes into account poems written in English, Italian and other languages, and compares them with their classical and Biblical ancestors as well as with their modern descendants.

This learned and stimulating collection will be read by students and scholars in a range of disciplines, and by all those with an interest in the literature discussed.